●●●●● soltbank 4G   0:00   100% ▰▰▰

‹ MEMO   END

Magical Girl Site

VOLUME 12

AUTHOR
KENTARO SATO

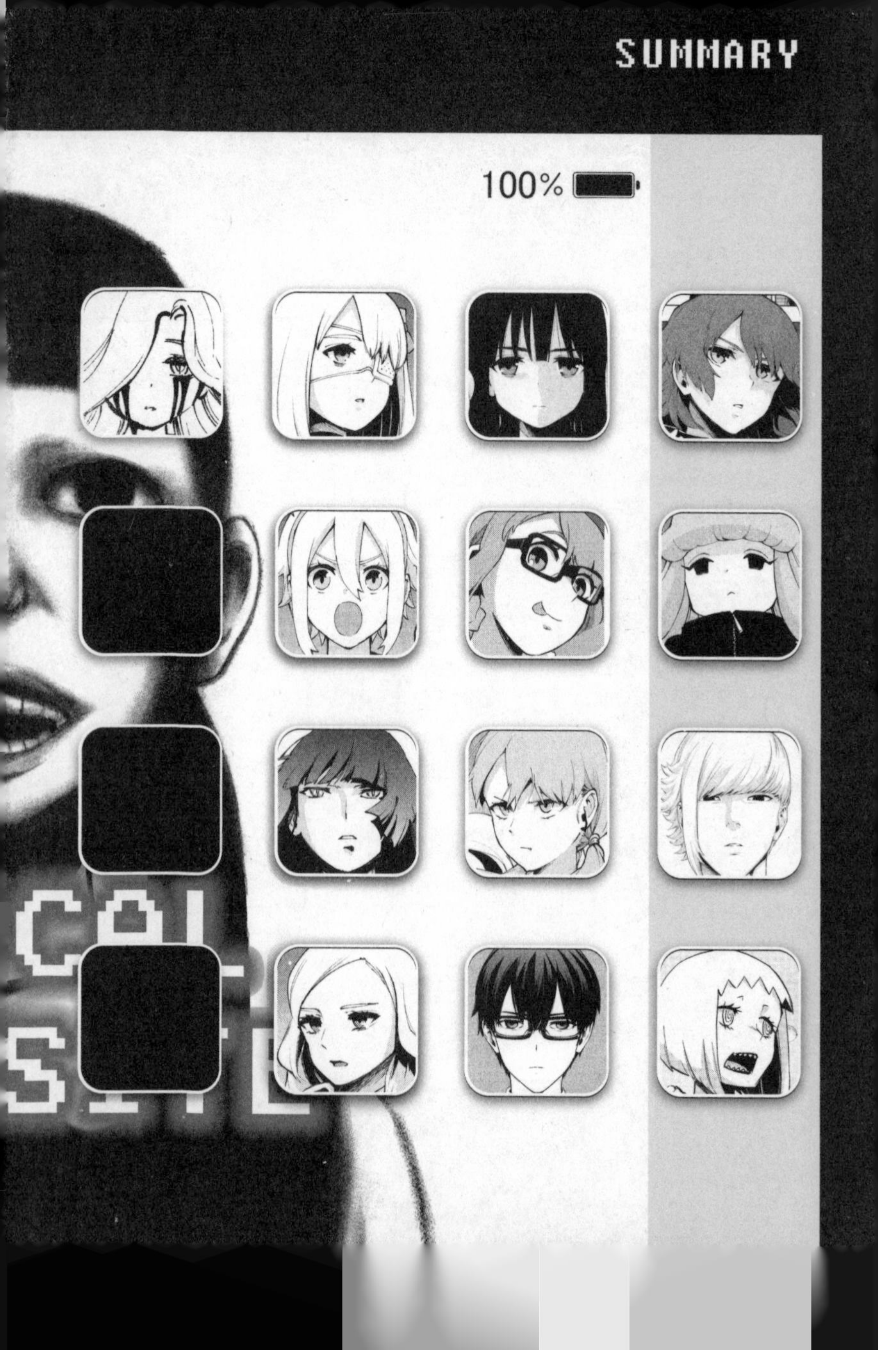
SUMMARY
100%

●●●●● soltbank 4G 0:00

MEMO END

It is August first, ten days before the Tempest. Ever since the night Maganuma Alice betrayed them, Asagiri Aya and the seven other magical girls who survived have been immersed in their efforts to crush the Magical Girl Site system—not to mention their brutal struggle with the managers. They strengthened themselves by increasing their understanding of their wands' abilities and crushing managers Hachi and Juushi, but trouble is still afoot.

Their rebellion did not go unnoticed by the other managers, who deployed Manager Juuroku and the newly reincarnated Manager Ni to kill them. Assassins were also sent out to kill the rebellious magical girls' families. As a result, six of the magical girls were caught in Ni's time stasis and killed by Juuroku. Manager Nana took some of the heat for this situation, as Misumi Kiichiro disappeared along with the numerous wands he had collected. Nana was deemed "unnecessary" by the King and slated for elimination.

The six magical girls killed by Juuroku and Ni were saved by a time reversal executed by Komura Kayo and Sakaki Sakura. Kayo and Sakaki faked their own deaths in order to protect their friends and loved ones from their involvement in the rebellion against Magical Girl Site. They went into hiding and gathered as much information as they could while waiting for the chance to strike back. Upon learning about Asagiri Aya, they sought to contact her and ask her to join the fight. When they go to meet her, they share memories—with the power of Aya's wand!

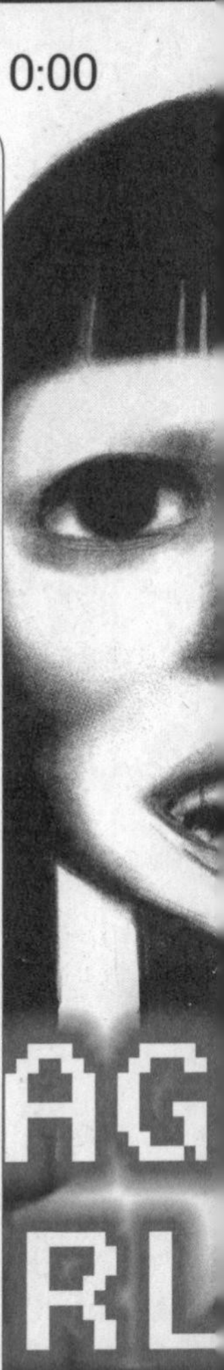

ENTER.87 CHANGING POINT

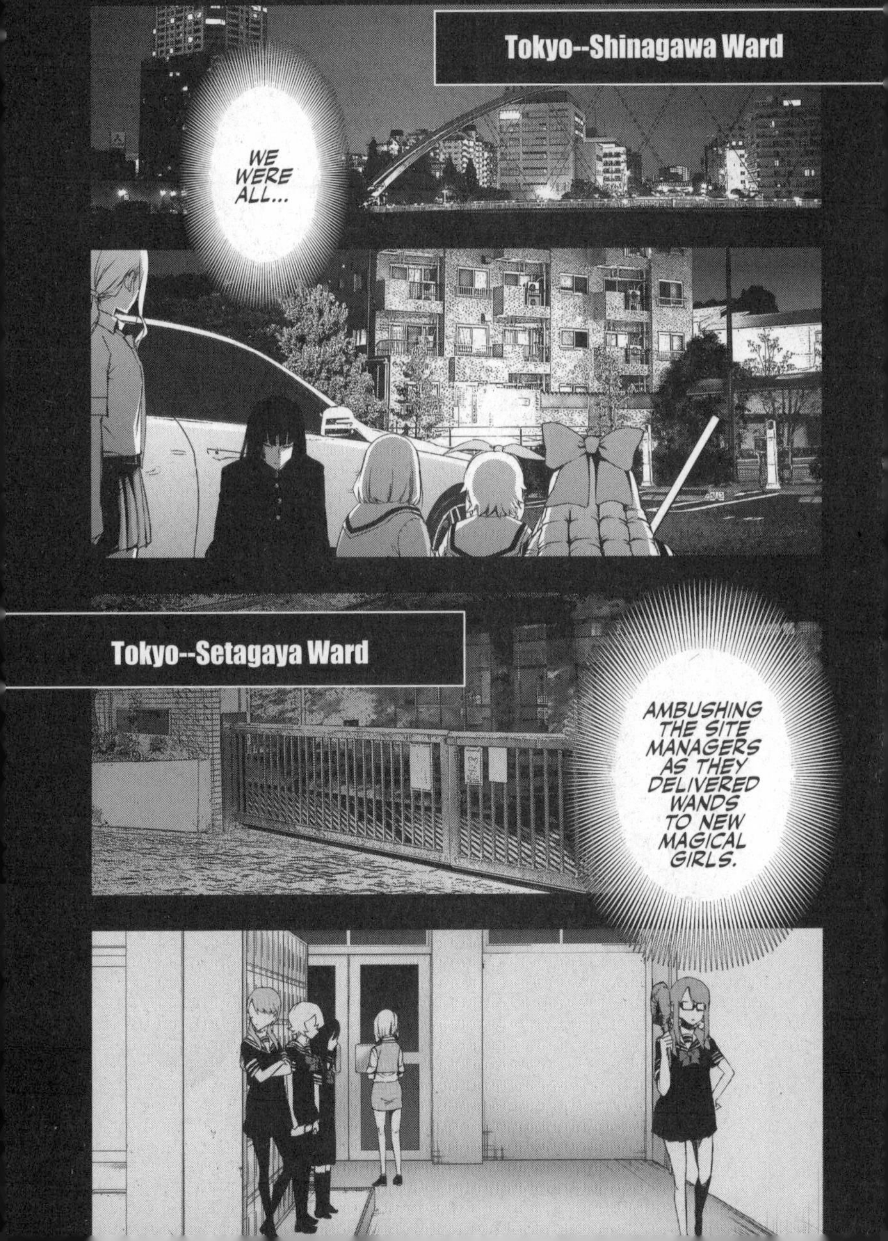
Tokyo--Shinagawa Ward
WE WERE ALL...
Tokyo--Setagaya Ward
AMBUSHING THE SITE MANAGERS AS THEY DELIVERED WANDS TO NEW MAGICAL GIRLS.

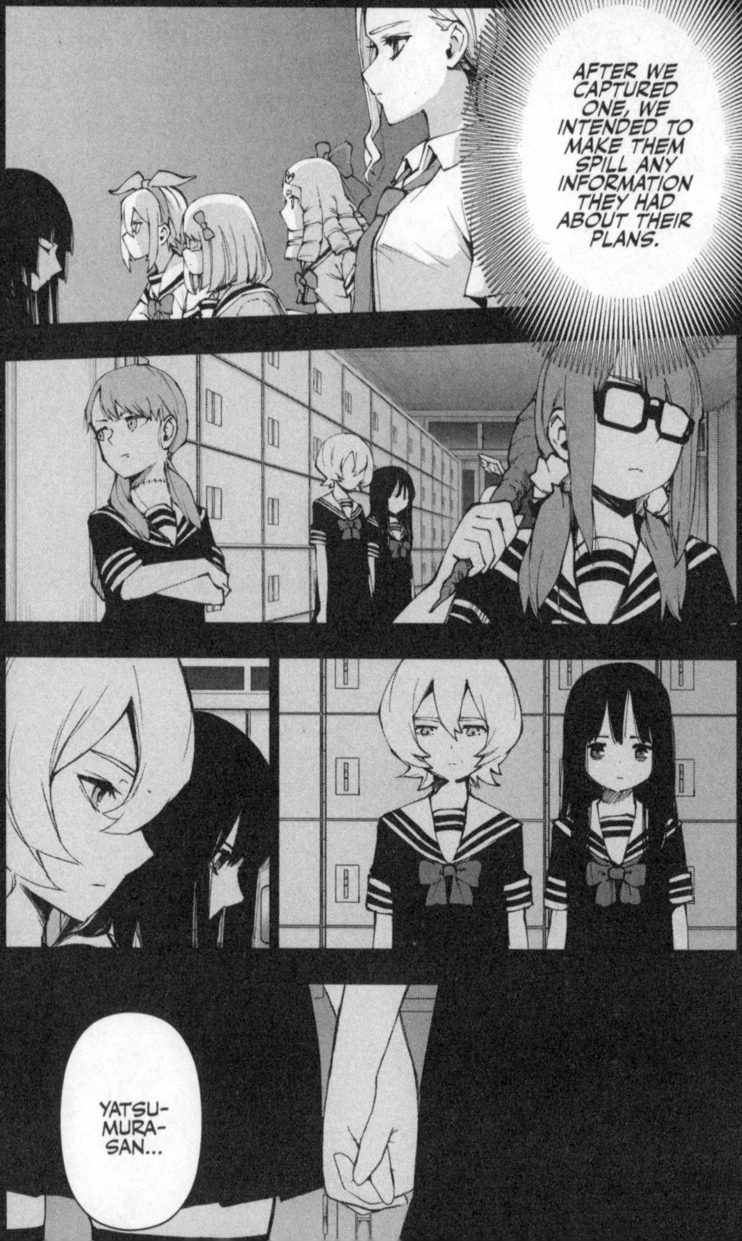
AFTER WE CAPTURED ONE, WE INTENDED TO MAKE THEM SPILL ANY INFORMATION THEY HAD ABOUT THEIR PLANS.
YATSU-MURA-SAN...

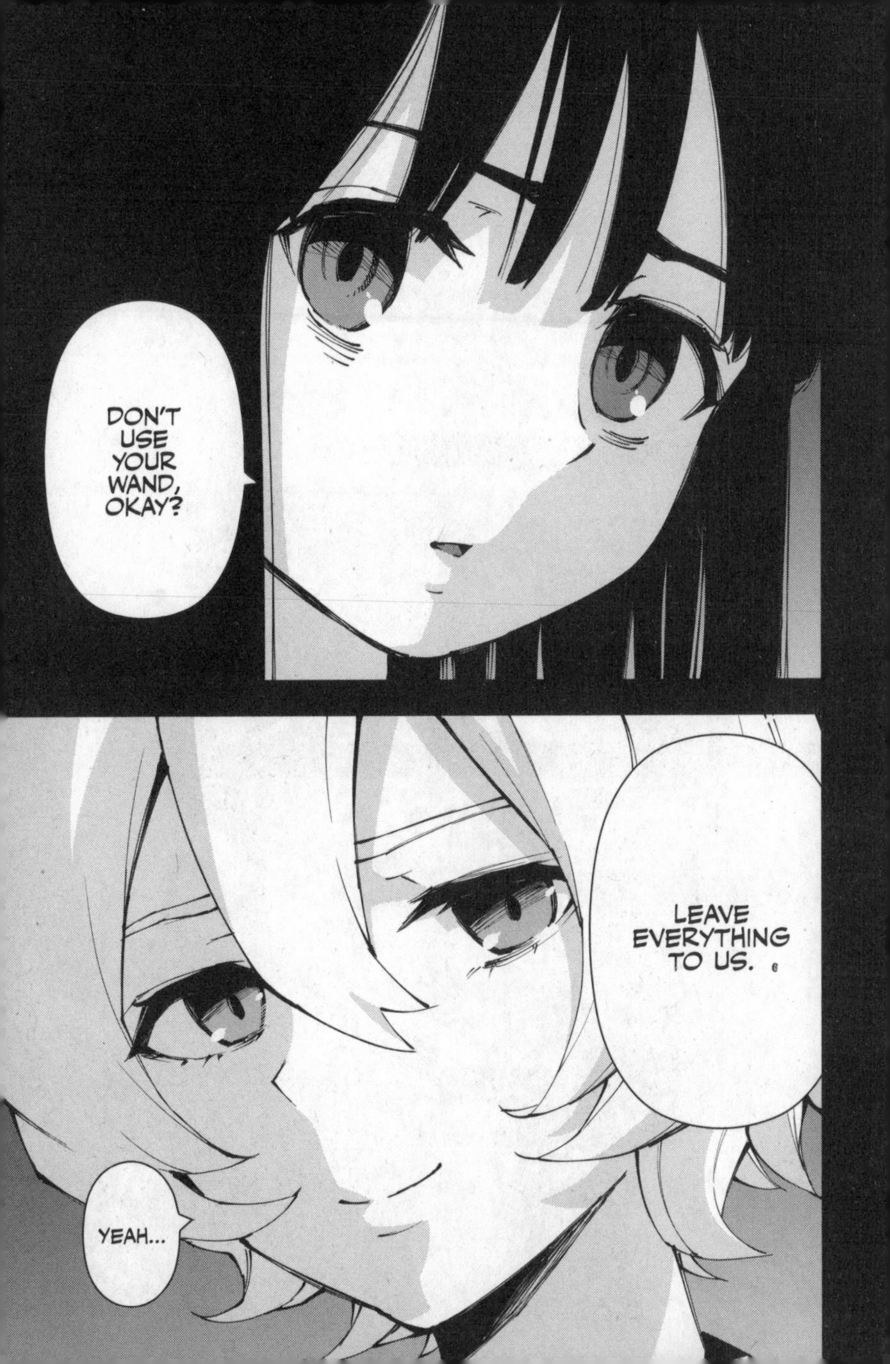
DON'T USE YOUR WAND, OKAY?
LEAVE EVERYTHING TO US.
YEAH...

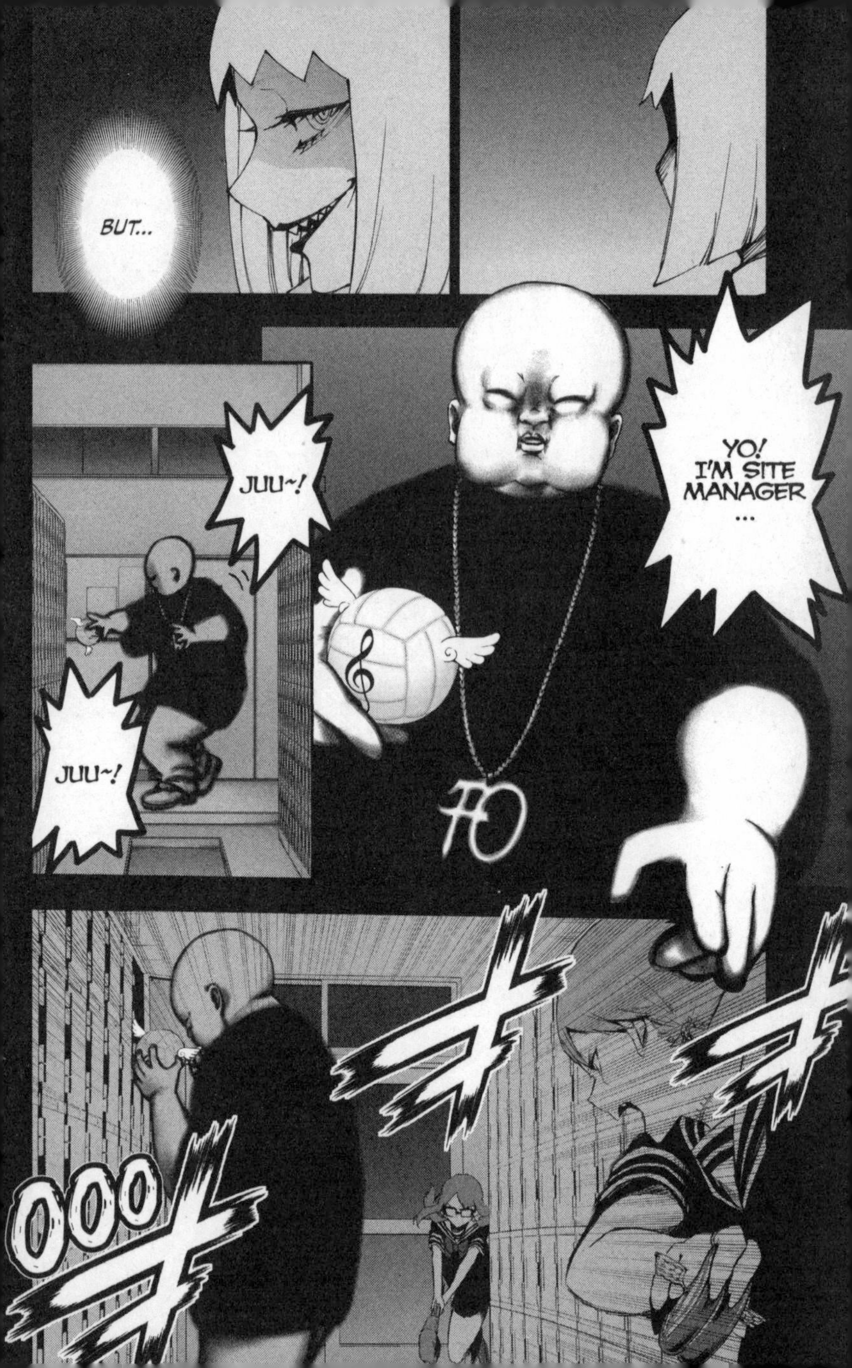
BUT...
YO! I'M SITE MANAGER ...
JUU~!
JUU~!
OOO

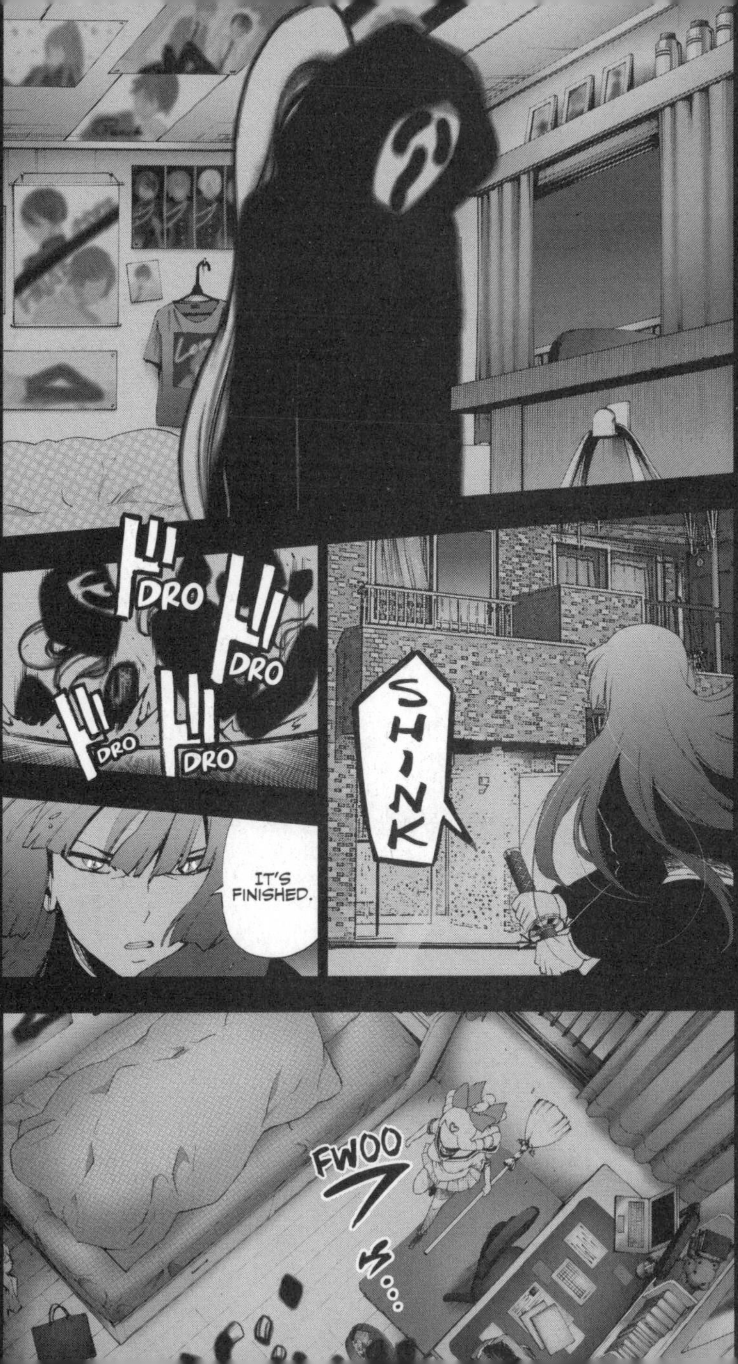
SHINK
DRO
DRO
DRO
DRO
IT'S FINISHED.
FWOO
S...

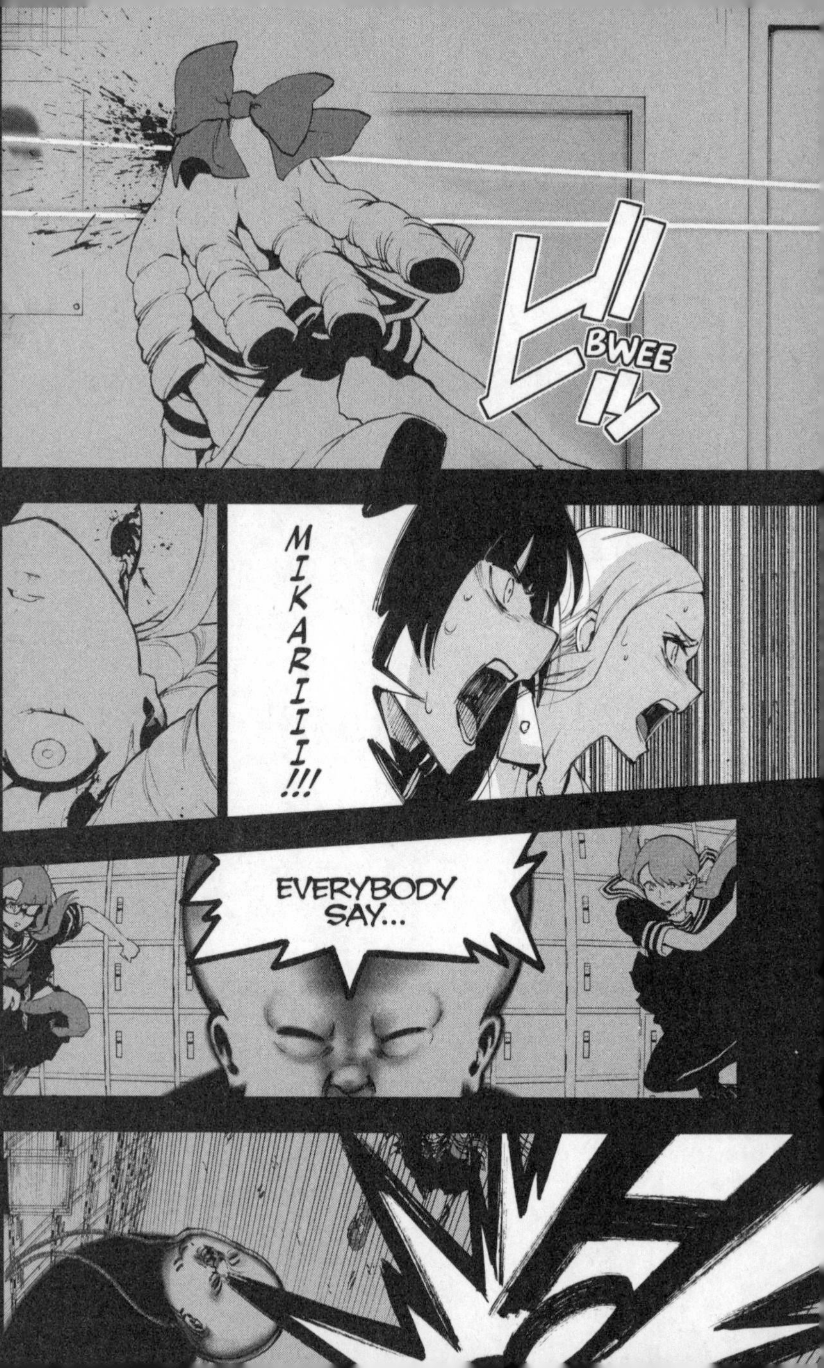
BWEE
MIKARIIII!!!
EVERYBODY SAY...

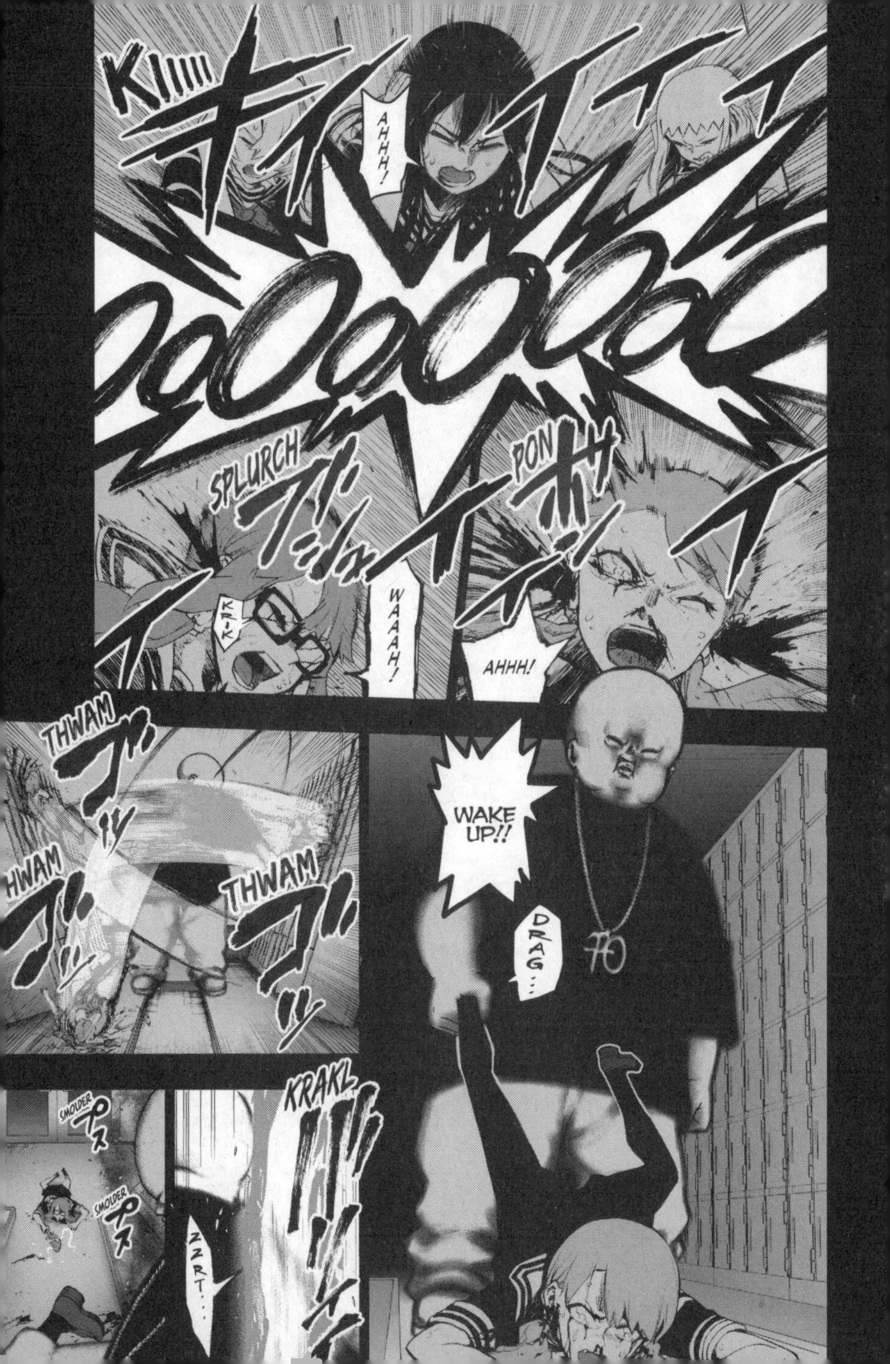
KI!!!!
AHHH!
PON
SPLURCH
AHHH!
WAAAAH!
KRIK
WAKE UP!!
DRAG...
THWAM
THWAM
THWAM
KRAKL
ZZRT...
SMOLDER
SMOLDER

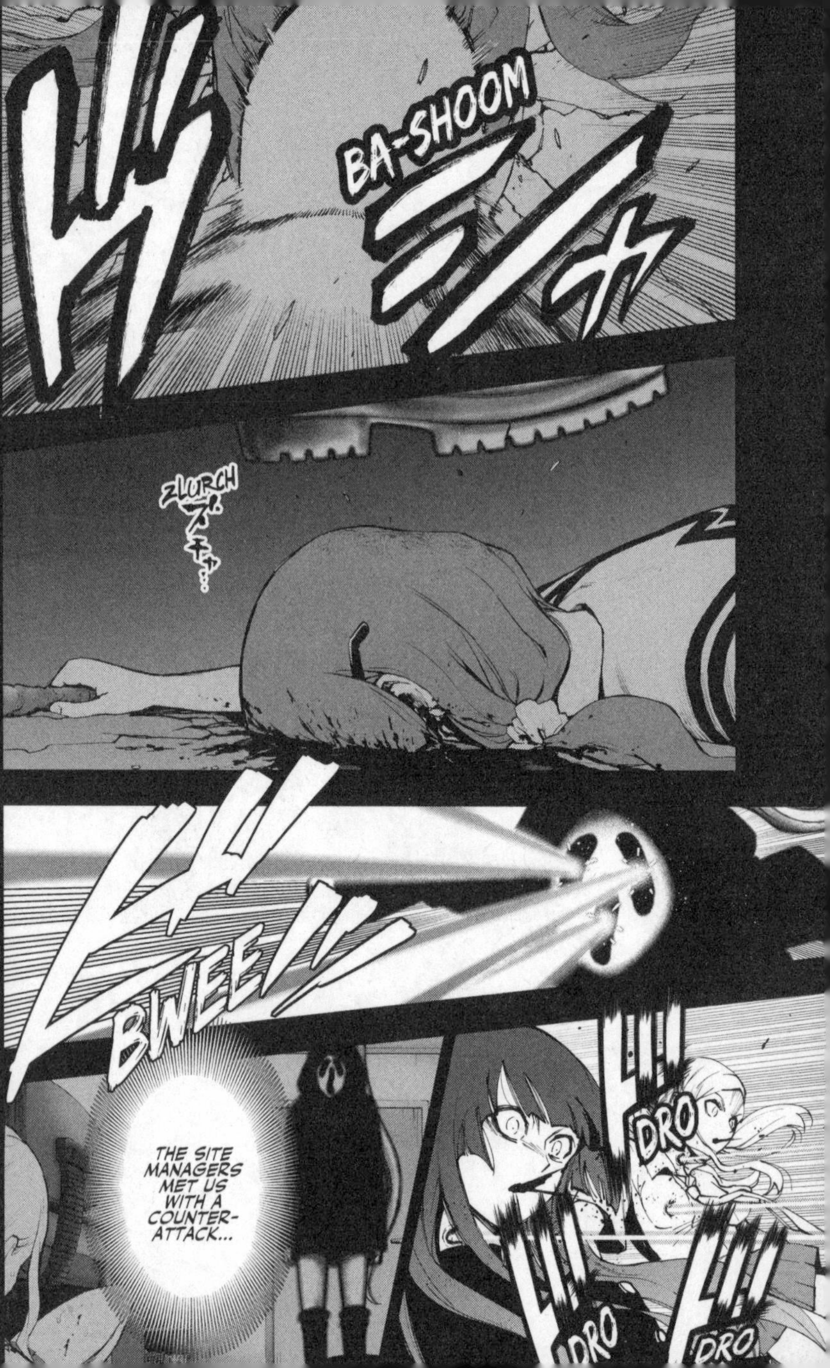
BA-SHOOM
ZLURCH
BWEE!!
DRO
THE SITE MANAGERS MET US WITH A COUNTER-ATTACK...
DRO
DRO

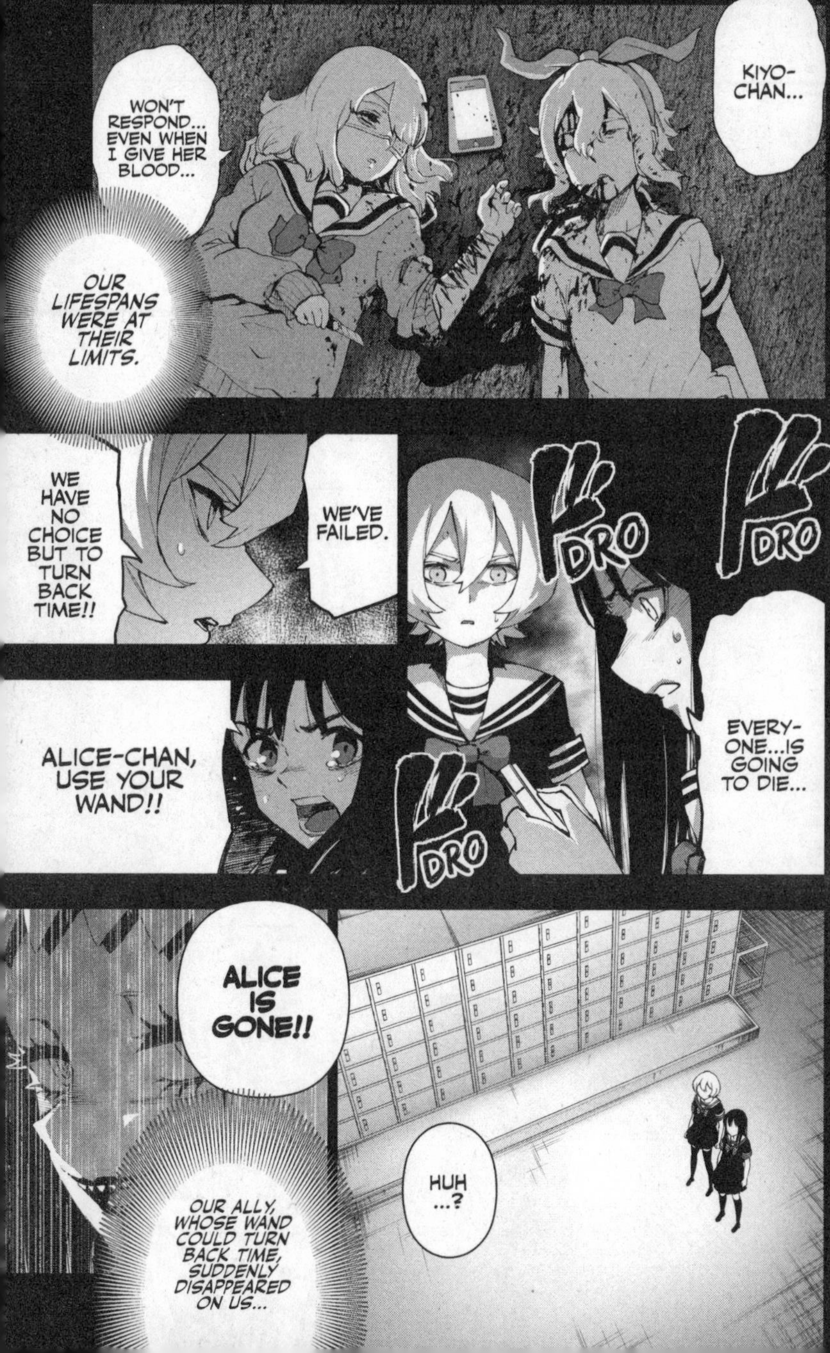
KIYO-CHAN...
WON'T RESPOND... EVEN WHEN I GIVE HER BLOOD...
OUR LIFESPANS WERE AT THEIR LIMITS.
WE'VE FAILED.
WE HAVE NO CHOICE BUT TO TURN BACK TIME!!
DRO
DRO
EVERY-ONE...IS GOING TO DIE...
DRO
ALICE-CHAN, USE YOUR WAND!!
HUH ...?
ALICE IS GONE!!
OUR ALLY, WHOSE WAND COULD TURN BACK TIME, SUDDENLY DISAPPEARED ON US...

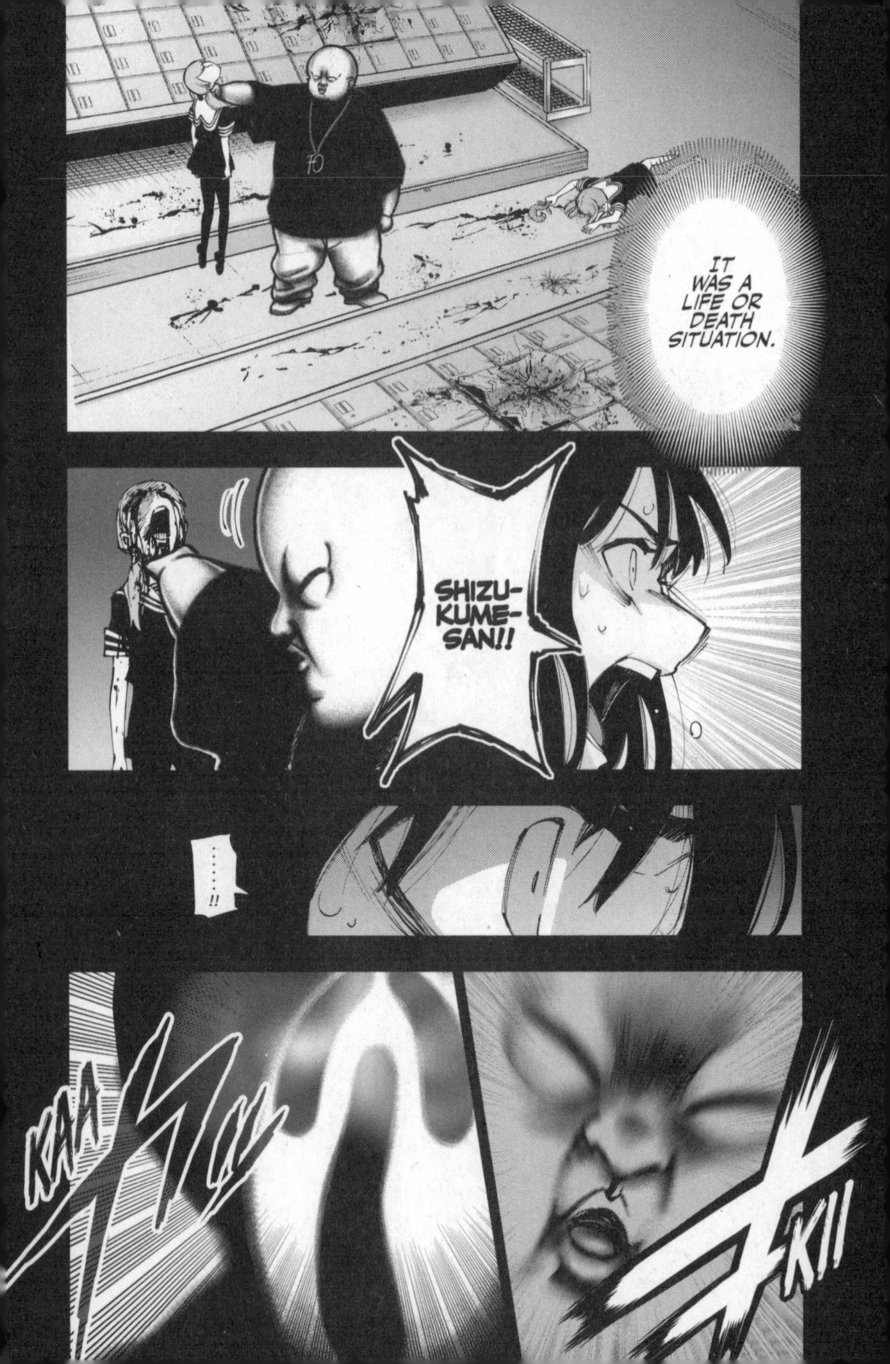
IT WAS A LIFE OR DEATH SITUATION.
SHIZU-KUME-SAN!!
......!!
KII
KAA

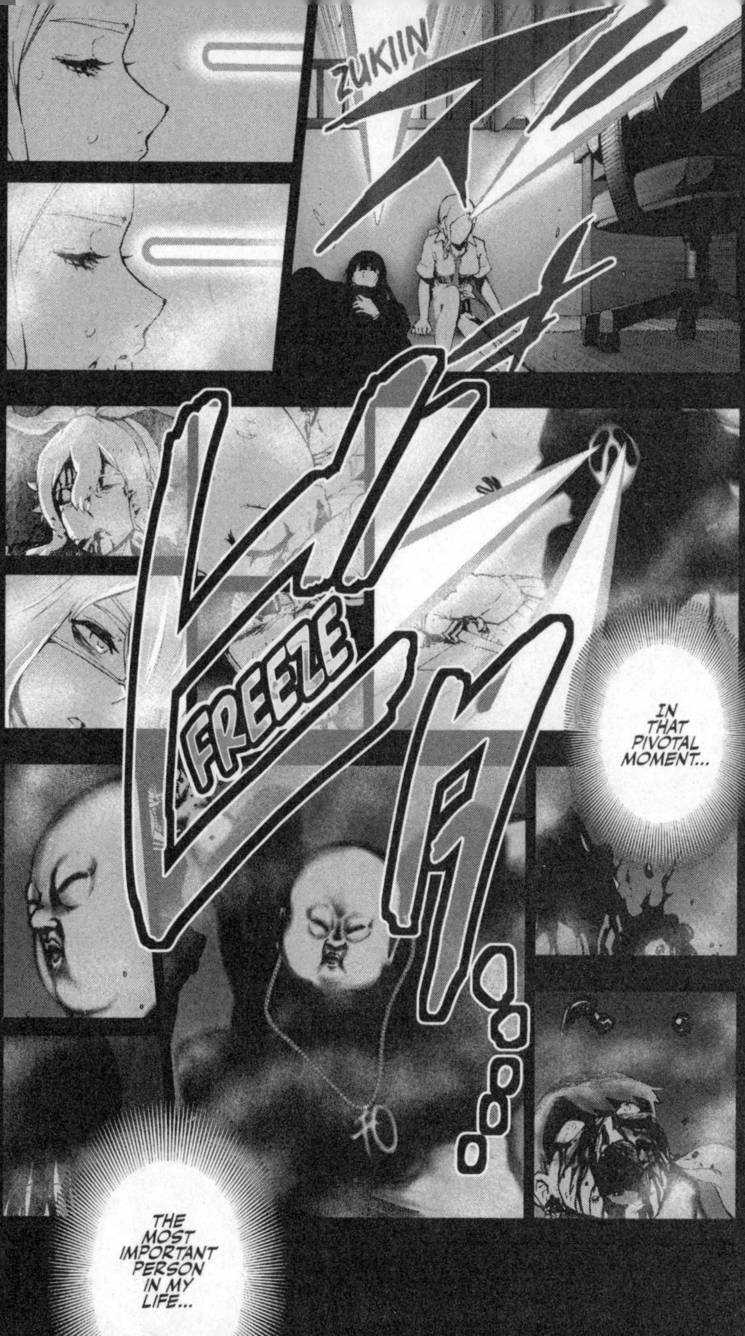
ZUKIIN
FREEZE
IN THAT PIVOTAL MOMENT...
THE MOST IMPORTANT PERSON IN MY LIFE...

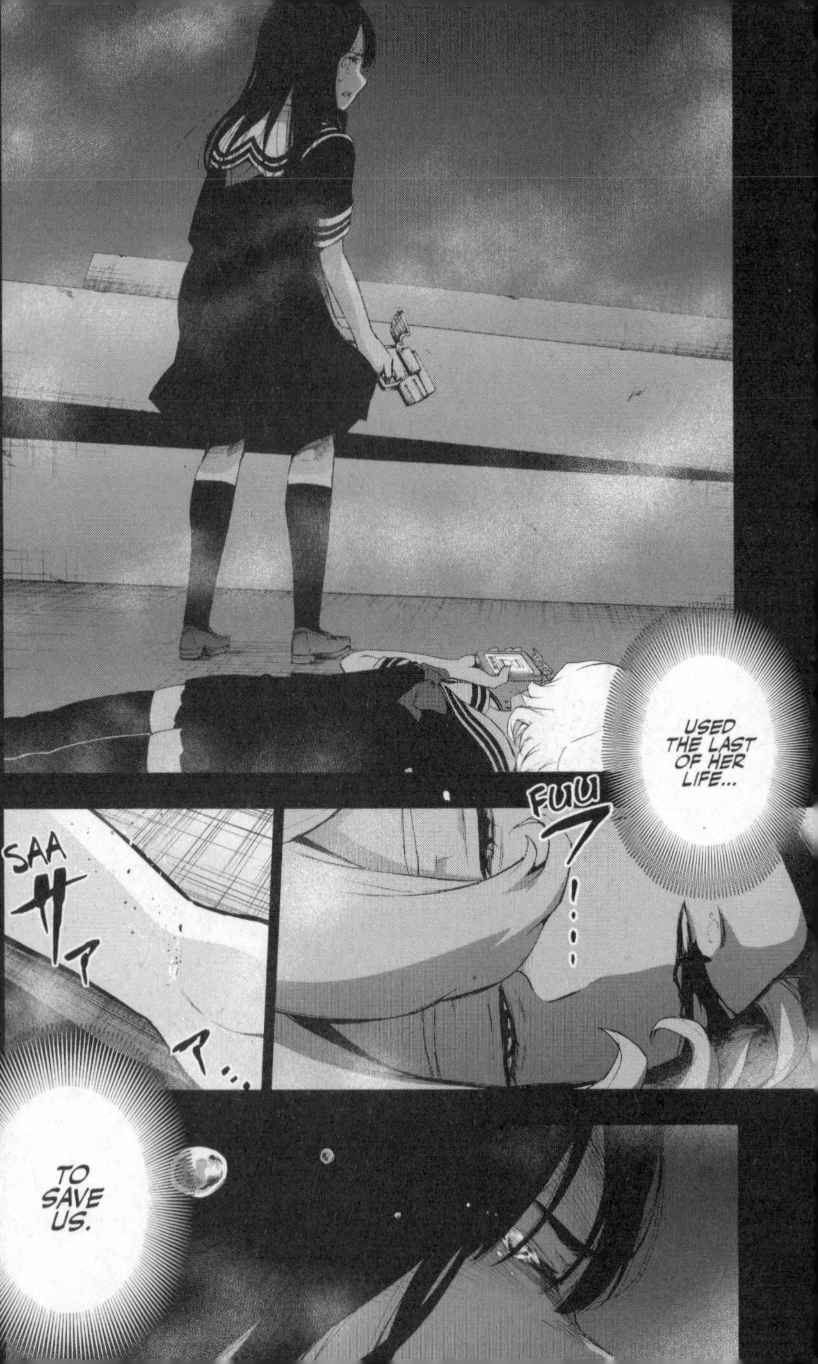
USED THE LAST OF HER LIFE...
FUU
!...
SAA
TO SAVE US.

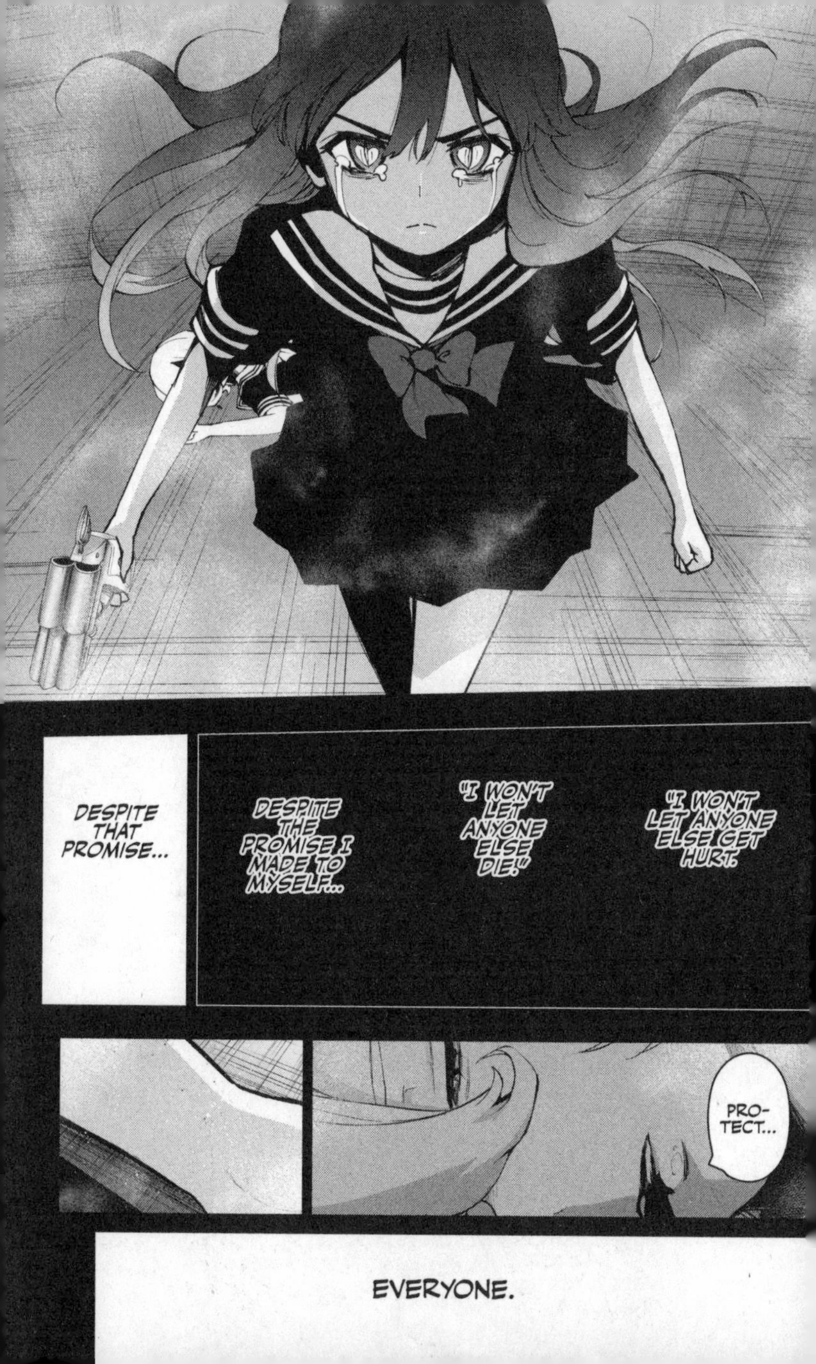
"I WON'T LET ANYONE ELSE GET HURT.
"I WON'T LET ANYONE ELSE DIE."
DESPITE THE PROMISE I MADE TO MYSELF...
DESPITE THAT PROMISE...
PRO-TECT...
EVERYONE.

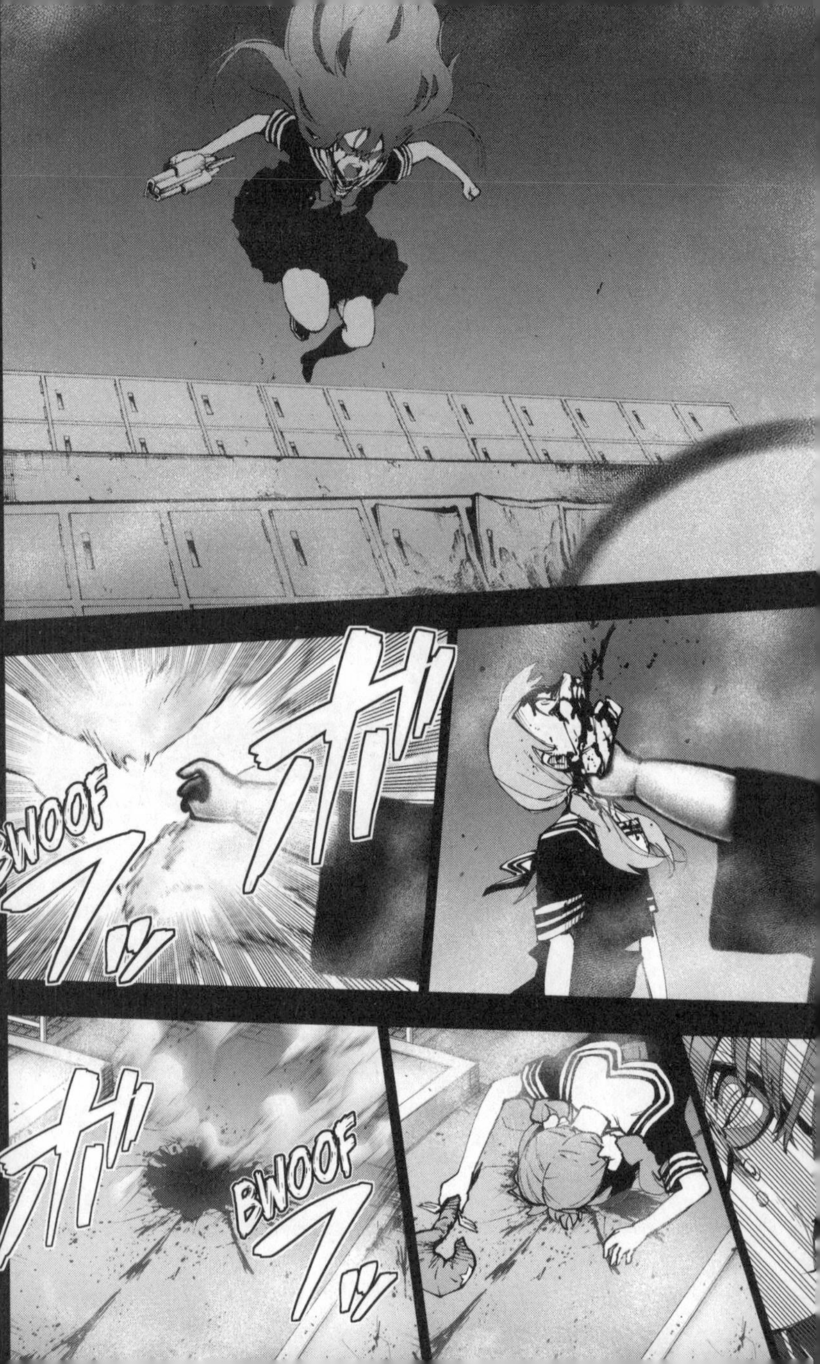
BWOOF
BWOOF

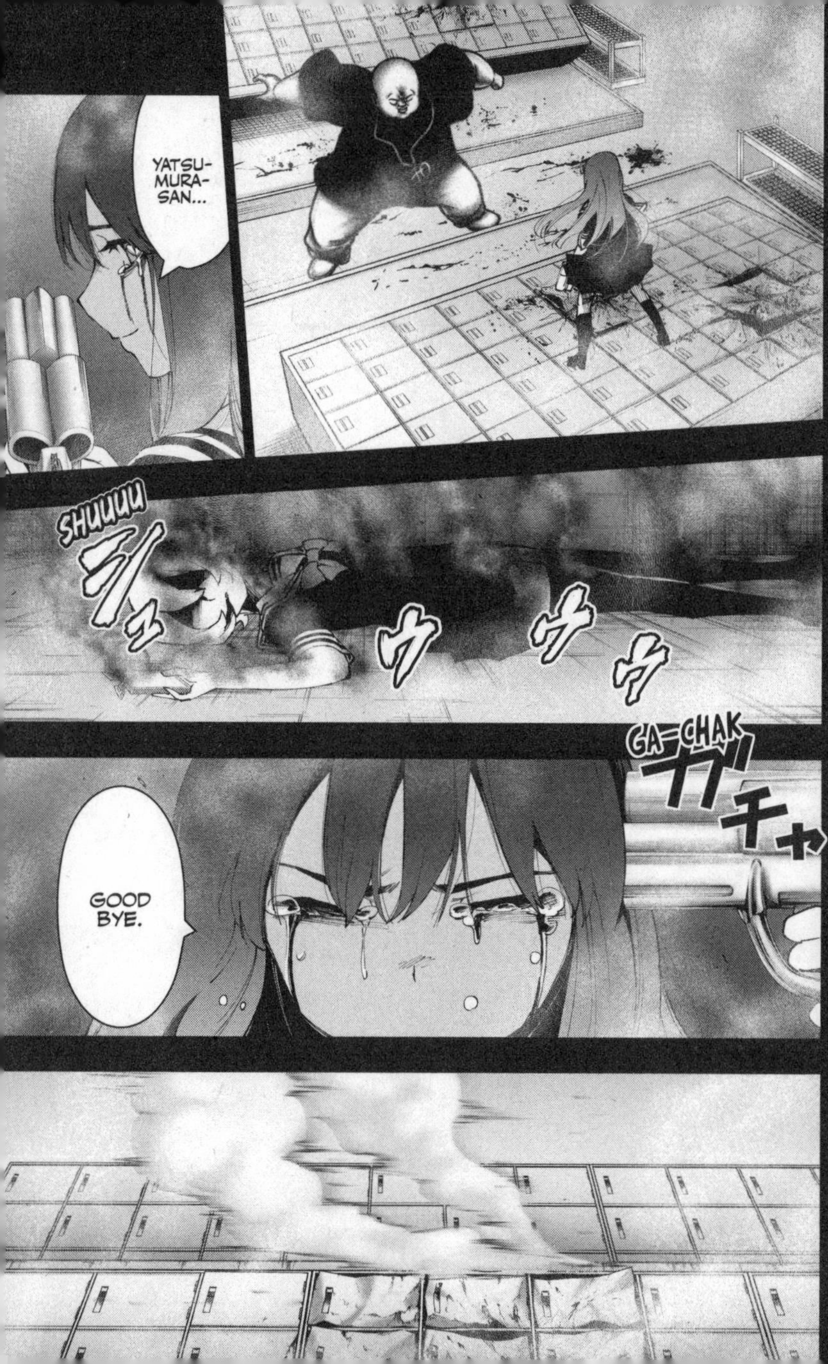
YATSU-MURA-SAN...
SHUUUU
GA-CHAK
GOOD BYE.

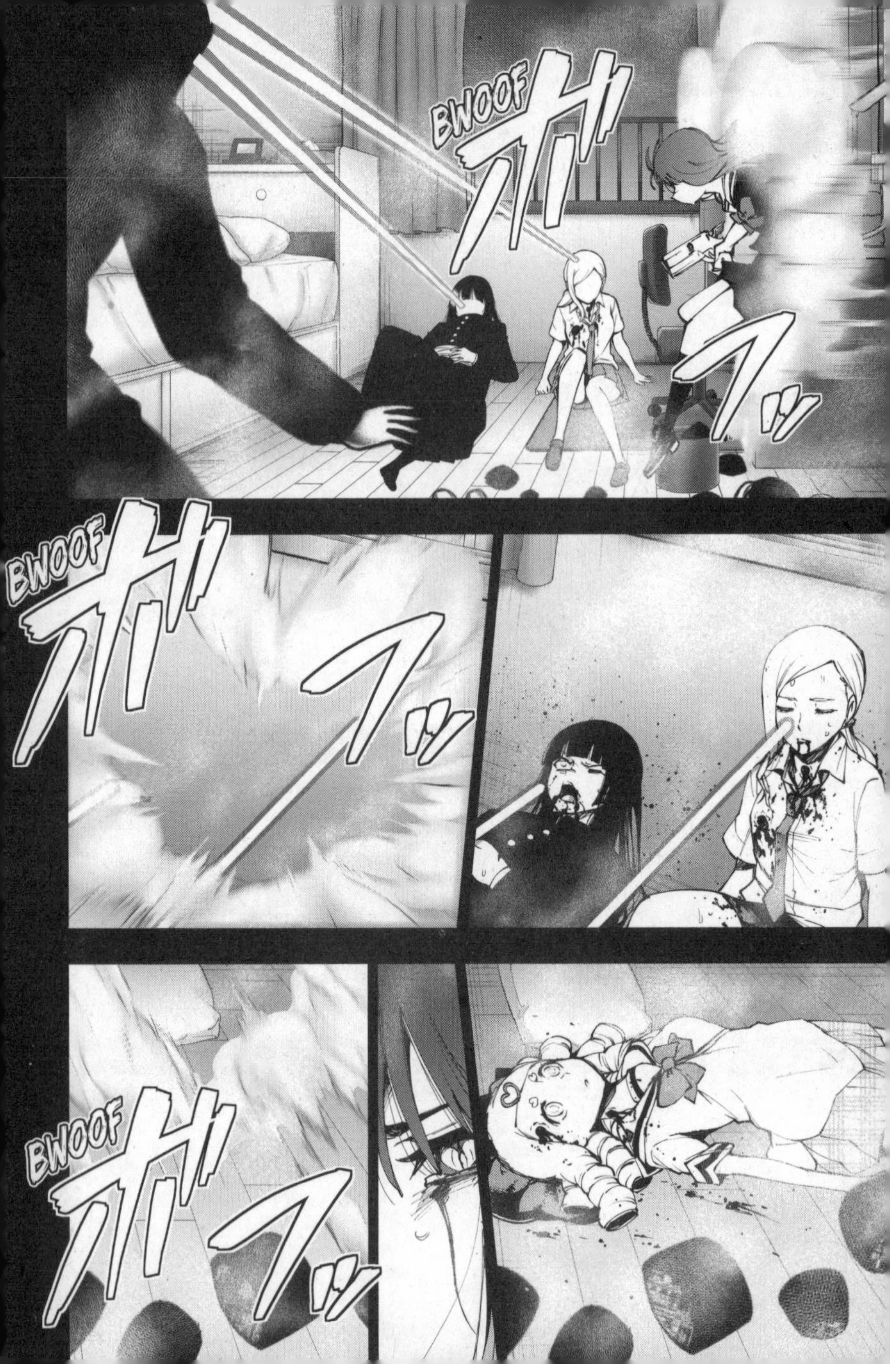
BWOOF
BWOOF
BWOOF

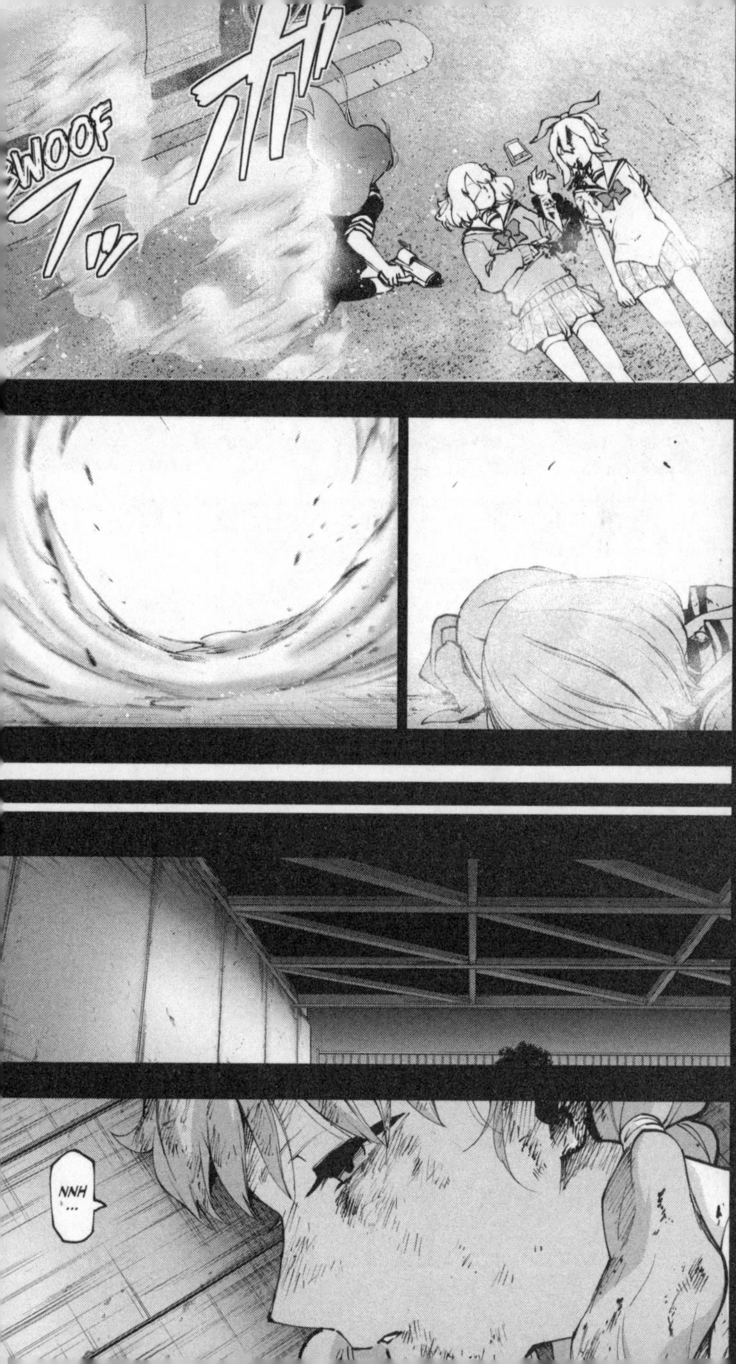
WOOF
NNH ...

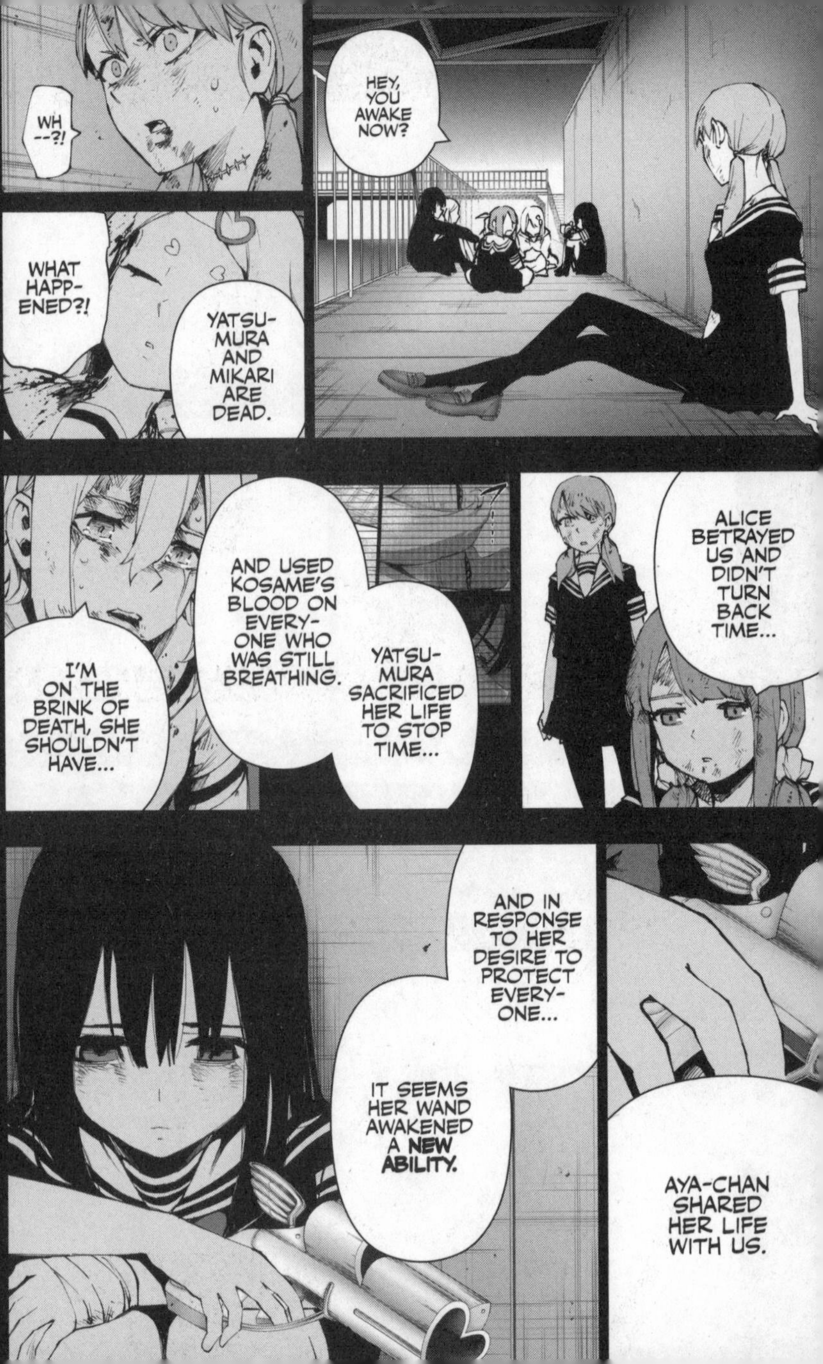
HEY, YOU AWAKE NOW?
WH--?!
WHAT HAPPENED?!
YATSUMURA AND MIKARI ARE DEAD.
ALICE BETRAYED US AND DIDN'T TURN BACK TIME...
YATSUMURA SACRIFICED HER LIFE TO STOP TIME...
AND USED KOSAME'S BLOOD ON EVERYONE WHO WAS STILL BREATHING.
I'M ON THE BRINK OF DEATH, SHE SHOULDN'T HAVE...
AYA-CHAN SHARED HER LIFE WITH US.
AND IN RESPONSE TO HER DESIRE TO PROTECT EVERYONE...
IT SEEMS HER WAND AWAKENED A **NEW ABILITY**.

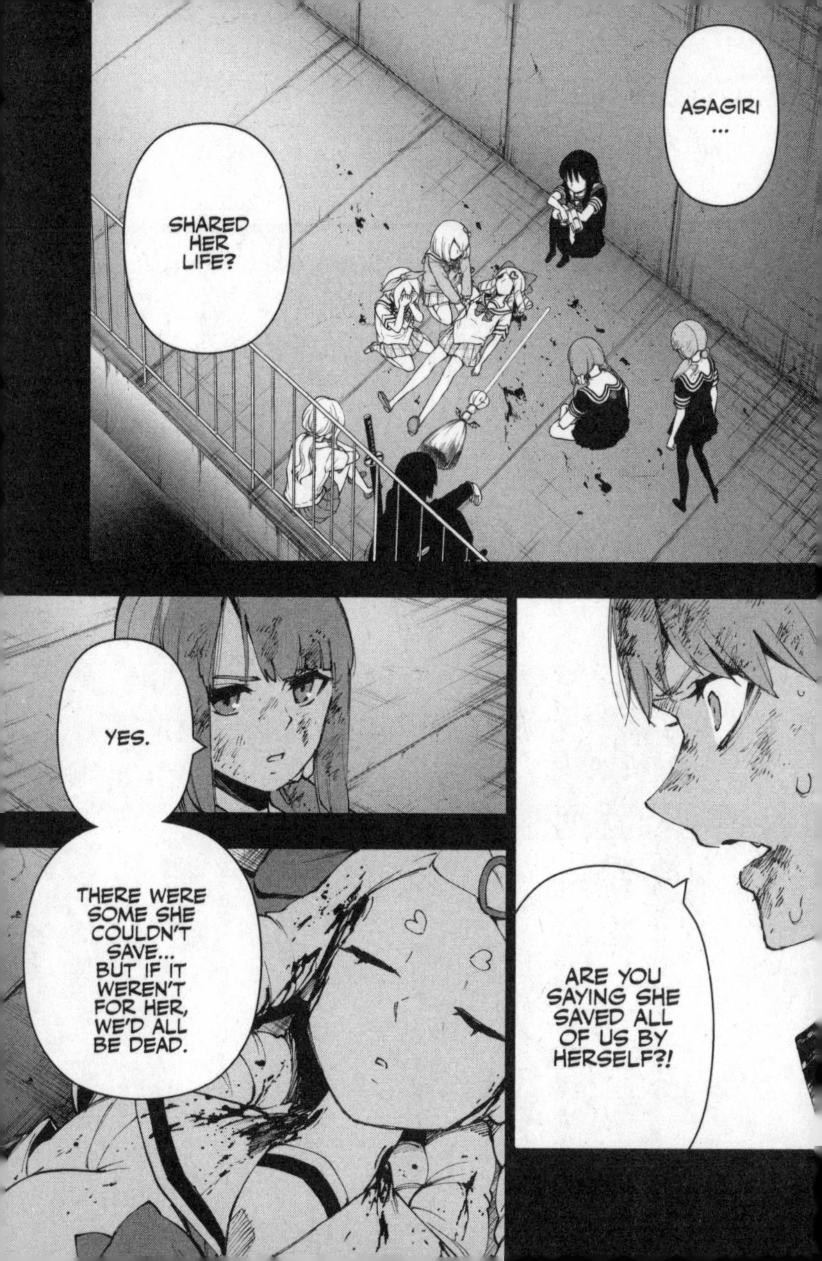
ASAGIRI ...
SHARED HER LIFE?
ARE YOU SAYING SHE SAVED ALL OF US BY HERSELF?!
YES.
THERE WERE SOME SHE COULDN'T SAVE... BUT IF IT WEREN'T FOR HER, WE'D ALL BE DEAD.

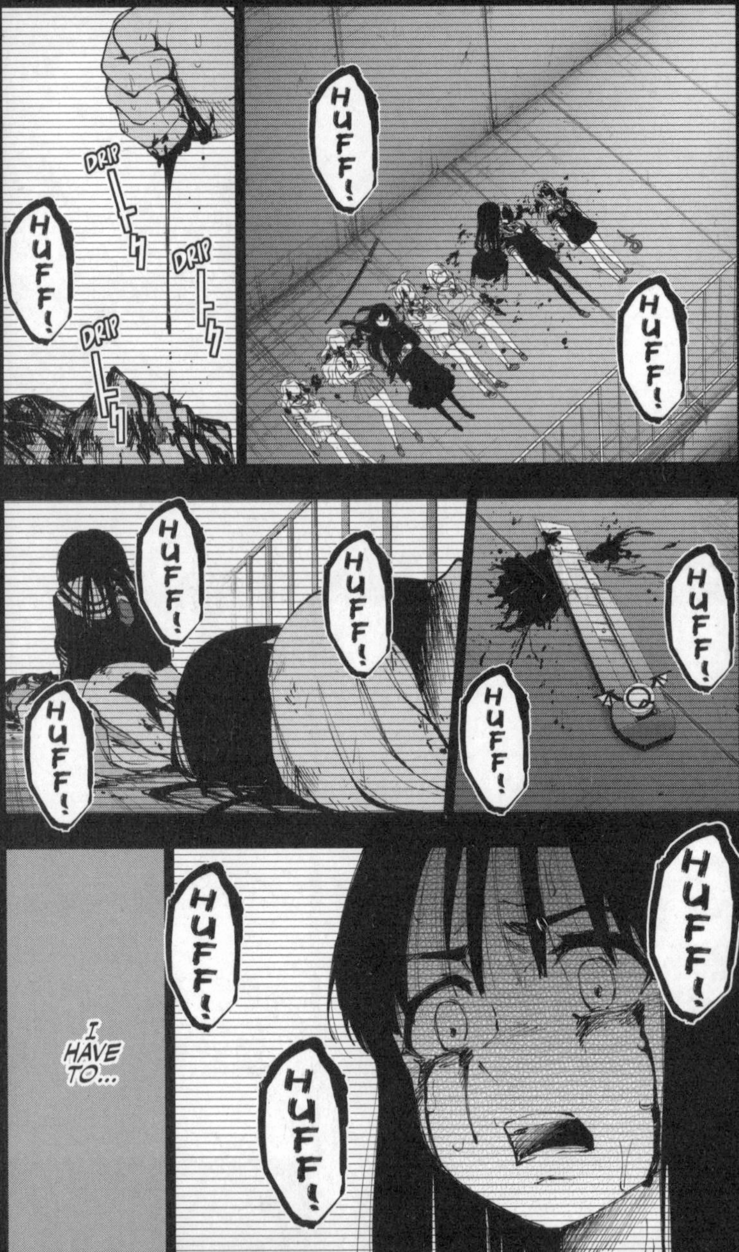
HUFF!
HUFF!
DRIP
DRIP
HUFF!
DRIP
HUFF!
HUFF!
HUFF!
HUFF!
HUFF!
HUFF!
HUFF!
HUFF!
I HAVE TO...

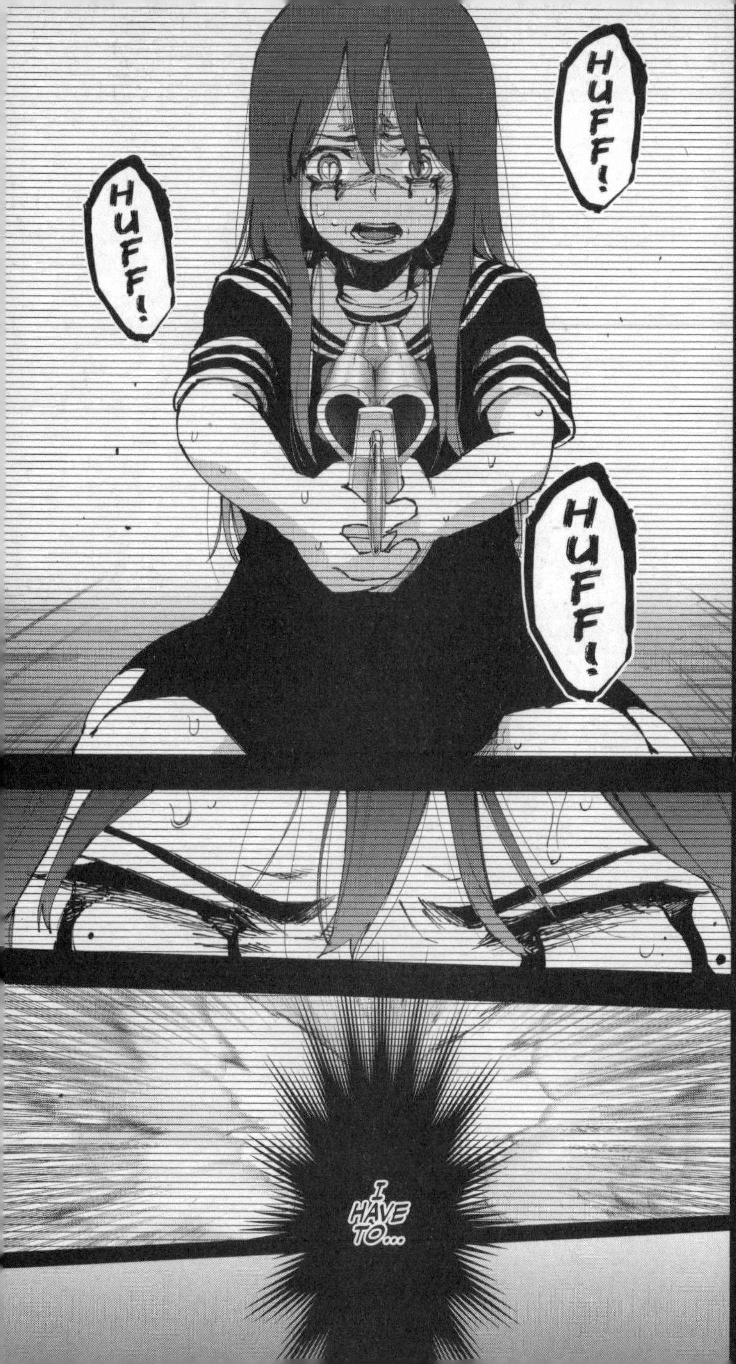
HUFF!
HUFF!
HUFF!
I HAVE TO...

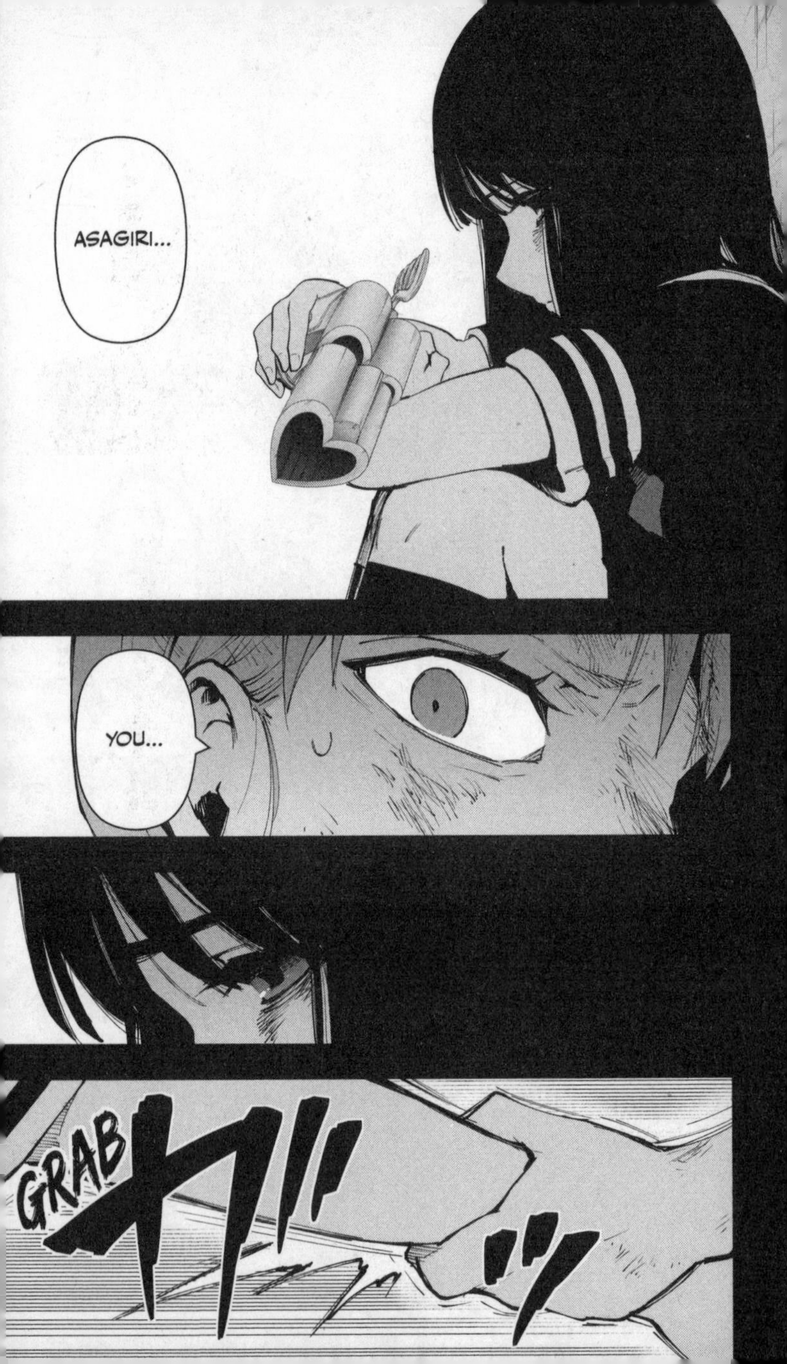
ASAGIRI...
YOU...
GRAB

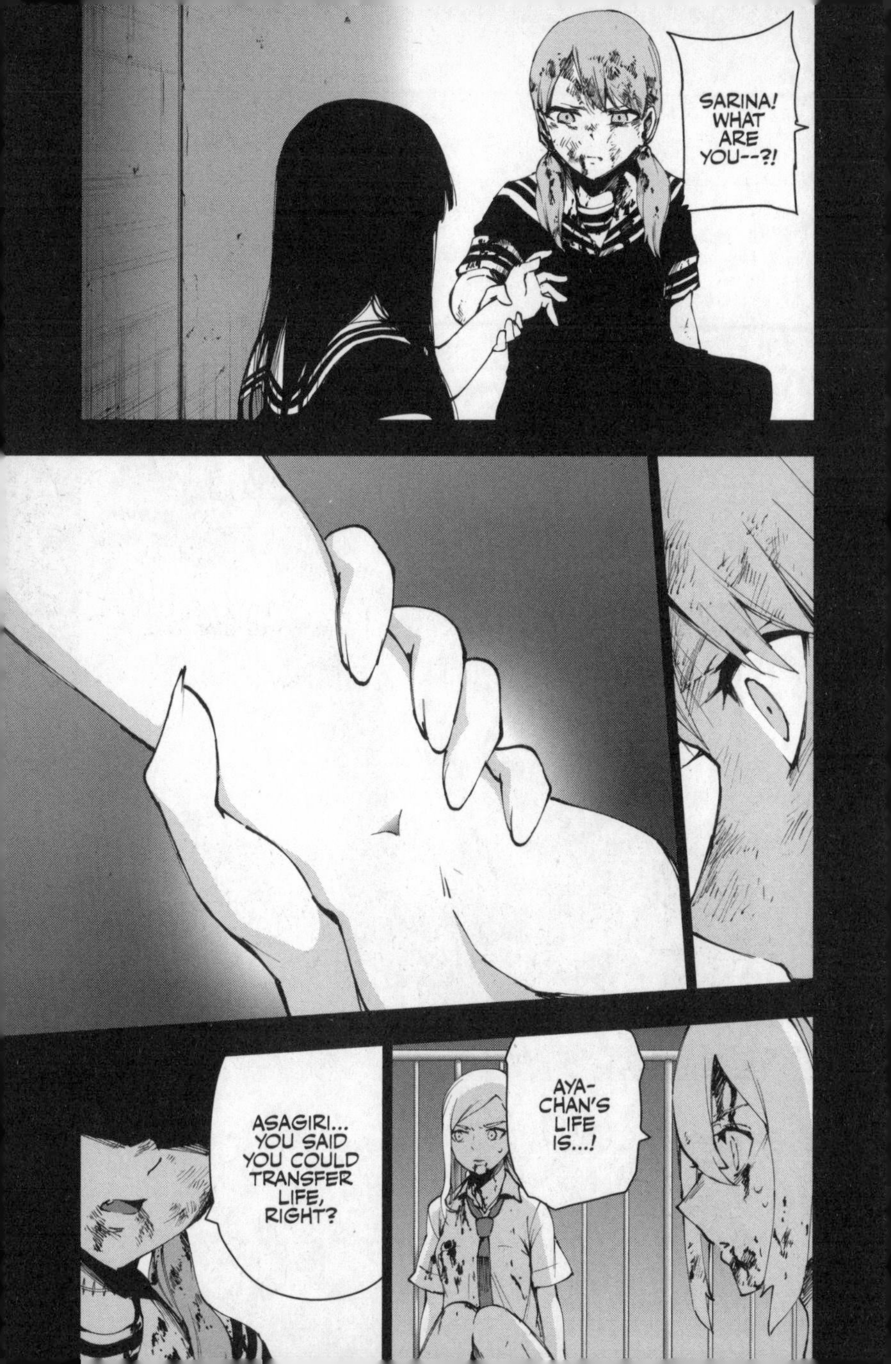
SARINA! WHAT ARE YOU--?!
AYA-CHAN'S LIFE IS...!
ASAGIRI... YOU SAID YOU COULD TRANSFER LIFE, RIGHT?

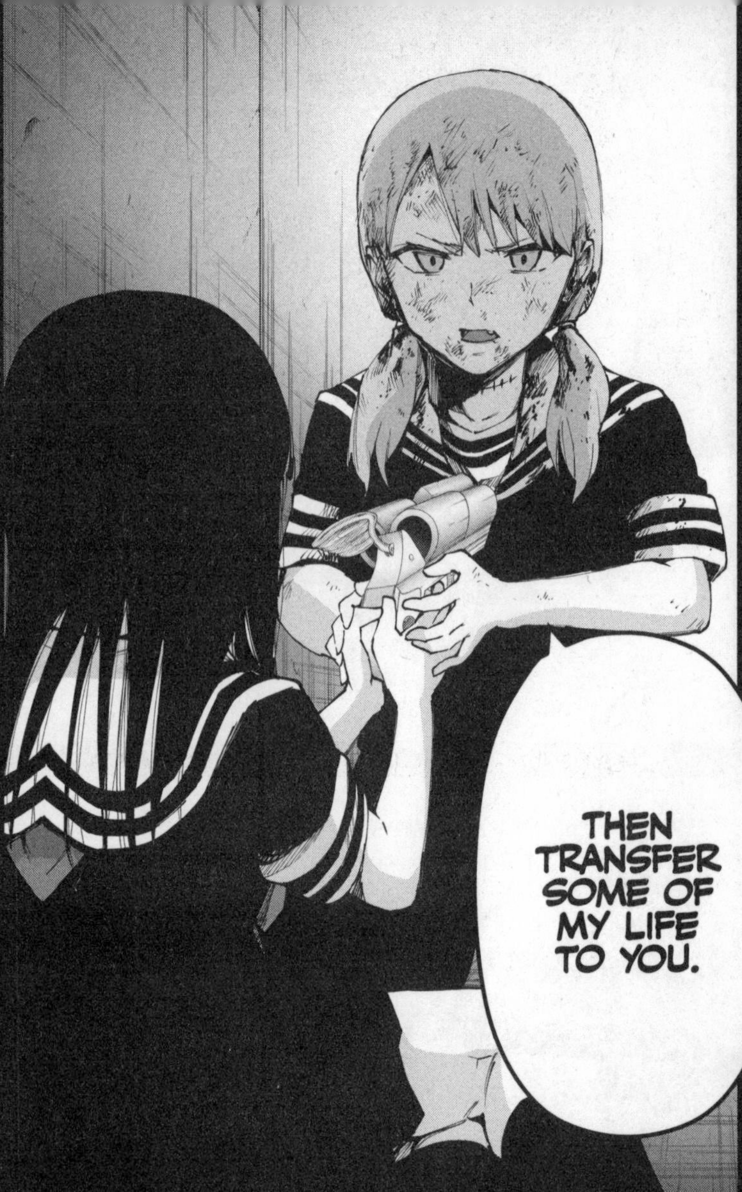
THEN TRANSFER SOME OF MY LIFE TO YOU.

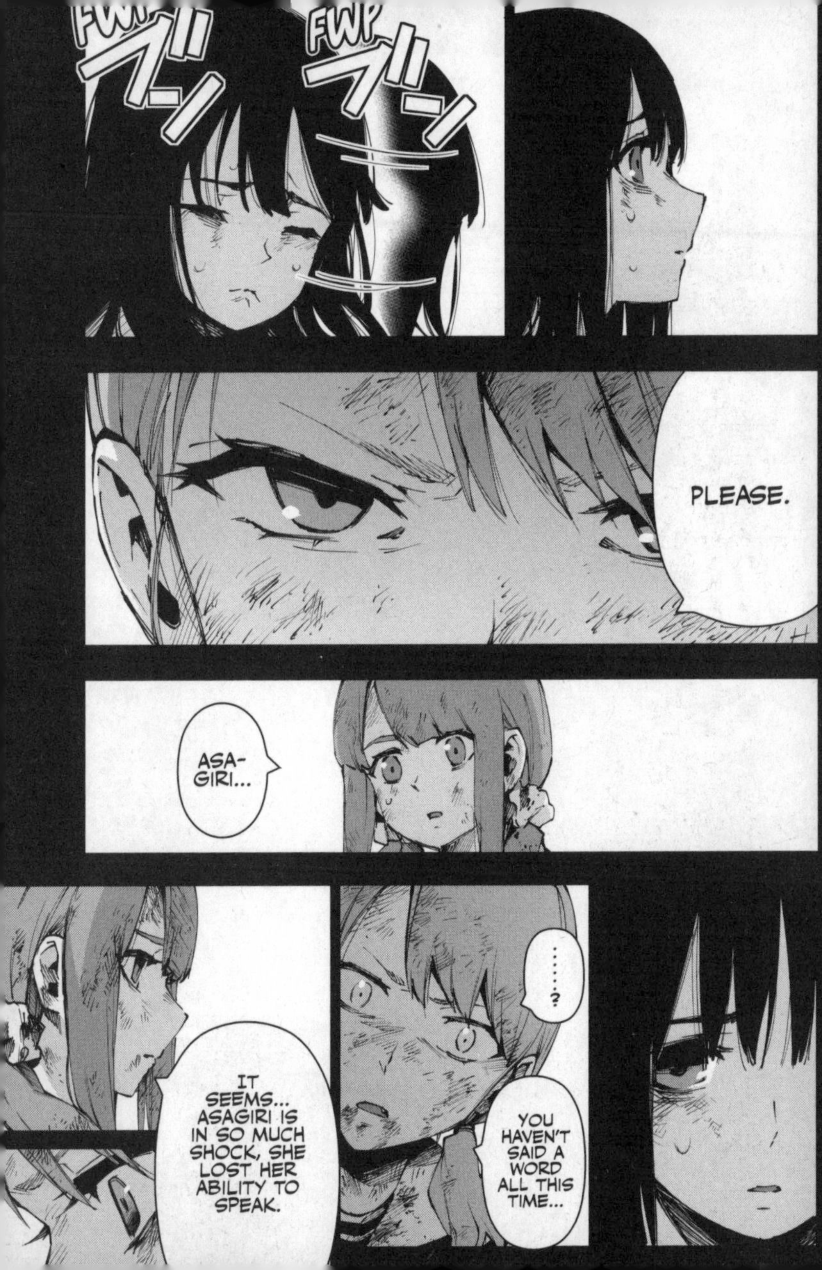
FWP
FWP
PLEASE.
ASA-GIRI...
......?
YOU HAVEN'T SAID A WORD ALL THIS TIME...
IT SEEMS... ASAGIRI IS IN SO MUCH SHOCK, SHE LOST HER ABILITY TO SPEAK.

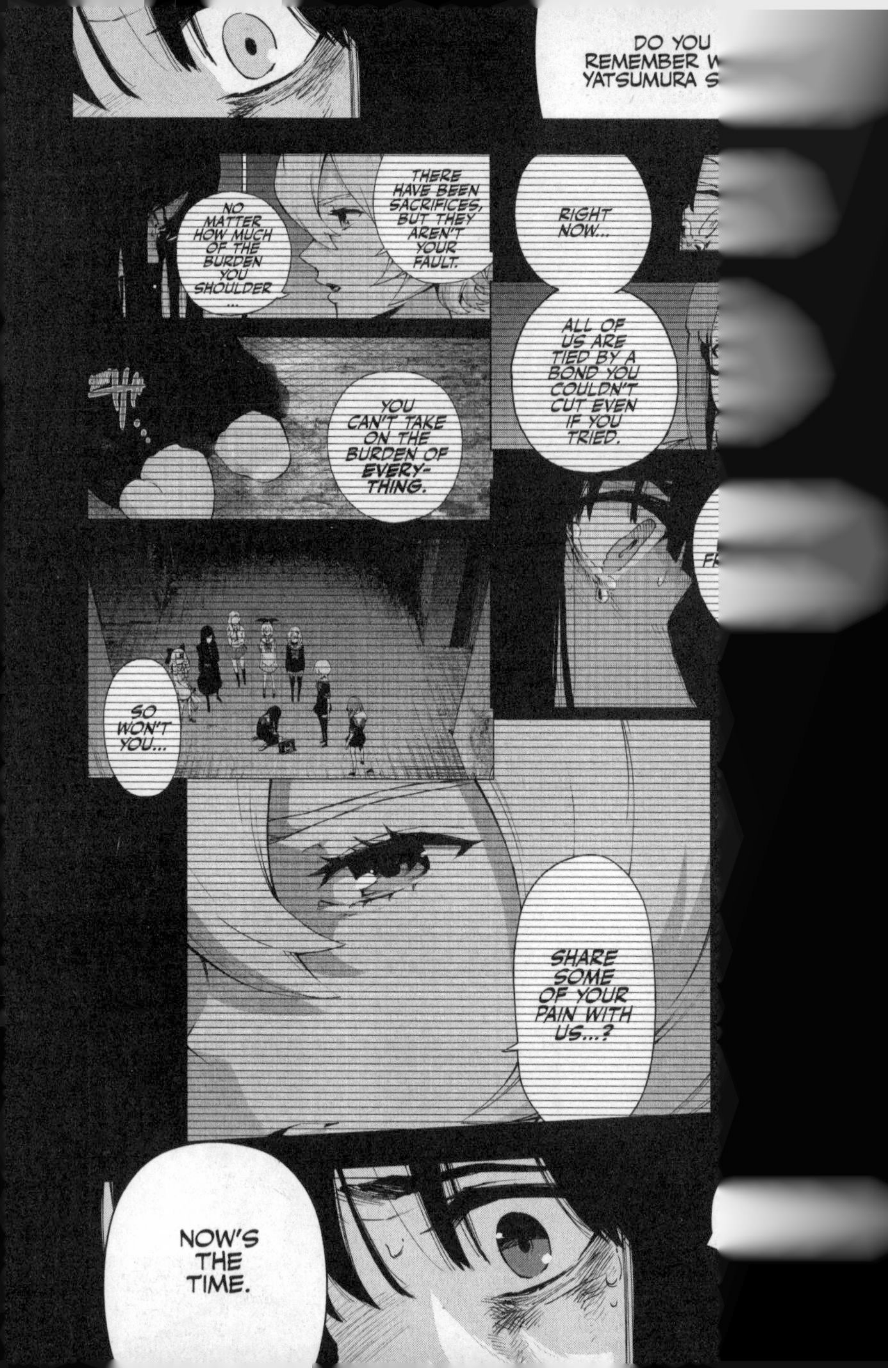

DO YOU REMEMBER
YATSUMURA
RIGHT NOW...
ALL OF US ARE TIED BY A BOND YOU COULDN'T CUT EVEN IF YOU TRIED.
THERE HAVE BEEN SACRIFICES, BUT THEY AREN'T YOUR FAULT.
NO MATTER HOW MUCH OF THE BURDEN YOU SHOULDER ...
YOU CAN'T TAKE ON THE BURDEN OF EVERYTHING.
SO WON'T YOU...
SHARE SOME OF YOUR PAIN WITH US...?
NOW'S THE TIME.

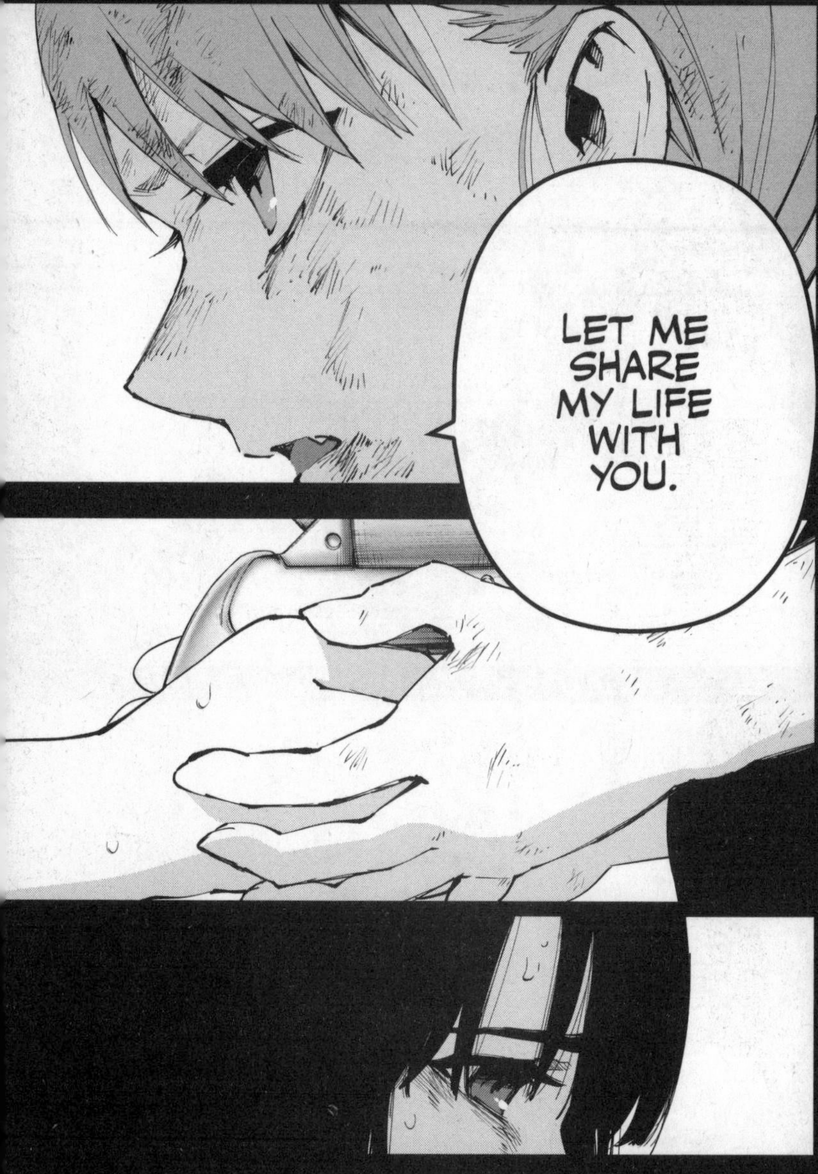
LET ME SHARE MY LIFE WITH YOU.

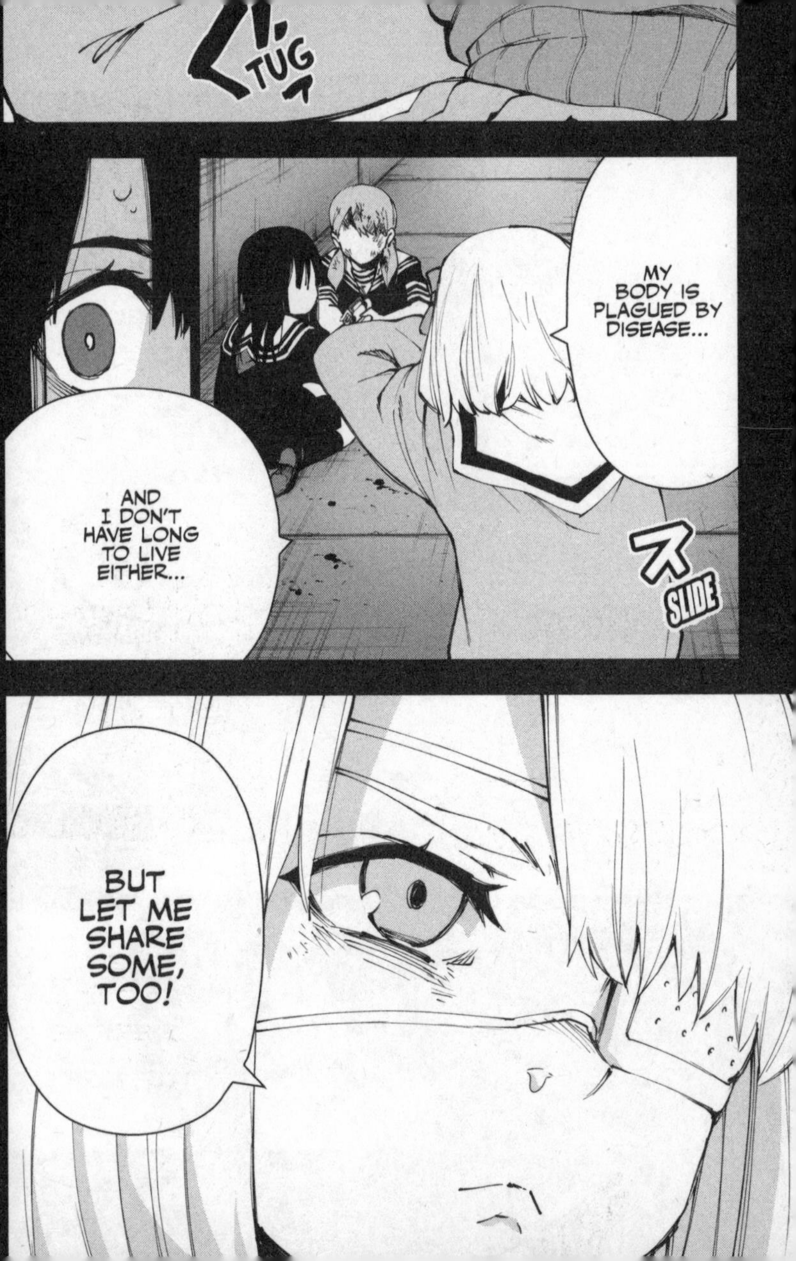
TUG
MY BODY IS PLAGUED BY DISEASE...
AND I DON'T HAVE LONG TO LIVE EITHER...
SLIDE
BUT LET ME SHARE SOME, TOO!

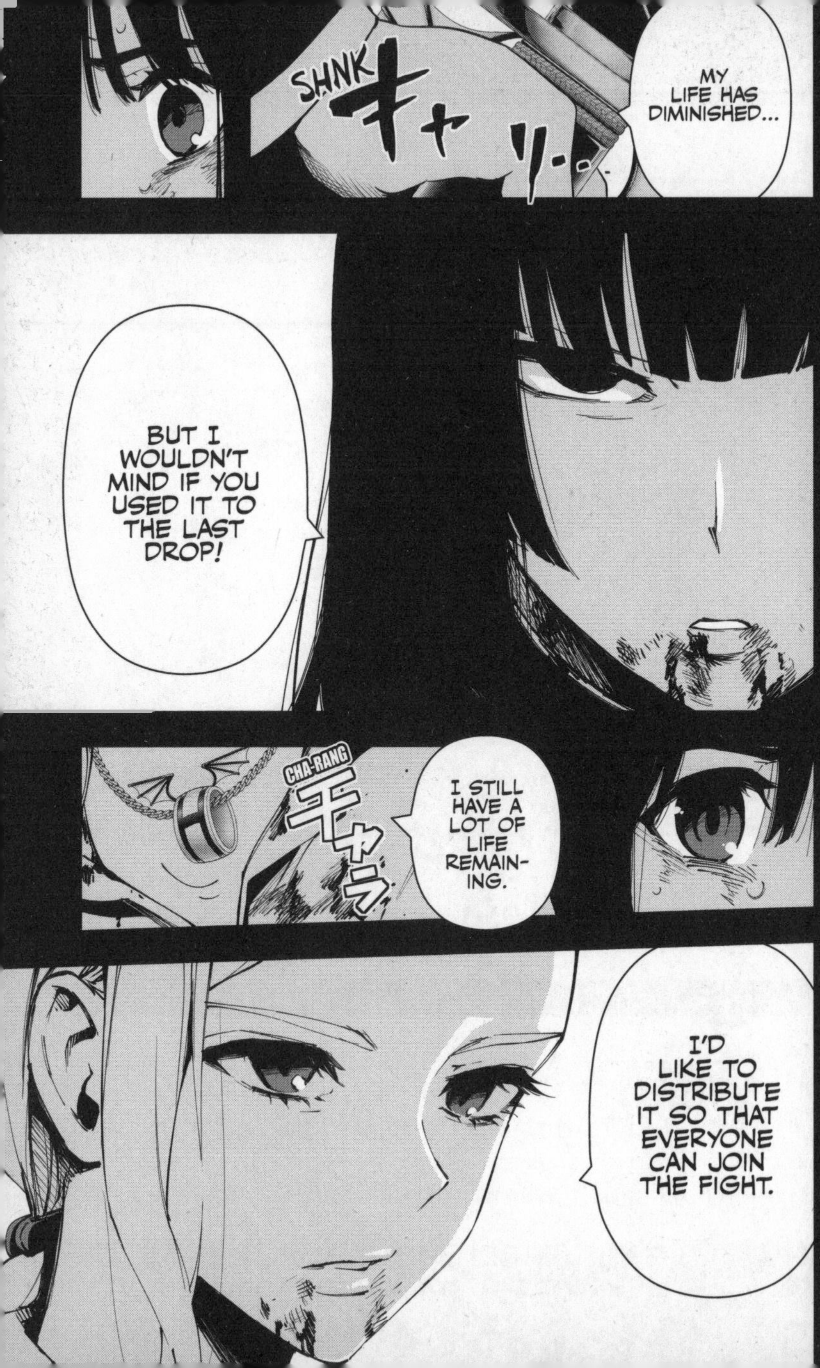
MY LIFE HAS DIMINISHED...
SHNK
BUT I WOULDN'T MIND IF YOU USED IT TO THE LAST DROP!
CHA-RANG
I STILL HAVE A LOT OF LIFE REMAIN-ING.
I'D LIKE TO DISTRIBUTE IT SO THAT EVERYONE CAN JOIN THE FIGHT.

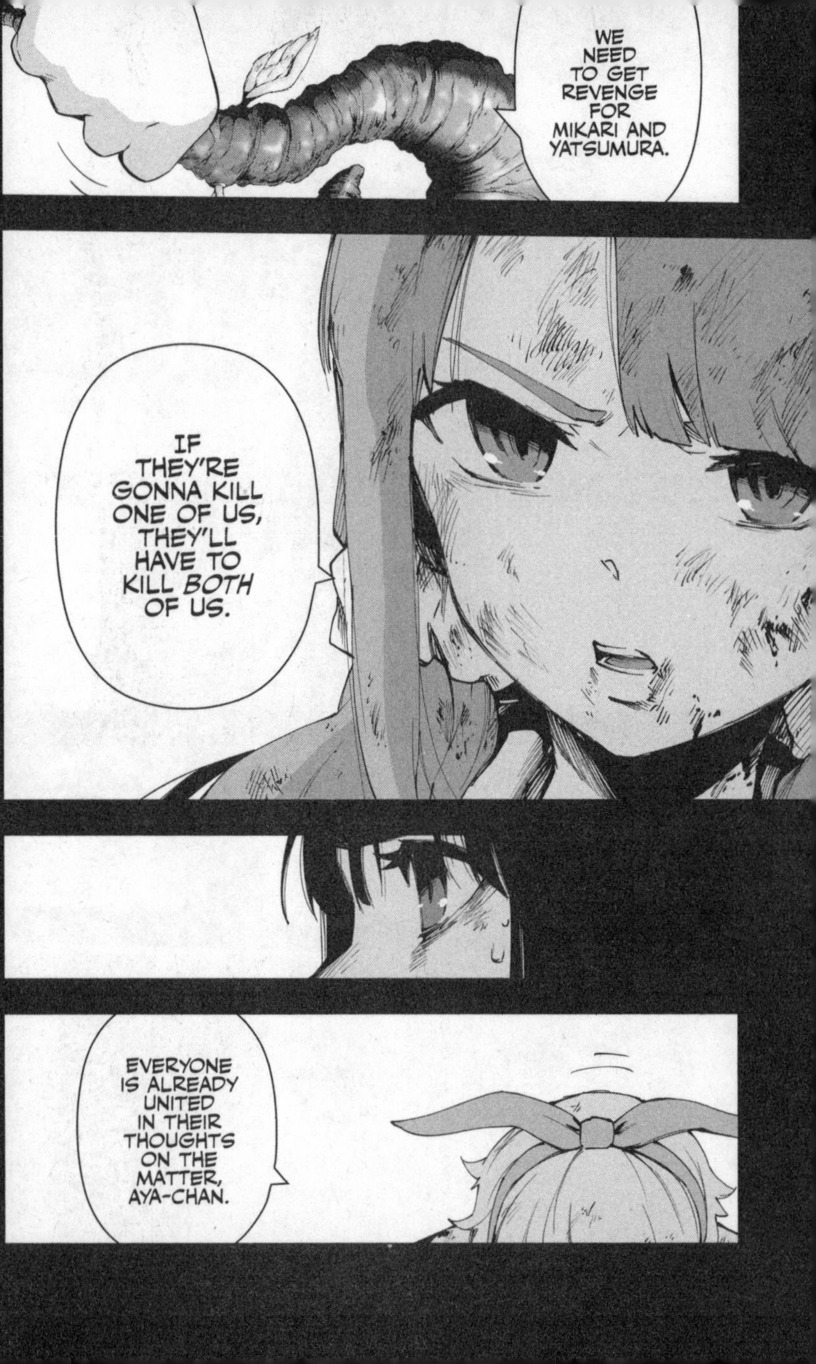
WE NEED TO GET REVENGE FOR MIKARI AND YATSUMURA.
IF THEY'RE GONNA KILL ONE OF US, THEY'LL HAVE TO KILL *BOTH* OF US.
EVERYONE IS ALREADY UNITED IN THEIR THOUGHTS ON THE MATTER, AYA-CHAN.

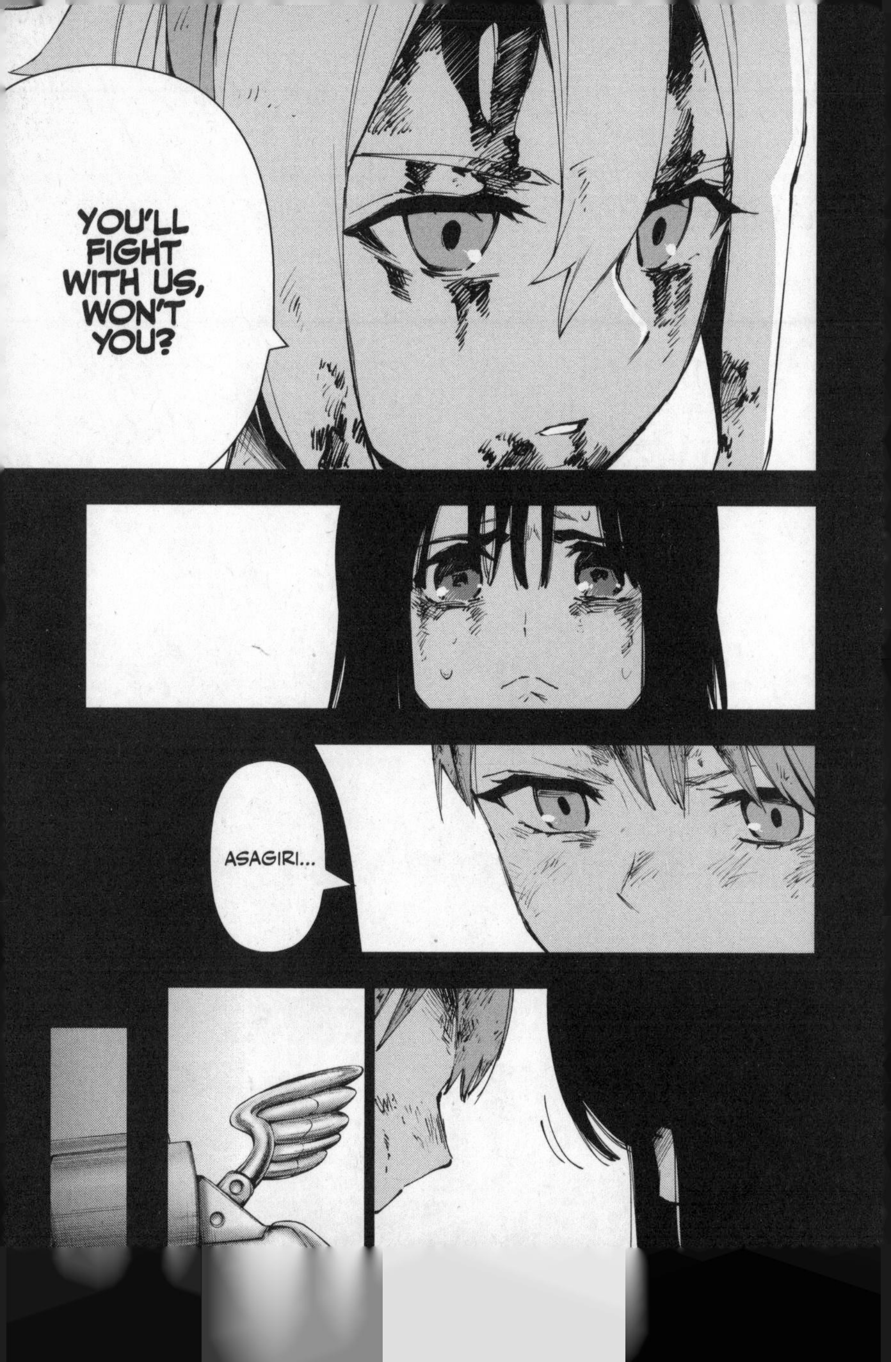
YOU'LL FIGHT WITH US, WON'T YOU?
ASAGIRI...

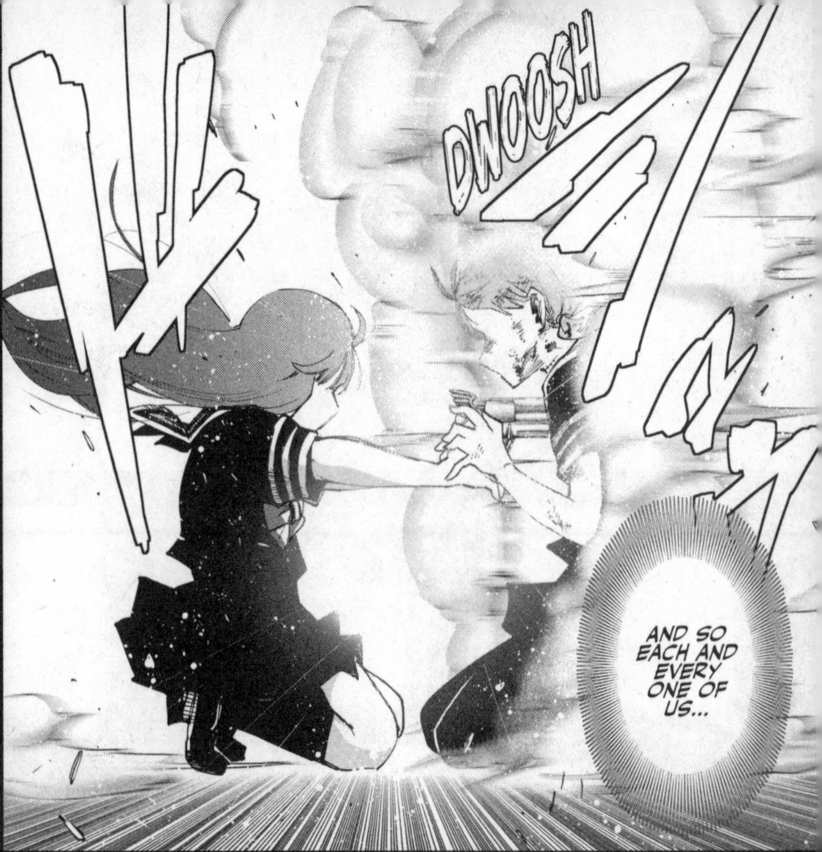
DWOOSH
AND SO EACH AND EVERY ONE OF US...
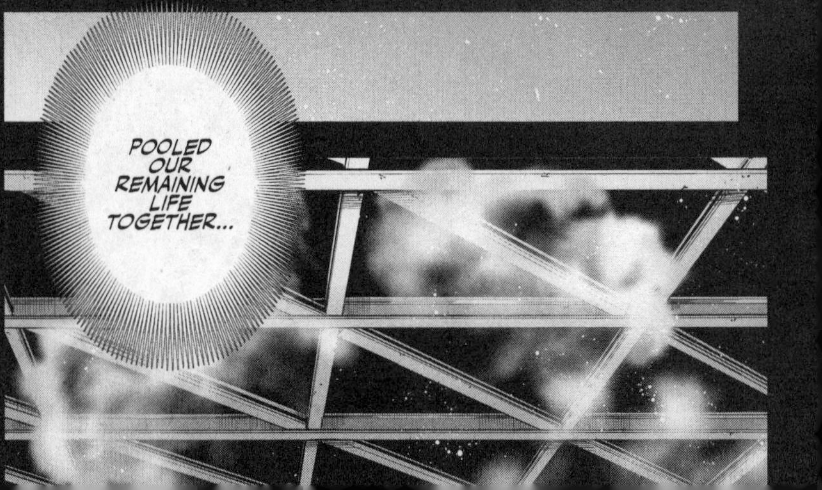
POOLED OUR REMAINING LIFE TOGETHER...

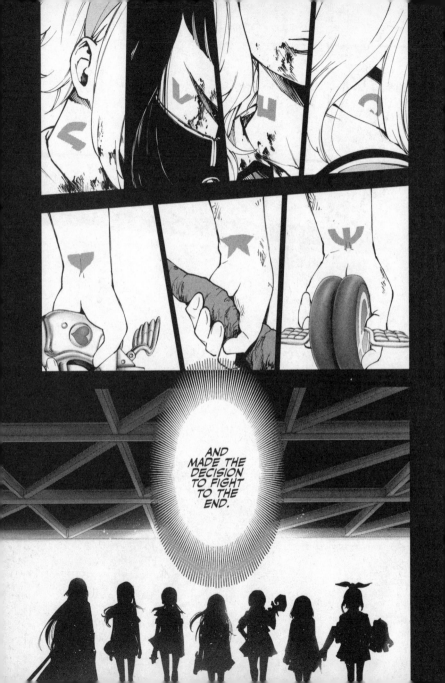

AND MADE THE DECISION TO FIGHT TO THE END.

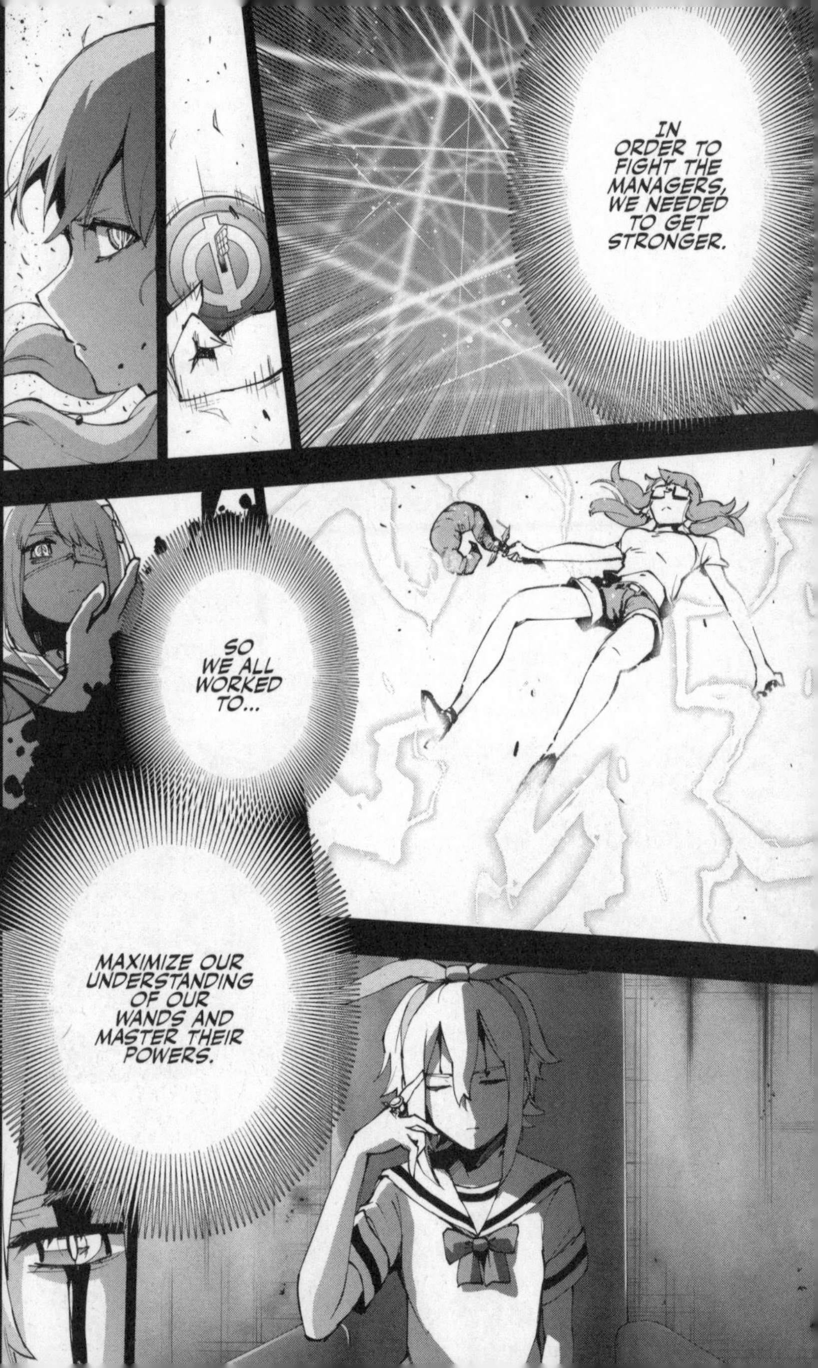
IN ORDER TO FIGHT THE MANAGERS, WE NEEDED TO GET STRONGER.
SO WE ALL WORKED TO...
MAXIMIZE OUR UNDERSTANDING OF OUR WANDS AND MASTER THEIR POWERS.

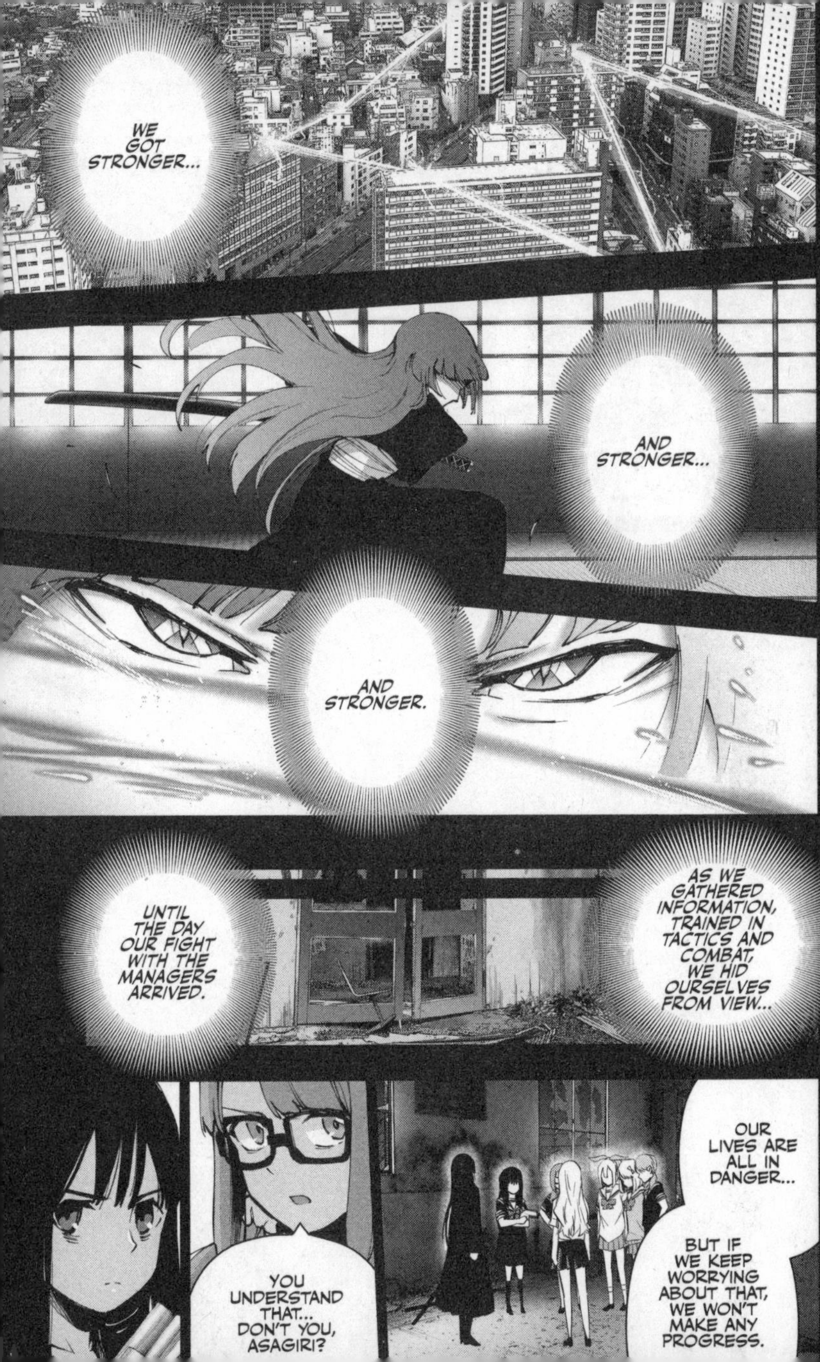
WE GOT STRONGER...
AND STRONGER...
AND STRONGER.
AS WE GATHERED INFORMATION, TRAINED IN TACTICS AND COMBAT, WE HID OURSELVES FROM VIEW...
UNTIL THE DAY OUR FIGHT WITH THE MANAGERS ARRIVED.
OUR LIVES ARE ALL IN DANGER...
BUT IF WE KEEP WORRYING ABOUT THAT, WE WON'T MAKE ANY PROGRESS.
YOU UNDERSTAND THAT... DON'T YOU, ASAGIRI?

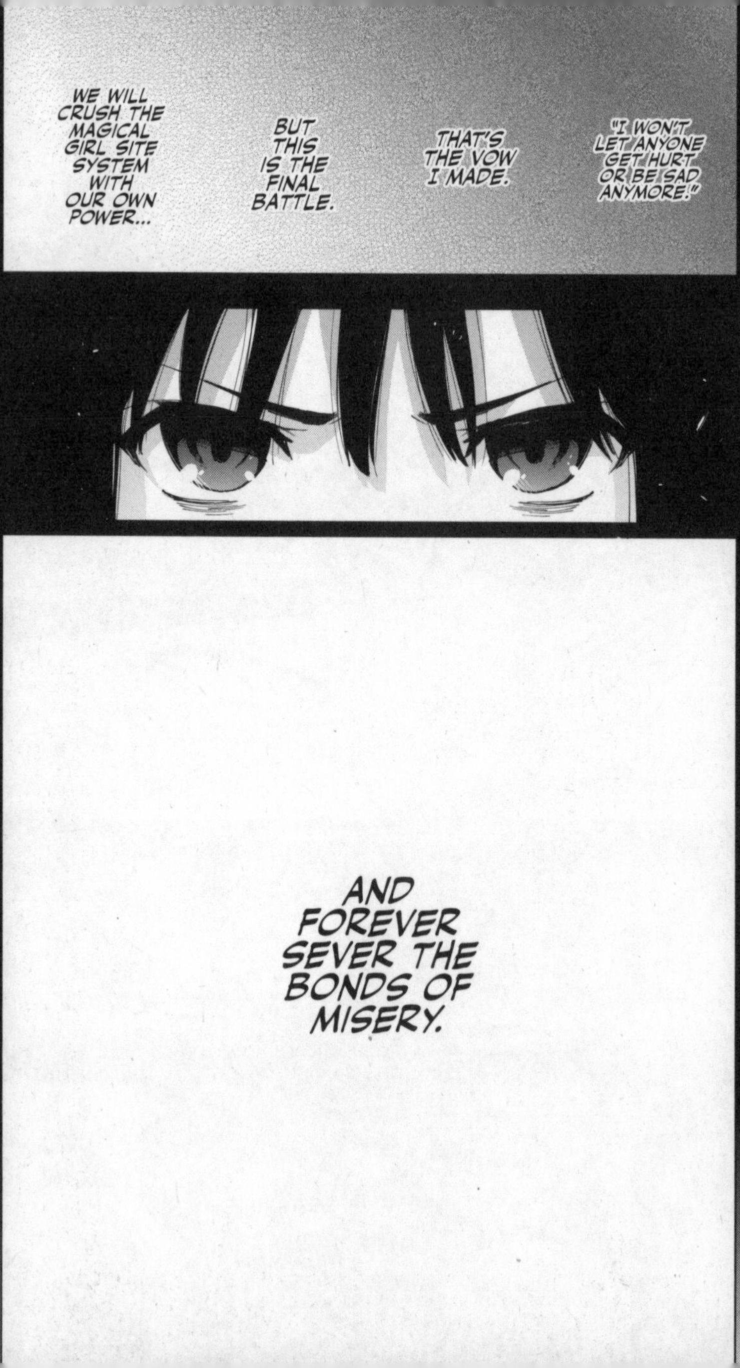
"I WON'T LET ANYONE GET HURT OR BE SAD ANYMORE."
THAT'S THE VOW I MADE.
BUT THIS IS THE FINAL BATTLE.
WE WILL CRUSH THE MAGICAL GIRL SITE SYSTEM WITH OUR OWN POWER...
AND FOREVER SEVER THE BONDS OF MISERY.

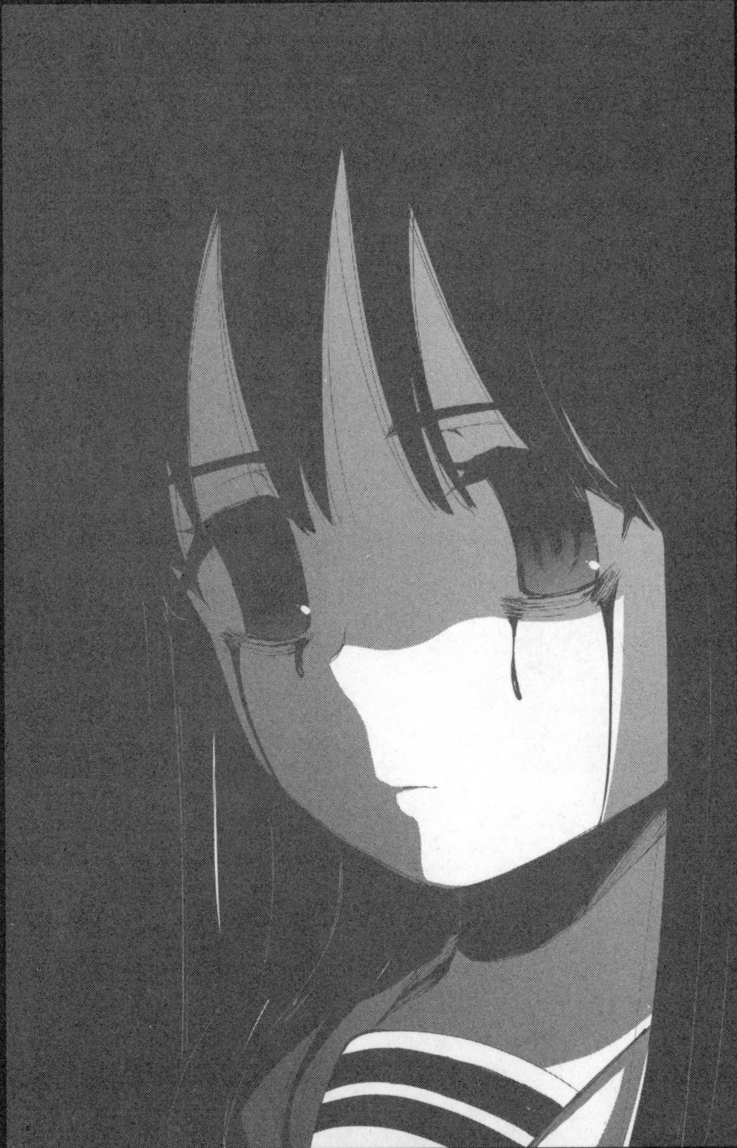

ENTER.89 BONDS OF MISERY

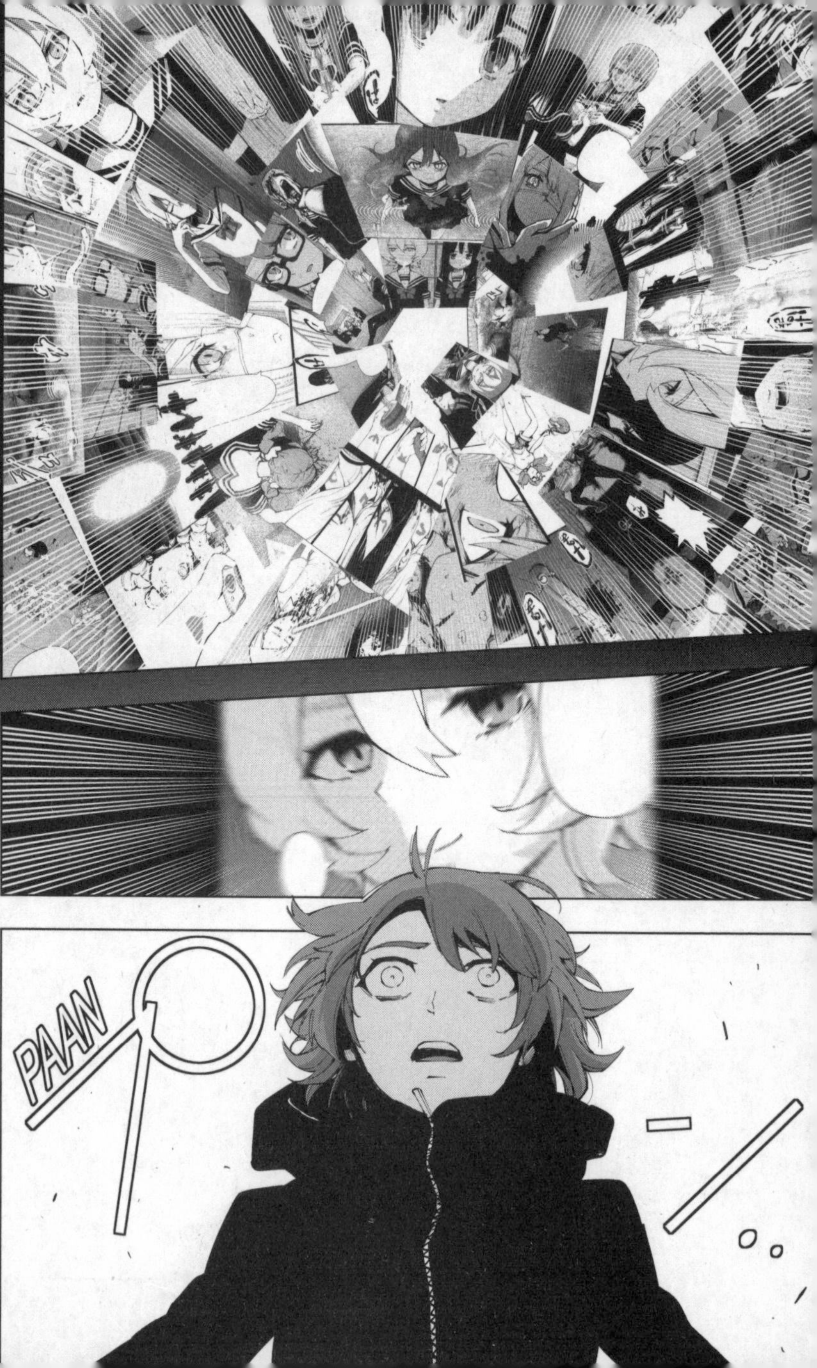
PAAN

PLIP..

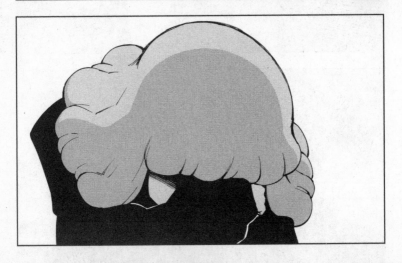

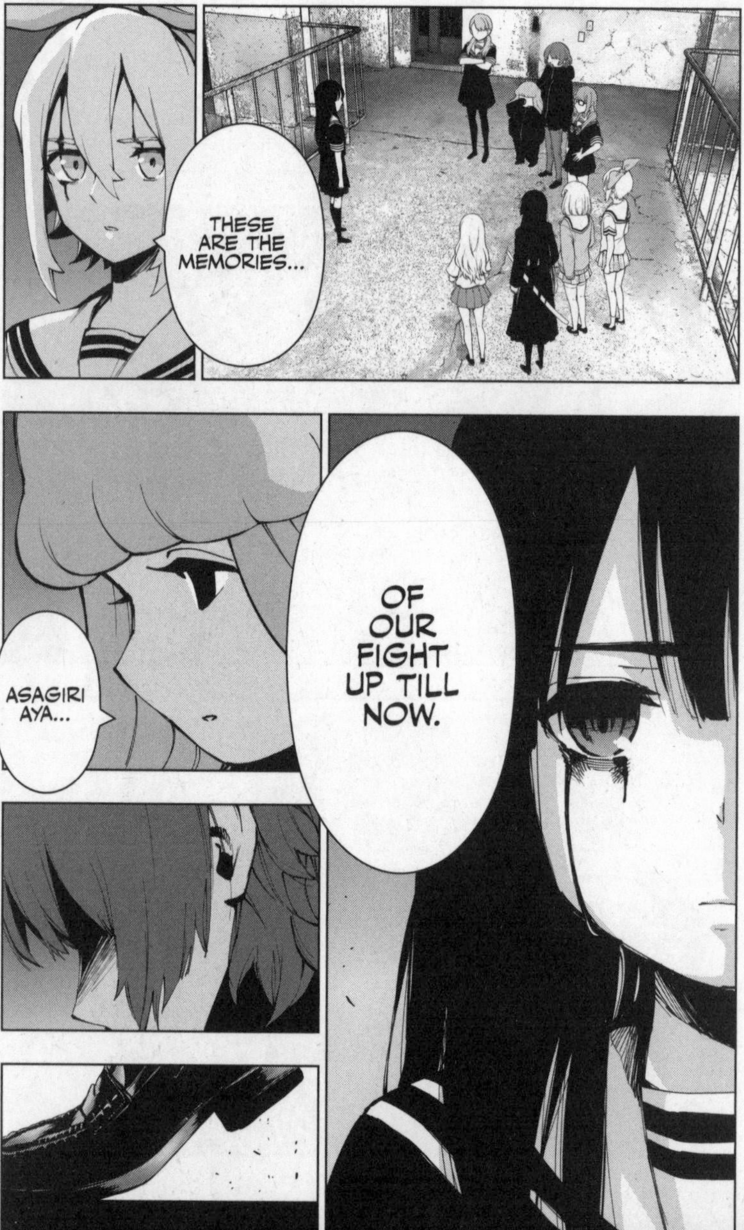
THESE ARE THE MEMORIES...
OF OUR FIGHT UP TILL NOW.
ASAGIRI AYA...

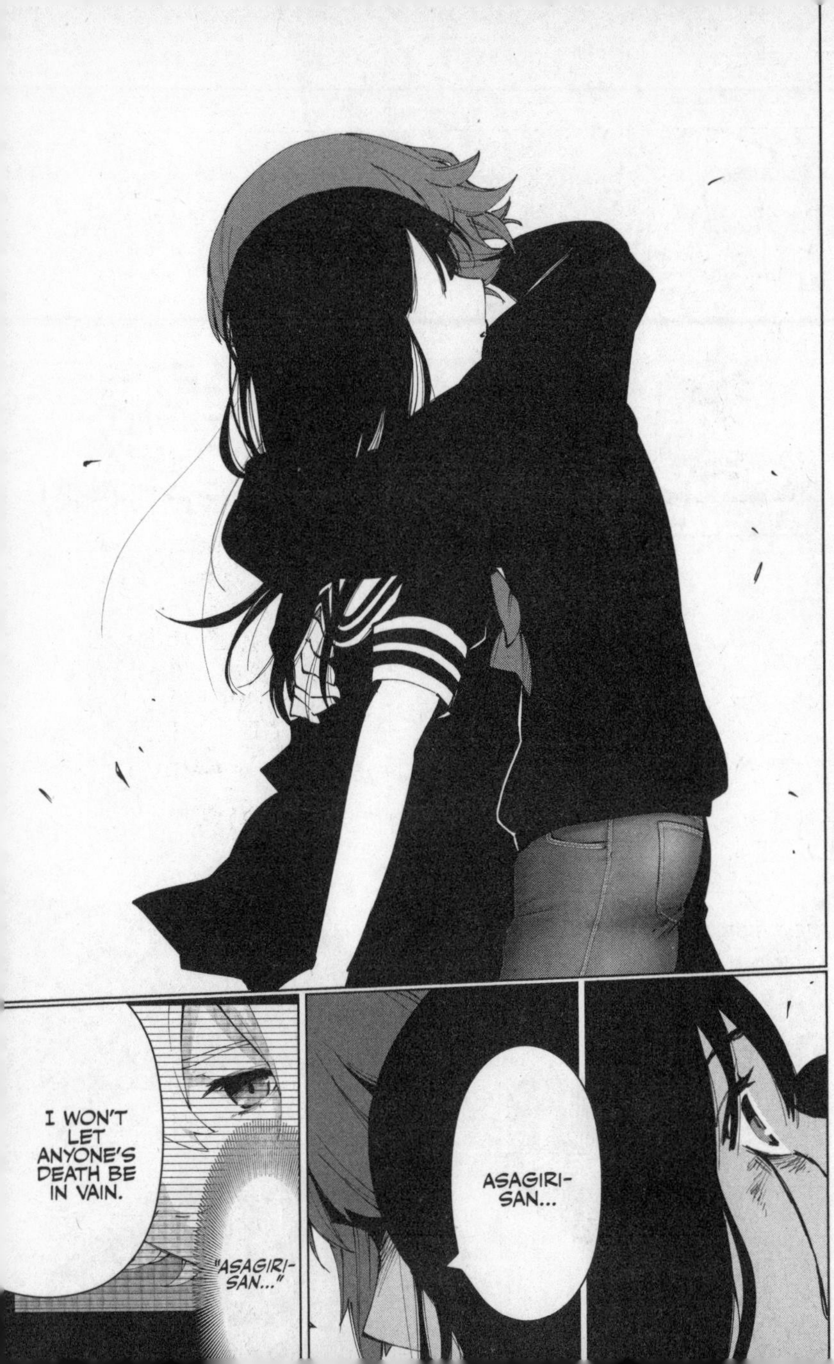
ASAGIRI-SAN...
I WON'T LET ANYONE'S DEATH BE IN VAIN.
"ASAGIRI-SAN..."

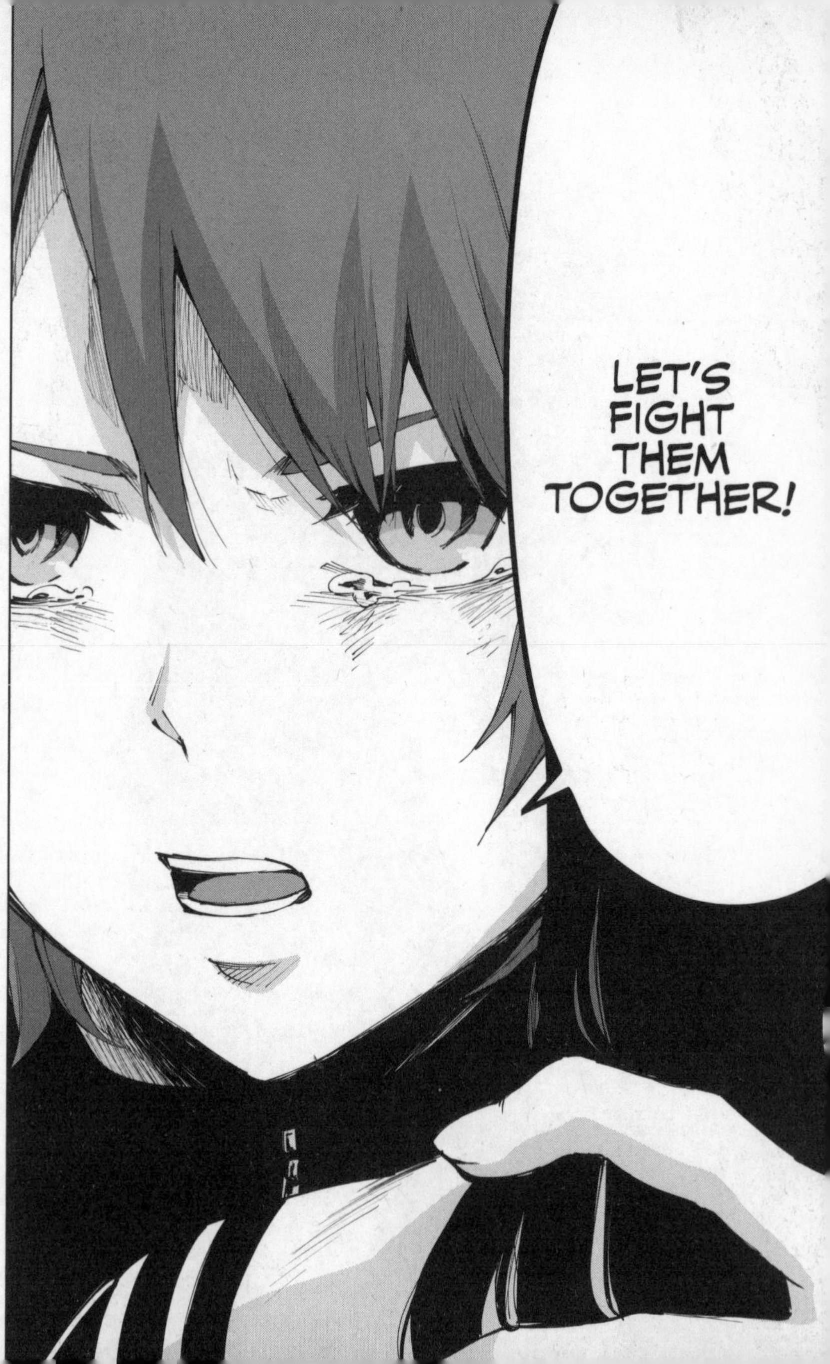
LET'S FIGHT THEM TOGETHER!

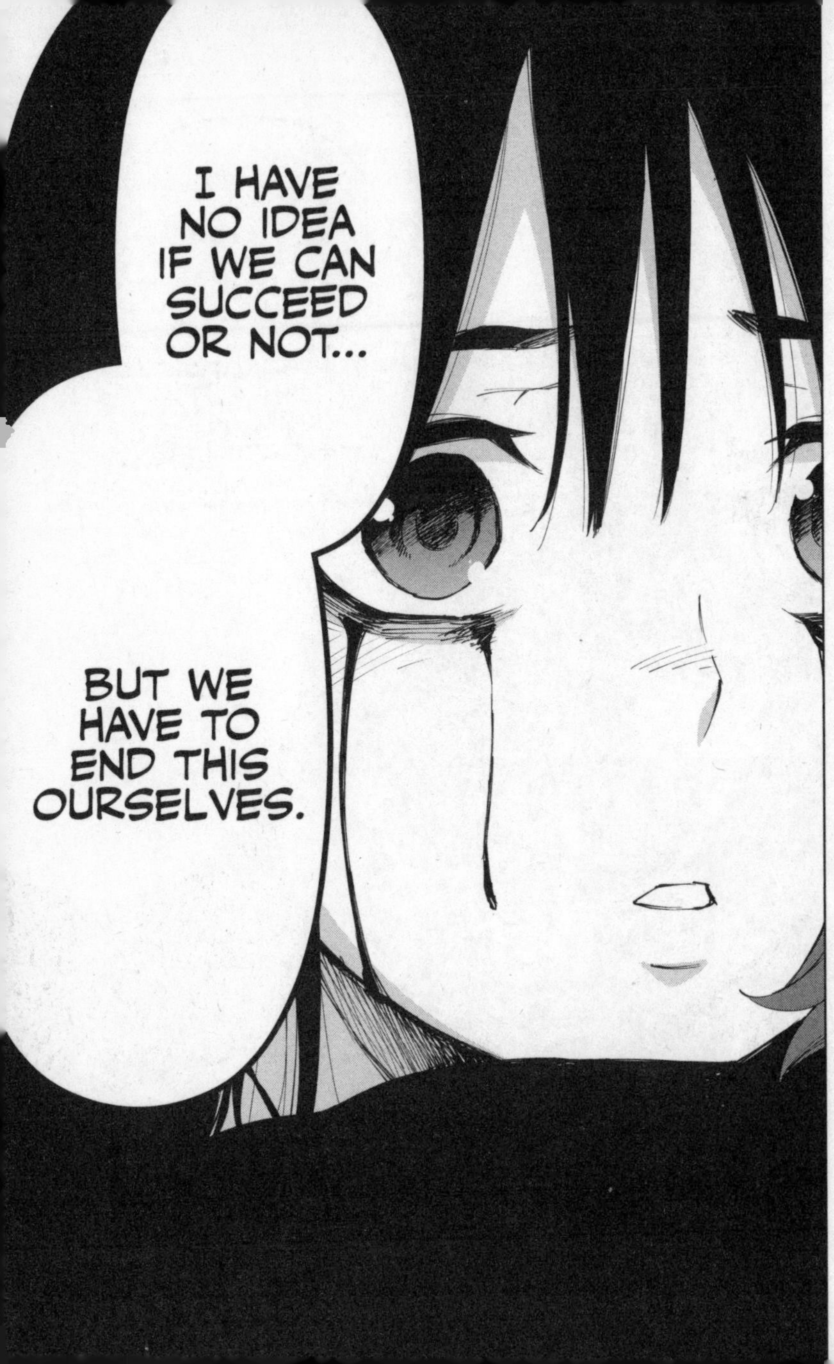
I HAVE NO IDEA IF WE CAN SUCCEED OR NOT...
BUT WE HAVE TO END THIS OURSELVES.

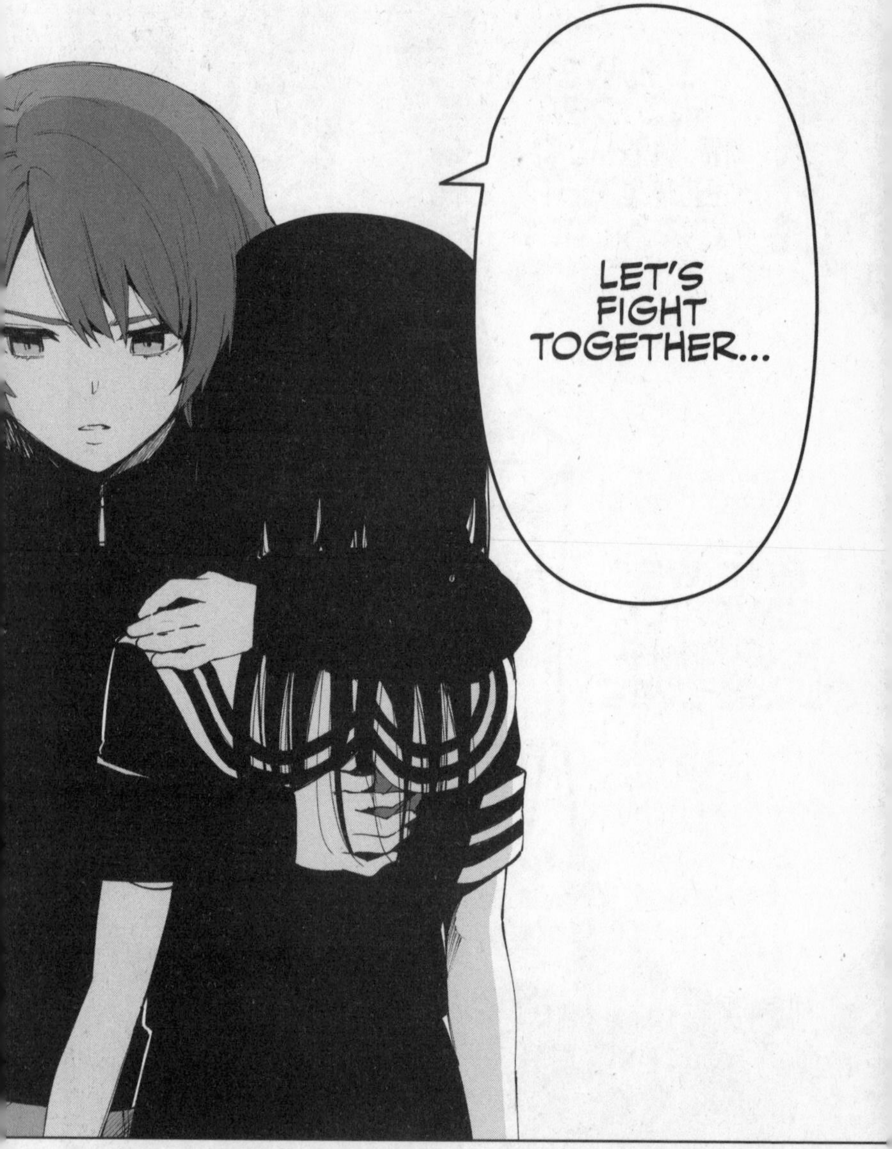
LET'S FIGHT TOGETHER...

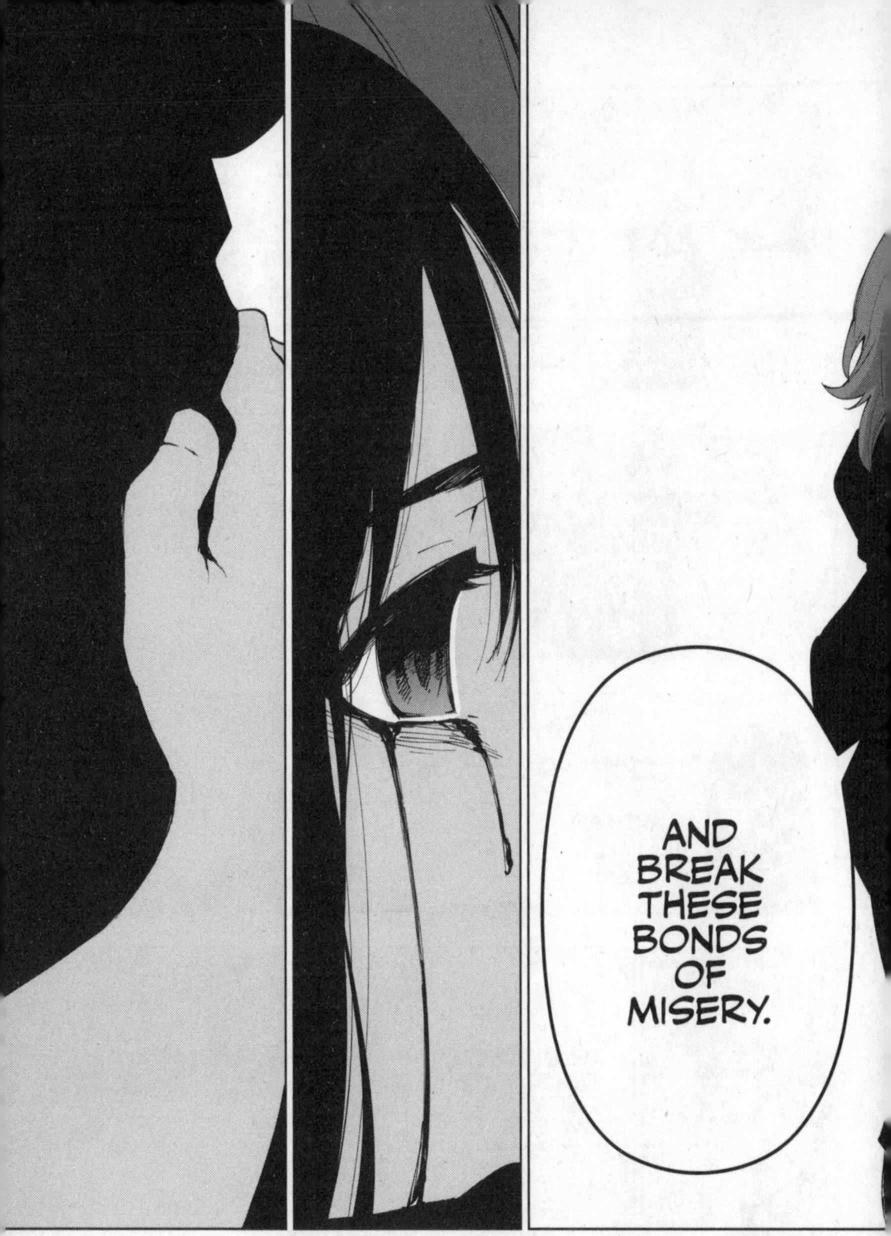
AND BREAK THESE BONDS OF MISERY.

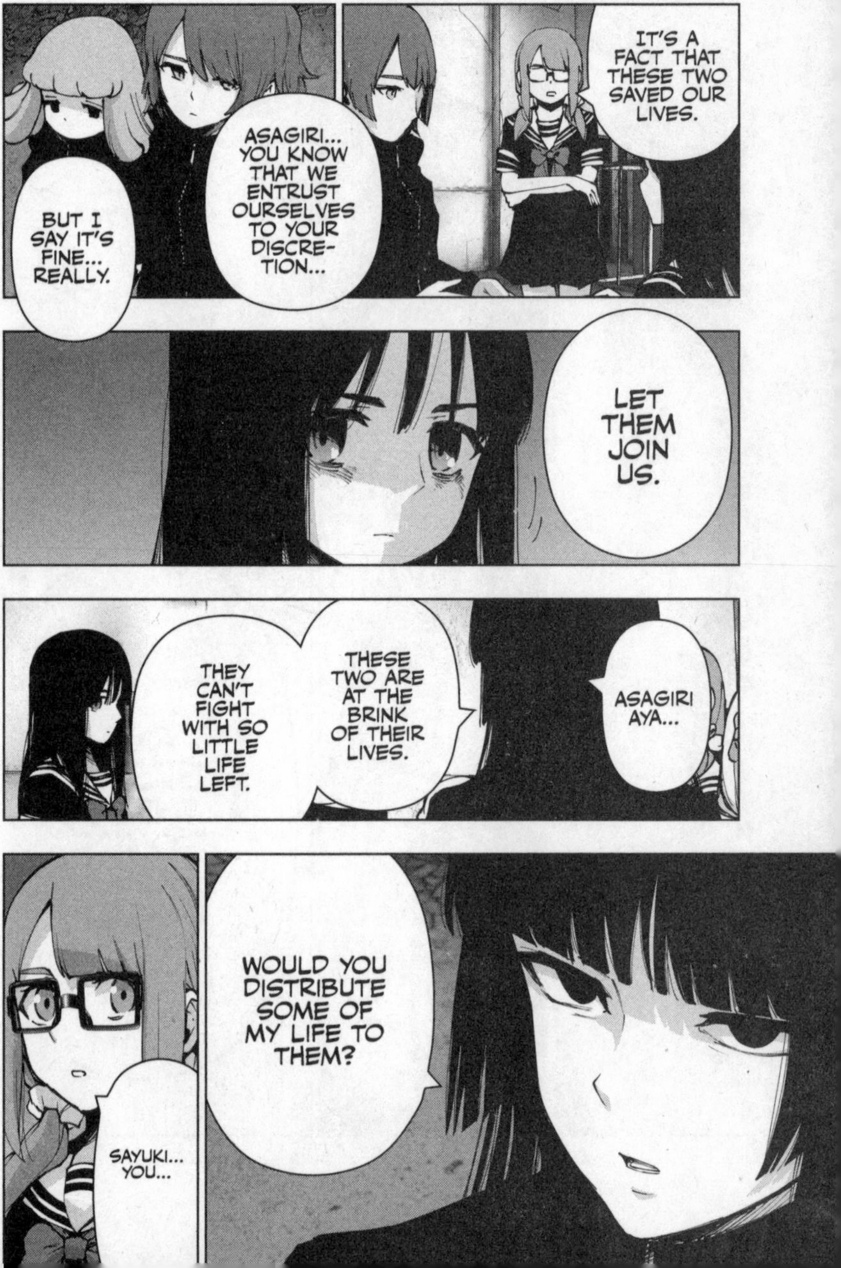
IT'S A FACT THAT THESE TWO SAVED OUR LIVES.
ASAGIRI... YOU KNOW THAT WE ENTRUST OURSELVES TO YOUR DISCRETION...
BUT I SAY IT'S FINE... REALLY.
LET THEM JOIN US.
ASAGIRI AYA...
THESE TWO ARE AT THE BRINK OF THEIR LIVES.
THEY CAN'T FIGHT WITH SO LITTLE LIFE LEFT.
WOULD YOU DISTRIBUTE SOME OF MY LIFE TO THEM?
SAYUKI... YOU...

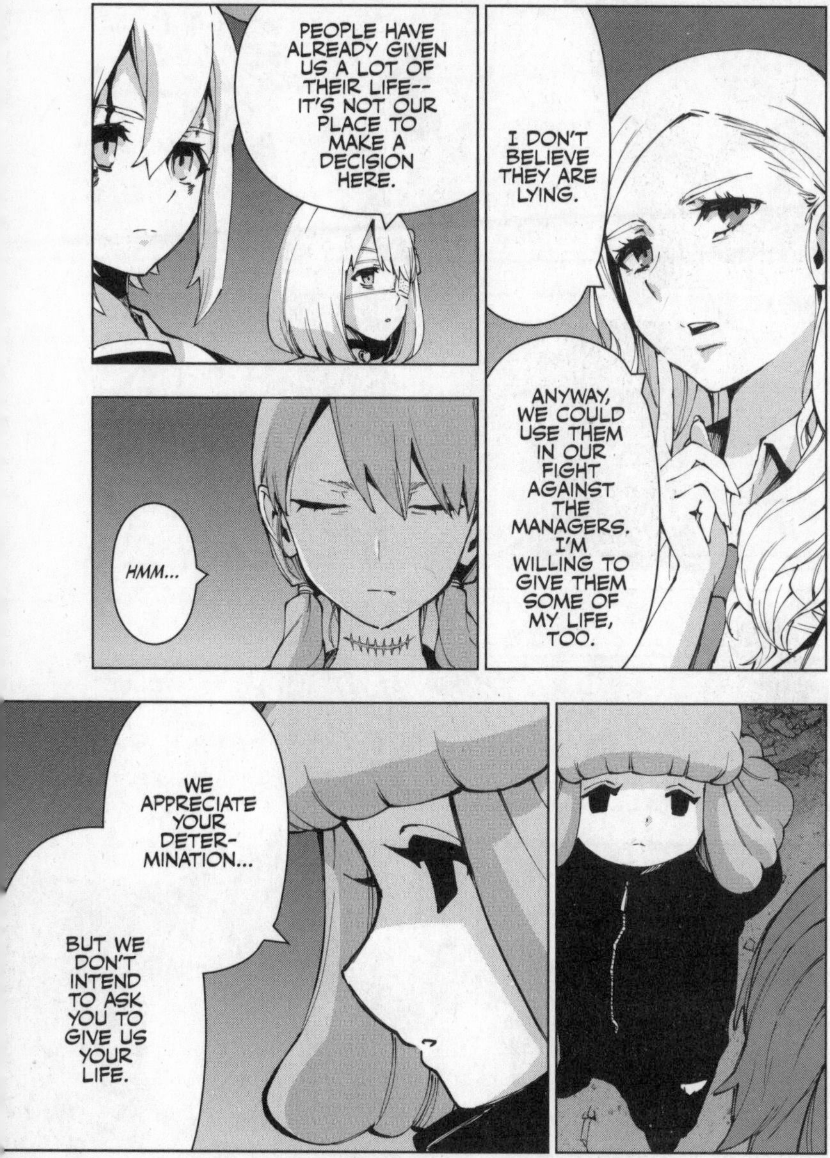
I DON'T BELIEVE THEY ARE LYING.
ANYWAY, WE COULD USE THEM IN OUR FIGHT AGAINST THE MANAGERS. I'M WILLING TO GIVE THEM SOME OF MY LIFE, TOO.
PEOPLE HAVE ALREADY GIVEN US A LOT OF THEIR LIFE-- IT'S NOT OUR PLACE TO MAKE A DECISION HERE.
HMM...
WE APPRECIATE YOUR DETER-MINATION...
BUT WE DON'T INTEND TO ASK YOU TO GIVE US YOUR LIFE.

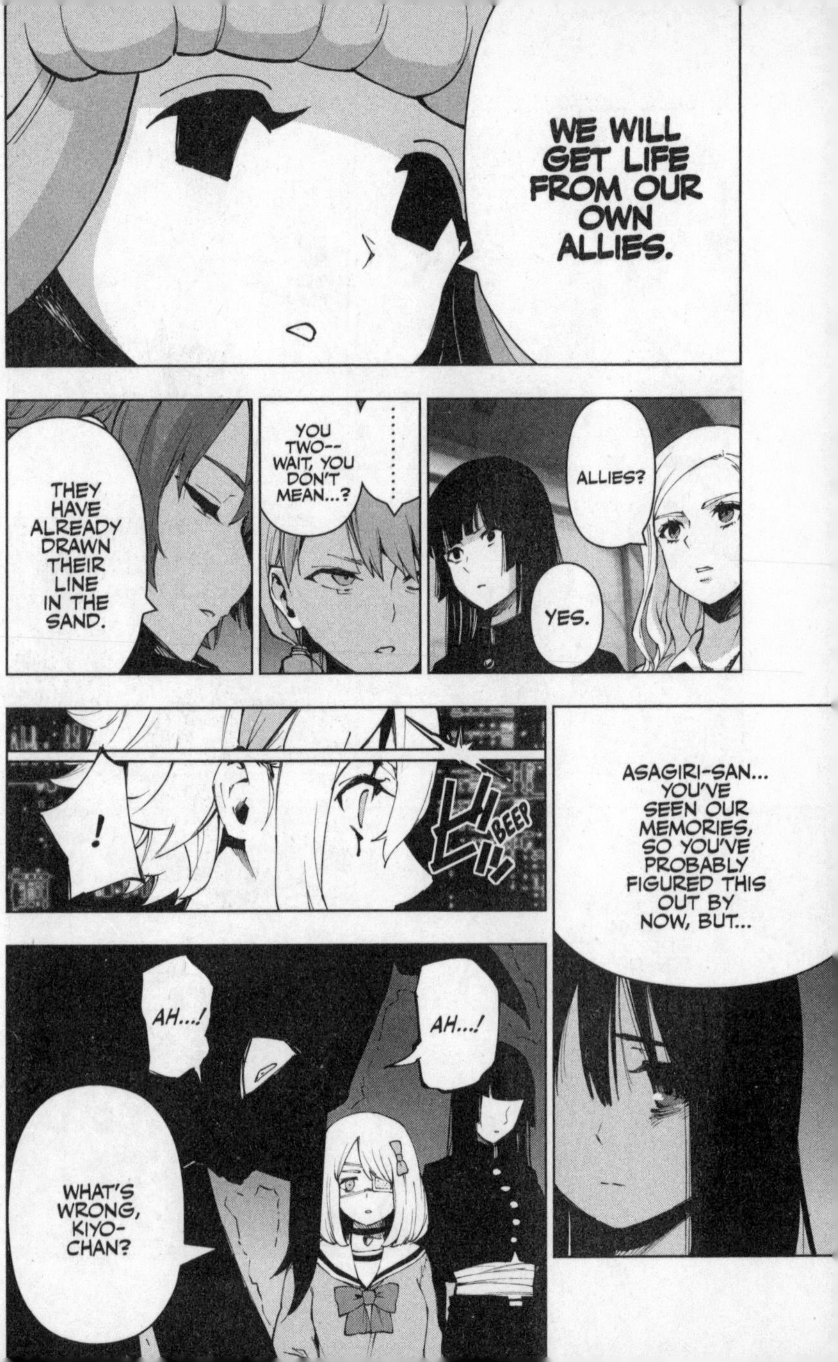
WE WILL GET LIFE FROM OUR OWN ALLIES.
ALLIES?
YES.
YOU TWO-- WAIT, YOU DON'T MEAN...?
THEY HAVE ALREADY DRAWN THEIR LINE IN THE SAND.
ASAGIRI-SAN... YOU'VE SEEN OUR MEMORIES, SO YOU'VE PROBABLY FIGURED THIS OUT BY NOW, BUT...
BEEP
!
AH...!
AH...!
WHAT'S WRONG, KIYO-CHAN?

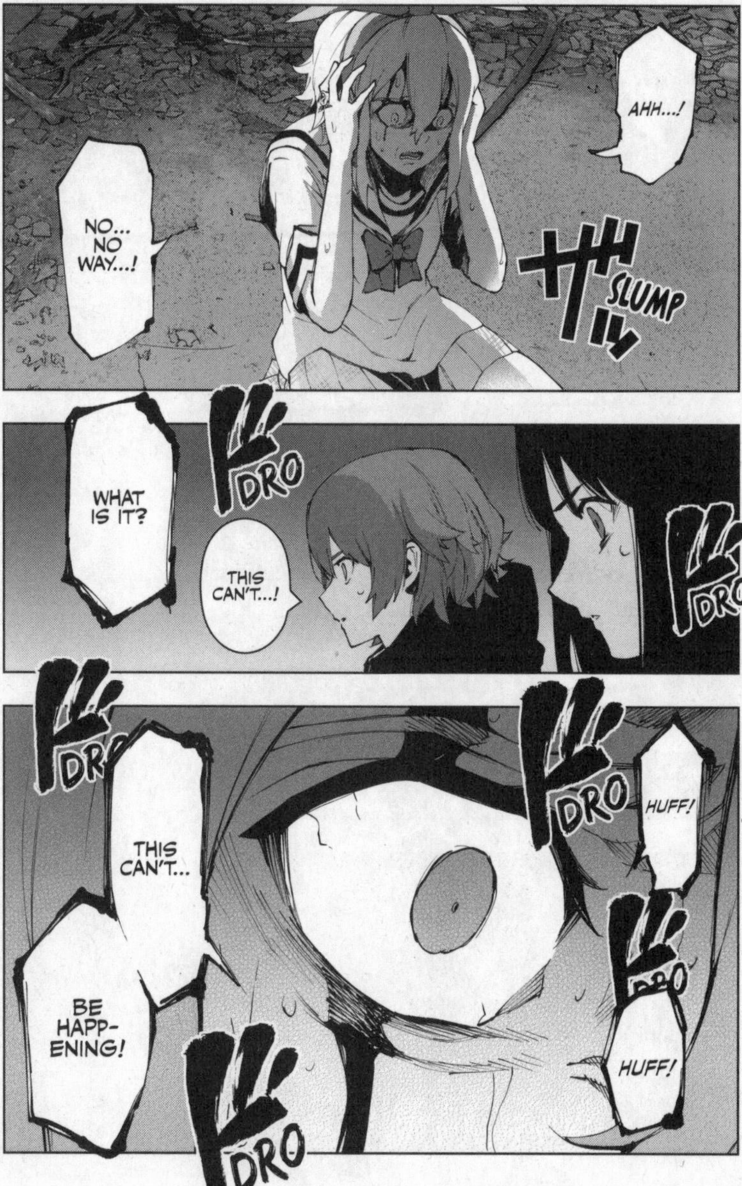
AHH...!
SLUMP
NO... NO WAY...!
DRO
THIS CAN'T...!
DRO
WHAT IS IT?
DRO
HUFF!
HUFF!
DRO
THIS CAN'T...
BE HAPP-ENING!
DRO
DRO

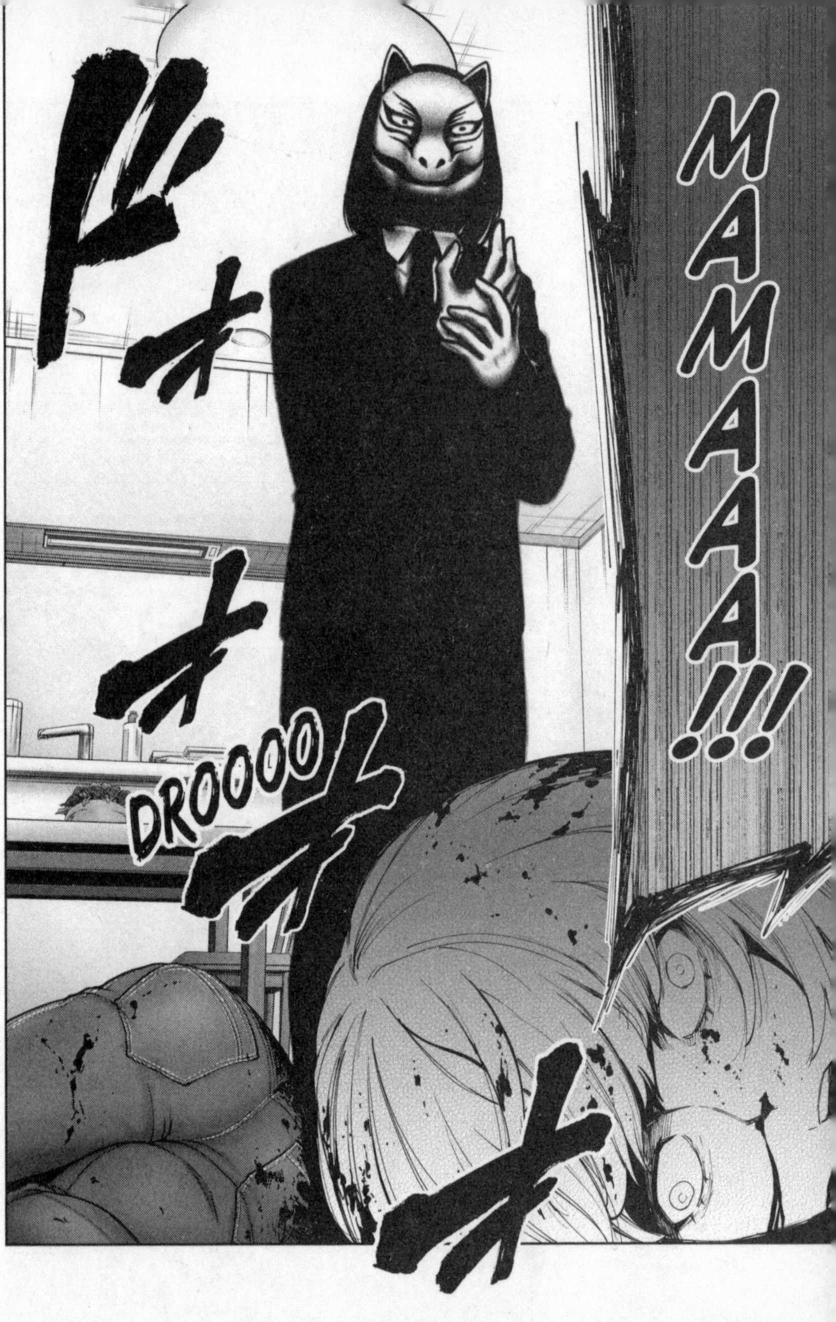
MAMAAA!!!
DROOOO

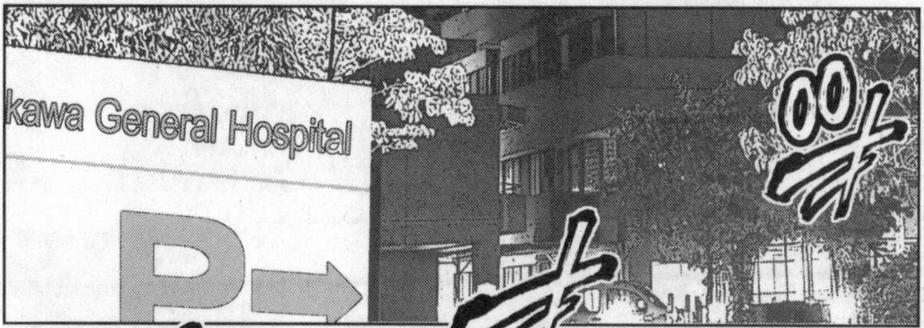
OO
kawa General Hospital
P

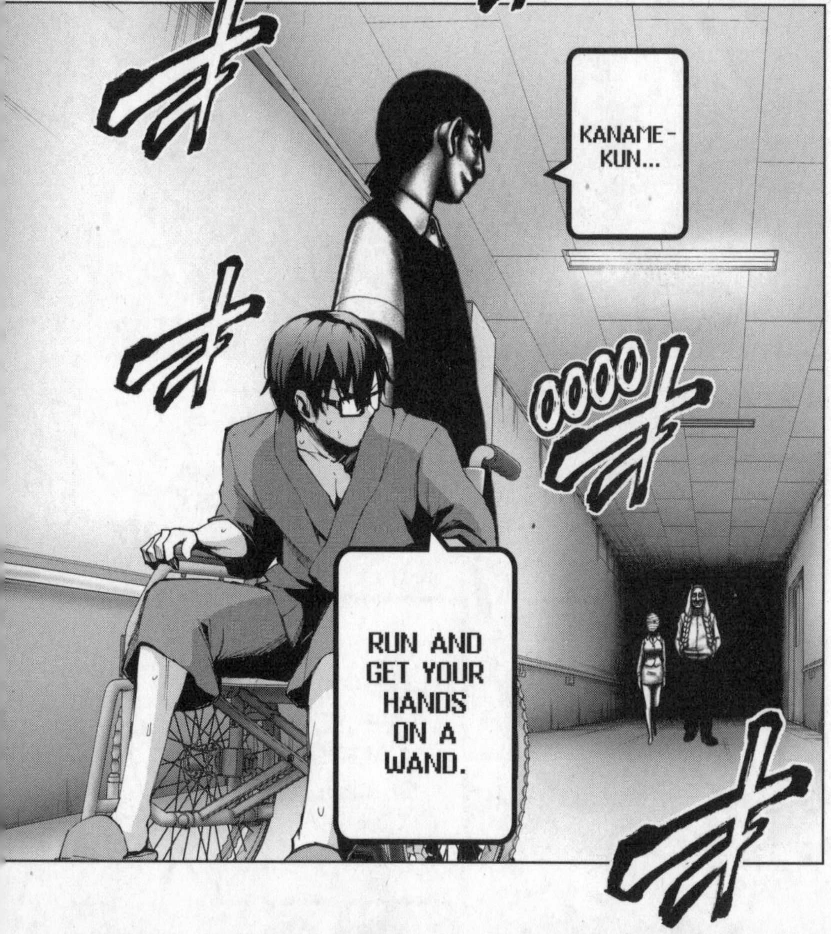
KANAME-KUN...
OOOO
RUN AND GET YOUR HANDS ON A WAND.

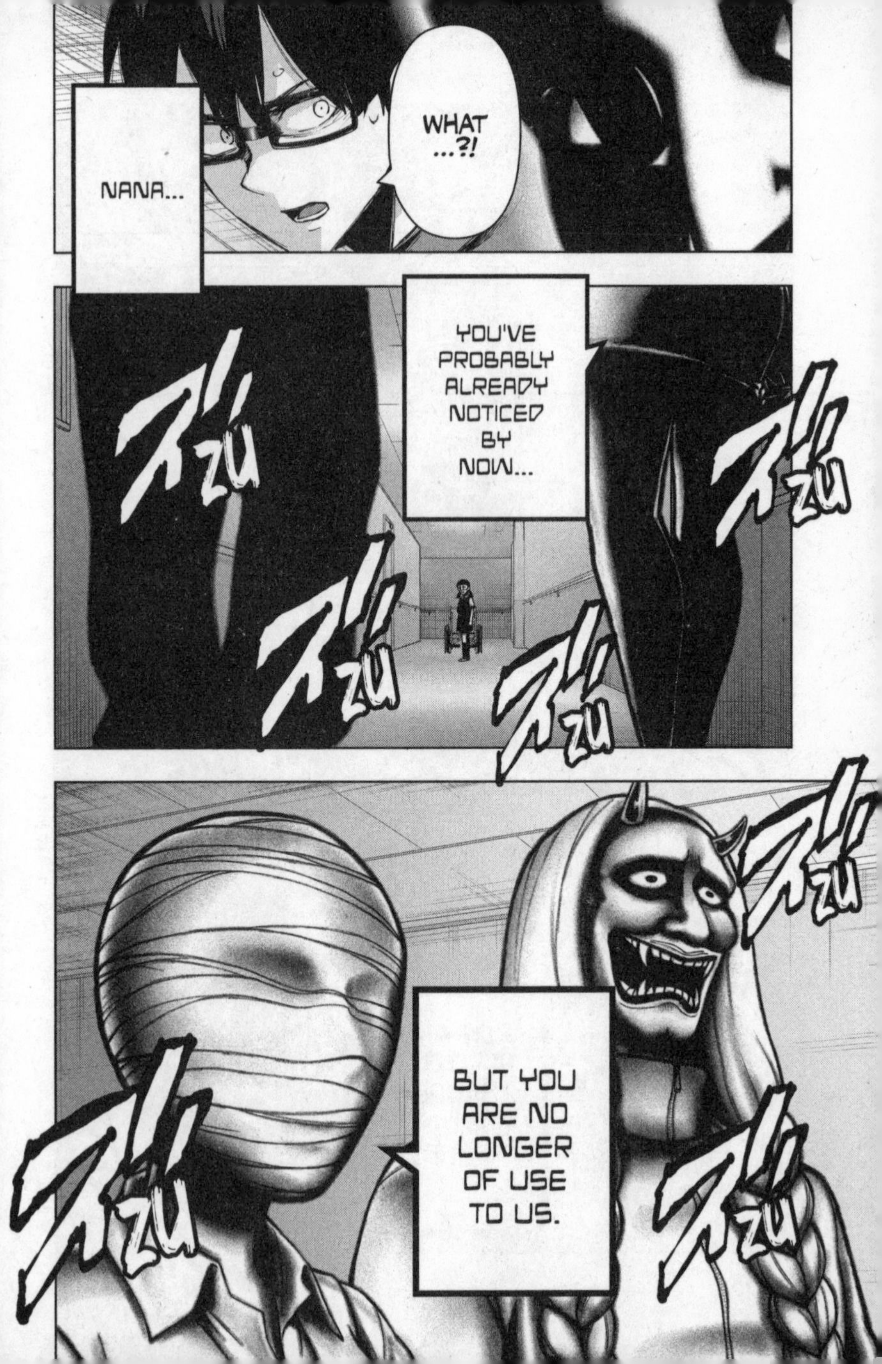
WHAT ...?!
NANA...
YOU'VE PROBABLY ALREADY NOTICED BY NOW...
ズ! zu
ズ! zu
ズ! zu
ズ! zu
ズ! zu
BUT YOU ARE NO LONGER OF USE TO US.
ズ! zu
ズ! zu

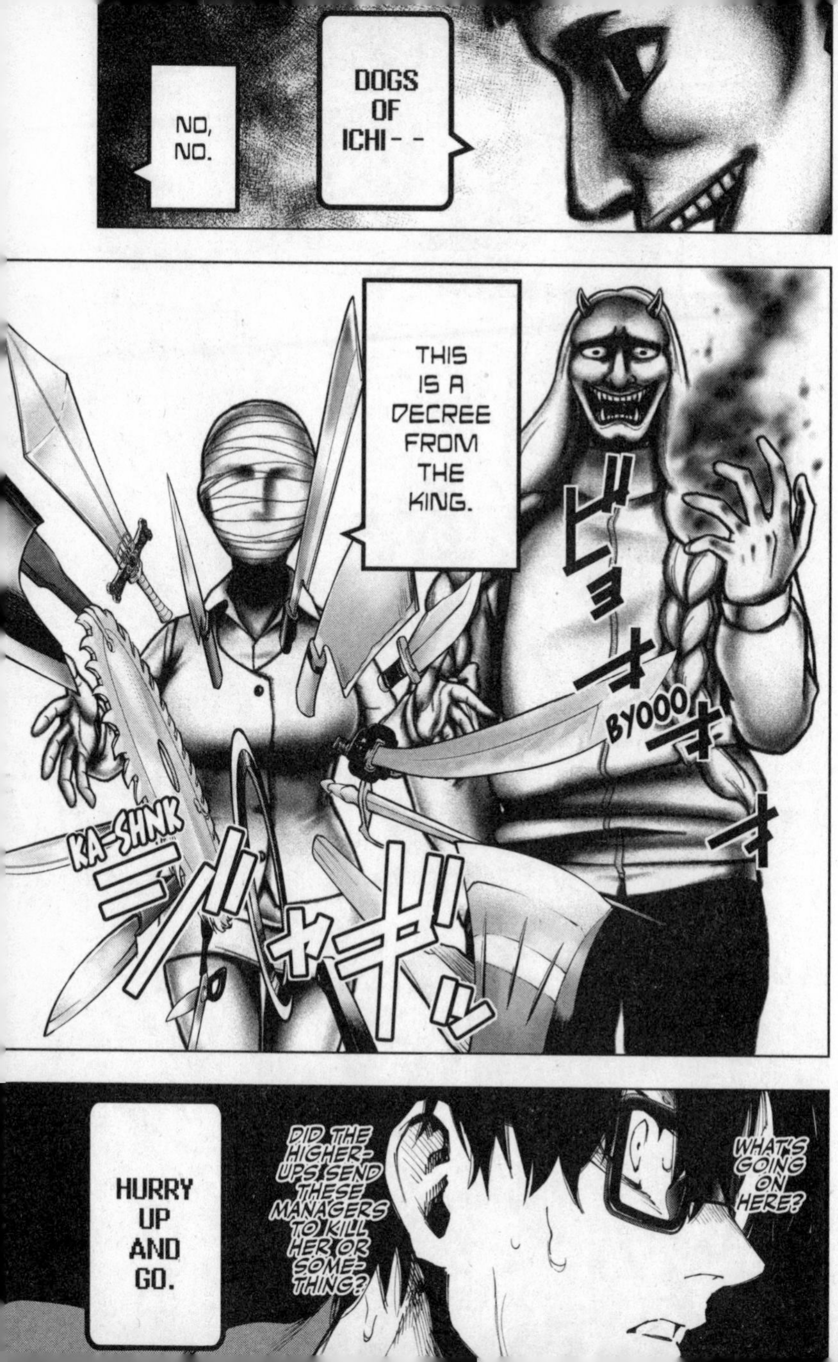
DOGS OF ICHI- -
NO, NO.
THIS IS A DECREE FROM THE KING.
BYOOO
KA-SHNK
WHAT'S GOING ON HERE?
DID THE HIGHER-UPS SEND THESE MANAGERS TO KILL HER OR SOME-THING?
HURRY UP AND GO.

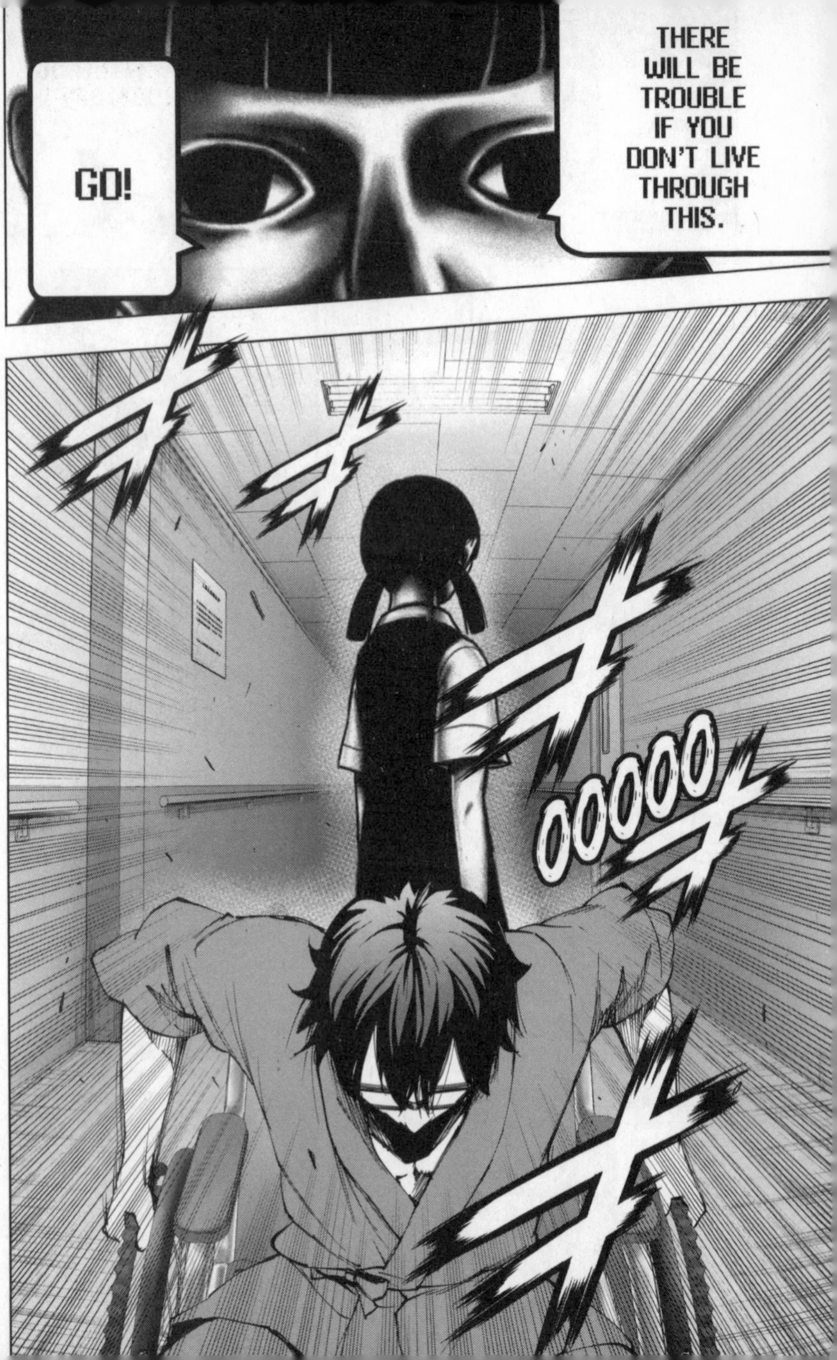
THERE WILL BE TROUBLE IF YOU DON'T LIVE THROUGH THIS.
GO!
OOOOO

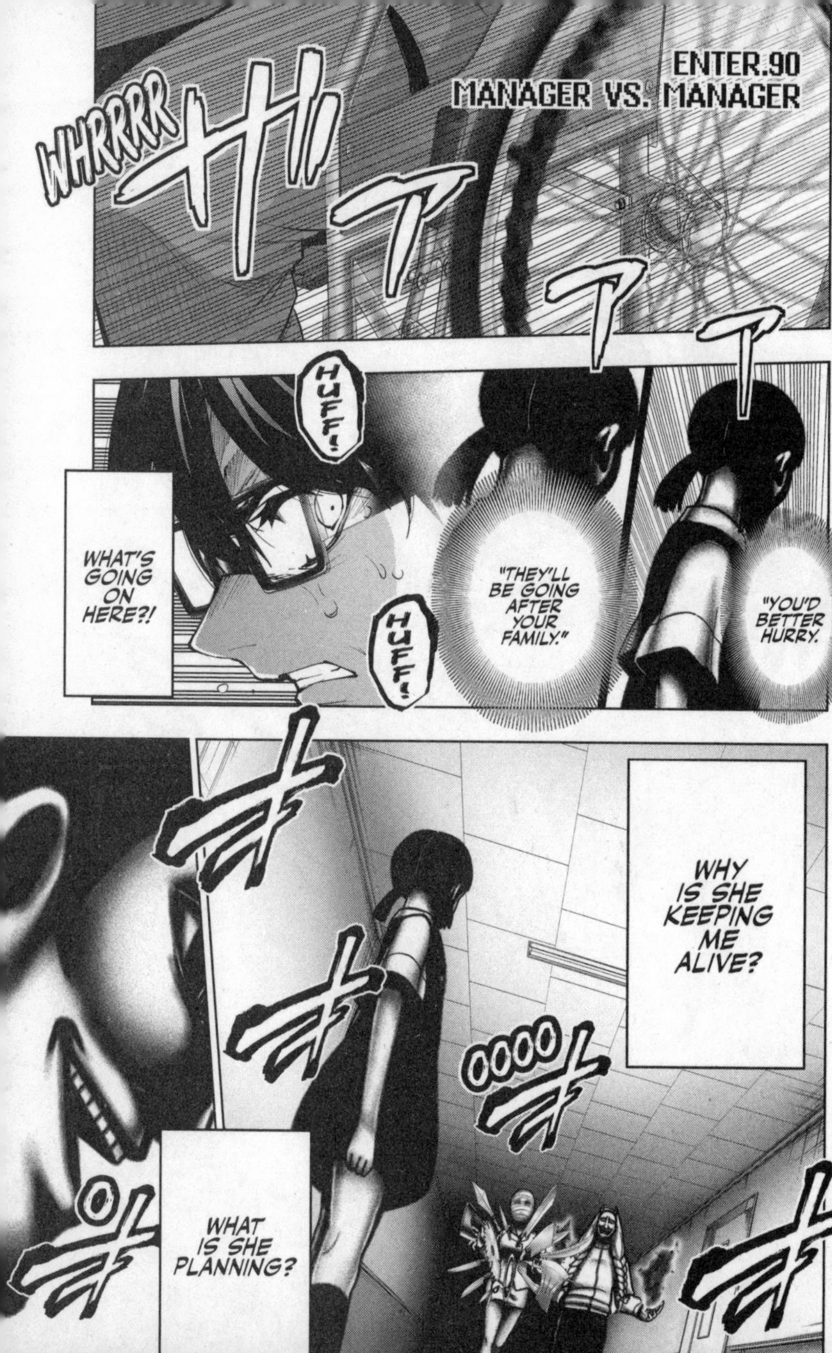
ENTER.90
MANAGER VS. MANAGER
WHRRRR
"YOU'D BETTER HURRY.
"THEY'LL BE GOING AFTER YOUR FAMILY."
HUFF!
HUFF!
WHAT'S GOING ON HERE?!
WHY IS SHE KEEPING ME ALIVE?
OOOO
WHAT IS SHE PLANNING?

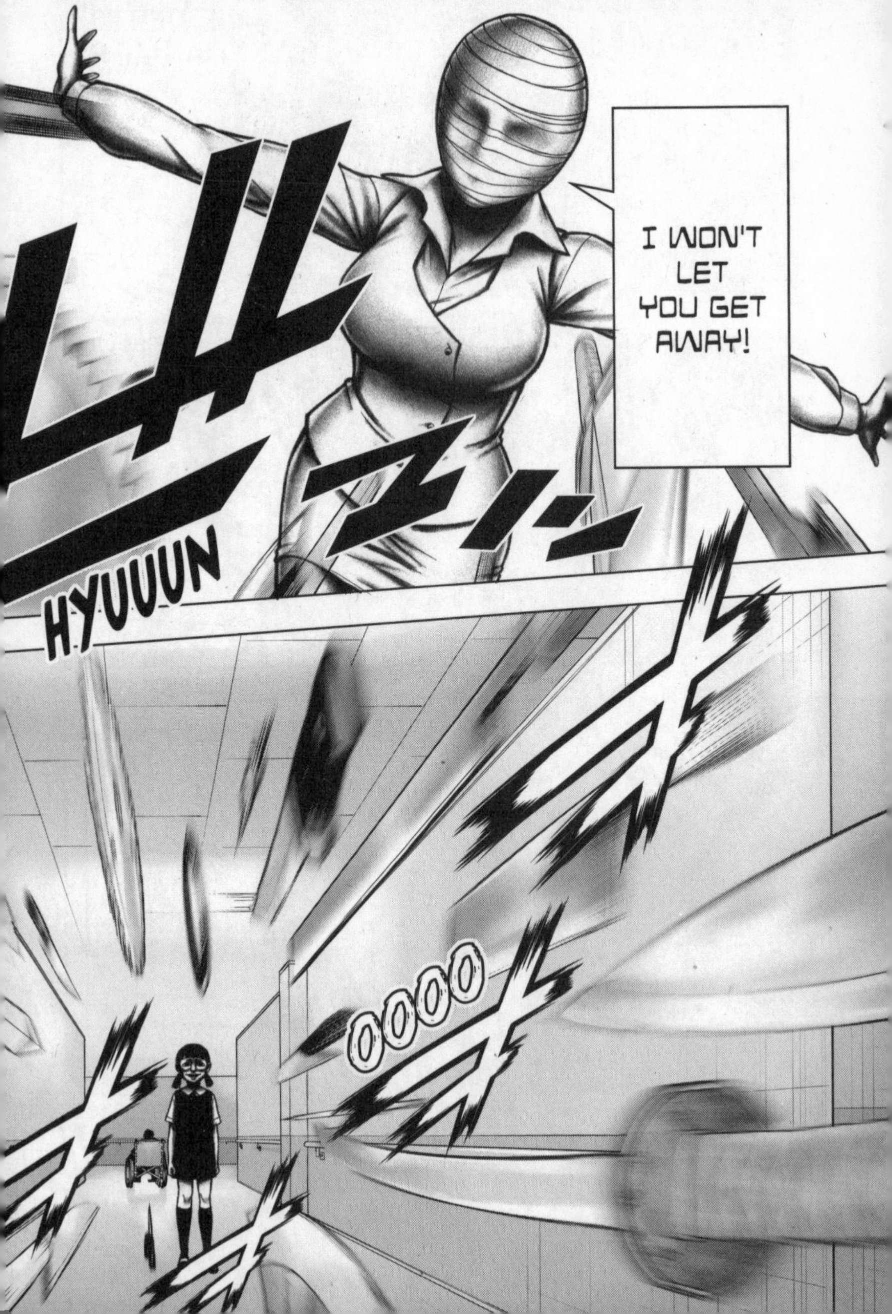
I WON'T LET YOU GET AWAY!
HYUUUN
OOOO

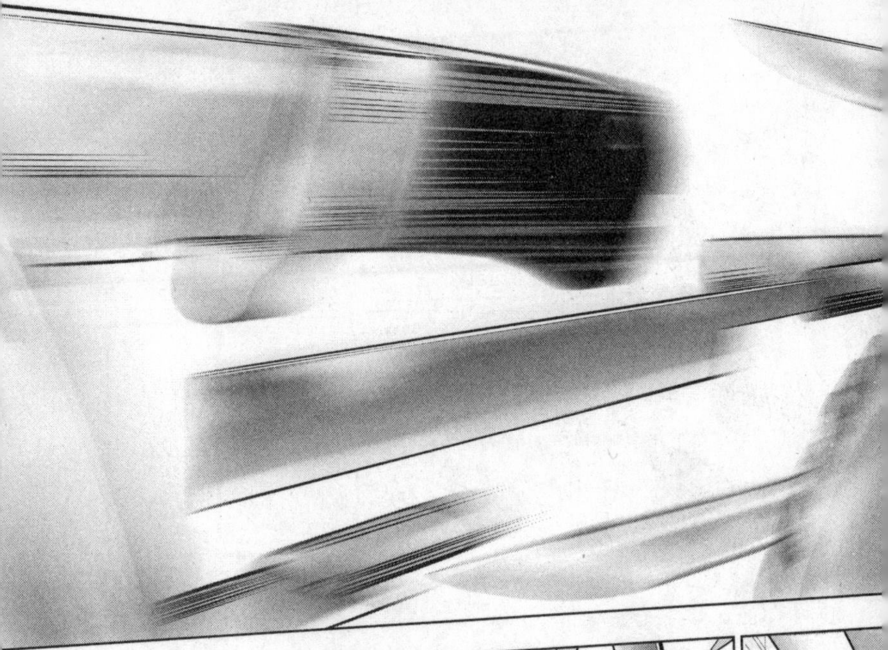
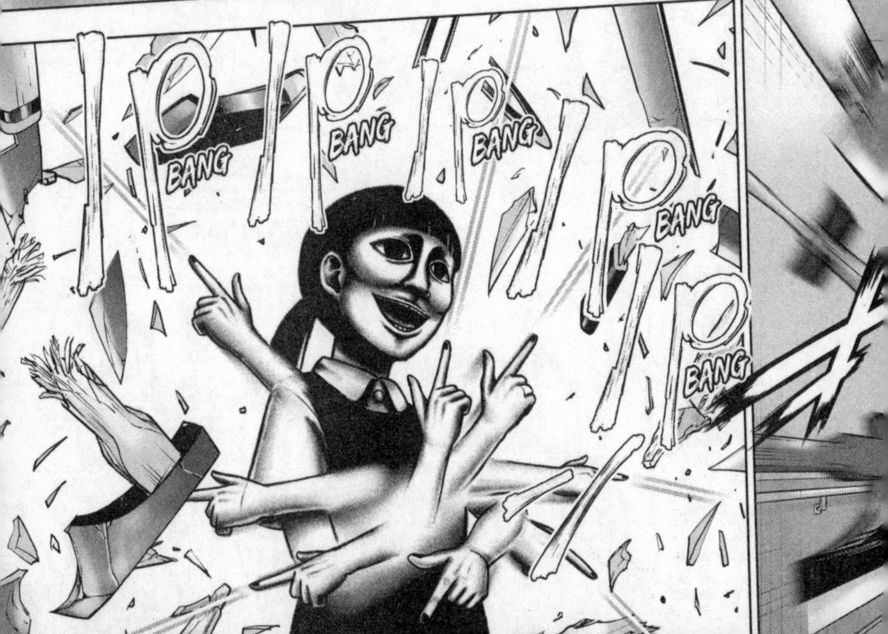
BANG
BANG
BANG
BANG
BANG
BANG

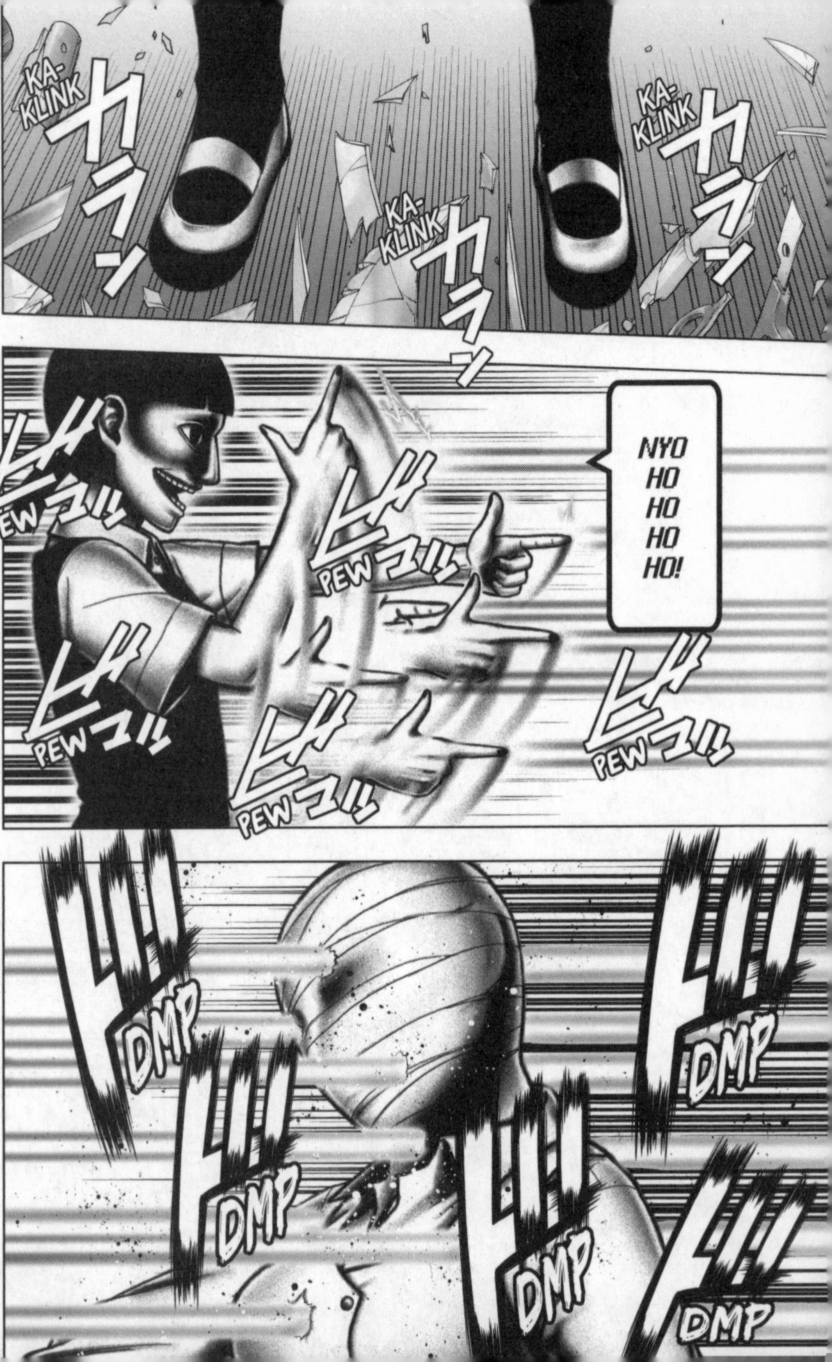
KA-KLINK
KA-KLINK
KA-KLINK
NYO HO HO HO HO!
PEW
PEW
PEW
PEW
PEW
DMP
DMP
DMP
DMP
DMP
DMP

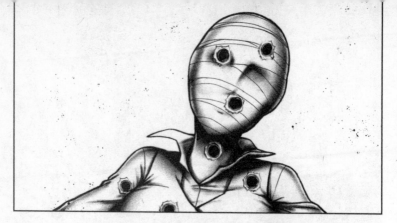

SHU

ZUOO

AH...
THIS
ONE'S
GOING
TO BE A
PAIN.

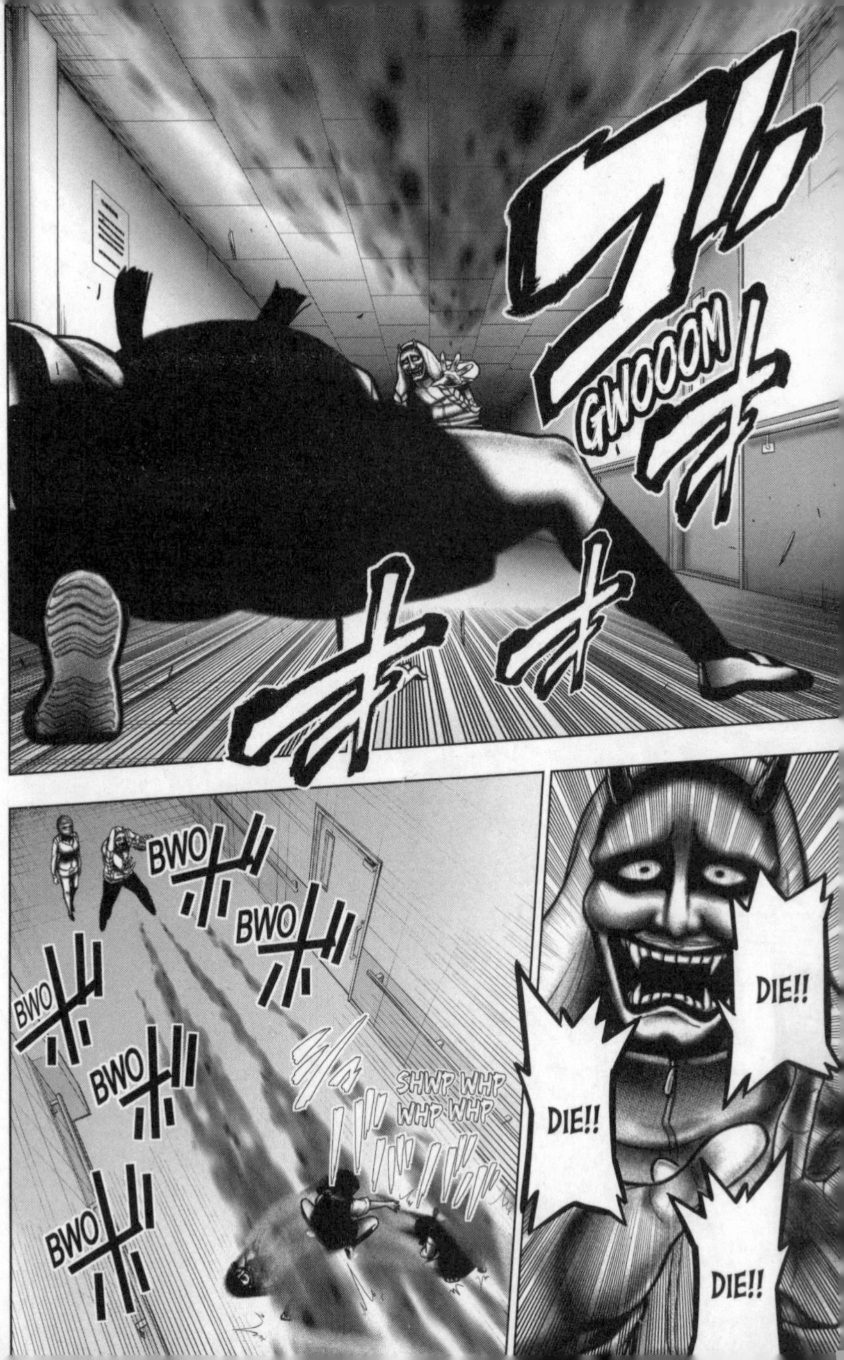
GWOOOM
DIE!!
DIE!!
DIE!!
BWO
BWO
BWO
BWO
BWO
SHWP WHP
WHP WHP

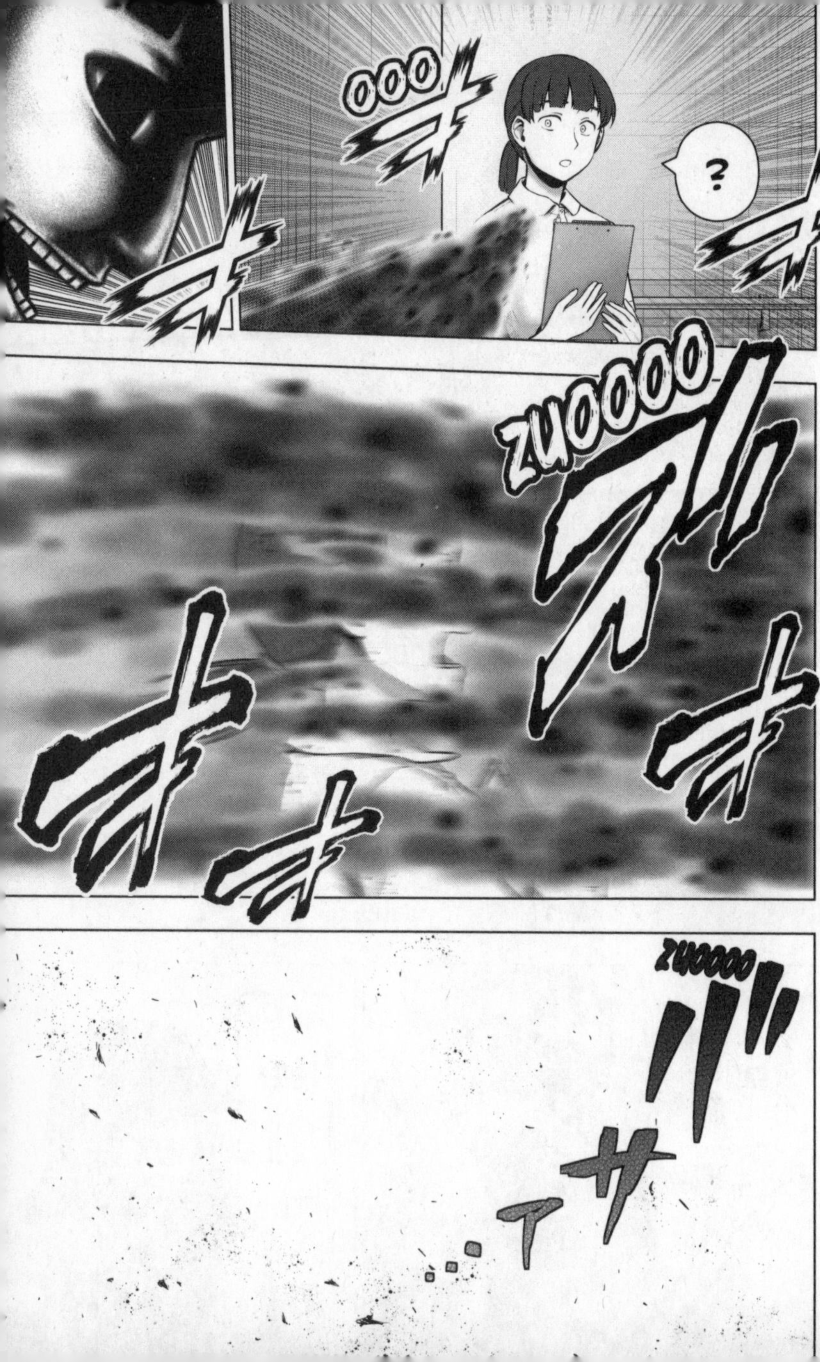
?
OOO
ZUOOOO
ZUOOOO

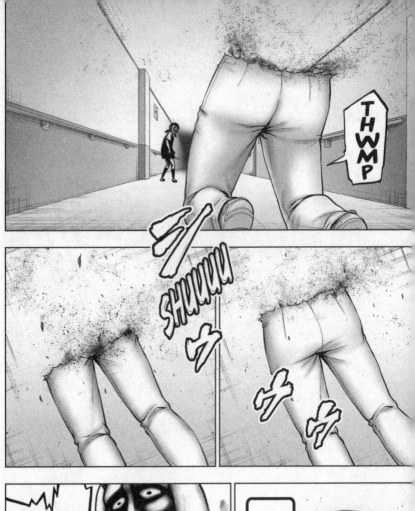

THWMP

SHUUUU

NANA!

HMPH!

OH?

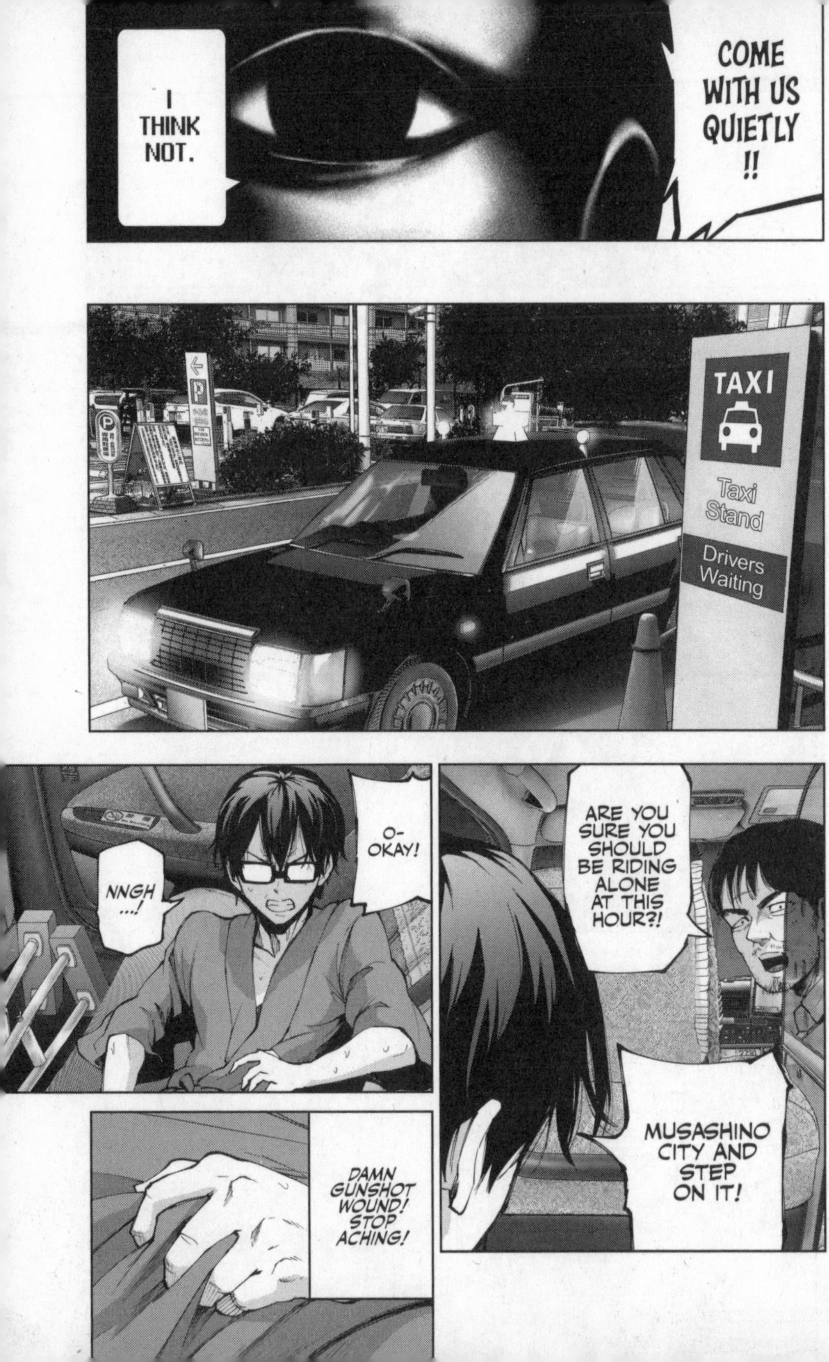
COME WITH US QUIETLY !!
I THINK NOT.
TAXI
Taxi Stand
Drivers Waiting
ARE YOU SURE YOU SHOULD BE RIDING ALONE AT THIS HOUR?!
MUSASHINO CITY AND STEP ON IT!
O-OKAY!
NNGH ...!
DAMN GUNSHOT WOUND! STOP ACHING!

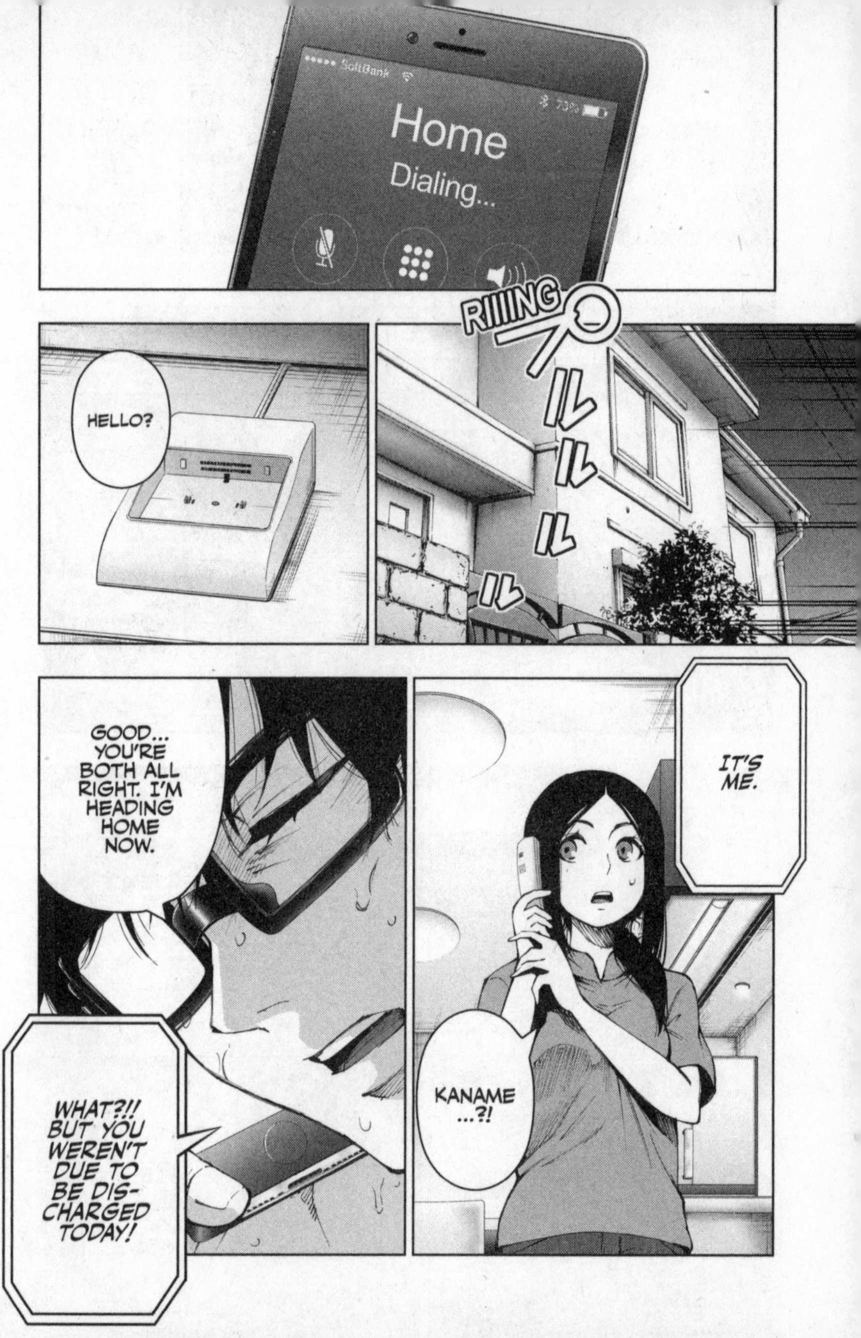
SoftBank
Home
Dialing...
RIIIING
ル
ル
ル
ル
HELLO?
IT'S ME.
KANAME ...?!
GOOD... YOU'RE BOTH ALL RIGHT. I'M HEADING HOME NOW.
WHAT?!! BUT YOU WEREN'T DUE TO BE DIS- CHARGED TODAY!

204
ASAGIRI KANAME...
YOU KEPT THEM SAFE FOR ME, DIDN'T YOU?
YES...
"WHERE ARE MY PANTIES?"
"WHERE ARE MY PANTIES?"
THOSE THINGS?
YOU DIDN'T WANT THE POLICE TO HAVE THEM, SO I PUT THEM IN YOUR ROOM.
BUT IS IT OKAY TO WITHHOLD EVIDENCE FROM THE POLICE LIKE THAT?
COULD YOU STOP ASKING ME QUESTIONS ABOUT THAT, MOM?
IF THAT'S WHAT YOU WANT...

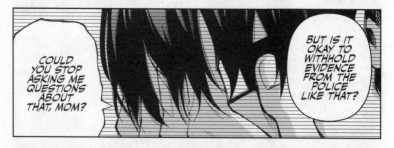

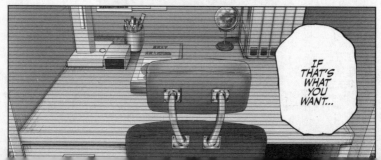

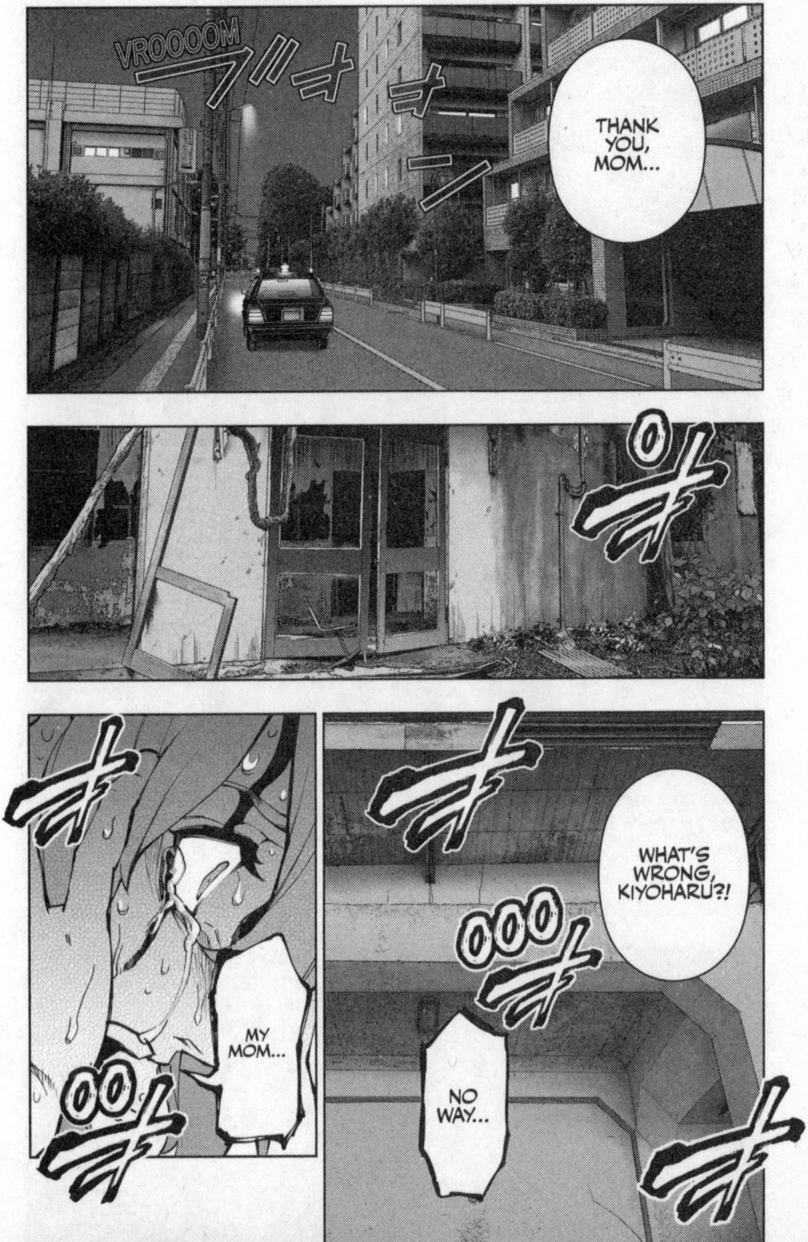
VROOOOM
THANK YOU, MOM...
O
WHAT'S WRONG, KIYOHARU?!
OOO
NO WAY...
MY MOM...
OO

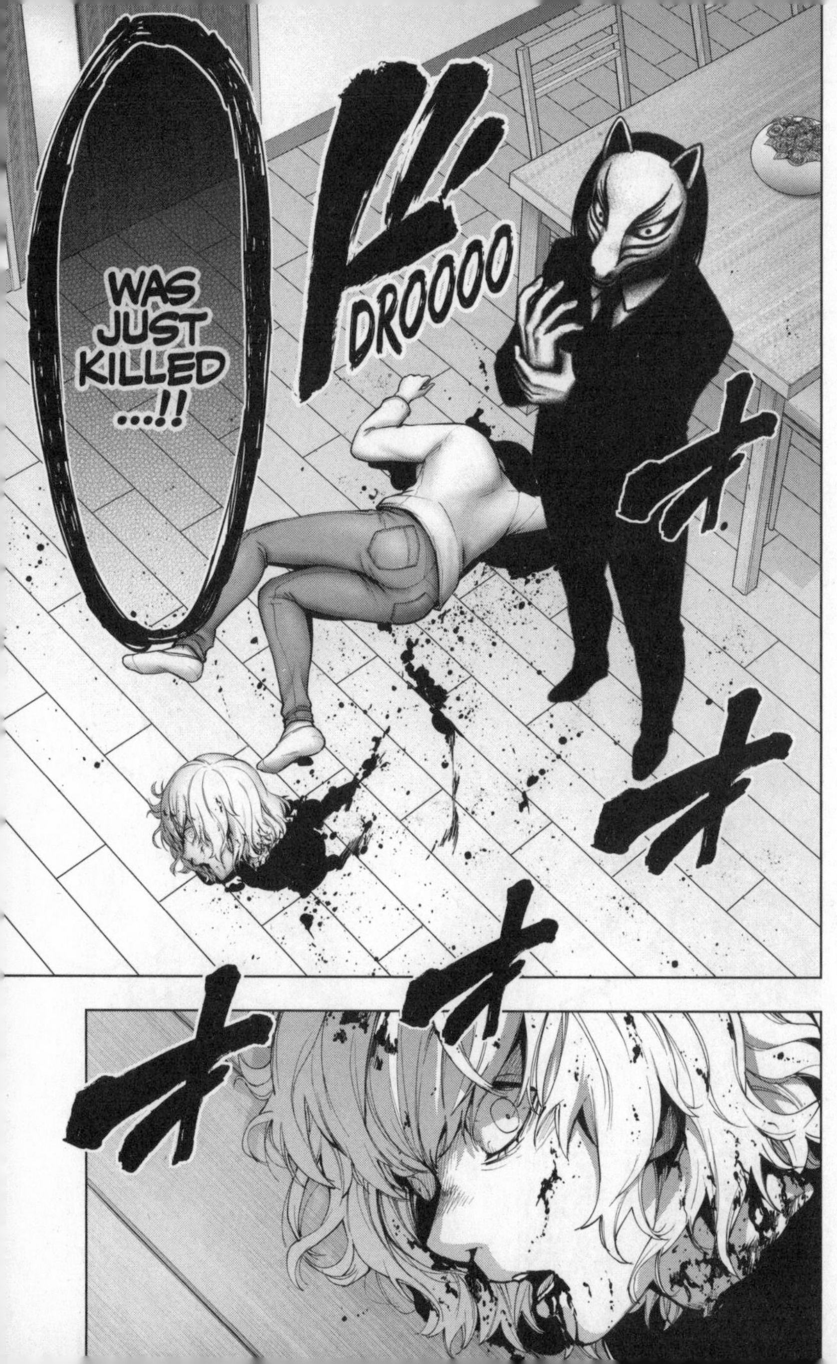
WAS JUST KILLED ...!!
DROOOO

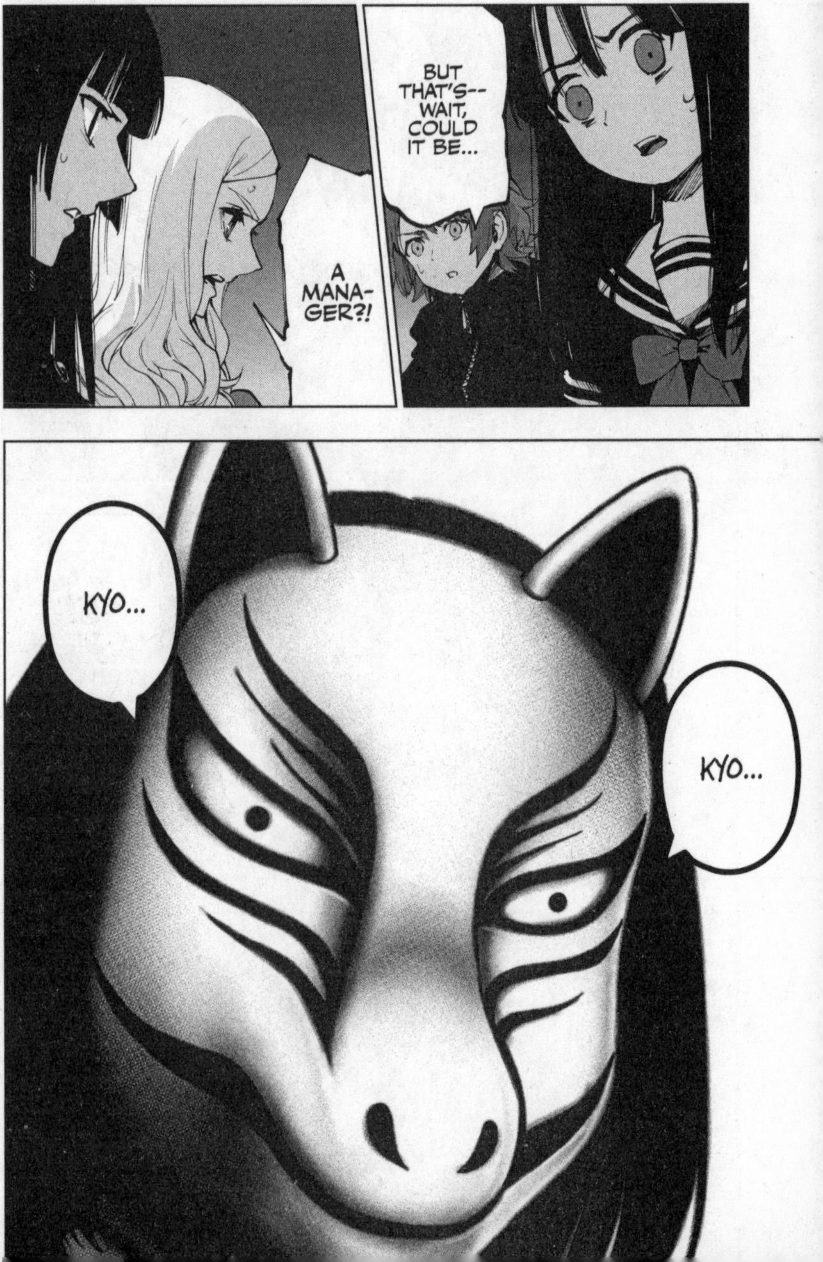
BUT THAT'S-- WAIT, COULD IT BE...
A MANA-GER?!
KYO...
KYO...

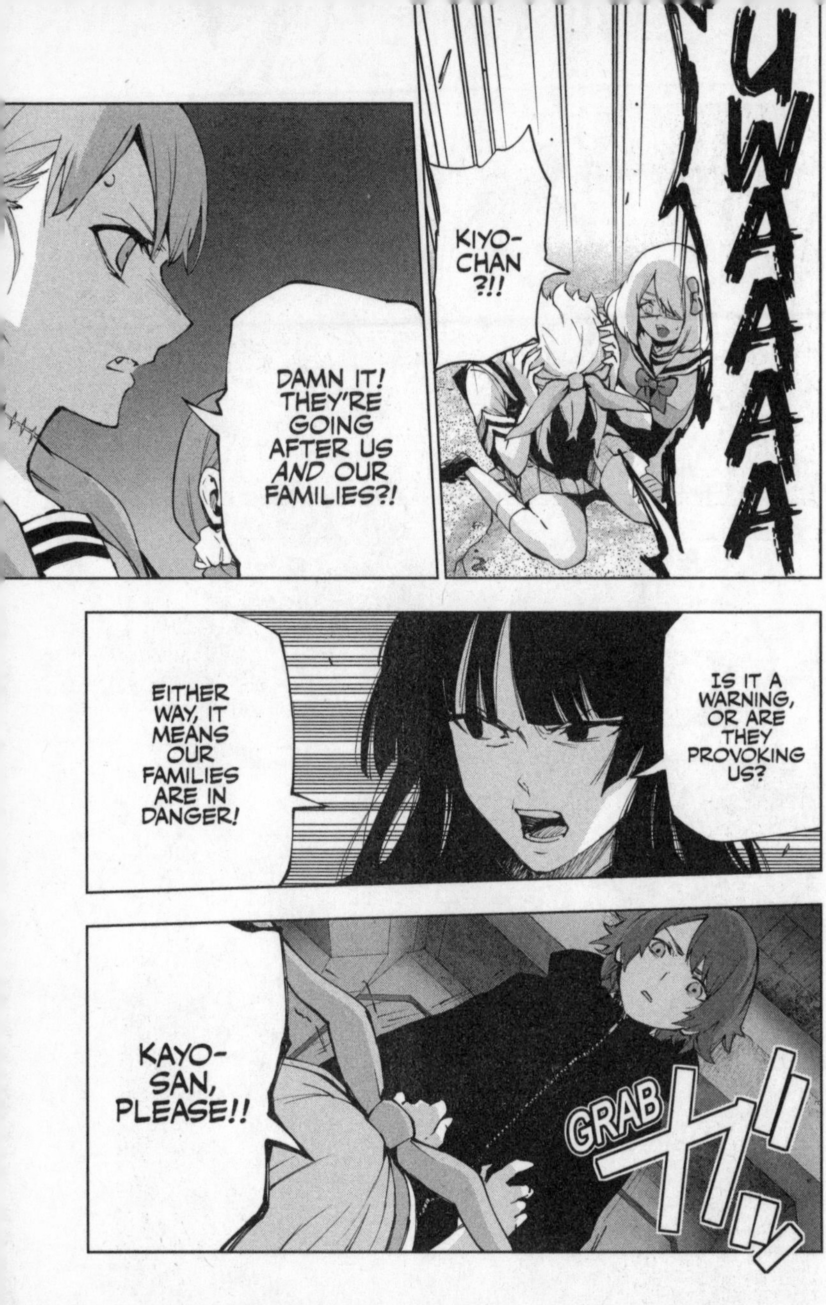
UWAAAAAA
KIYO-CHAN?!!
DAMN IT! THEY'RE GOING AFTER US *AND* OUR FAMILIES?!
IS IT A WARNING, OR ARE THEY PROVOKING US?
EITHER WAY, IT MEANS OUR FAMILIES ARE IN DANGER!
KAYO-SAN, PLEASE!!
GRAB

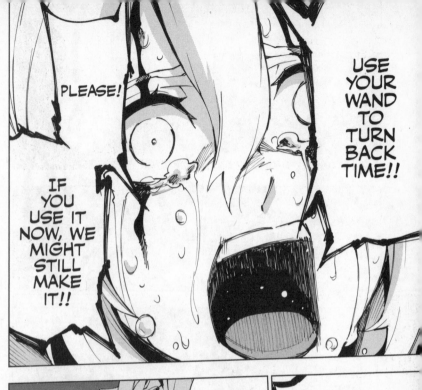

PLEASE!

USE YOUR WAND TO TURN BACK TIME!!

IF YOU USE IT NOW, WE MIGHT STILL MAKE IT!!

WE COULD SAVE MY MOM!!

KAYO'S WAND CAN ONLY BE USED ONCE PER POWER.

AFTER IT'S BEEN USED, SHE HAS TO TOUCH THE MAGICAL GIRL TO COPY THEIR ABILITY AGAIN.

THAT MEANS...

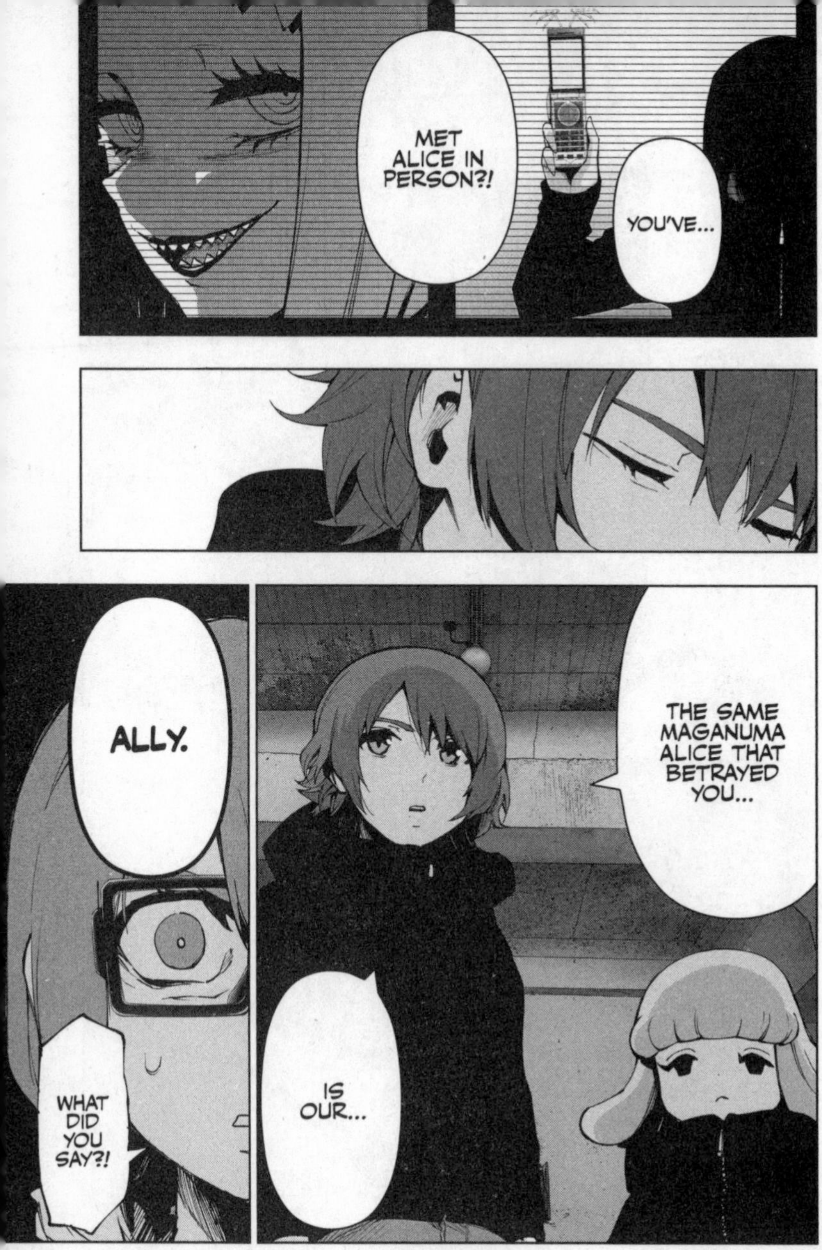
YOU'VE...
MET ALICE IN PERSON?!
THE SAME MAGANUMA ALICE THAT BETRAYED YOU...
IS OUR...
ALLY.
WHAT DID YOU SAY?!

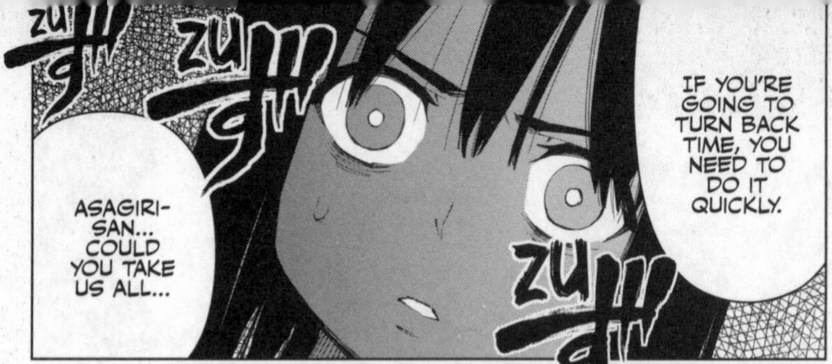
ZU
ZU
IF YOU'RE GOING TO TURN BACK TIME, YOU NEED TO DO IT QUICKLY.
ZU
ASAGIRI-SAN... COULD YOU TAKE US ALL...
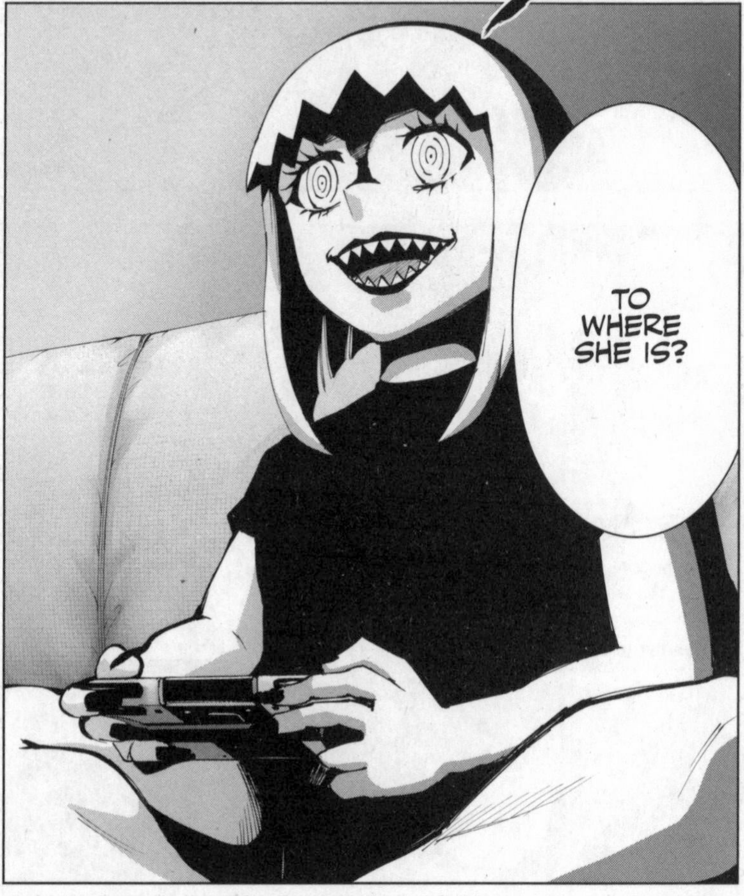
TO WHERE SHE IS?

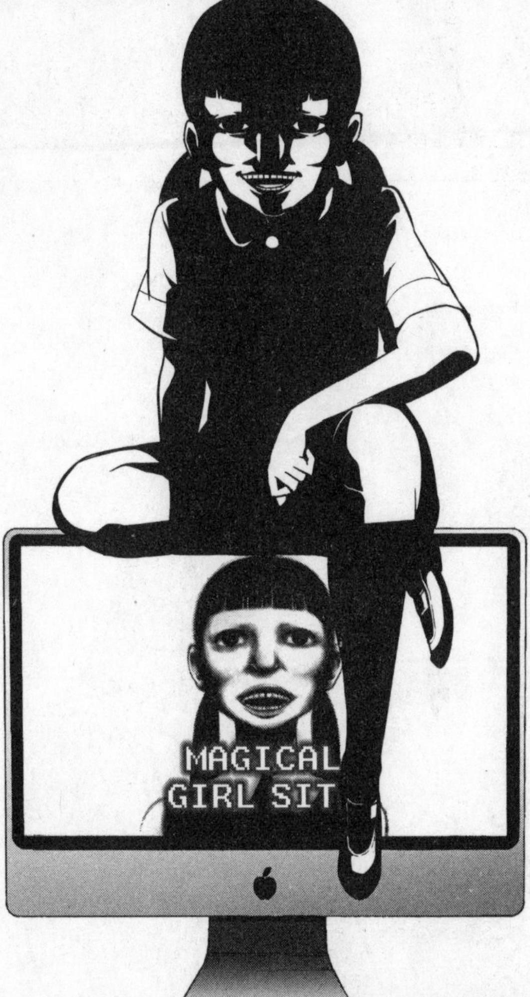
MAGICAL
GIRL SIT

ENTER.91 UNDERESTIMATE

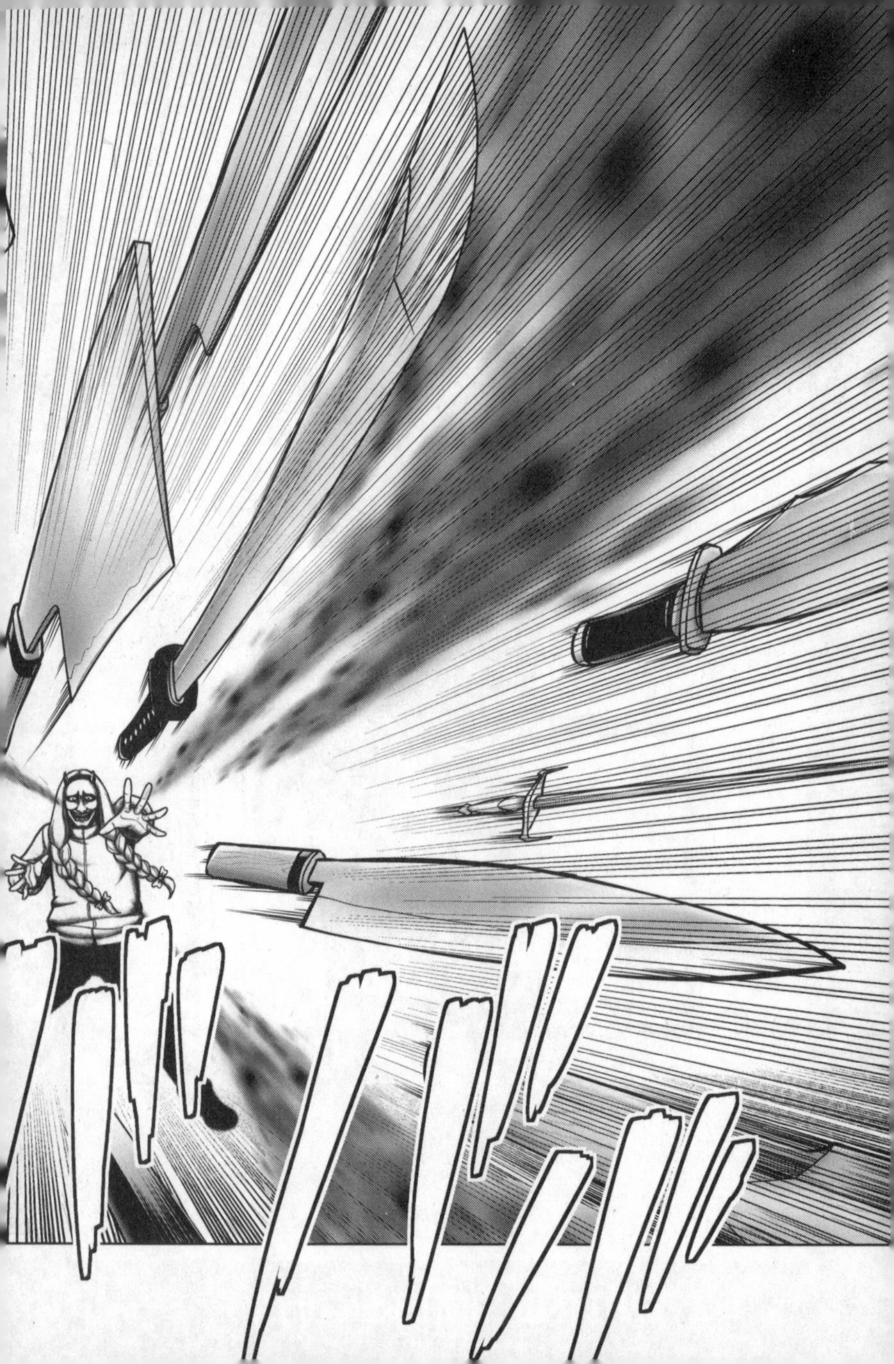

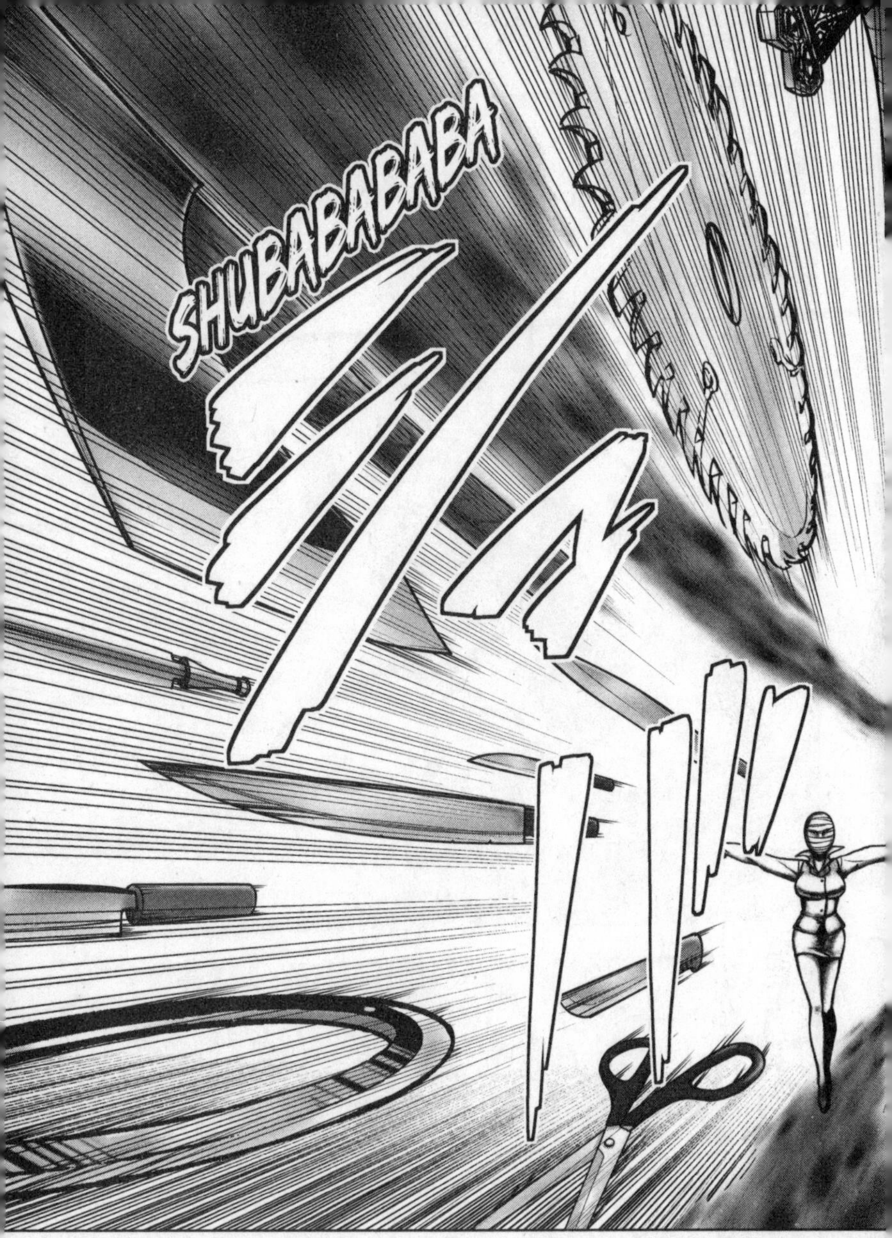
SHUBABABABA

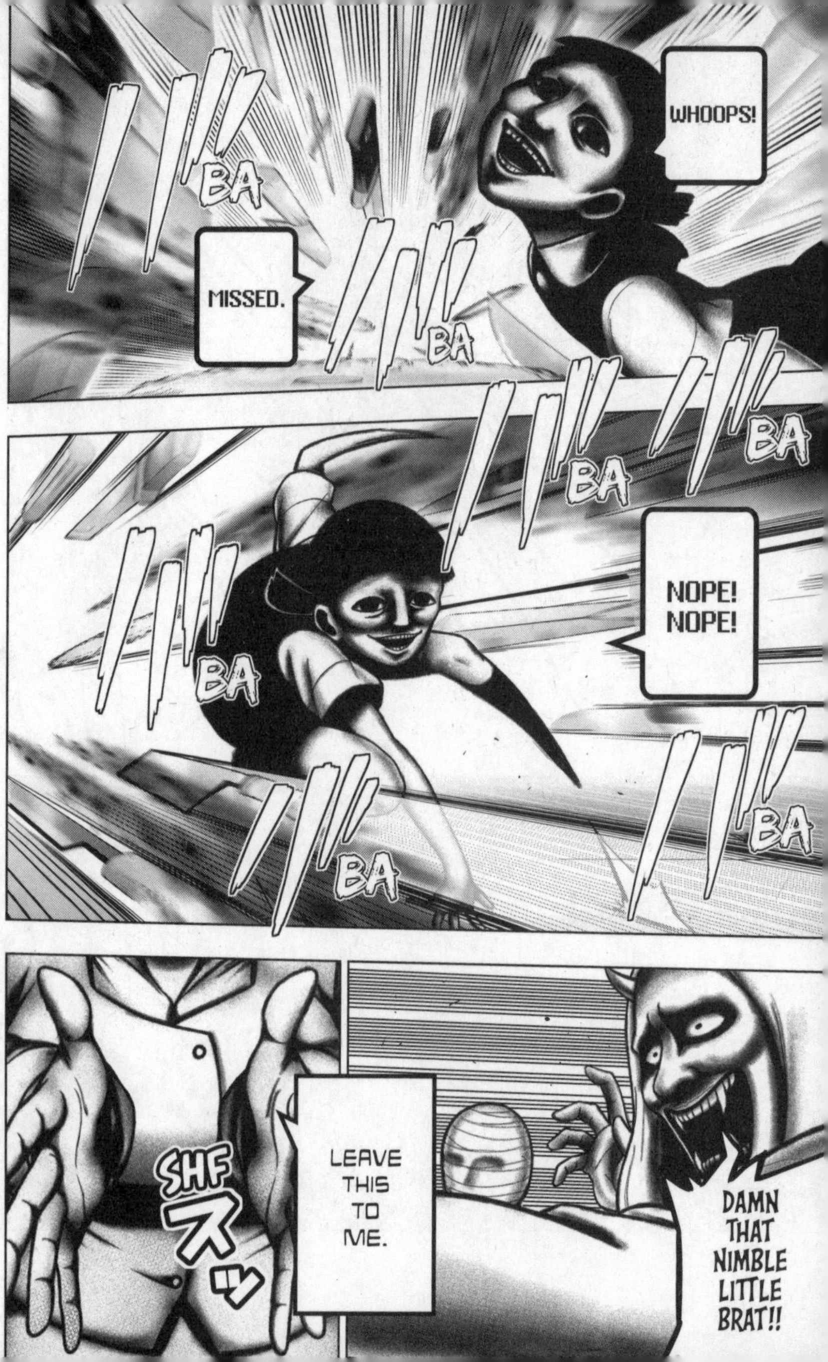
WHOOPS!
BA
MISSED.
BA
BA
BA
NOPE! NOPE!
BA
BA
BA
DAMN THAT NIMBLE LITTLE BRAT!!
LEAVE THIS TO ME.
SHF
スッ

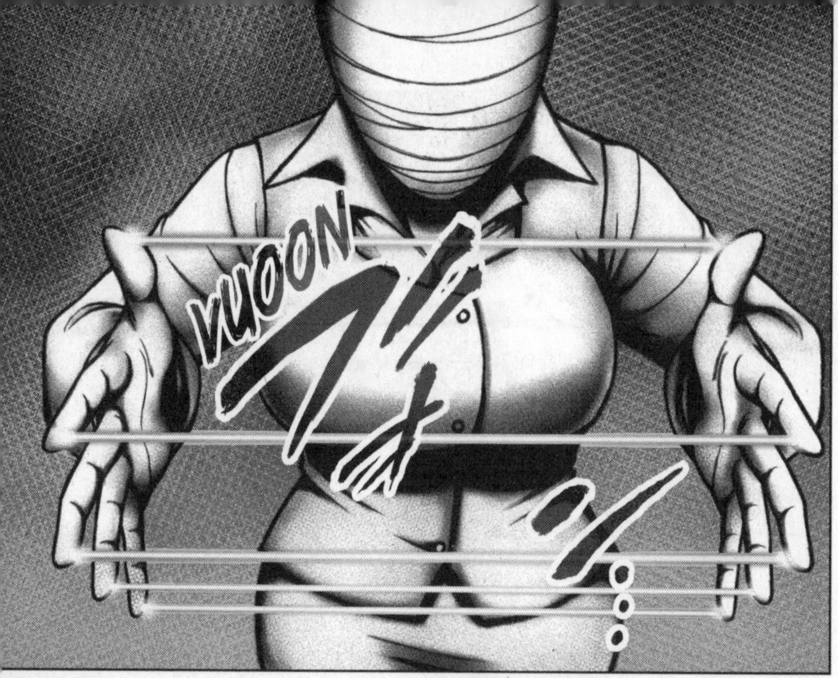
VUOON
ブォッ…
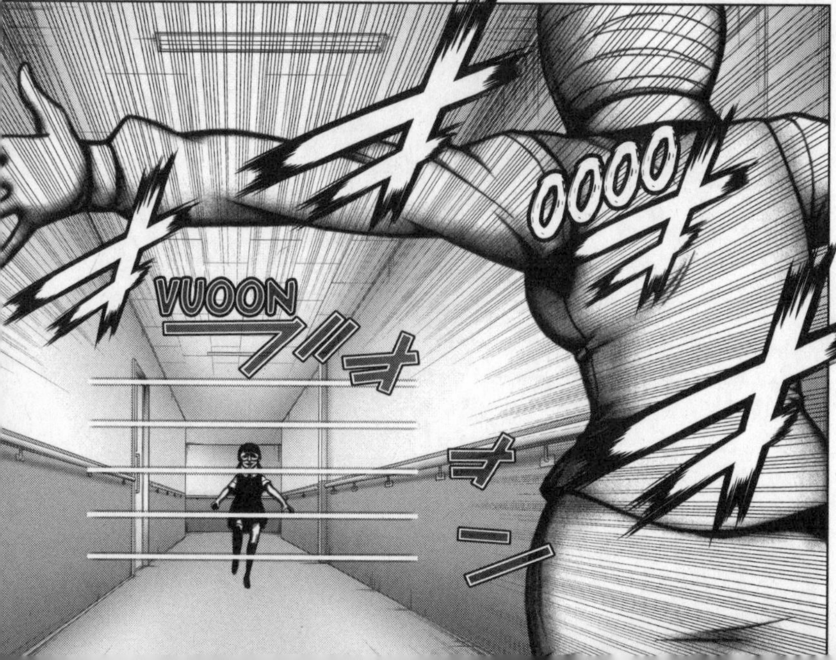
オオオオ
OOOO
VUOON
ブォォーー

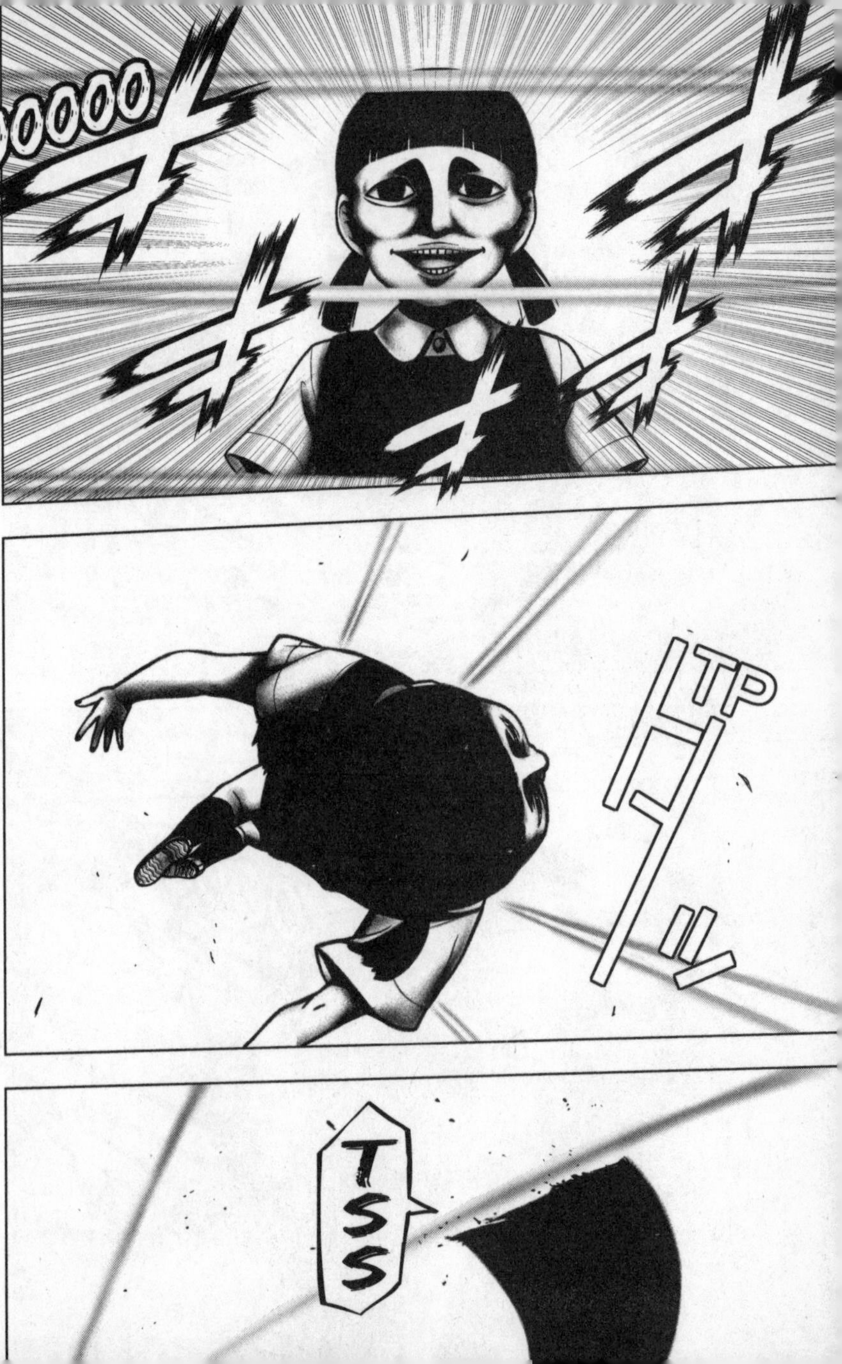
OOOOO
TP
TSS

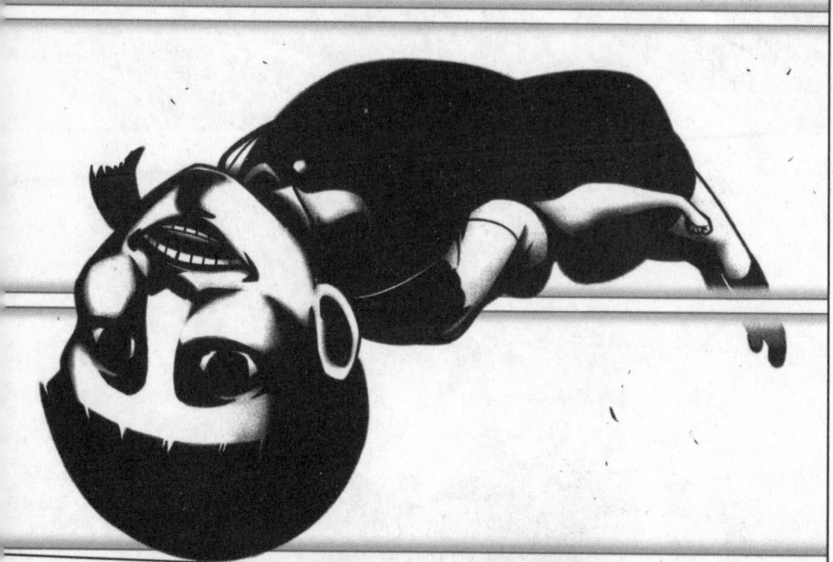

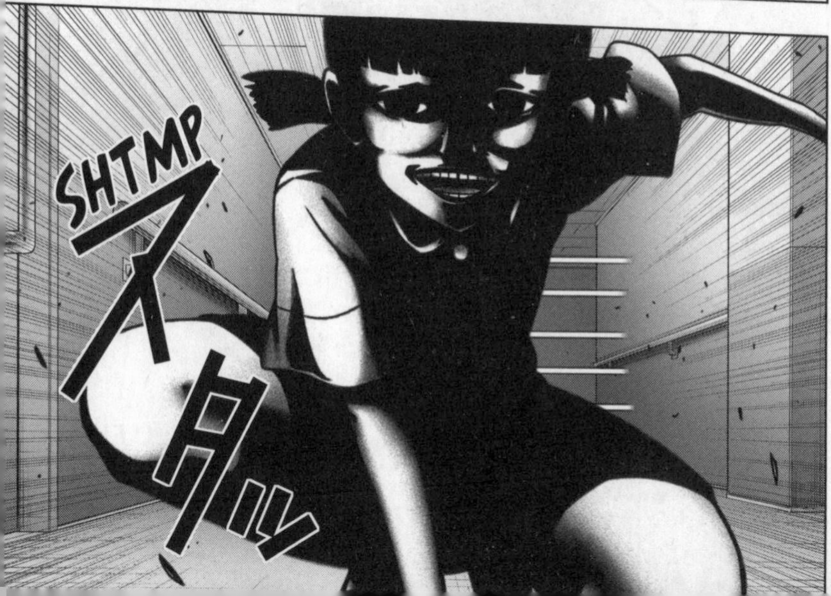
SHTMP

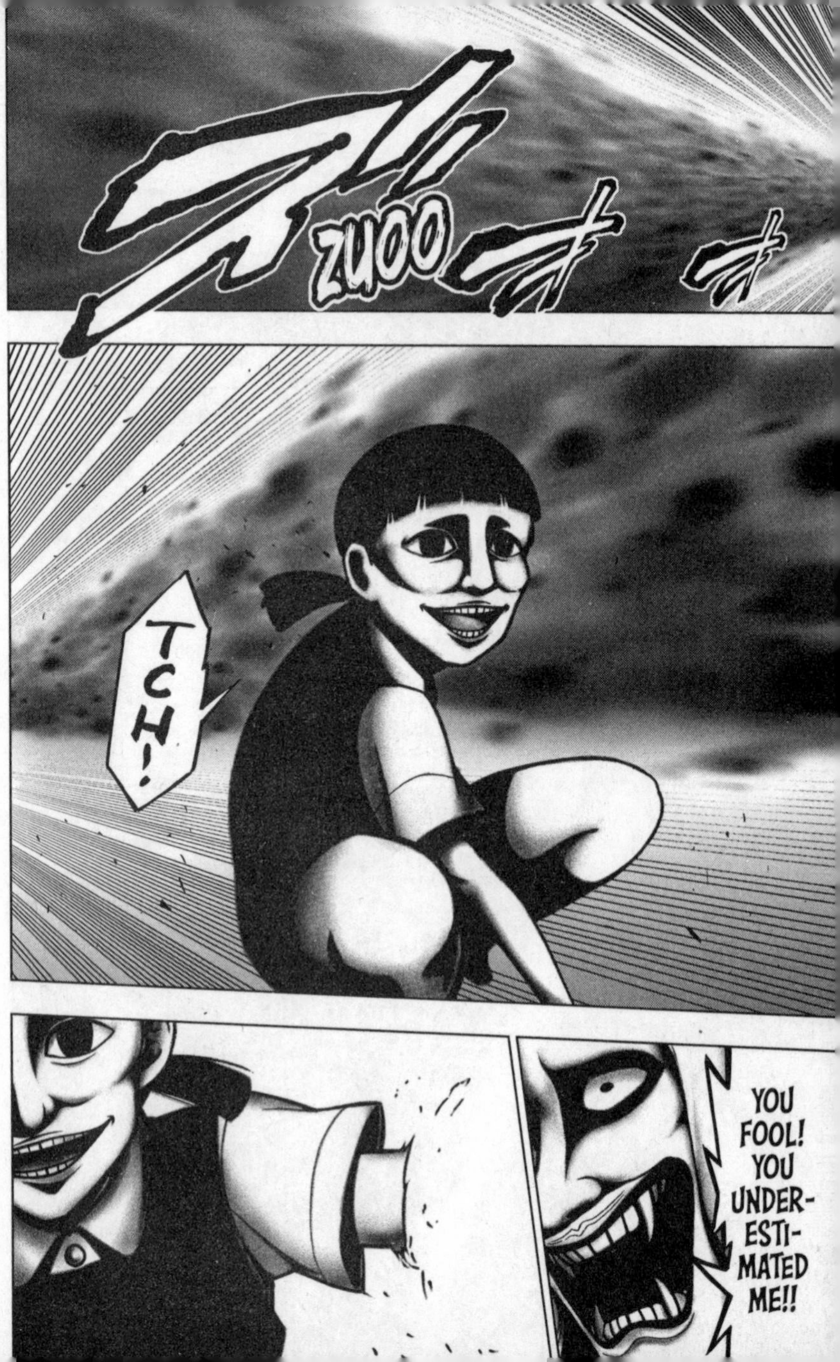
ZUOO
TCH!
YOU FOOL! YOU UNDER-ESTI-MATED ME!!

ZZRT...
THWOP
スパッ
KERTHUNK
ゴトン
SHUUUUU
シュウウウ
TMP TMP TMP TMP TMP
ダダダダダ

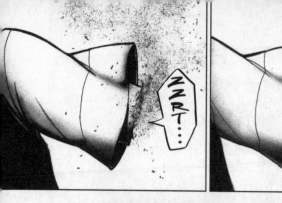

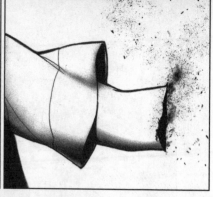

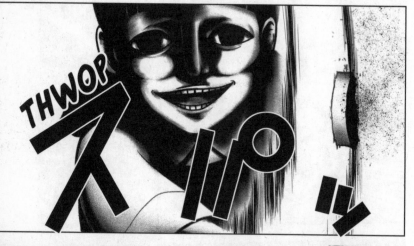

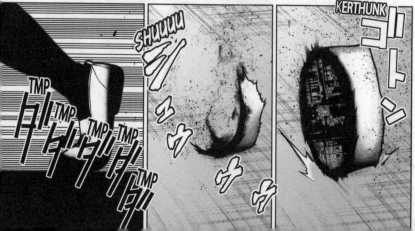

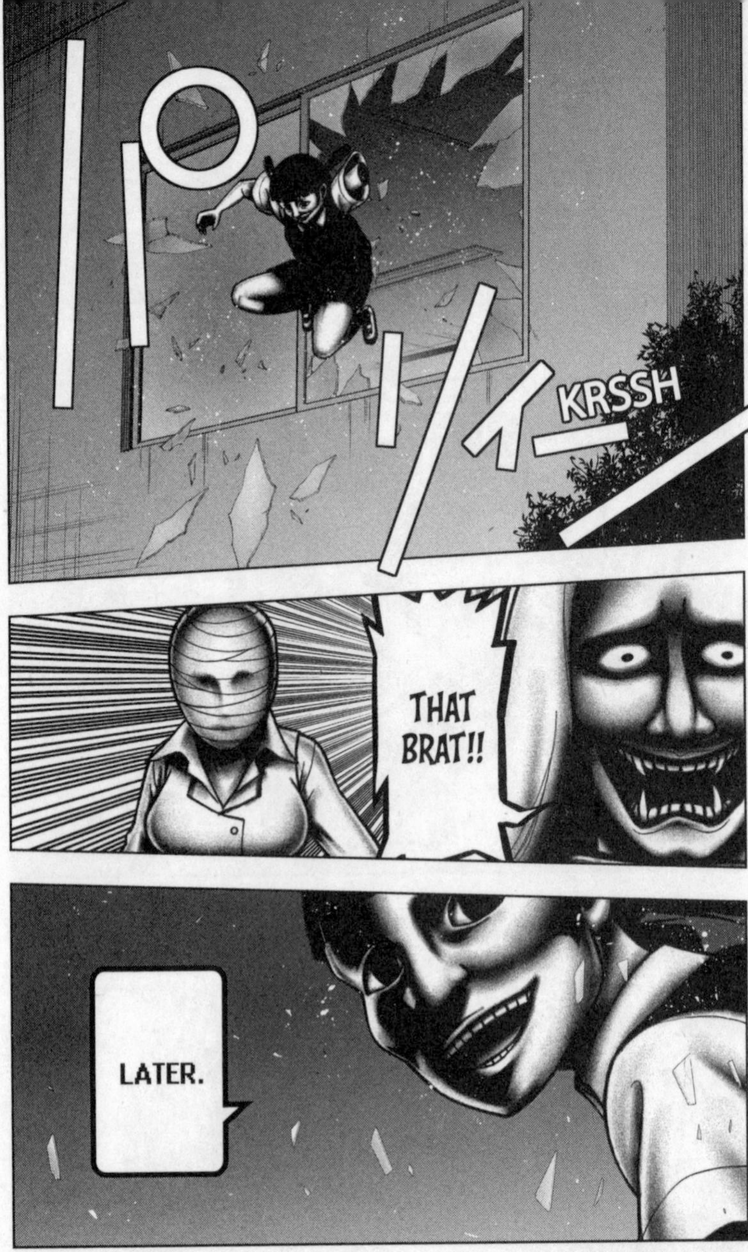
KRSSH
THAT BRAT!!
LATER.

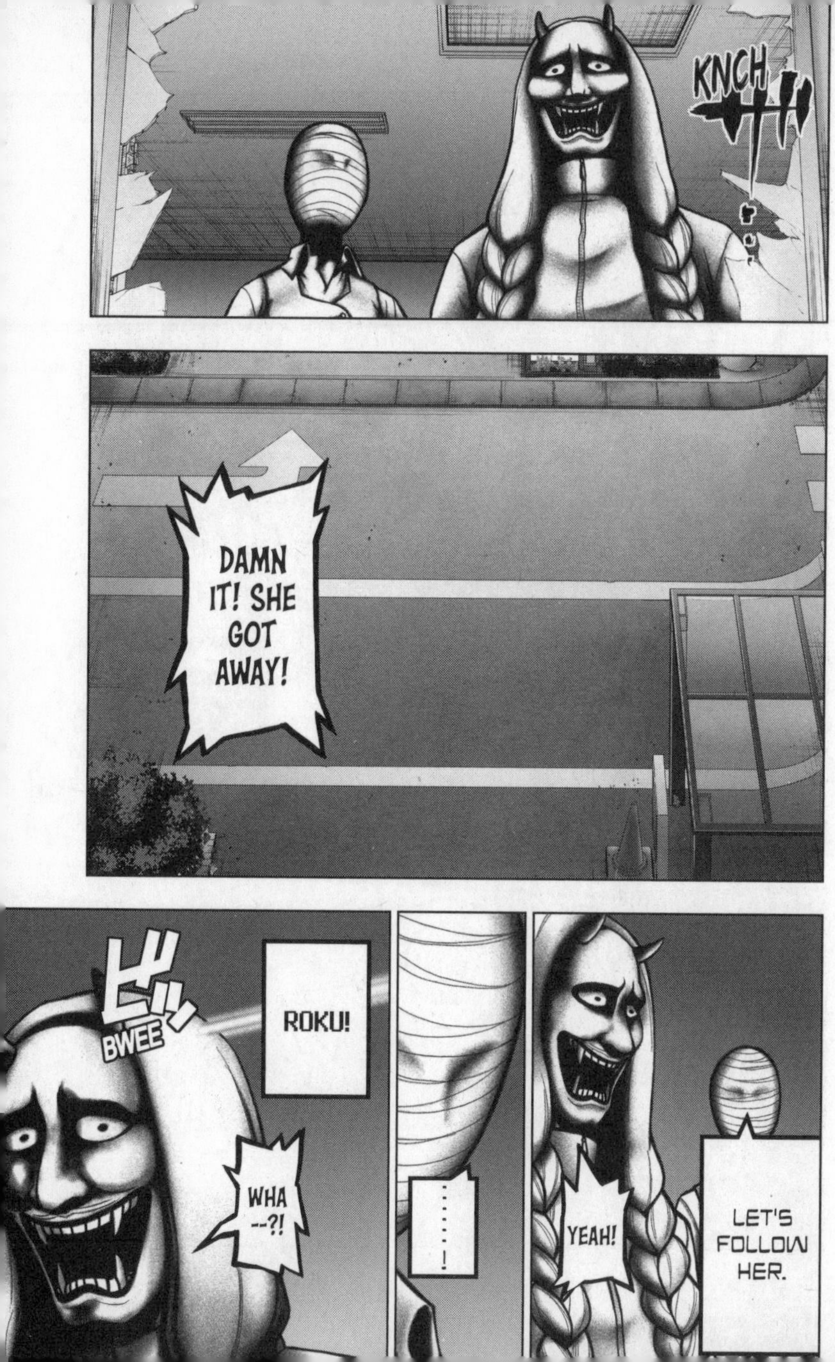
KNCH
DAMN IT! SHE GOT AWAY!
LET'S FOLLOW HER.
YEAH!
......!
ROKU!
ビッ
BWEE
WHA--?!

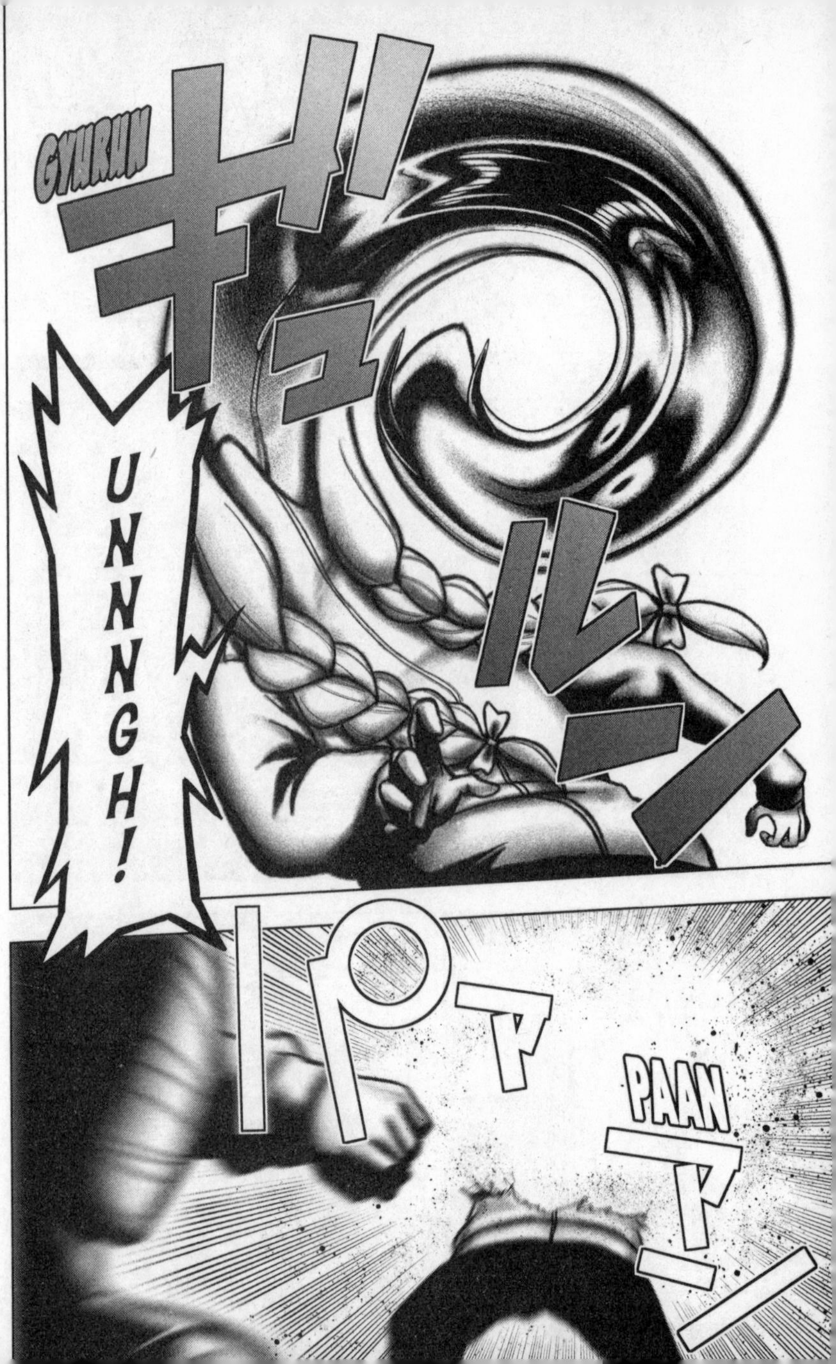
GYURUN
ギュルーン
UNNNGH!
PAAN

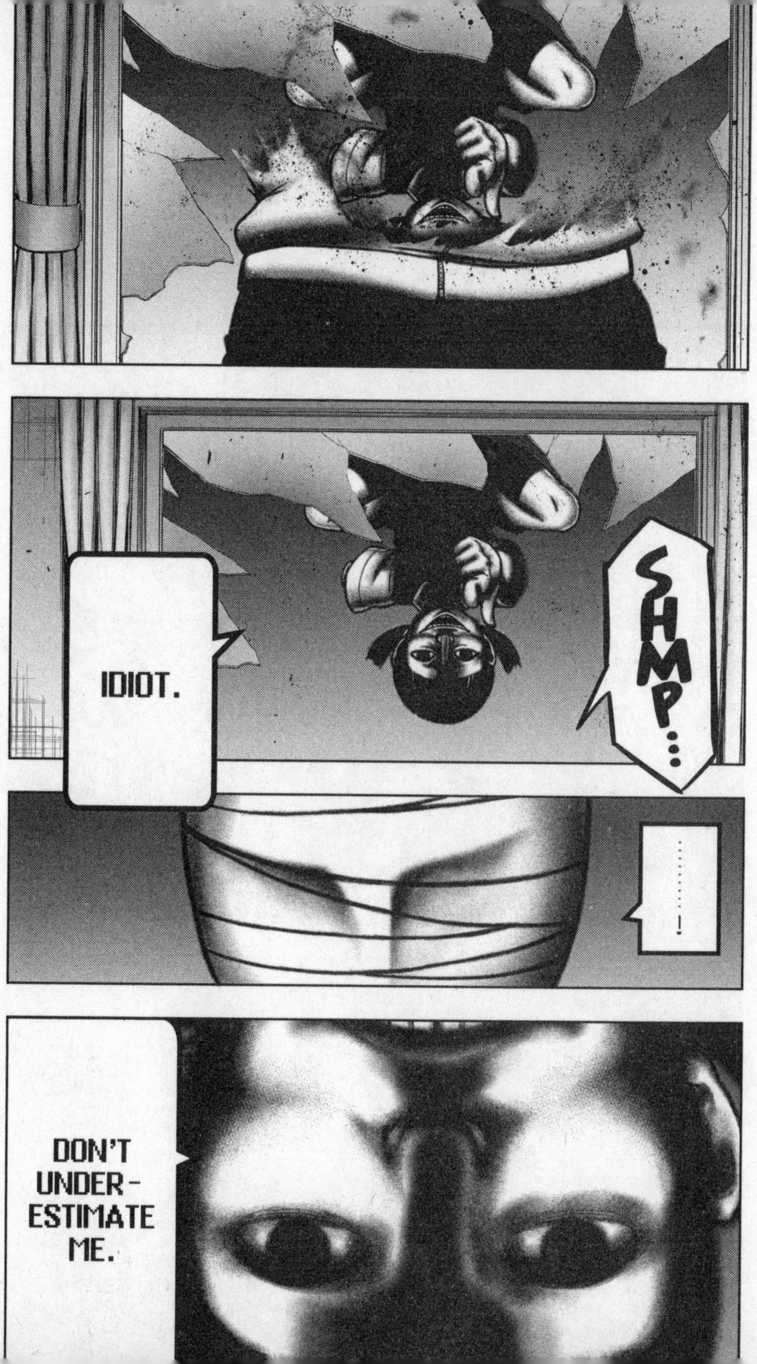
SHMP...
IDIOT.
......!
DON'T UNDER-ESTIMATE ME.

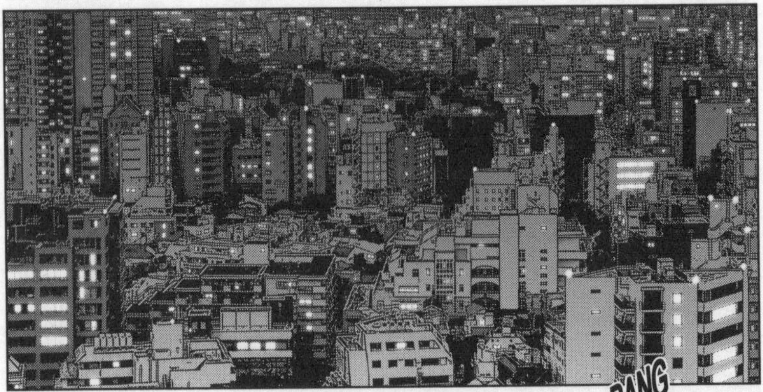

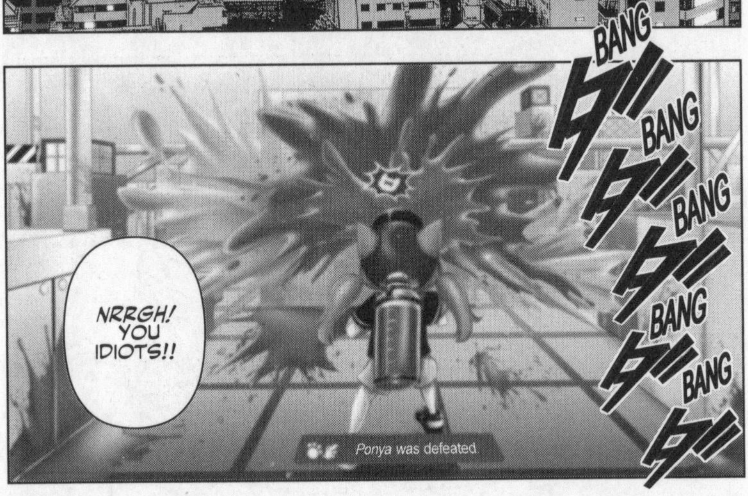
BANG ダ
BANG ダ
BANG ダ
BANG ダ
BANG ダ
BANG ダ
NRRGH! YOU IDIOTS!!
Ponya was defeated.

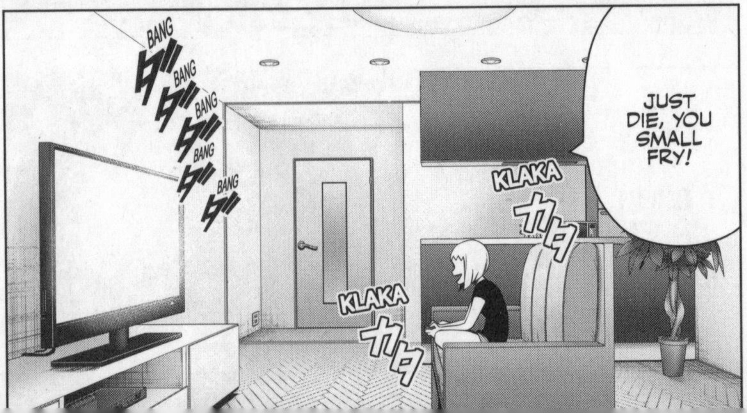
JUST DIE, YOU SMALL FRY!
KLAKA カタ
KLAKA カタ
BANG ダ
BANG ダ
BANG ダ
BANG ダ
BANG ダ

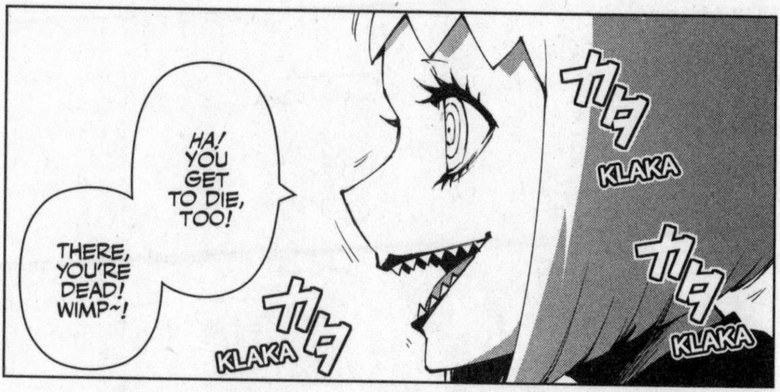
カタ
KLAKA
カタ
KLAKA
HA! YOU GET TO DIE, TOO!
THERE, YOU'RE DEAD! WIMP~!
カタ
KLAKA

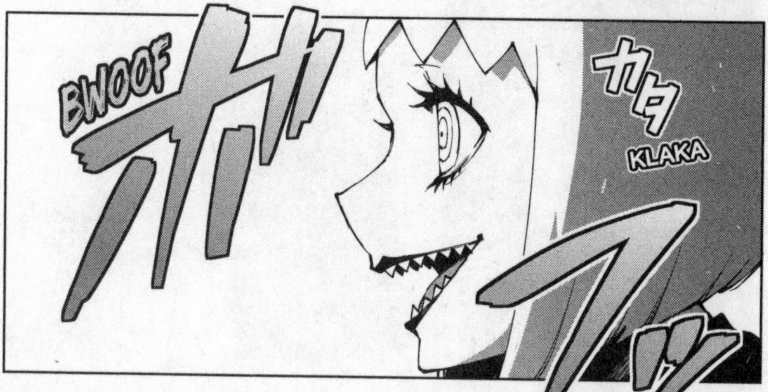
カタ
KLAKA
BWOOF

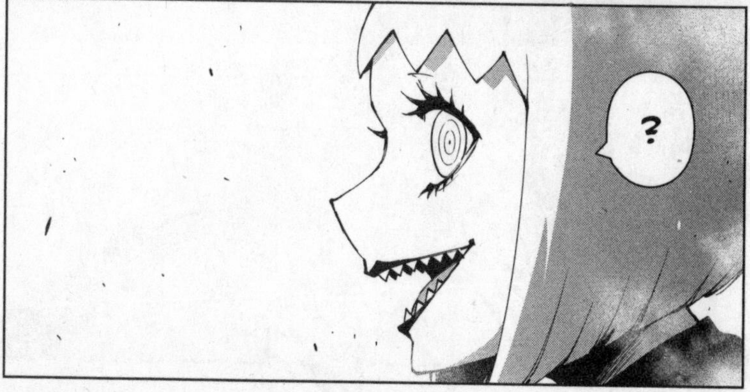
?

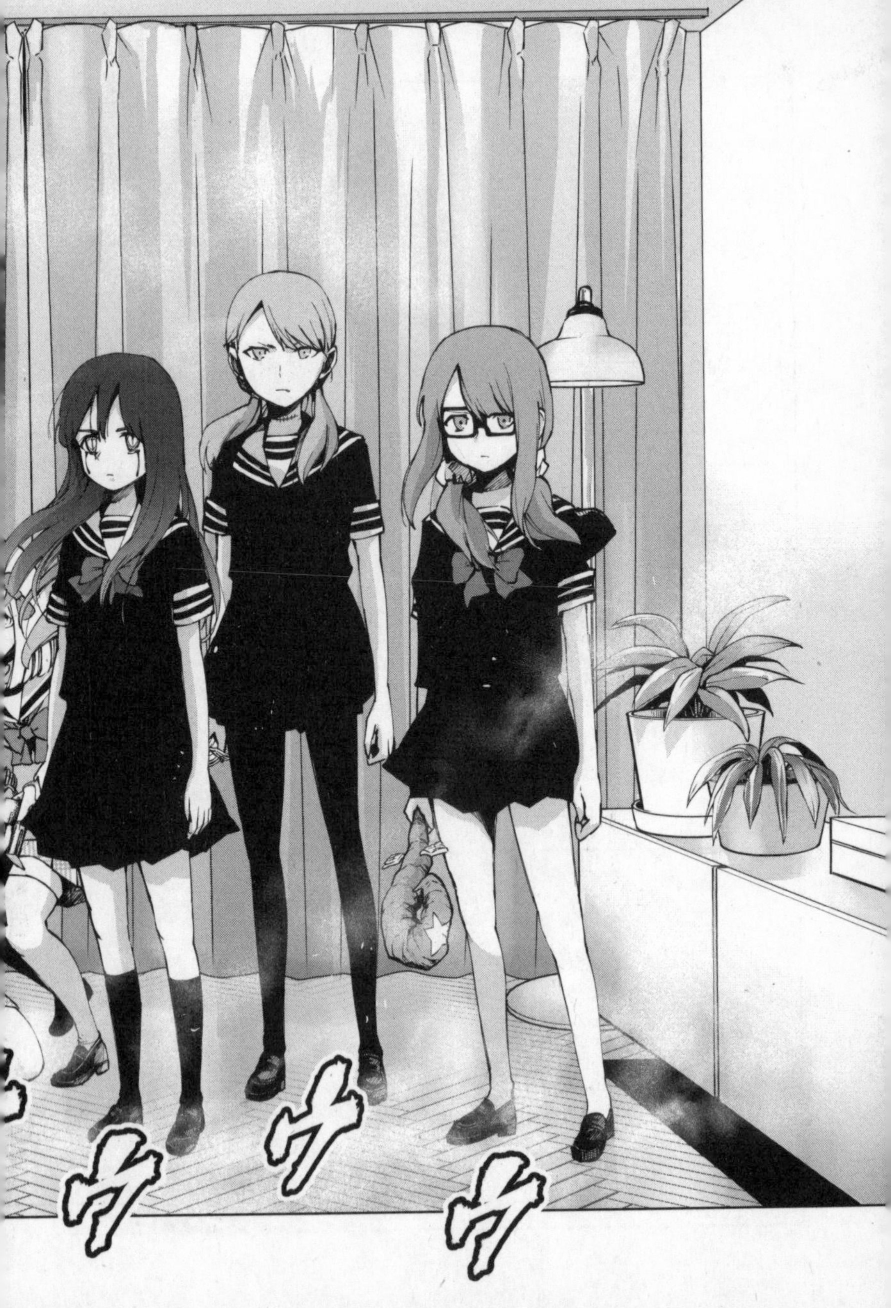

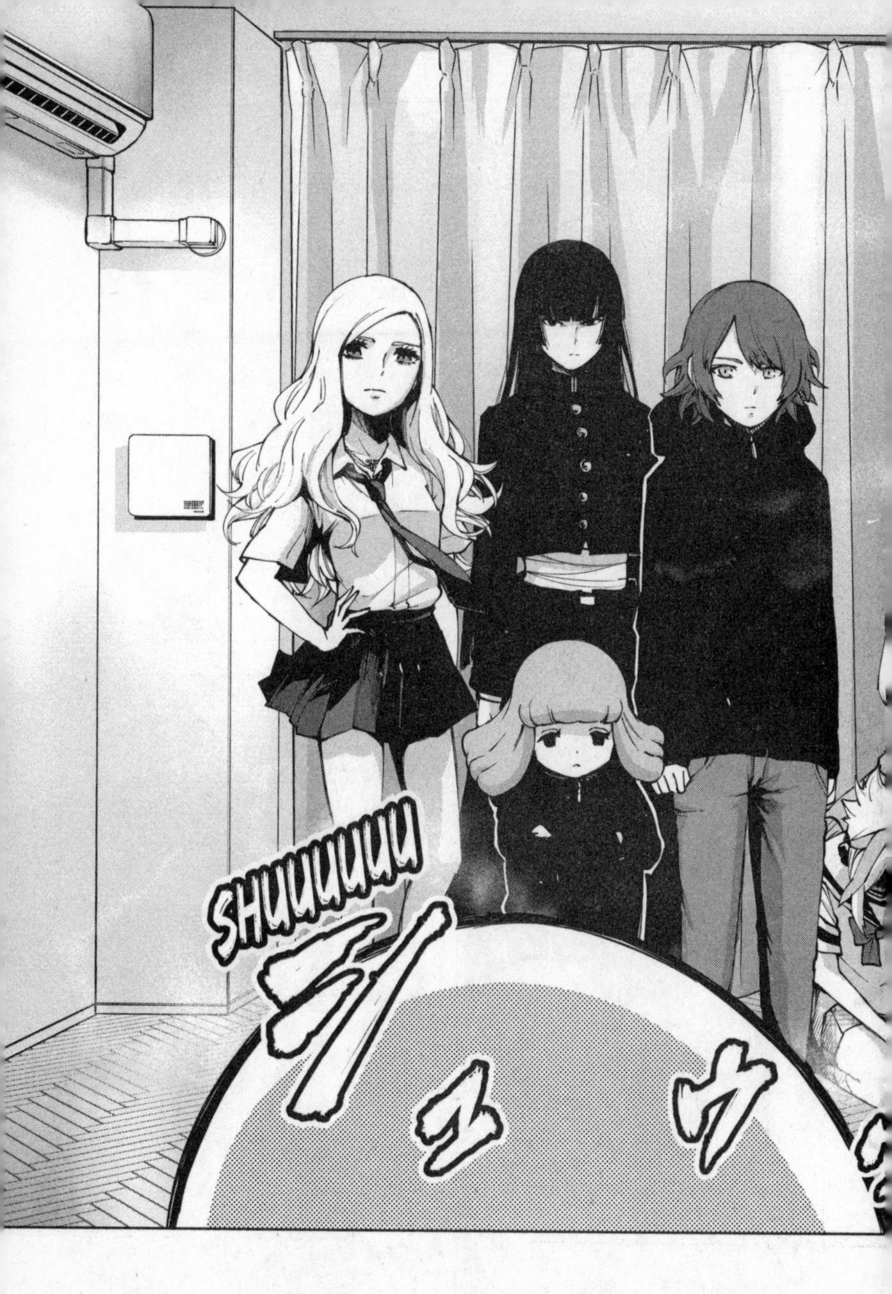
SHUUUUUU

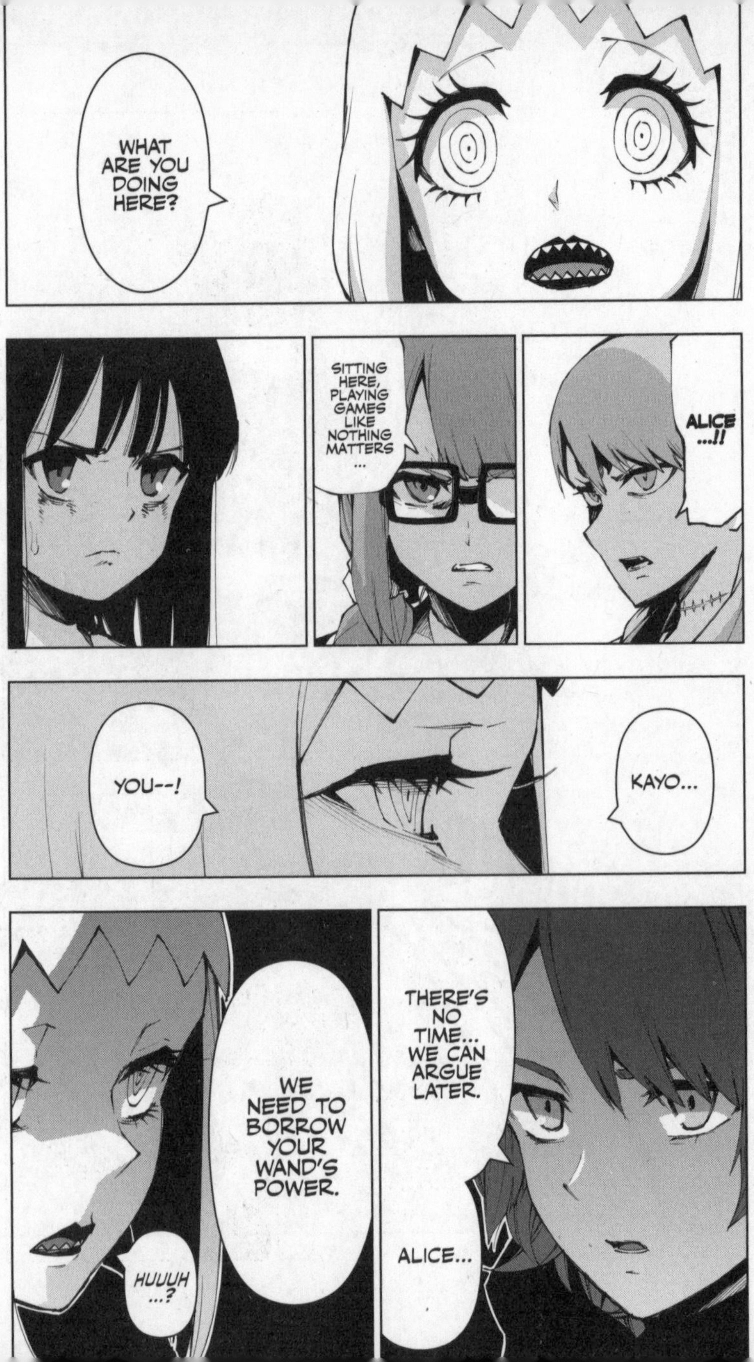
WHAT ARE YOU DOING HERE?
ALICE ...!!
SITTING HERE, PLAYING GAMES LIKE NOTHING MATTERS ...
KAYO...
YOU--!
THERE'S NO TIME... WE CAN ARGUE LATER.
WE NEED TO BORROW YOUR WAND'S POWER.
ALICE...
HUUUH ...?

ENTER.92 COTTON CANDY

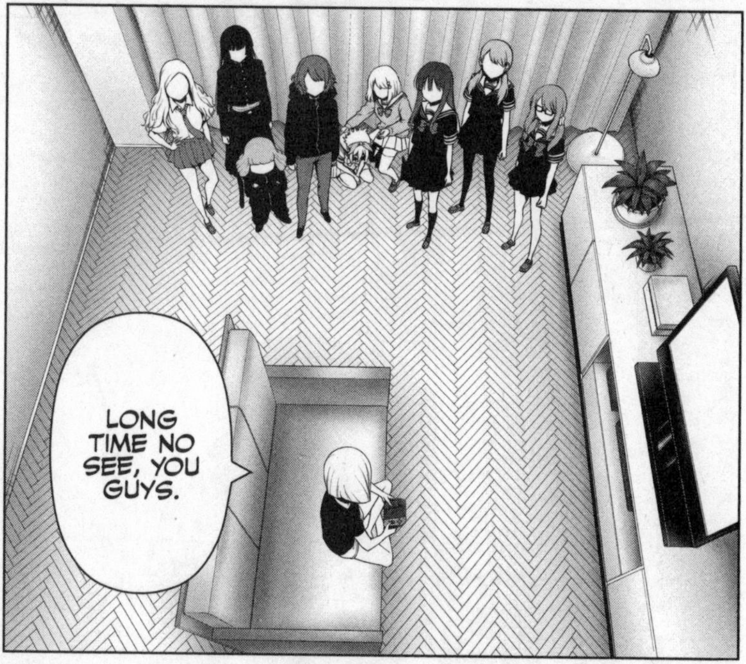
LONG TIME NO SEE, YOU GUYS.

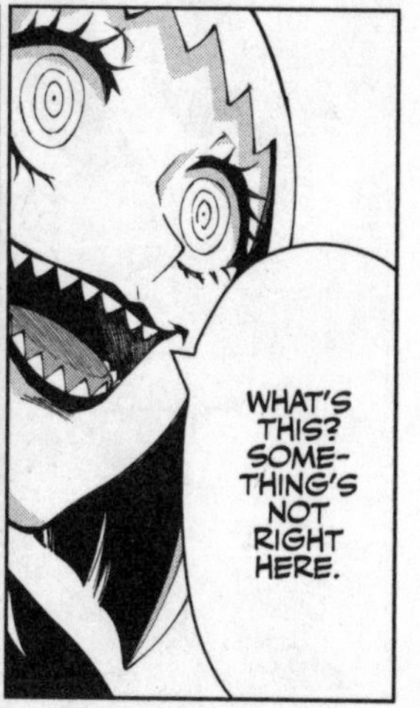
WHAT'S THIS? SOME-THING'S NOT RIGHT HERE.

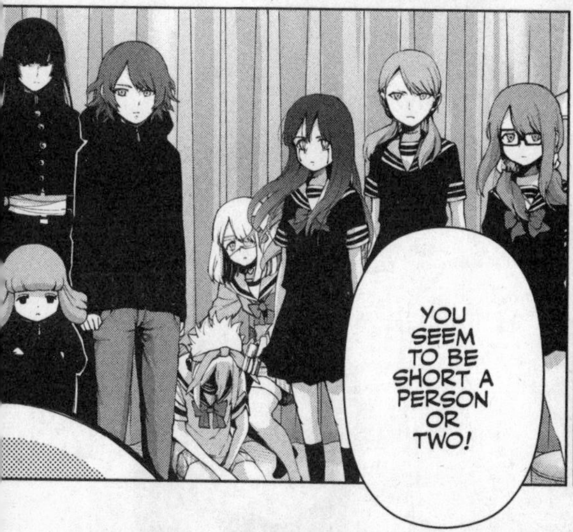
YOU SEEM TO BE SHORT A PERSON OR TWO!

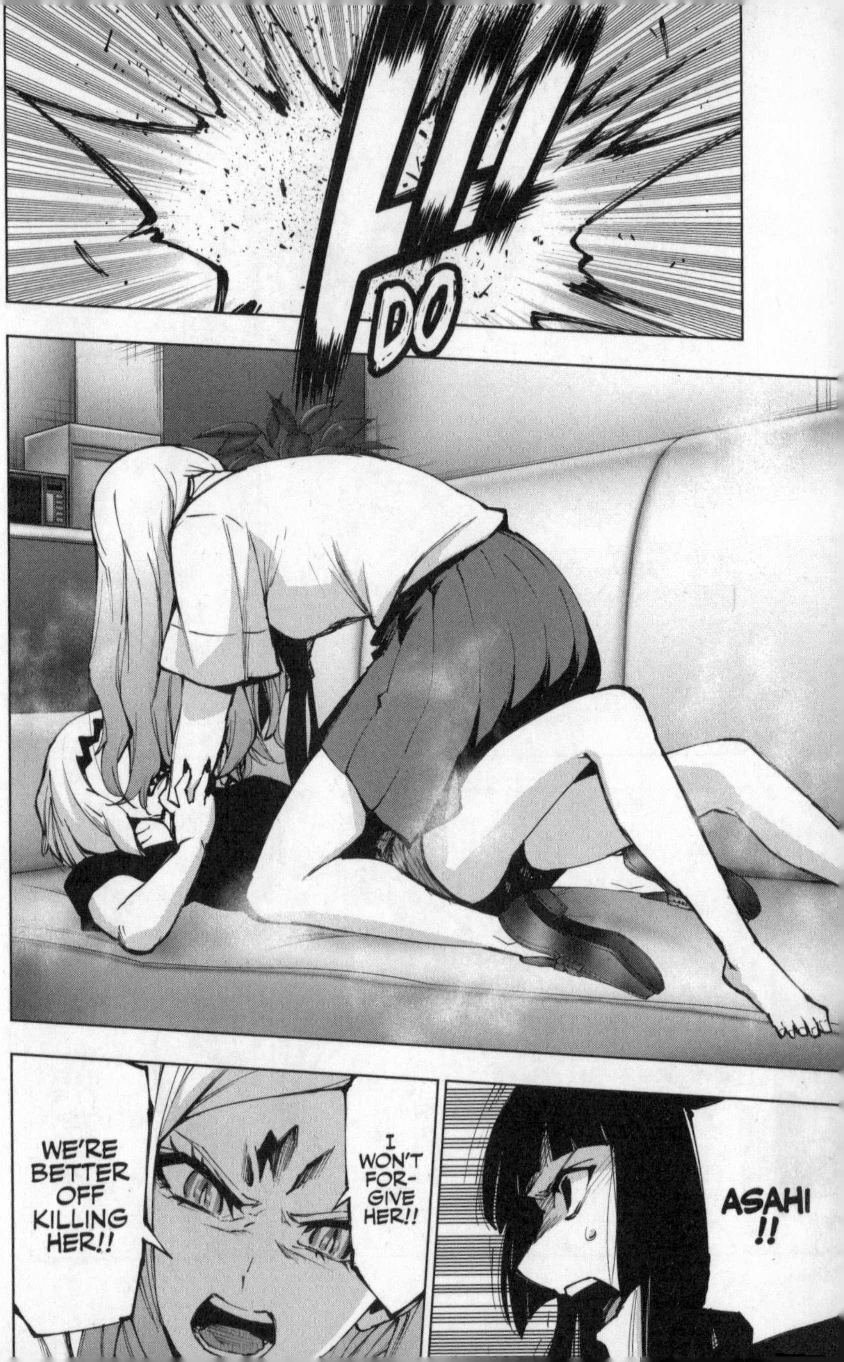
DO
ASAHI!!
I WON'T FOR-GIVE HER!!
WE'RE BETTER OFF KILLING HER!!

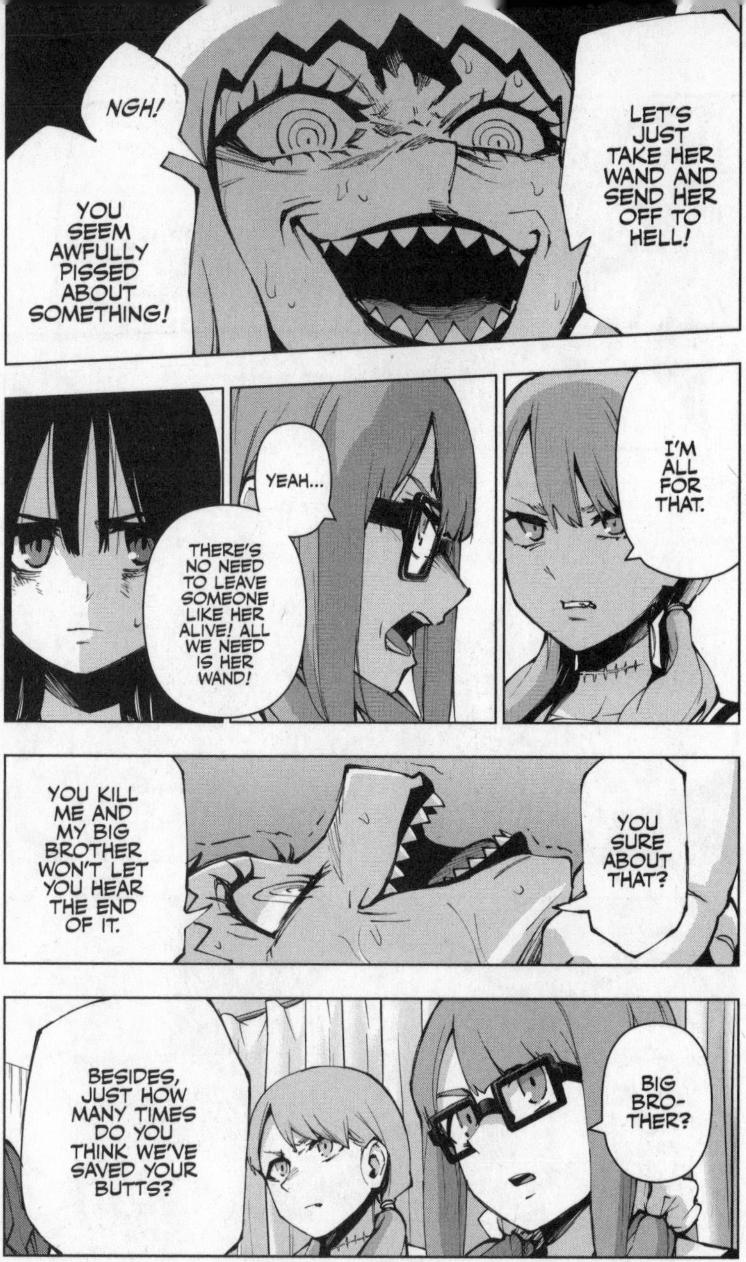
LET'S JUST TAKE HER WAND AND SEND HER OFF TO HELL!
NGH!
YOU SEEM AWFULLY PISSED ABOUT SOMETHING!
I'M ALL FOR THAT.
YEAH...
THERE'S NO NEED TO LEAVE SOMEONE LIKE HER ALIVE! ALL WE NEED IS HER WAND!
YOU SURE ABOUT THAT?
YOU KILL ME AND MY BIG BROTHER WON'T LET YOU HEAR THE END OF IT.
BIG BRO-THER?
BESIDES, JUST HOW MANY TIMES DO YOU THINK WE'VE SAVED YOUR BUTTS?

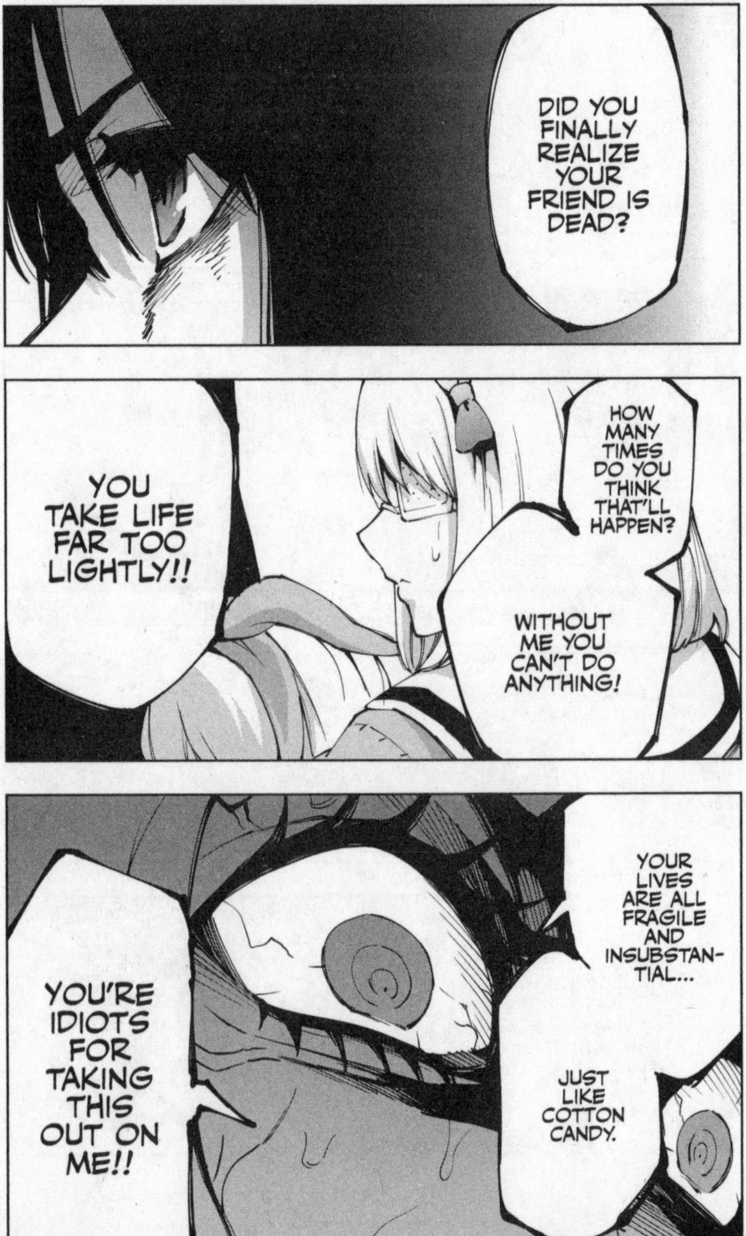
DID YOU FINALLY REALIZE YOUR FRIEND IS DEAD?
HOW MANY TIMES DO YOU THINK THAT'LL HAPPEN?
WITHOUT ME YOU CAN'T DO ANYTHING!
YOU TAKE LIFE FAR TOO LIGHTLY!!
YOUR LIVES ARE ALL FRAGILE AND INSUBSTANTIAL...
JUST LIKE COTTON CANDY.
YOU'RE IDIOTS FOR TAKING THIS OUT ON ME!!

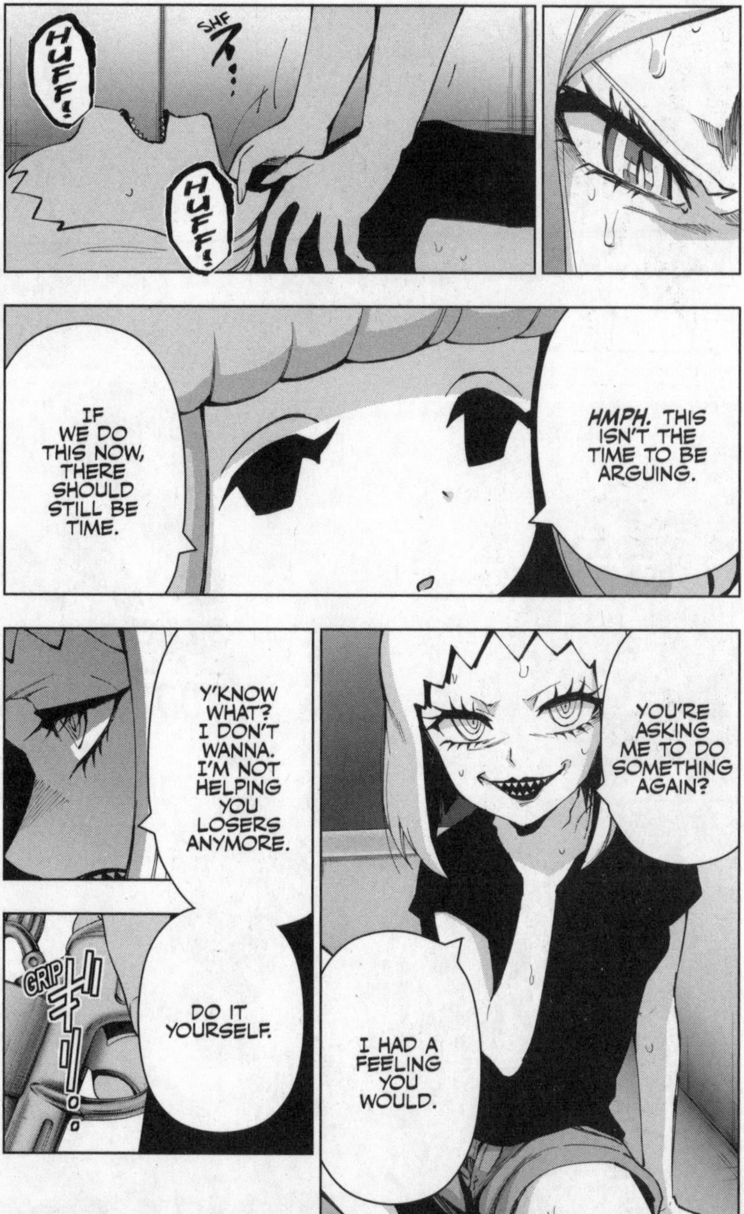
SHF
HUFF!
HUFF!
HMPH. THIS ISN'T THE TIME TO BE ARGUING.
IF WE DO THIS NOW, THERE SHOULD STILL BE TIME.
YOU'RE ASKING ME TO DO SOMETHING AGAIN?
Y'KNOW WHAT? I DON'T WANNA. I'M NOT HELPING YOU LOSERS ANYMORE.
GRIP
DO IT YOURSELF.
I HAD A FEELING YOU WOULD.

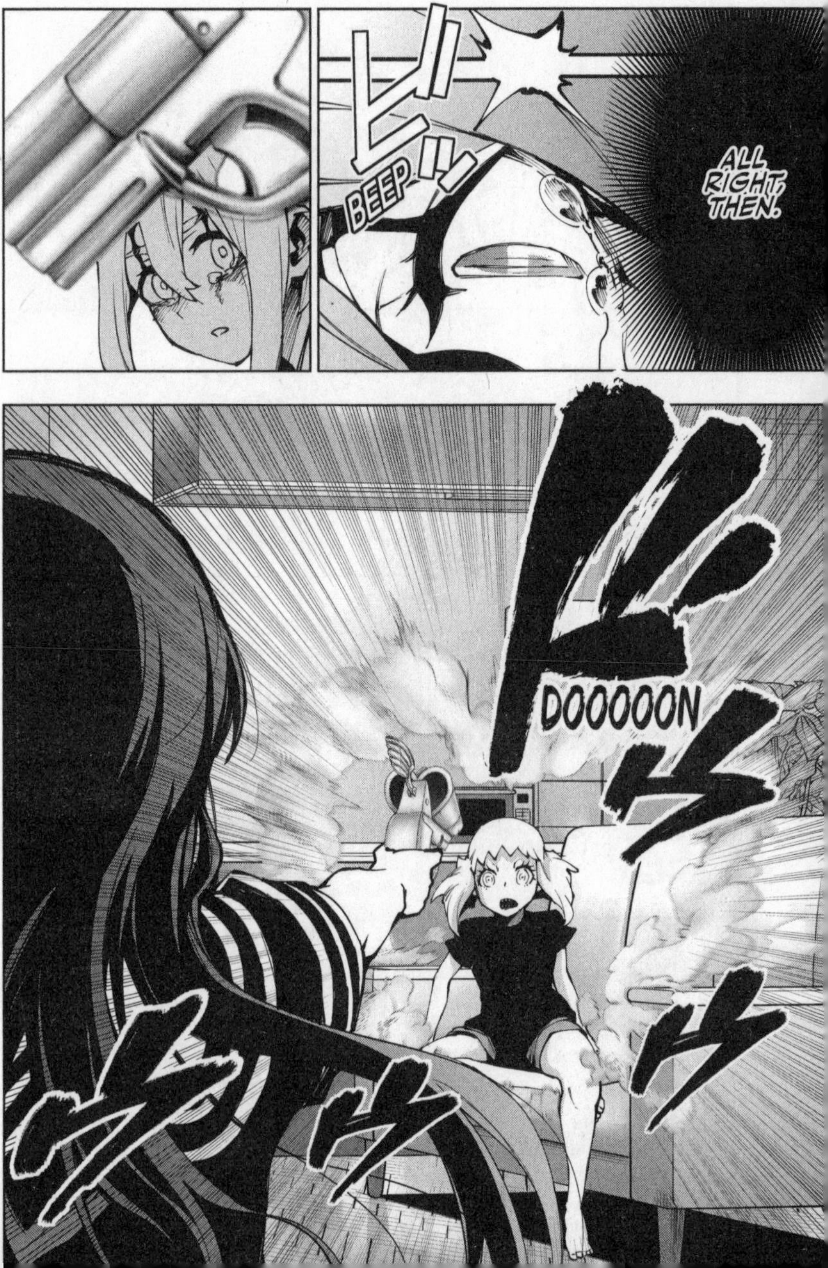
ALL RIGHT, THEN.
BEEP
DOOOOON

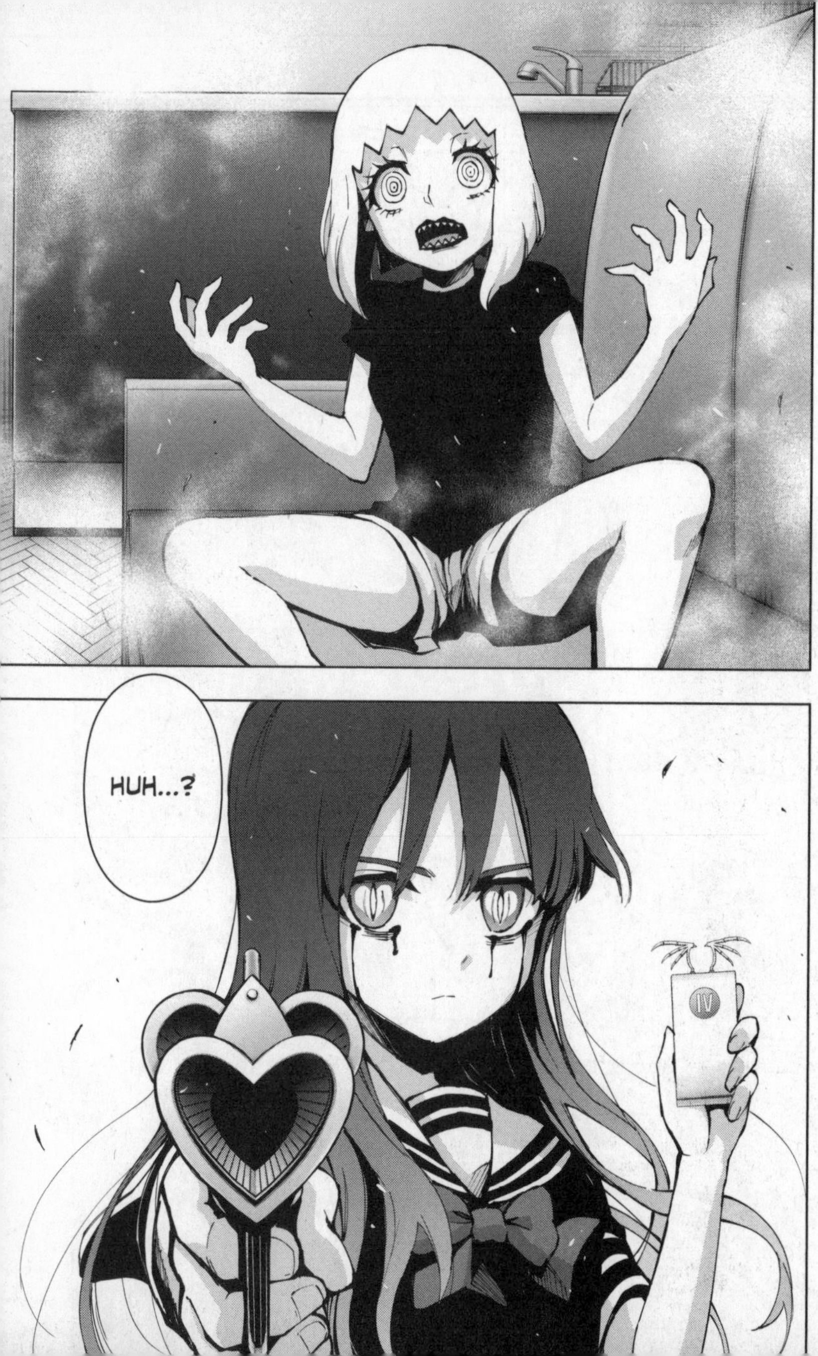
HUH...?

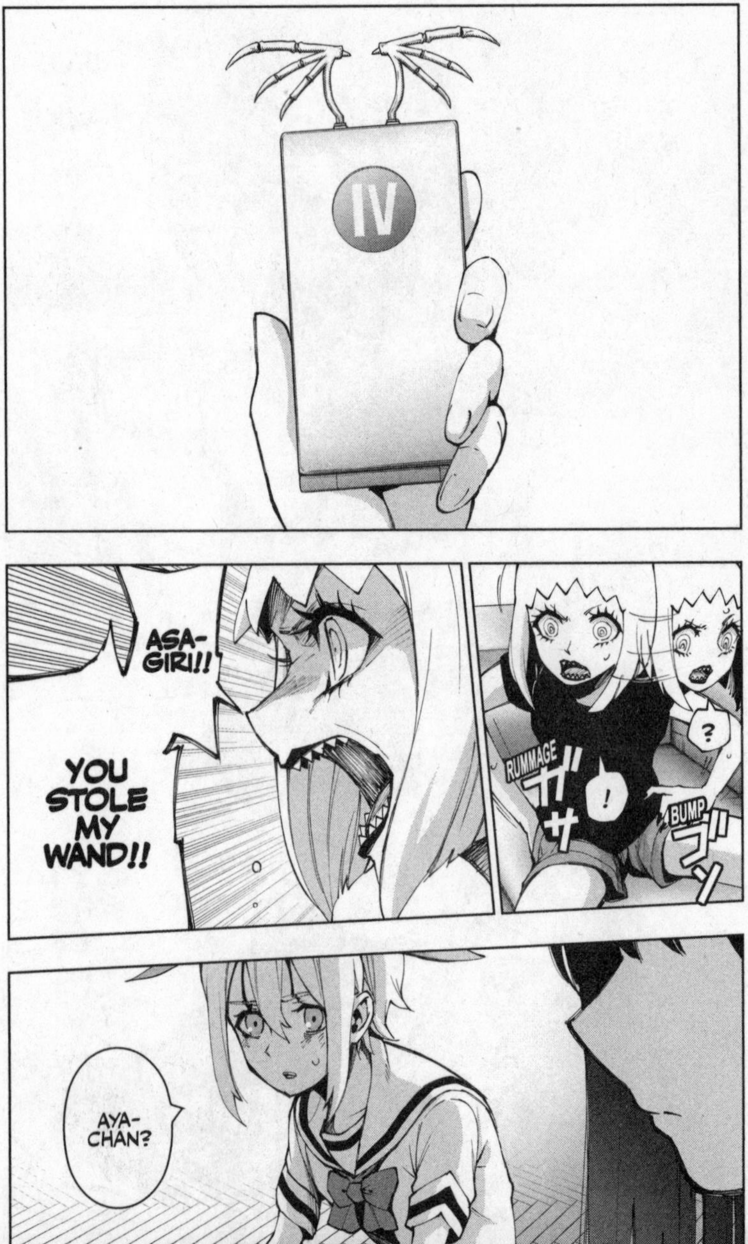
IV
?
RUMMAGE
ガサ
!
BUMP
ASA-GIRI!!
YOU STOLE MY WAND!!
AYA-CHAN?

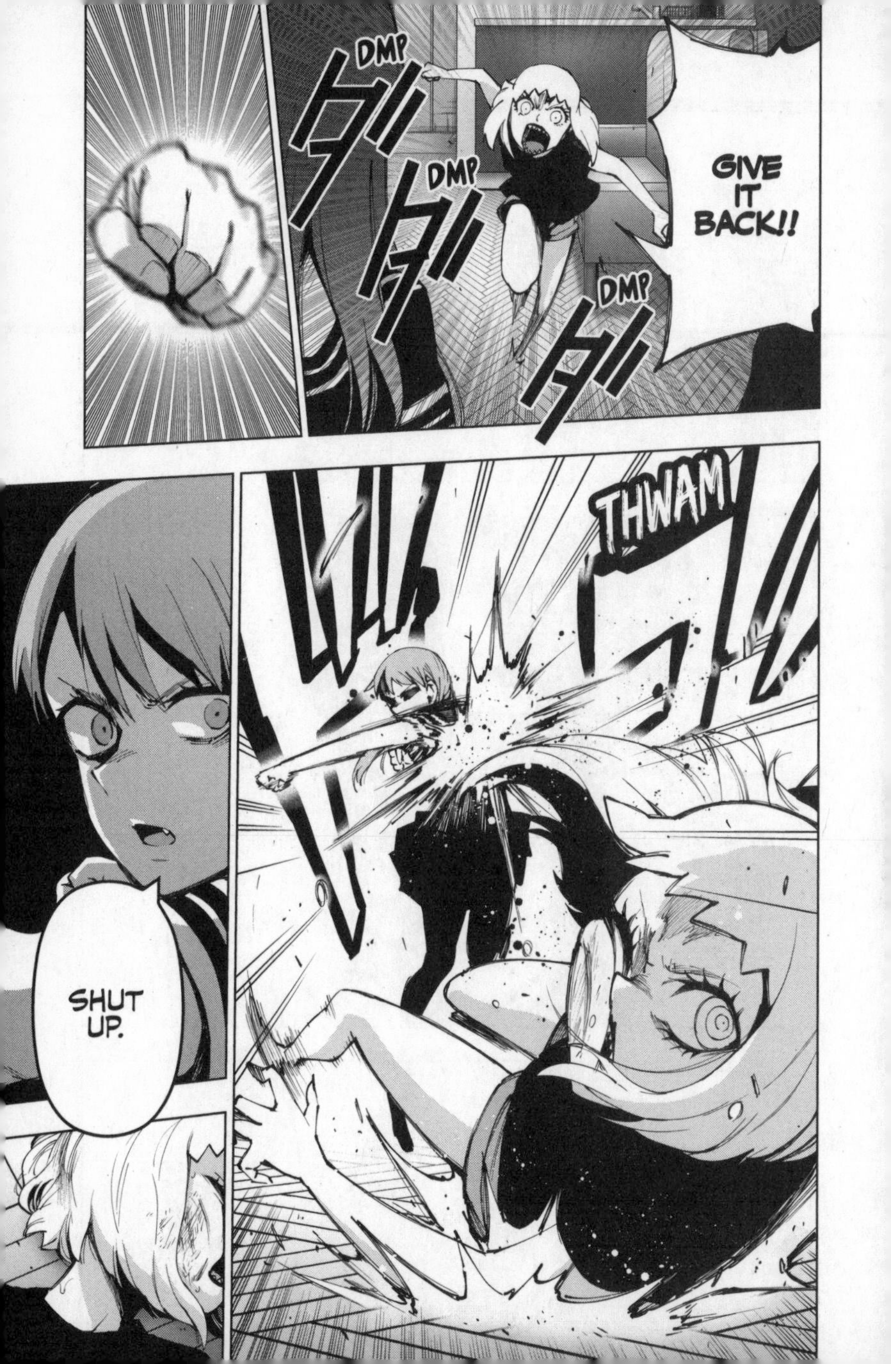
DMP
DMP
DMP
GIVE IT BACK!!
THWAM
SHUT UP.

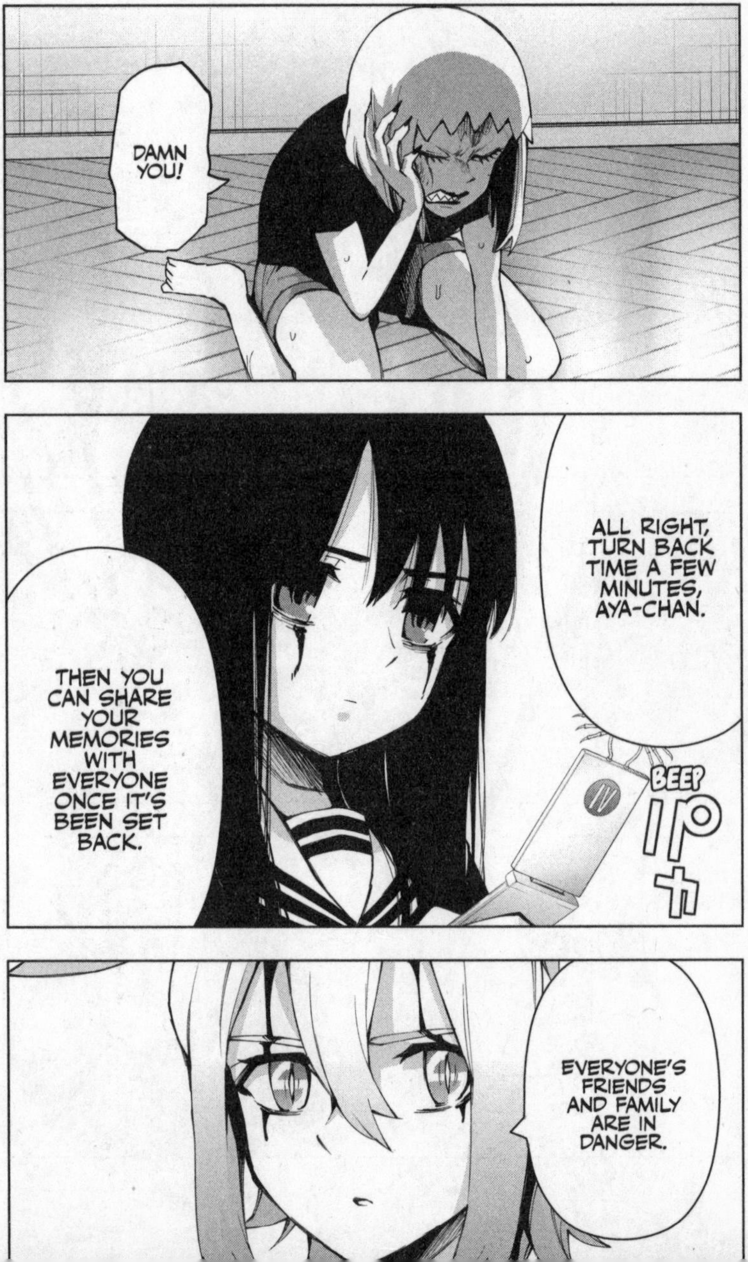
DAMN YOU!
ALL RIGHT, TURN BACK TIME A FEW MINUTES, AYA-CHAN.
THEN YOU CAN SHARE YOUR MEMORIES WITH EVERYONE ONCE IT'S BEEN SET BACK.
BEEP
EVERYONE'S FRIENDS AND FAMILY ARE IN DANGER.

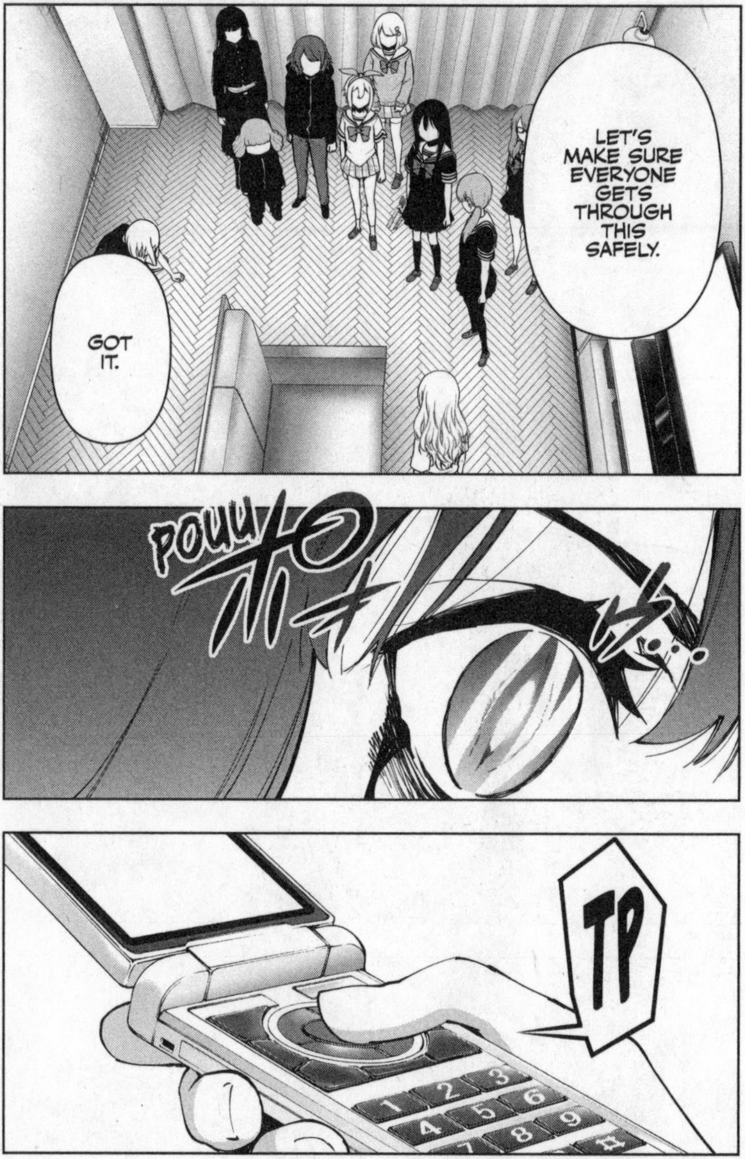
LET'S MAKE SURE EVERYONE GETS THROUGH THIS SAFELY.
GOT IT.
TP

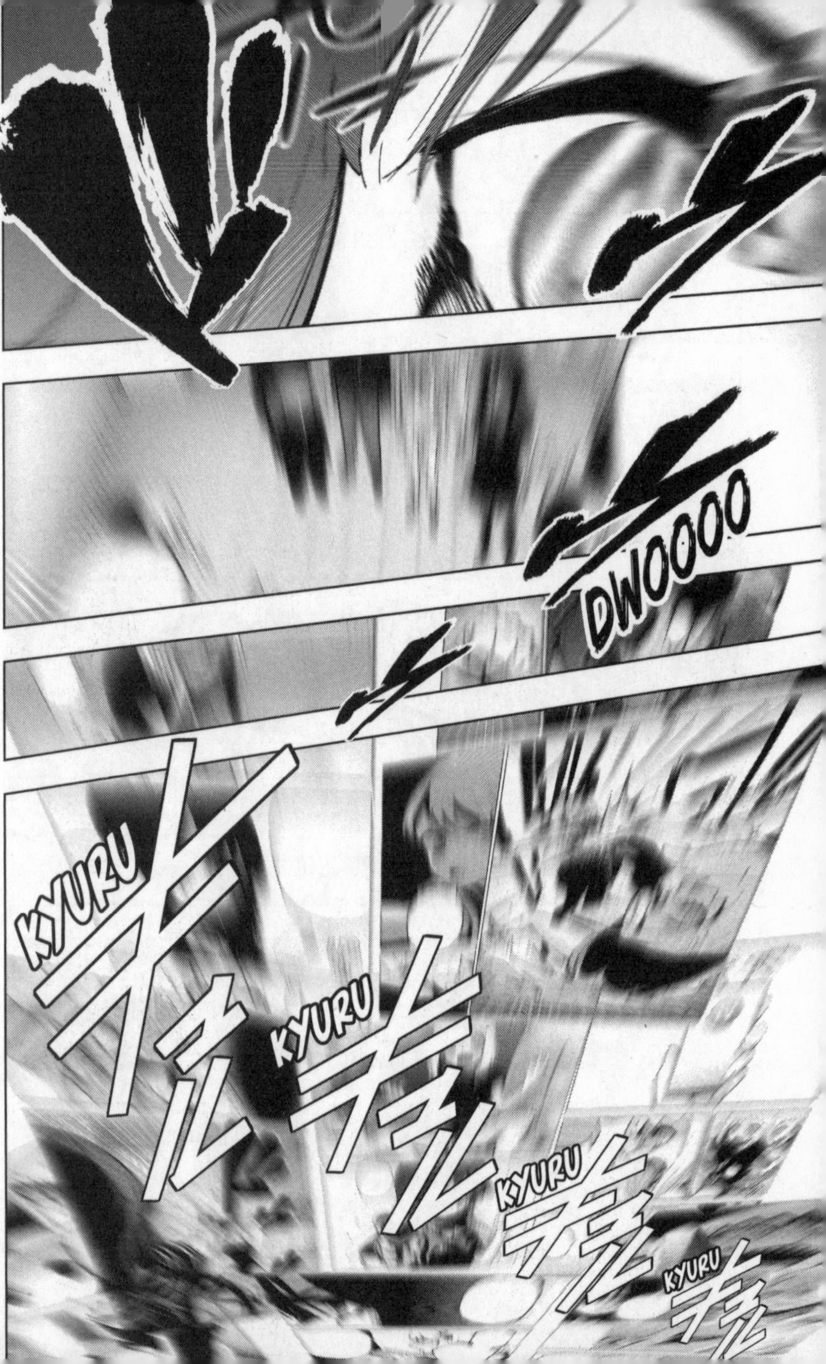
DWOOOO
KYURU
KYURU
KYURU
KYURU

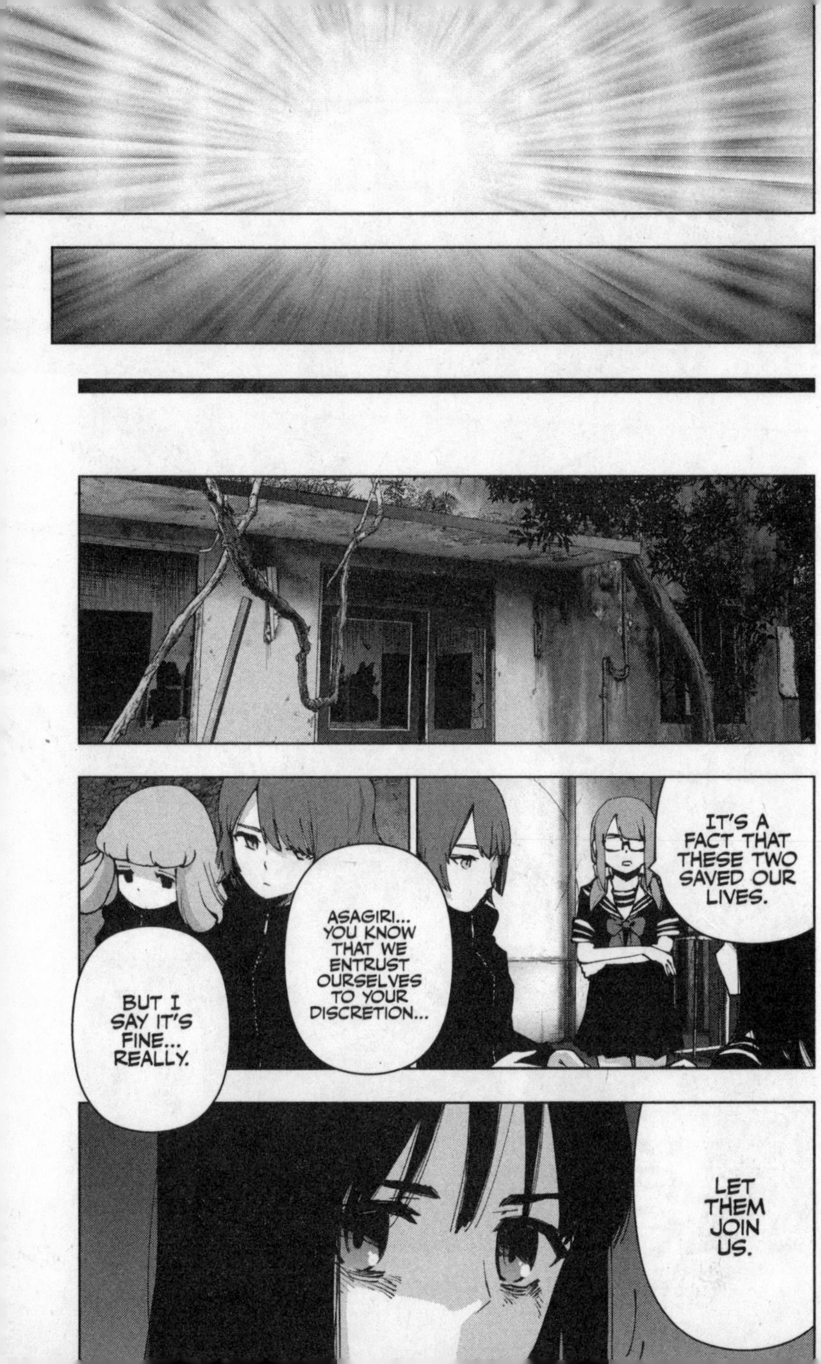
IT'S A FACT THAT THESE TWO SAVED OUR LIVES.
ASAGIRI... YOU KNOW THAT WE ENTRUST OURSELVES TO YOUR DISCRETION...
BUT I SAY IT'S FINE... REALLY.
LET THEM JOIN US.

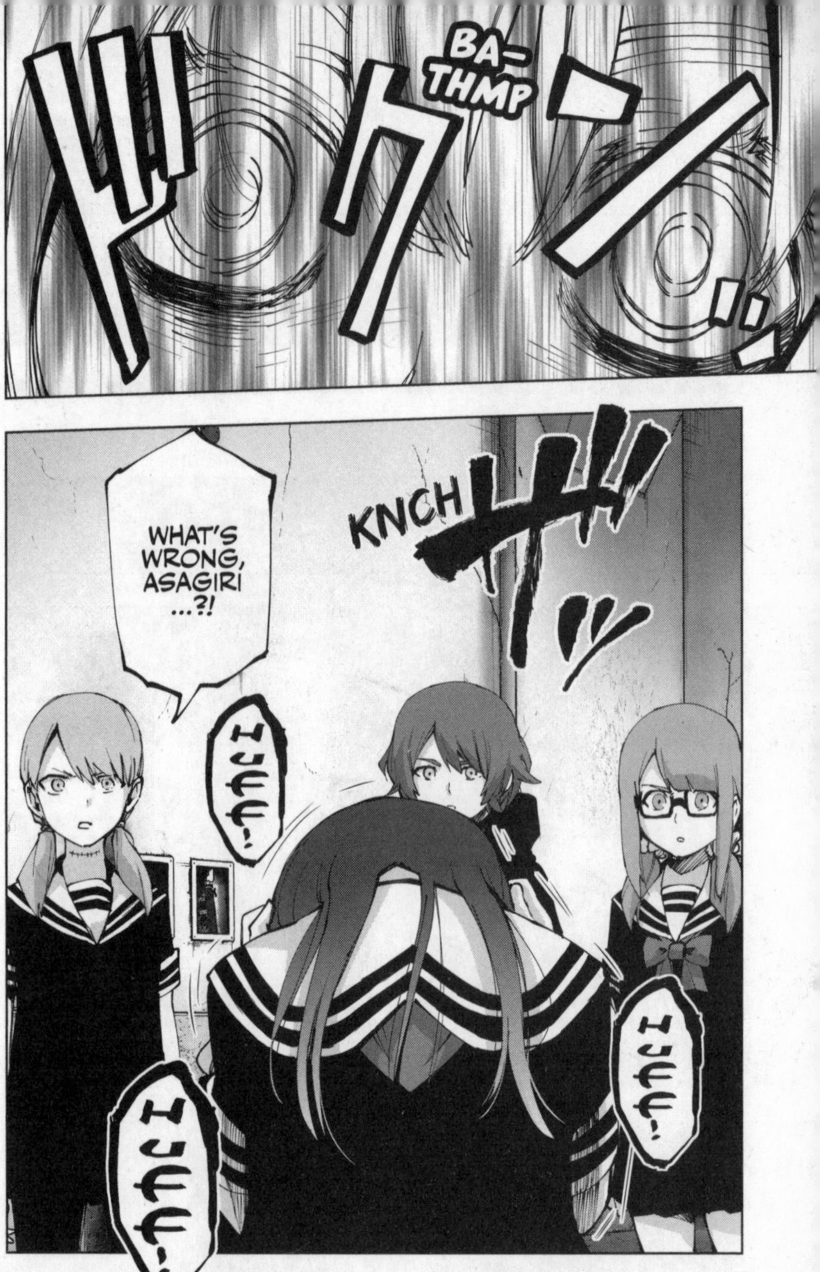
BA-THMP
KNCH
WHAT'S WRONG, ASAGIRI ...?!
HUFF,
HUFF,
HUFF,

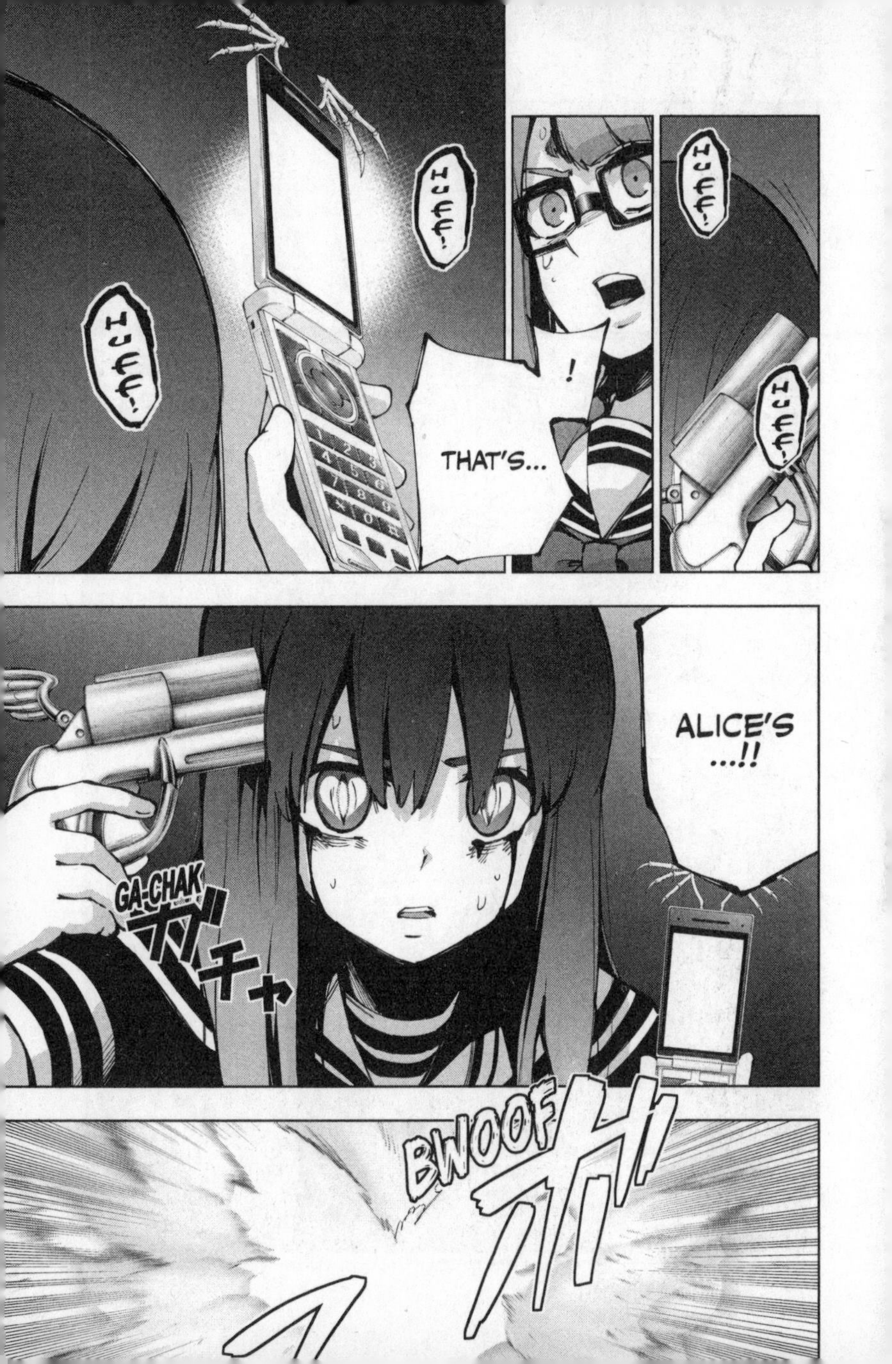
HUFF!
HUFF!
!
THAT'S...
HUFF!
HUFF!
ALICE'S ...!!
GA-CHAK
BWOOF

ピー　ピー　ピー　ピー　ピー　ピー　ピー　ピー
BEEP　BEEP　BEEP　BEEP　　BEEP　BEEP　BEEP　BEEP

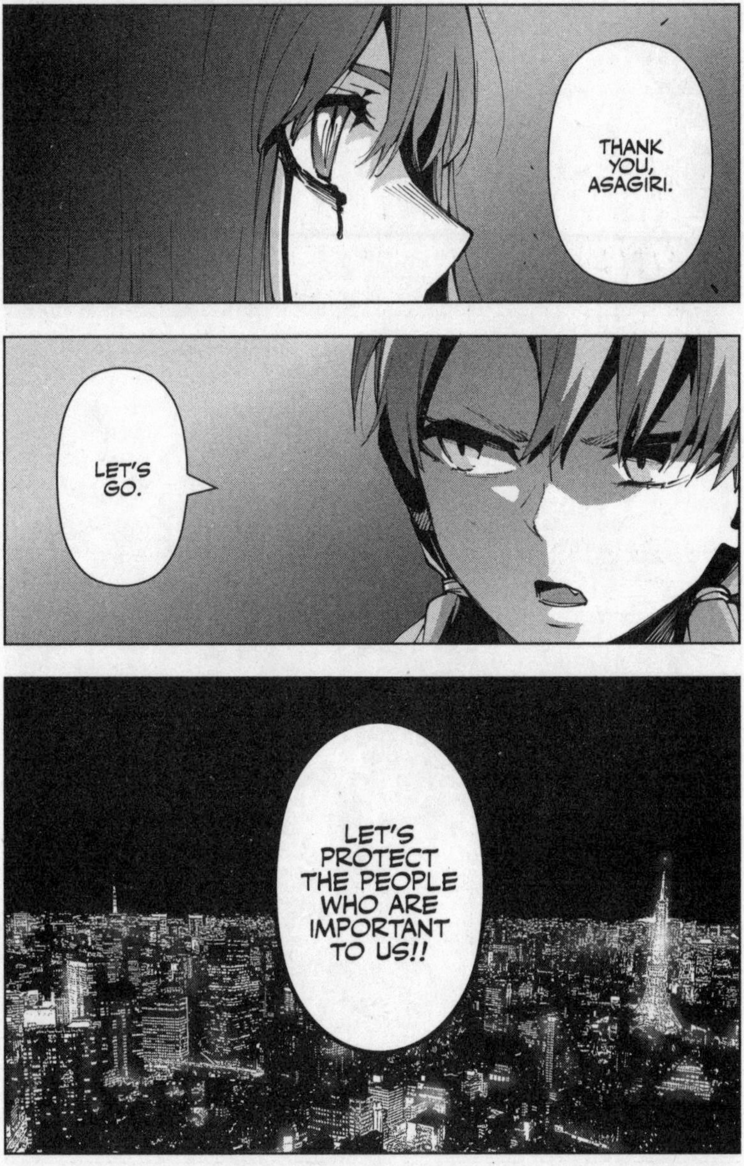
THANK YOU, ASAGIRI.
LET'S GO.
LET'S PROTECT THE PEOPLE WHO ARE IMPORTANT TO US!!

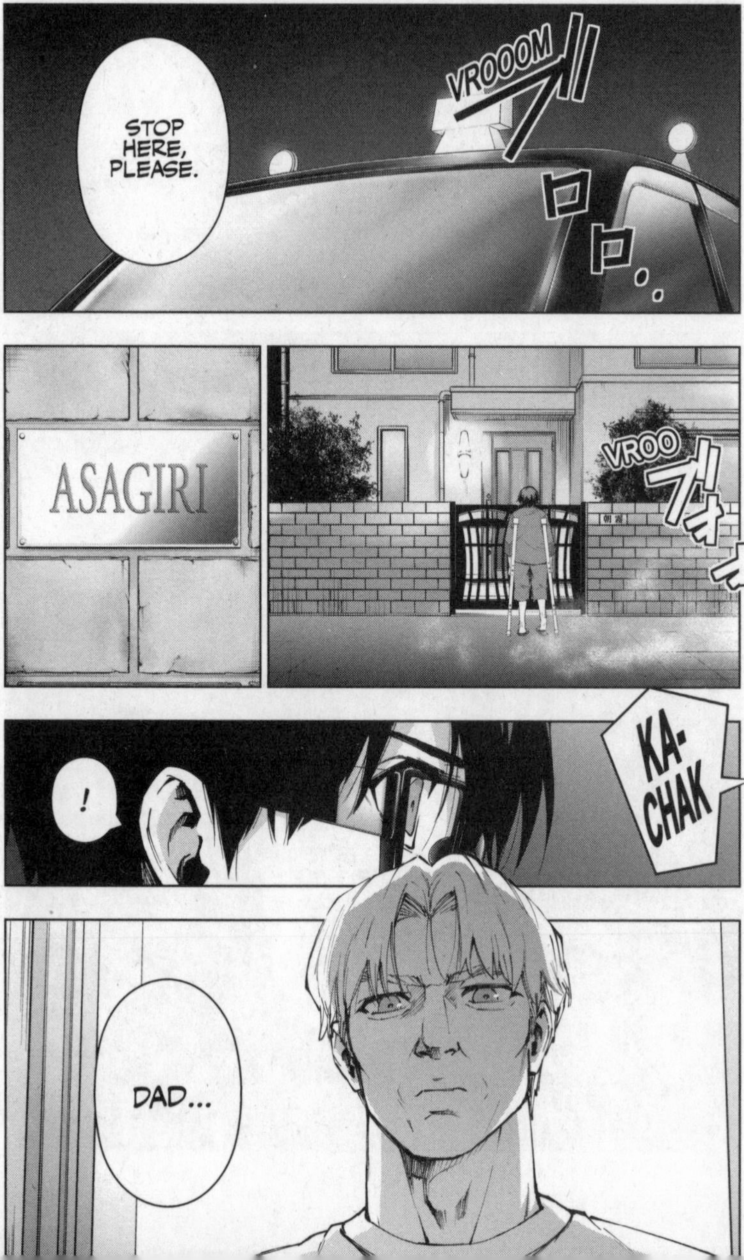
VROOOM
STOP HERE, PLEASE.
VROO
ブォォ
ASAGIRI
KA-CHAK
!
DAD...

ENTER.93 SCUMBAG FATHER

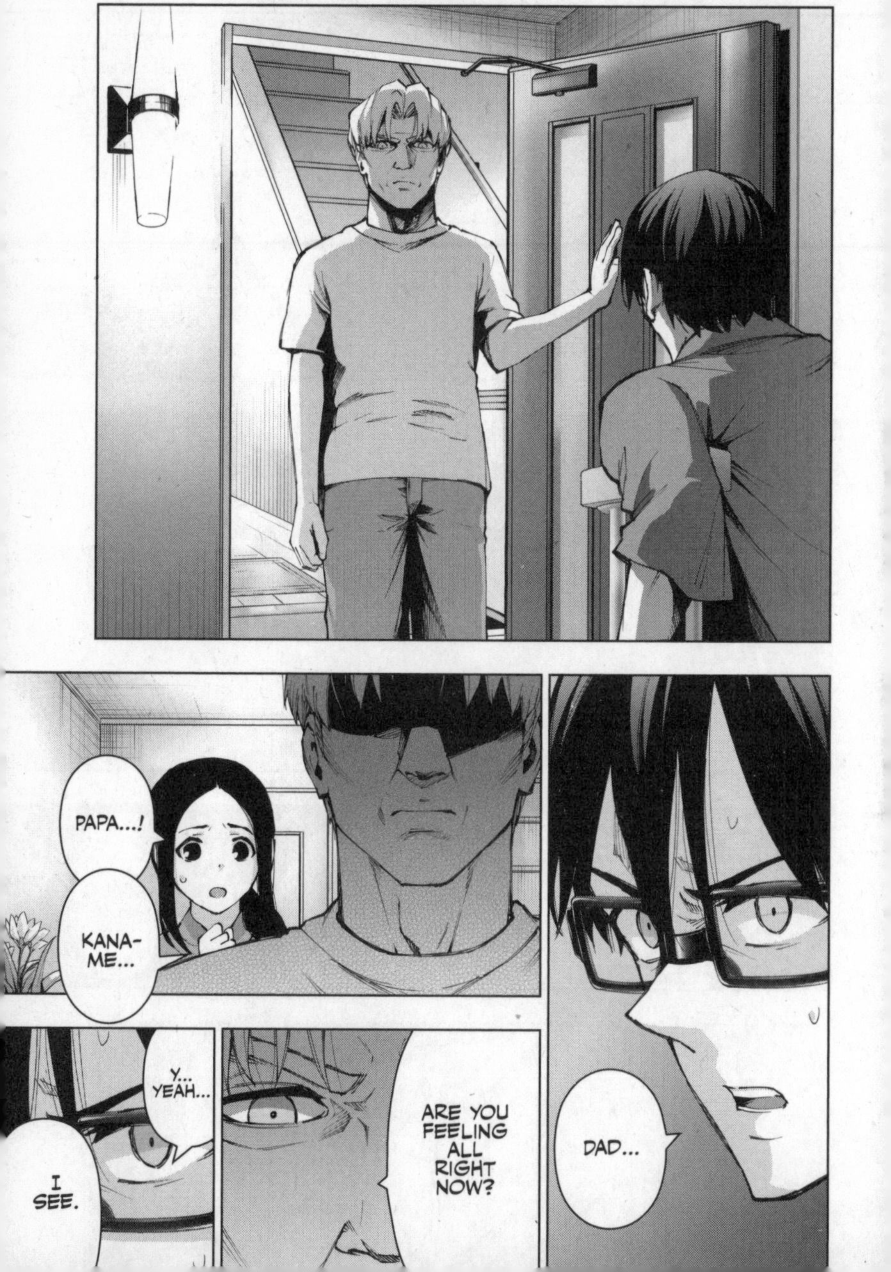
DAD...
PAPA...!
KANA-ME...
ARE YOU FEELING ALL RIGHT NOW?
Y... YEAH...
I SEE.

IT'S TIME YOU MADE UP FOR ALL THE TIME YOU LOST.

HUH? WHAT ARE YOU...?

STUDYING.

TIME TO STUDY!

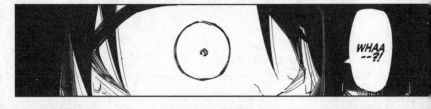

WHAA --?!

NOW, COME IN.

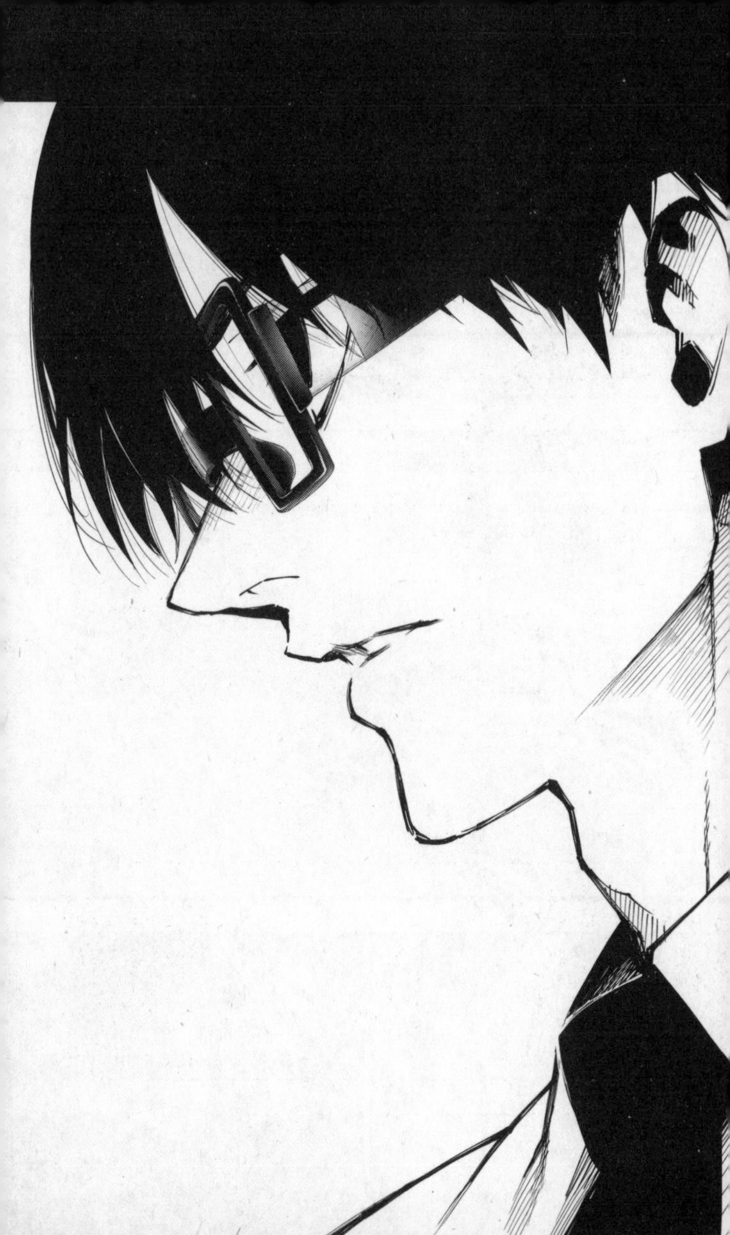

ENTER.93 SCUMBAG FATHER

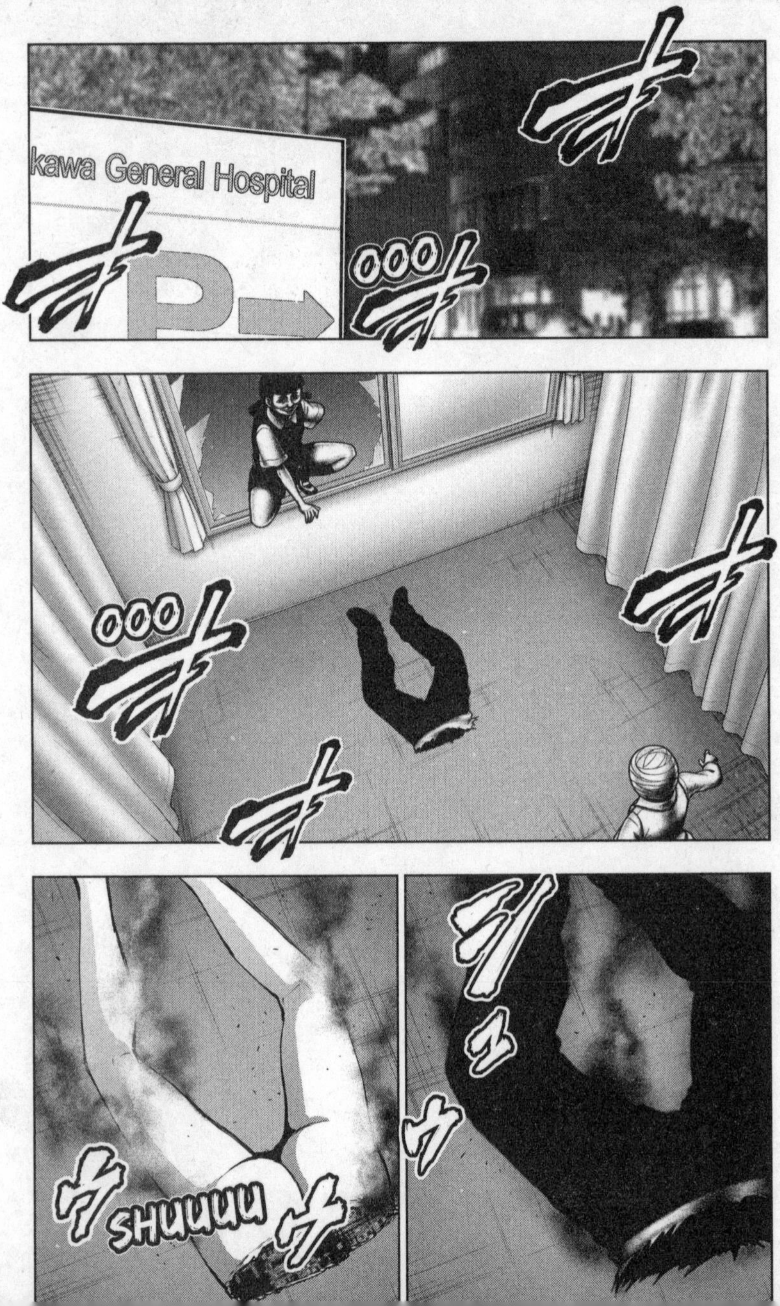
kawa General Hospital
P
ooo
ooo
SHuuuuu

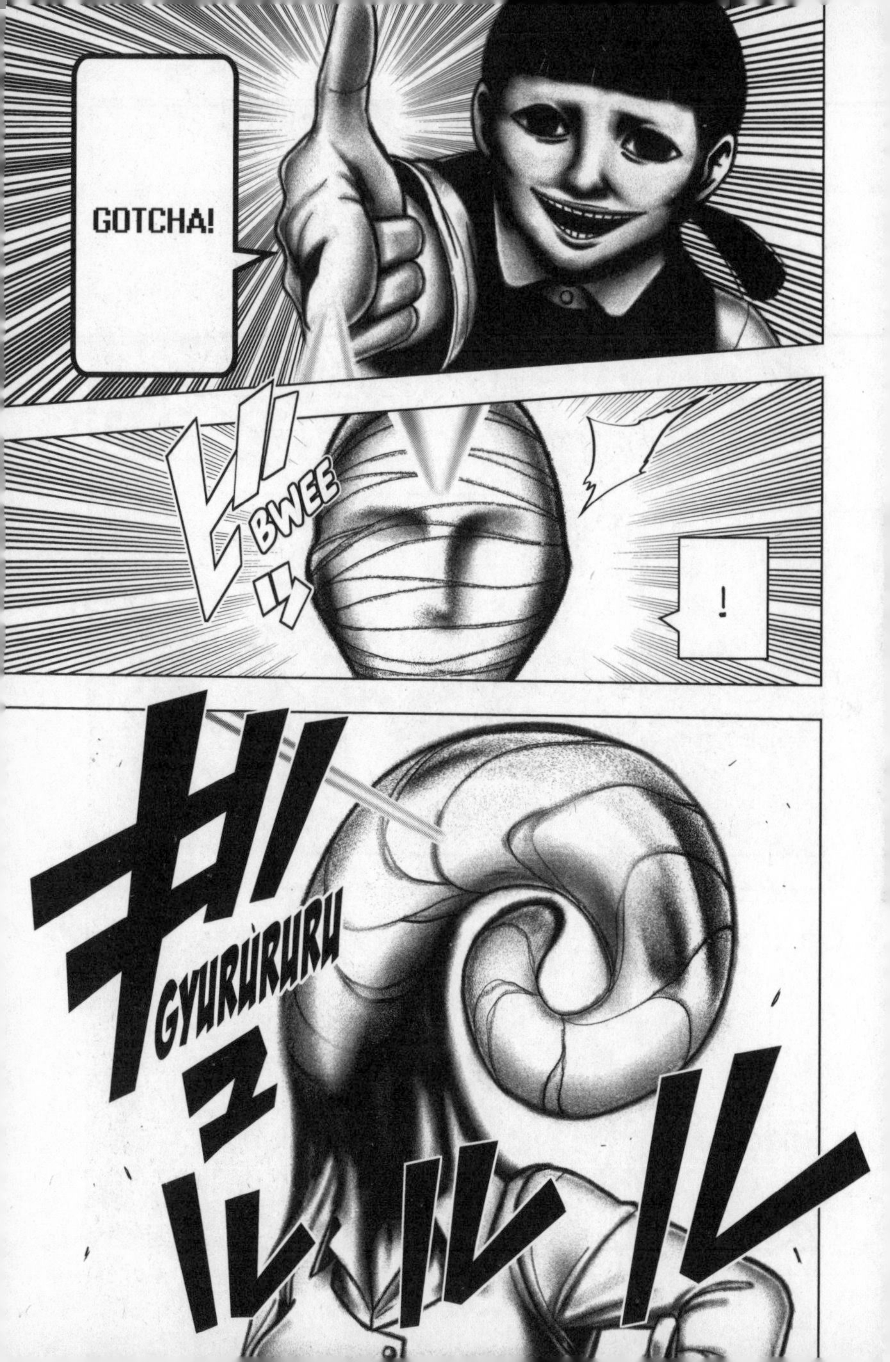
GOTCHA!
BWEE
!
GYURURURU

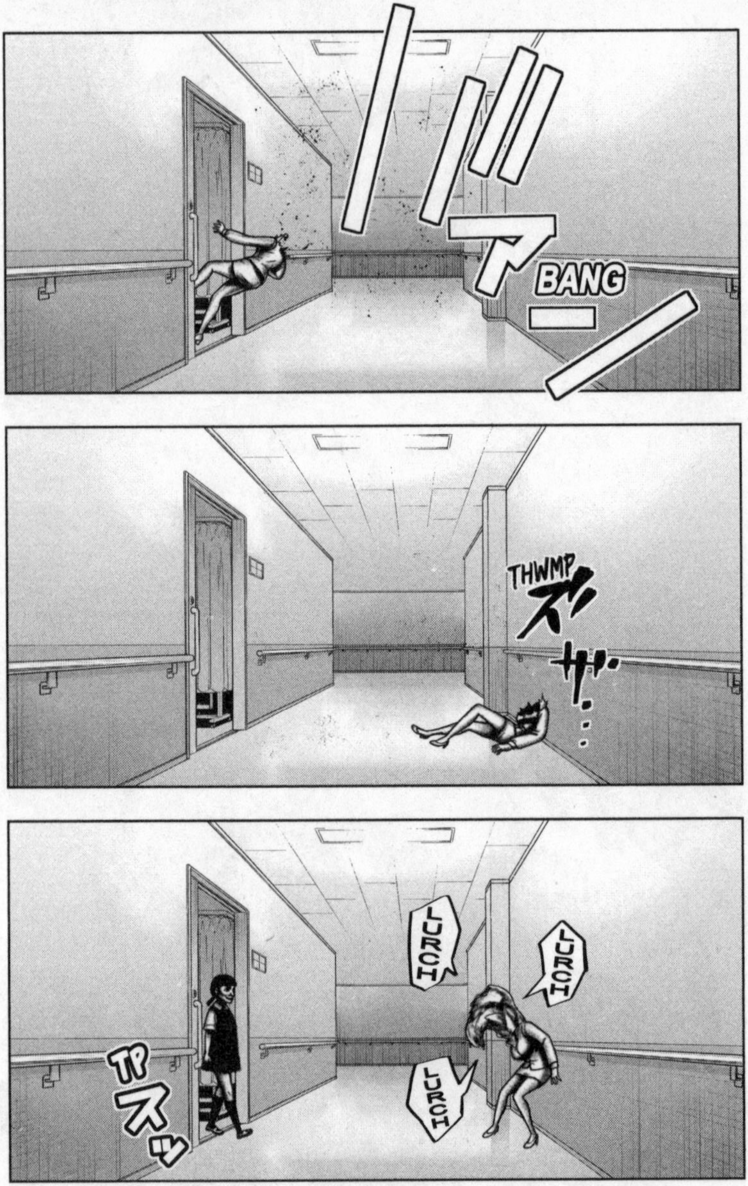
BANG
THWMP
ズッ
ザ…
LURCH
LURCH
LURCH
TP
スッ

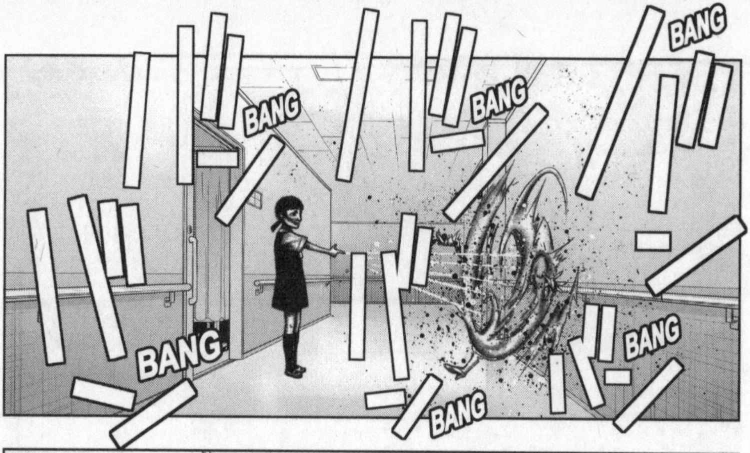
BANG
BANG
BANG
BANG
BANG
BANG

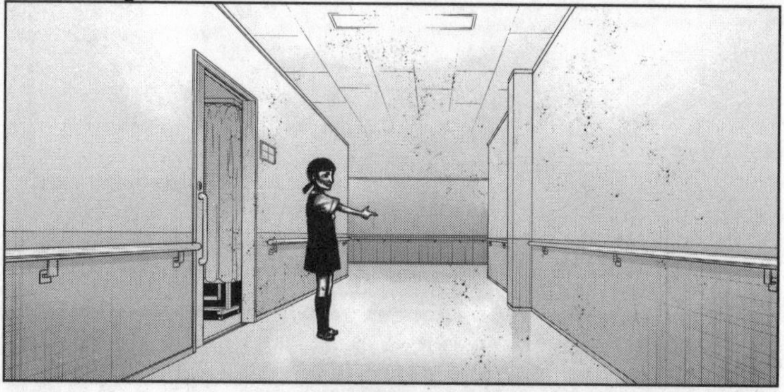

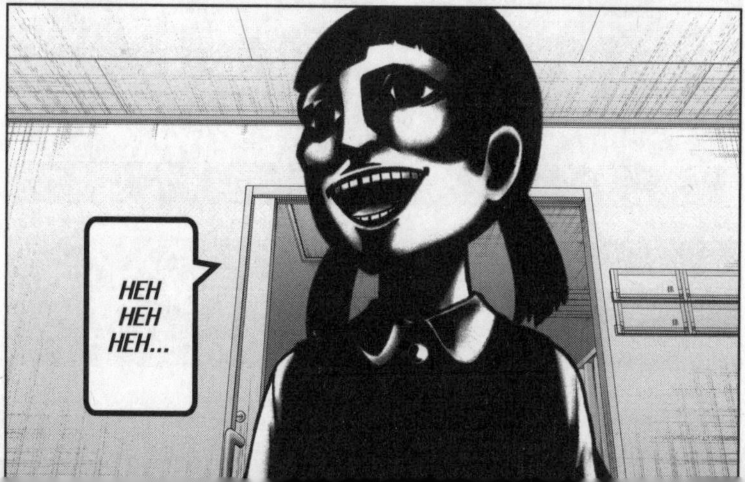
HEH HEH HEH...

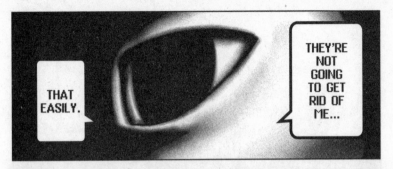

THEY'RE NOT GOING TO GET RID OF ME...

THAT EASILY.

ARE THEY TAKING ME FOR A FOOL?

SHWF

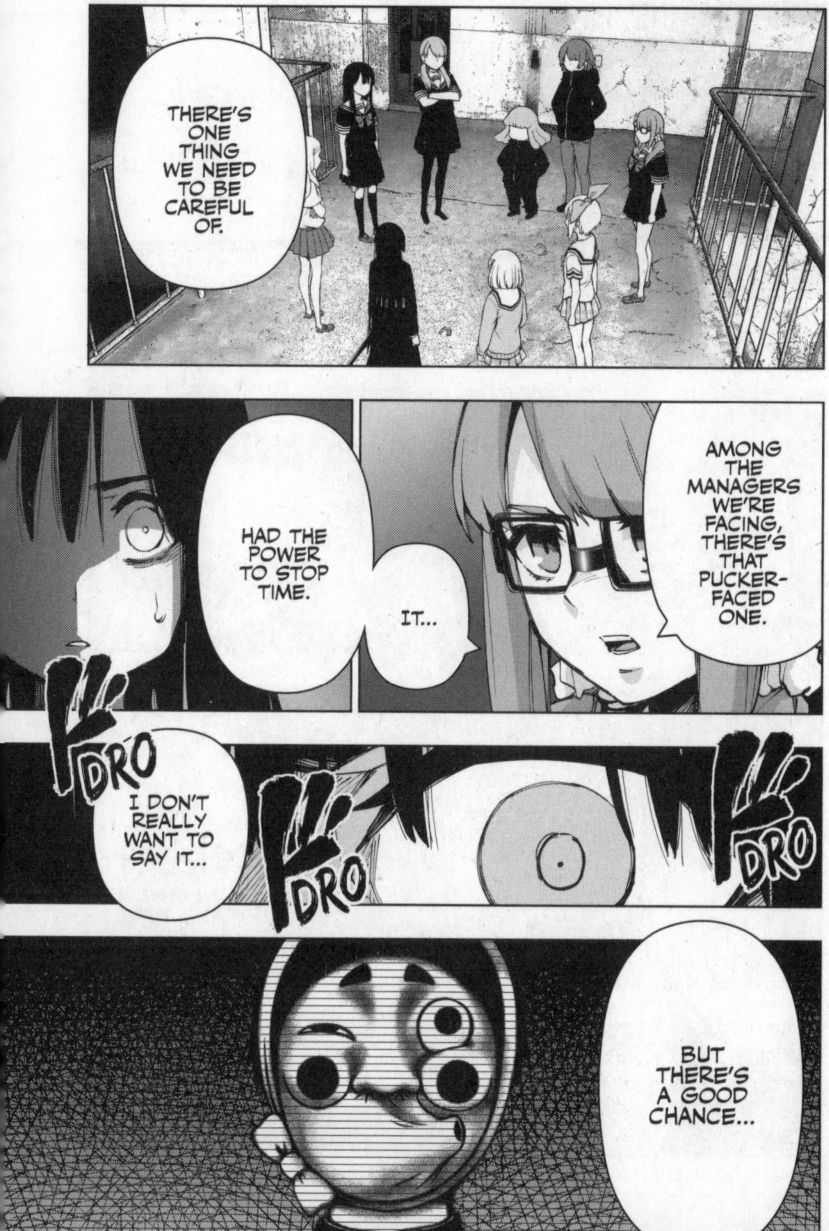
THERE'S ONE THING WE NEED TO BE CAREFUL OF.
AMONG THE MANAGERS WE'RE FACING, THERE'S THAT PUCKER-FACED ONE.
IT...
HAD THE POWER TO STOP TIME.
DRO
DRO
I DON'T REALLY WANT TO SAY IT...
DRO
BUT THERE'S A GOOD CHANCE...

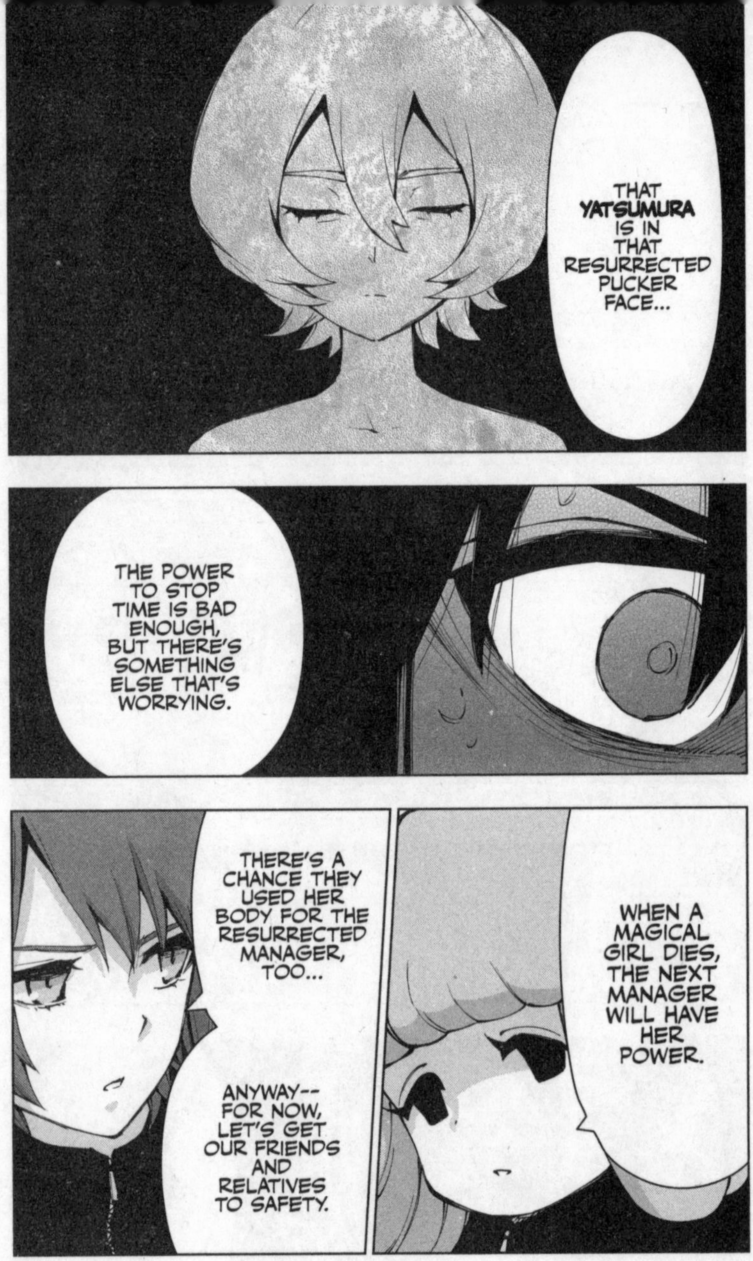
THAT YATSUMURA IS IN THAT RESURRECTED PUCKER FACE...
THE POWER TO STOP TIME IS BAD ENOUGH, BUT THERE'S SOMETHING ELSE THAT'S WORRYING.
WHEN A MAGICAL GIRL DIES, THE NEXT MANAGER WILL HAVE HER POWER.
THERE'S A CHANCE THEY USED HER BODY FOR THE RESURRECTED MANAGER, TOO...
ANYWAY-- FOR NOW, LET'S GET OUR FRIENDS AND RELATIVES TO SAFETY.

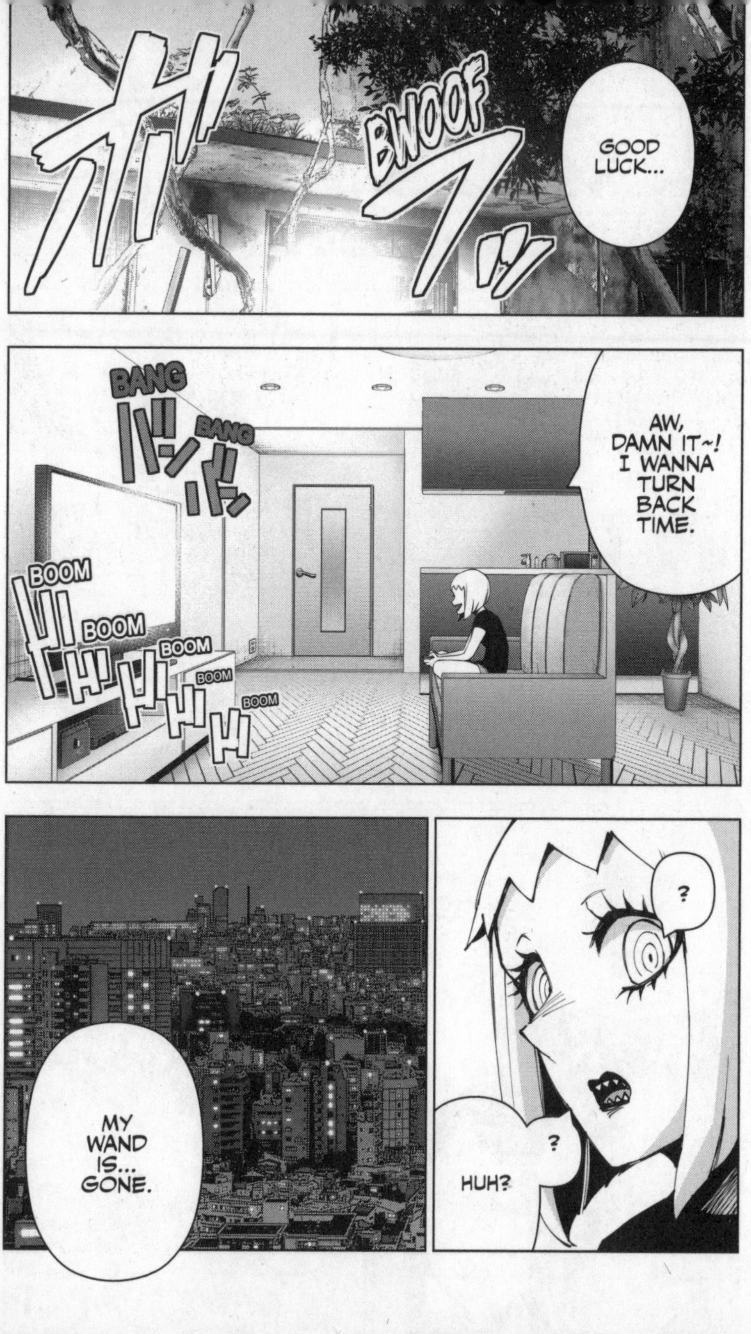
GOOD LUCK...
BWOOF
AW, DAMN IT~! I WANNA TURN BACK TIME.
BANG
BANG
BOOM
BOOM
BOOM
BOOM
BOOM
?
?
HUH?
MY WAND IS... GONE.

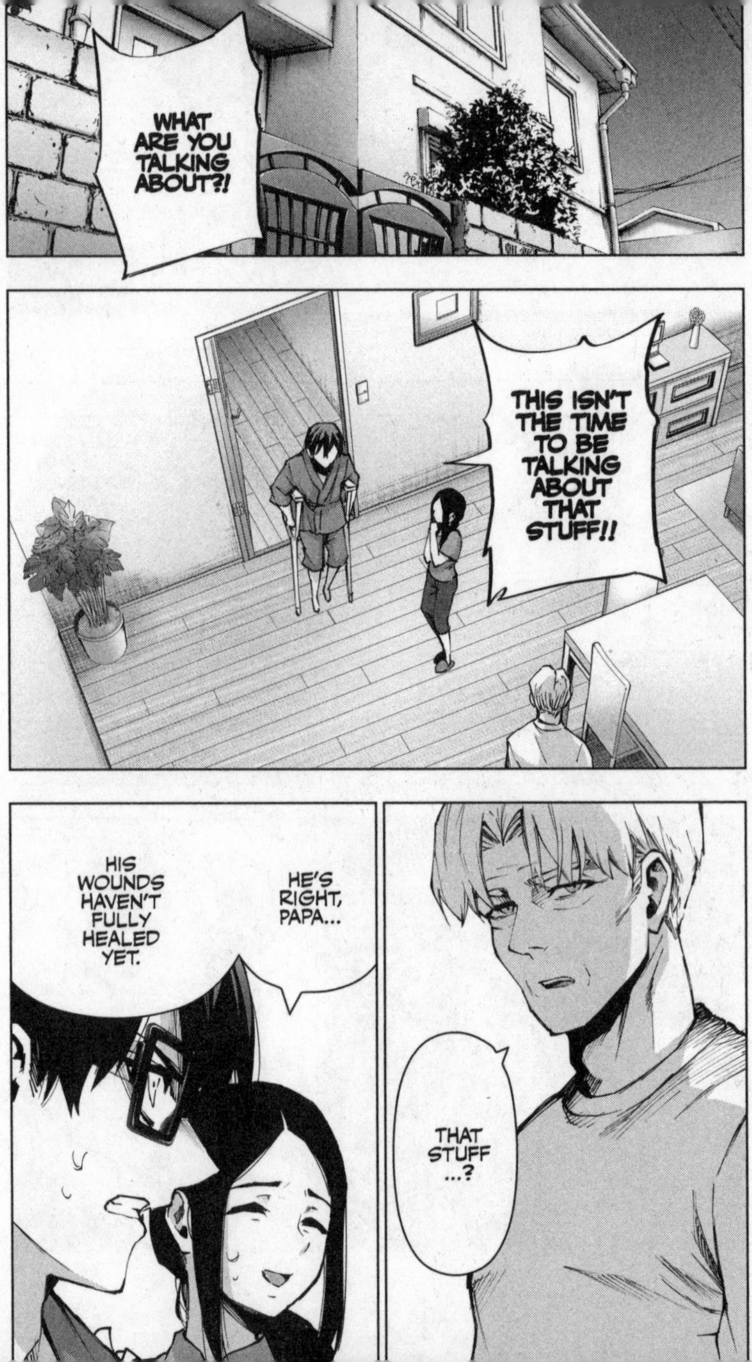
WHAT ARE YOU TALKING ABOUT?!
THIS ISN'T THE TIME TO BE TALKING ABOUT THAT STUFF!!
THAT STUFF ...?
HE'S RIGHT, PAPA...
HIS WOUNDS HAVEN'T FULLY HEALED YET.

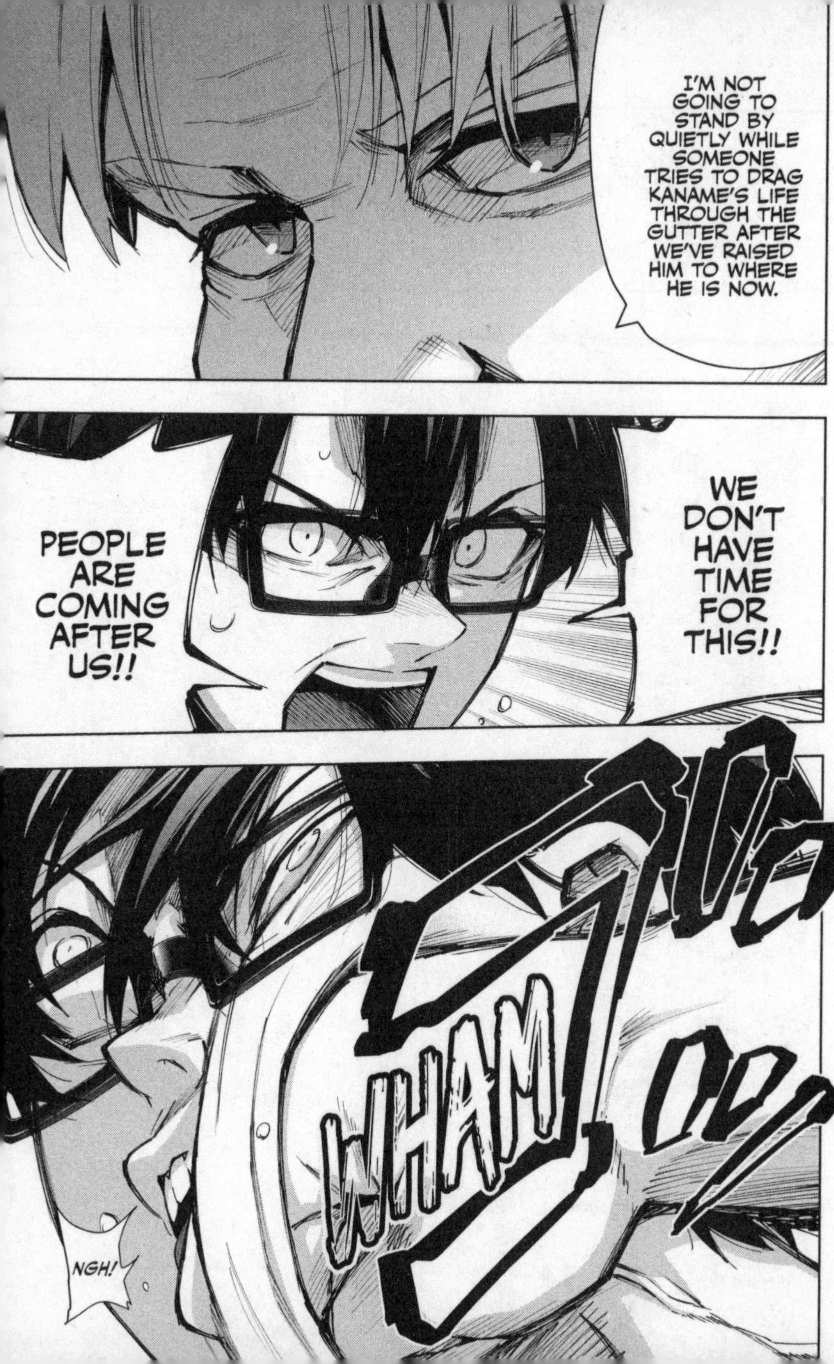
I'M NOT GOING TO STAND BY QUIETLY WHILE SOMEONE TRIES TO DRAG KANAME'S LIFE THROUGH THE GUTTER AFTER WE'VE RAISED HIM TO WHERE HE IS NOW.
WE DON'T HAVE TIME FOR THIS!!
PEOPLE ARE COMING AFTER US!!
WHAM
NGH!

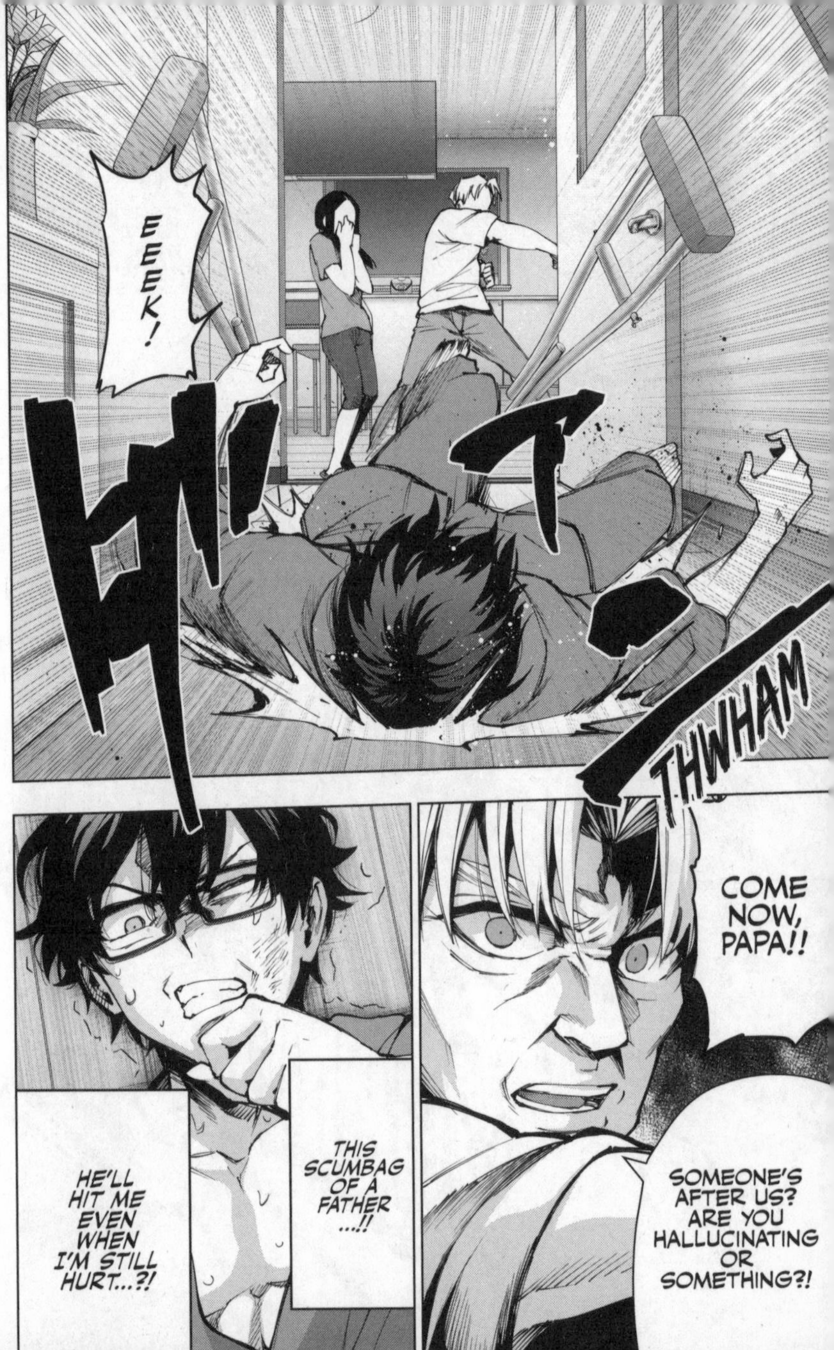
EEEK!
THWHAM
COME NOW, PAPA!!
SOMEONE'S AFTER US? ARE YOU HALLUCINATING OR SOMETHING?!
THIS SCUMBAG OF A FATHER ...!!
HE'LL HIT ME EVEN WHEN I'M STILL HURT...?!

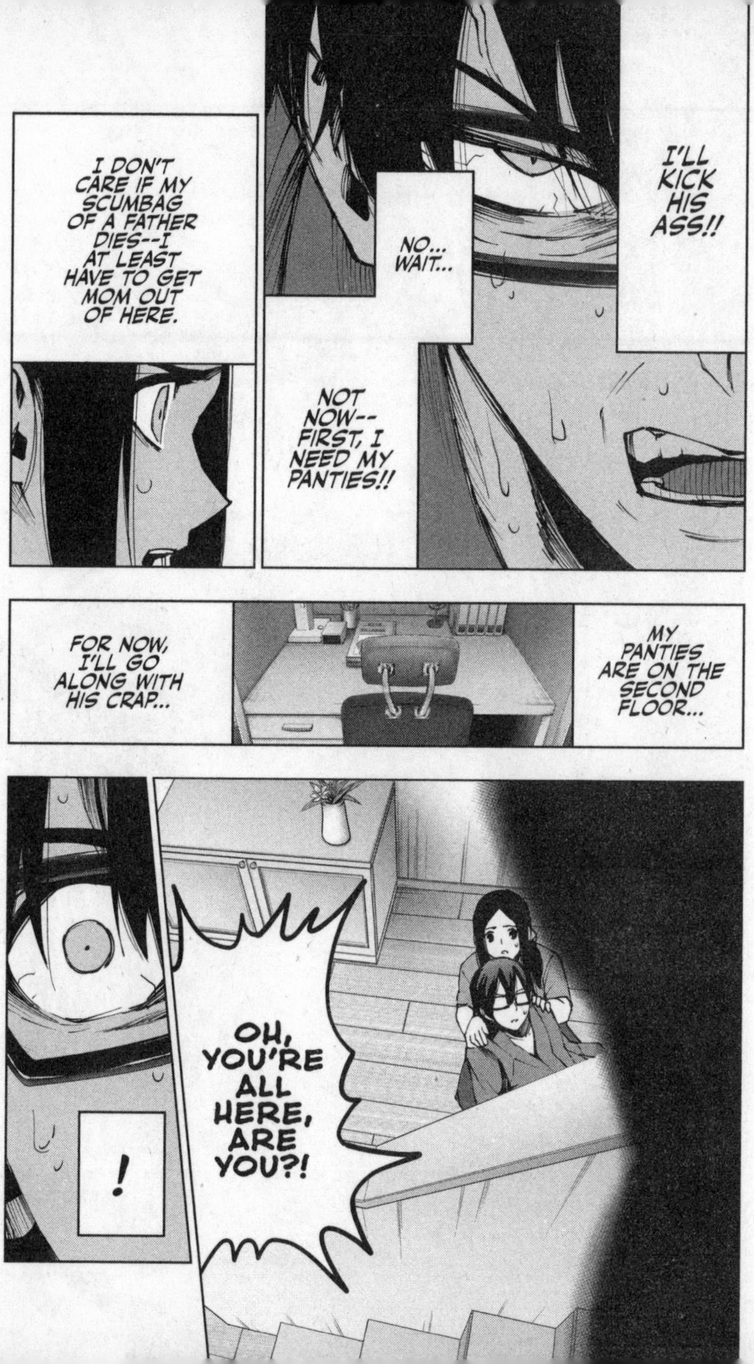
I'LL KICK HIS ASS!!
NO... WAIT...
NOT NOW--FIRST, I NEED MY PANTIES!!
I DON'T CARE IF MY SCUMBAG OF A FATHER DIES--I AT LEAST HAVE TO GET MOM OUT OF HERE.
MY PANTIES ARE ON THE SECOND FLOOR...
FOR NOW, I'LL GO ALONG WITH HIS CRAP...
OH, YOU'RE ALL HERE, ARE YOU?!
!

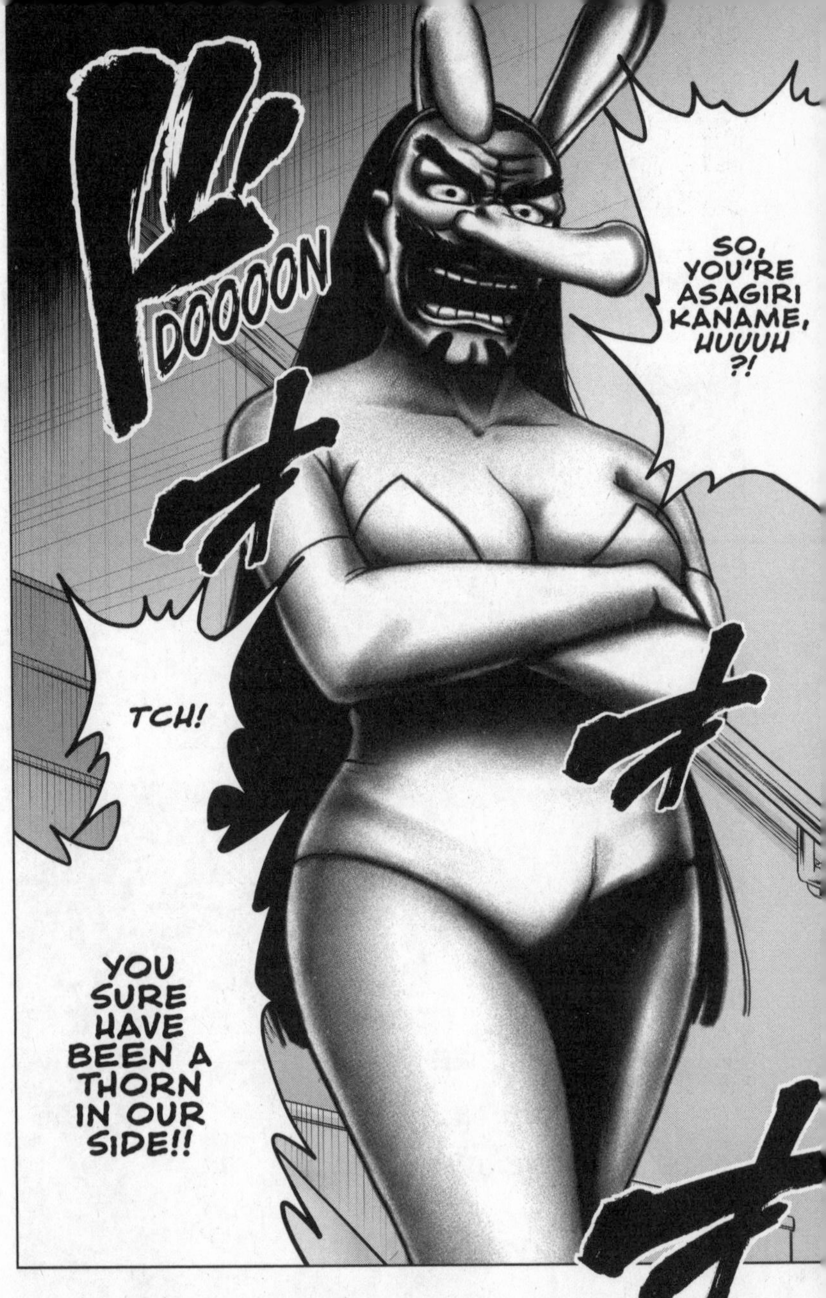
DOOOON
SO, YOU'RE ASAGIRI KANAME, HUUUH ?!
TCH!
YOU SURE HAVE BEEN A THORN IN OUR SIDE!!

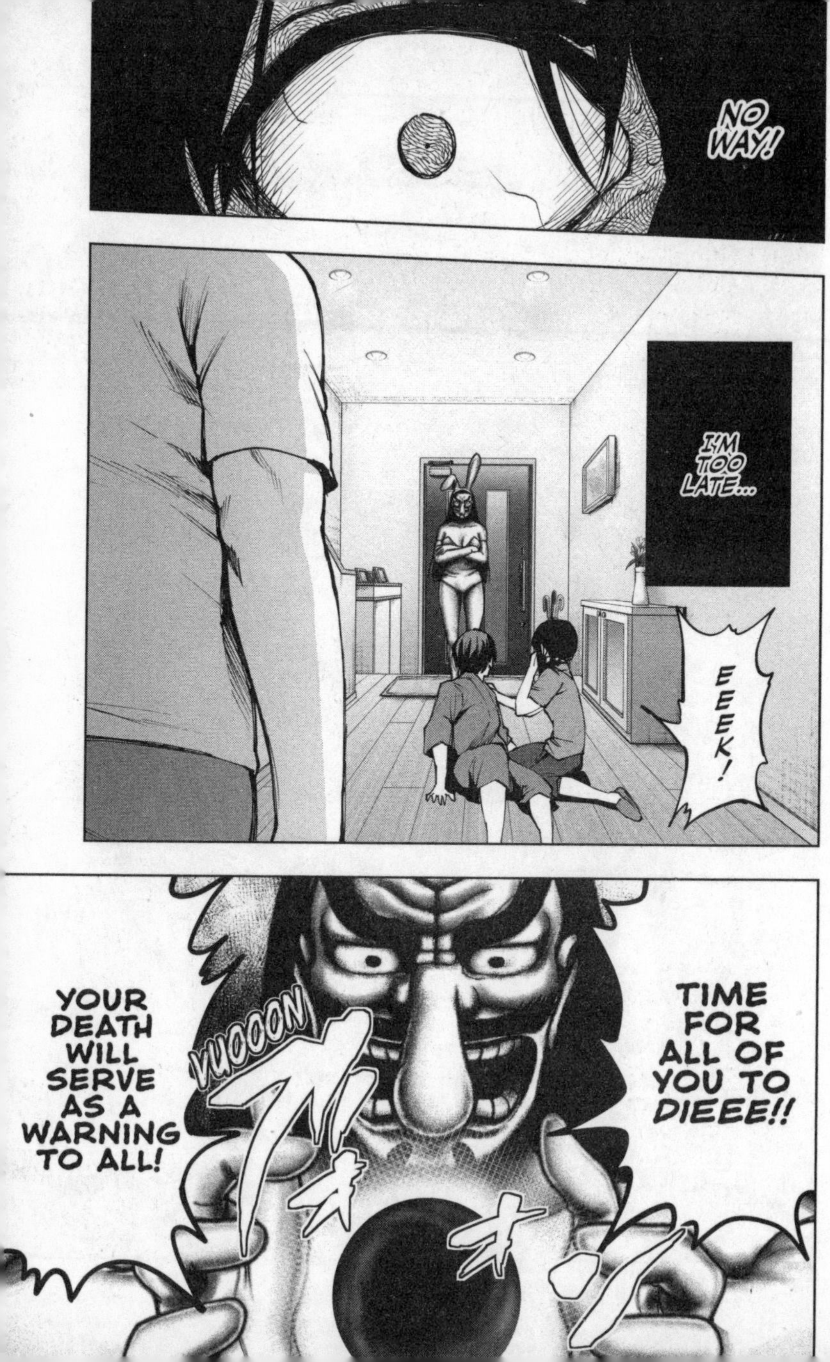
NO WAY!
I'M TOO LATE...
EEEEK!
TIME FOR ALL OF YOU TO DIEEE!!
VUOOON
YOUR DEATH WILL SERVE AS A WARNING TO ALL!

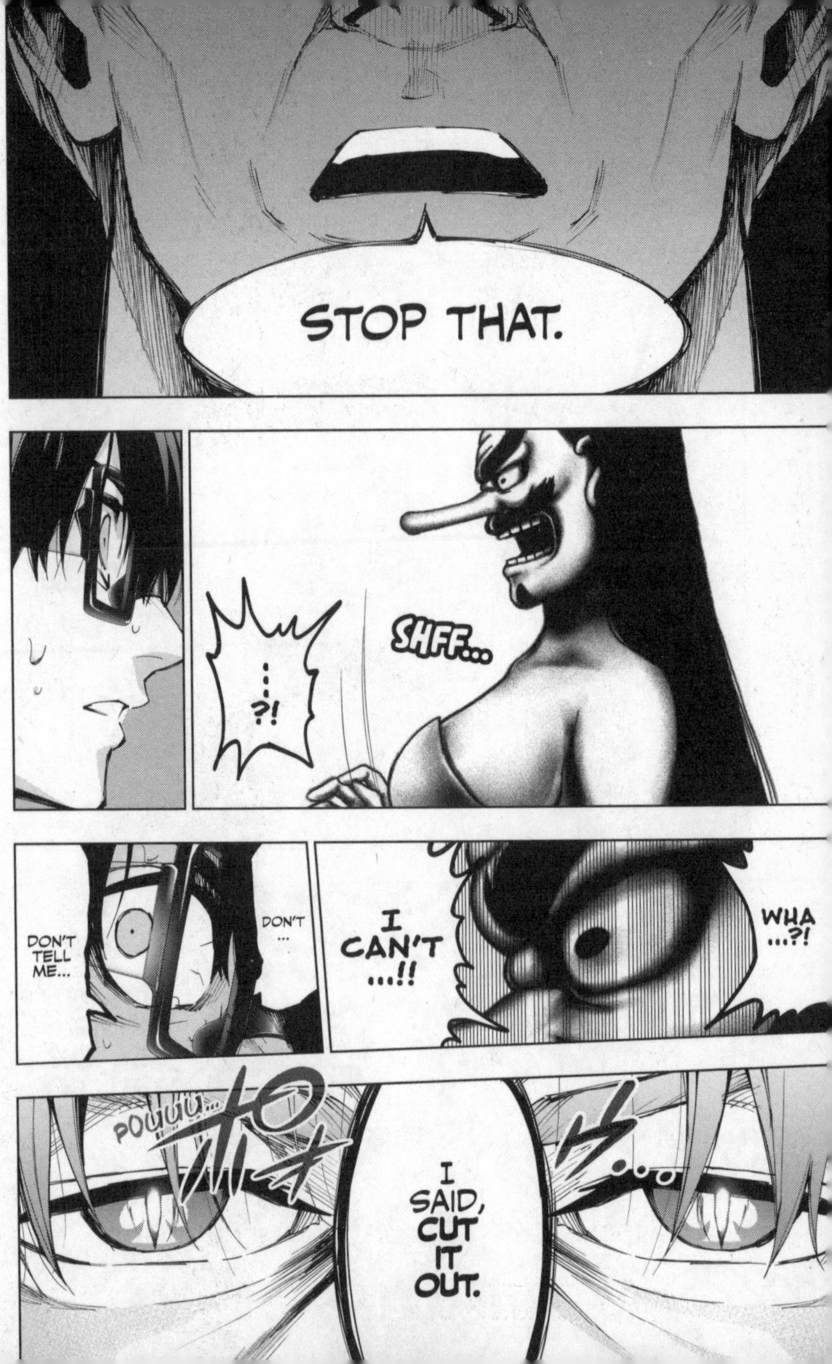
STOP THAT.
SHFF...
...?!
WHA ...?!
I CAN'T ...!!
DON'T ...
DON'T TELL ME...
POUUU...
I SAID, CUT IT OUT.

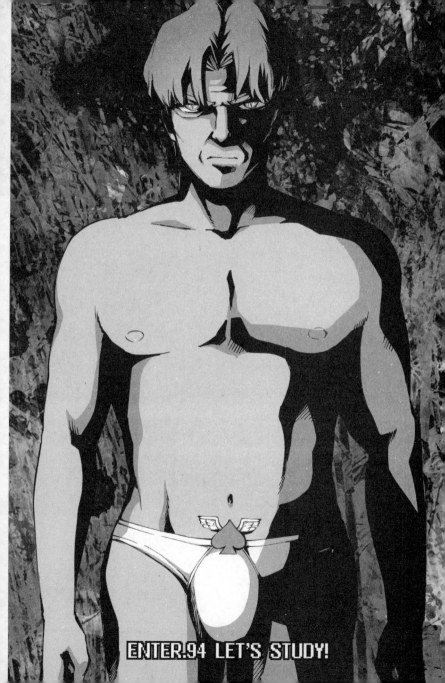

ENTER.94 LET'S STUDY!

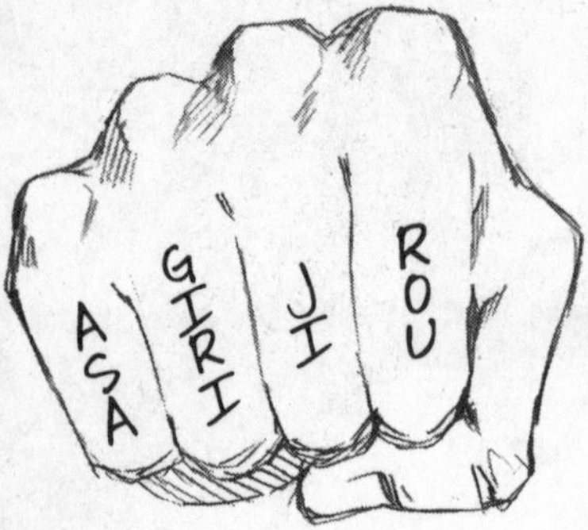
ASA
GIRI
JI
ROU

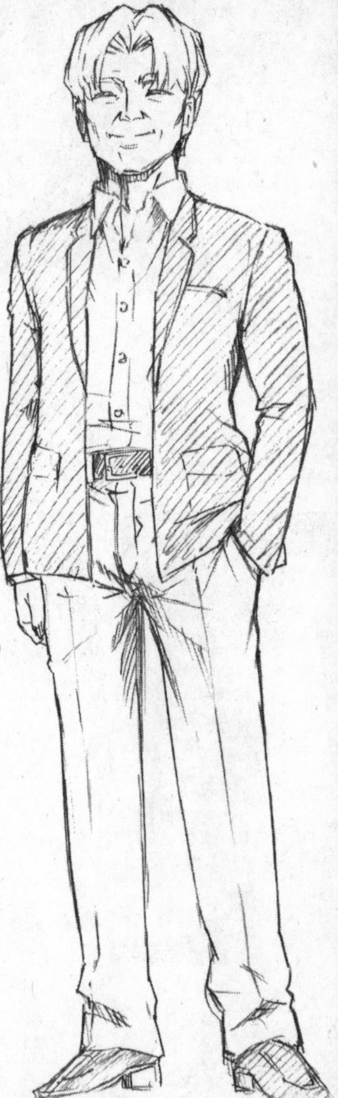

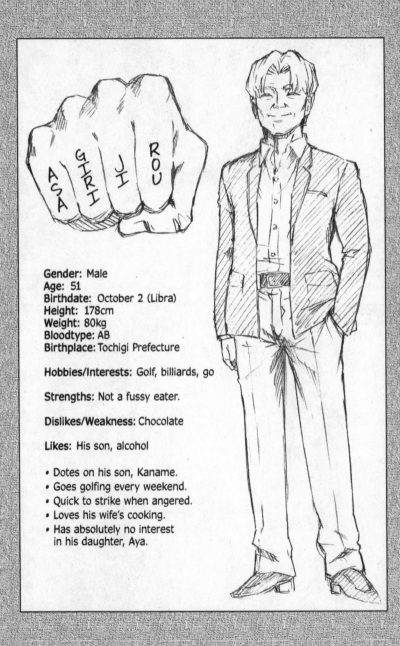

Gender: Male
Age: 51
Birthdate: October 2 (Libra)
Height: 178cm
Weight: 80kg
Bloodtype: AB
Birthplace: Tochigi Prefecture

Hobbies/Interests: Golf, billiards, go

Strengths: Not a fussy eater.

Dislikes/Weakness: Chocolate

Likes: His son, alcohol

- Dotes on his son, Kaname.
- Goes golfing every weekend.
- Quick to strike when angered.
- Loves his wife's cooking.
- Has absolutely no interest in his daughter, Aya.

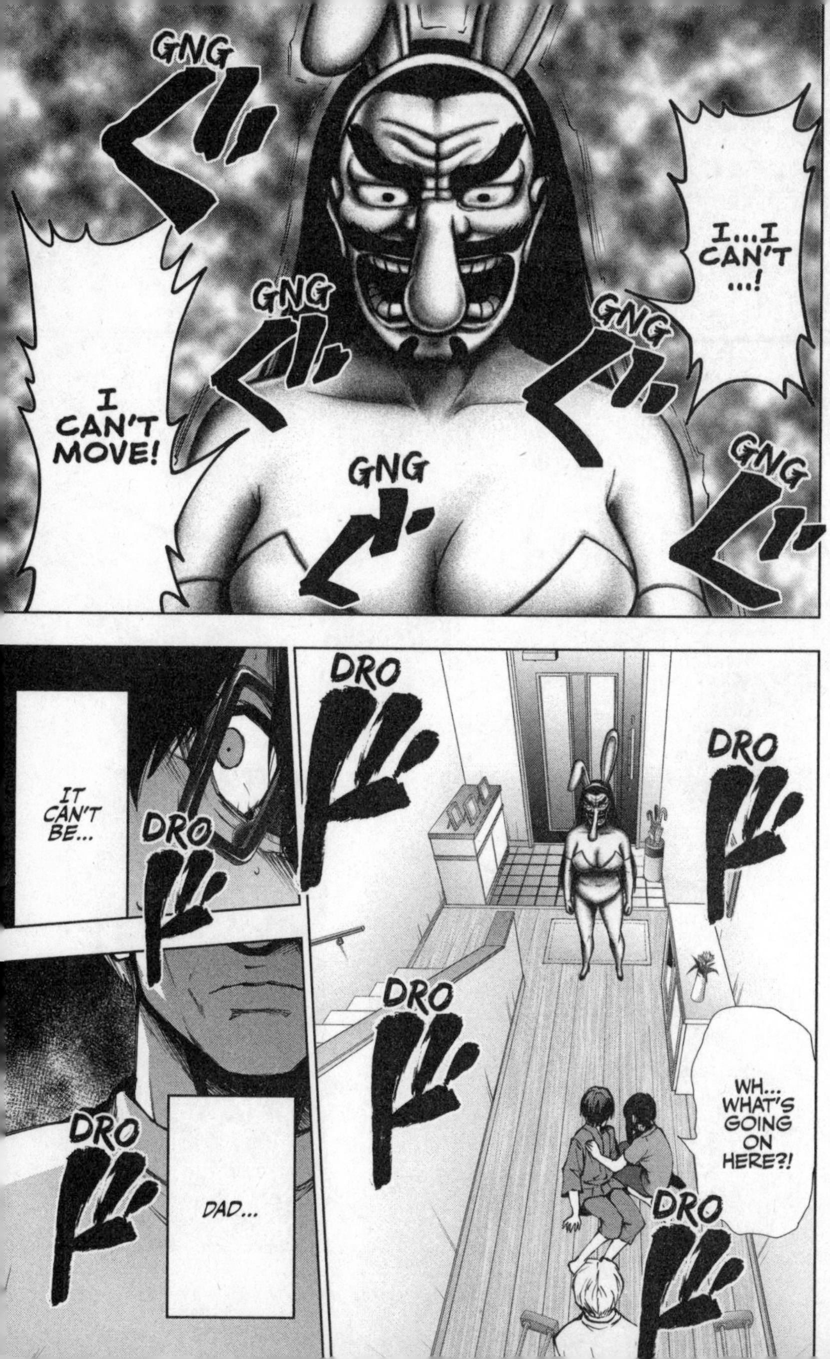
GNG
GNG
GNG
GNG
GNG
I...I CAN'T ...!
I CAN'T MOVE!
DRO
DRO
DRO
DRO
WH... WHAT'S GOING ON HERE?!
DRO
IT CAN'T BE...
DRO
DAD...

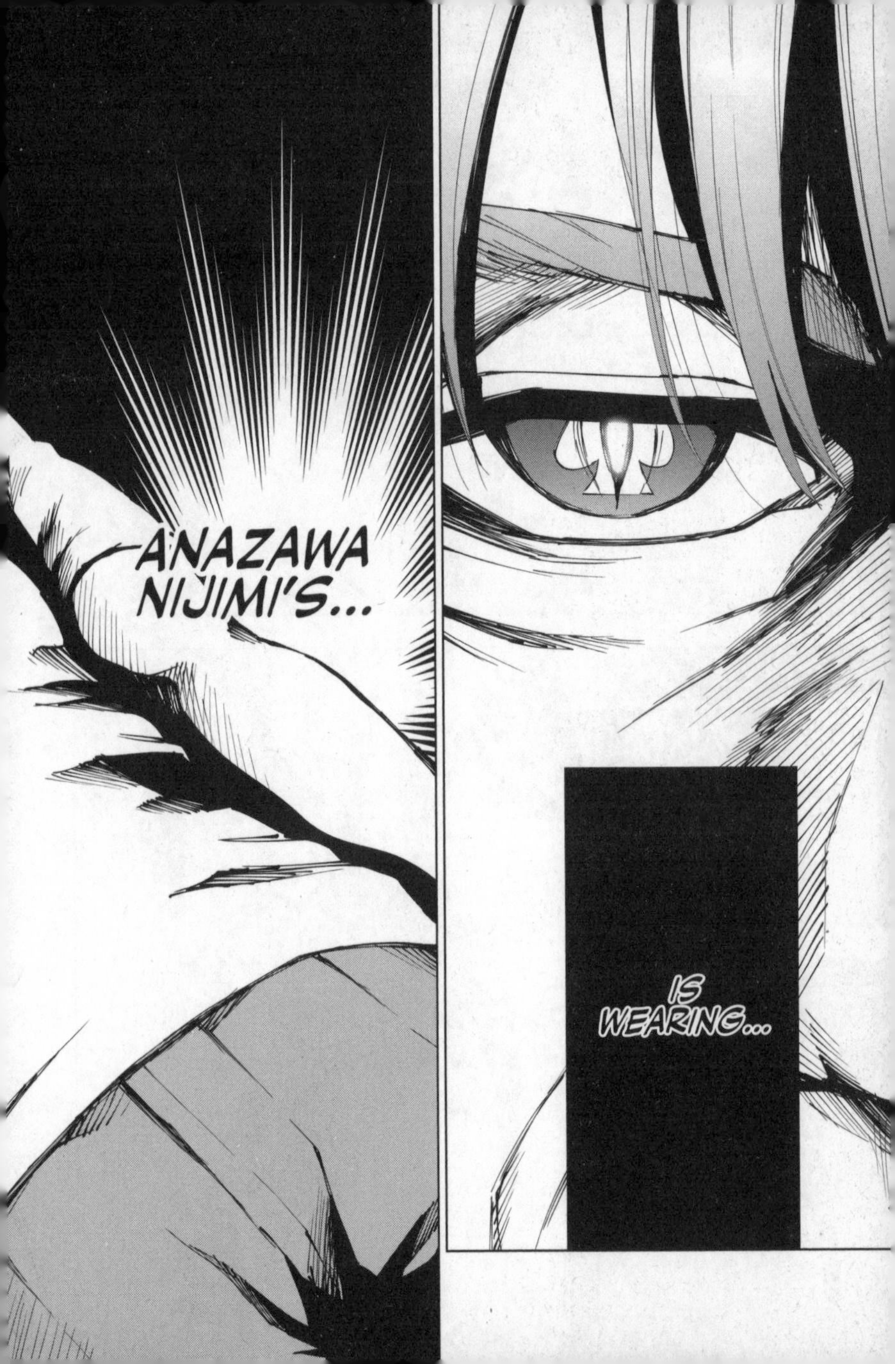
ANAZAWA NIJIMI'S...
IS WEARING...

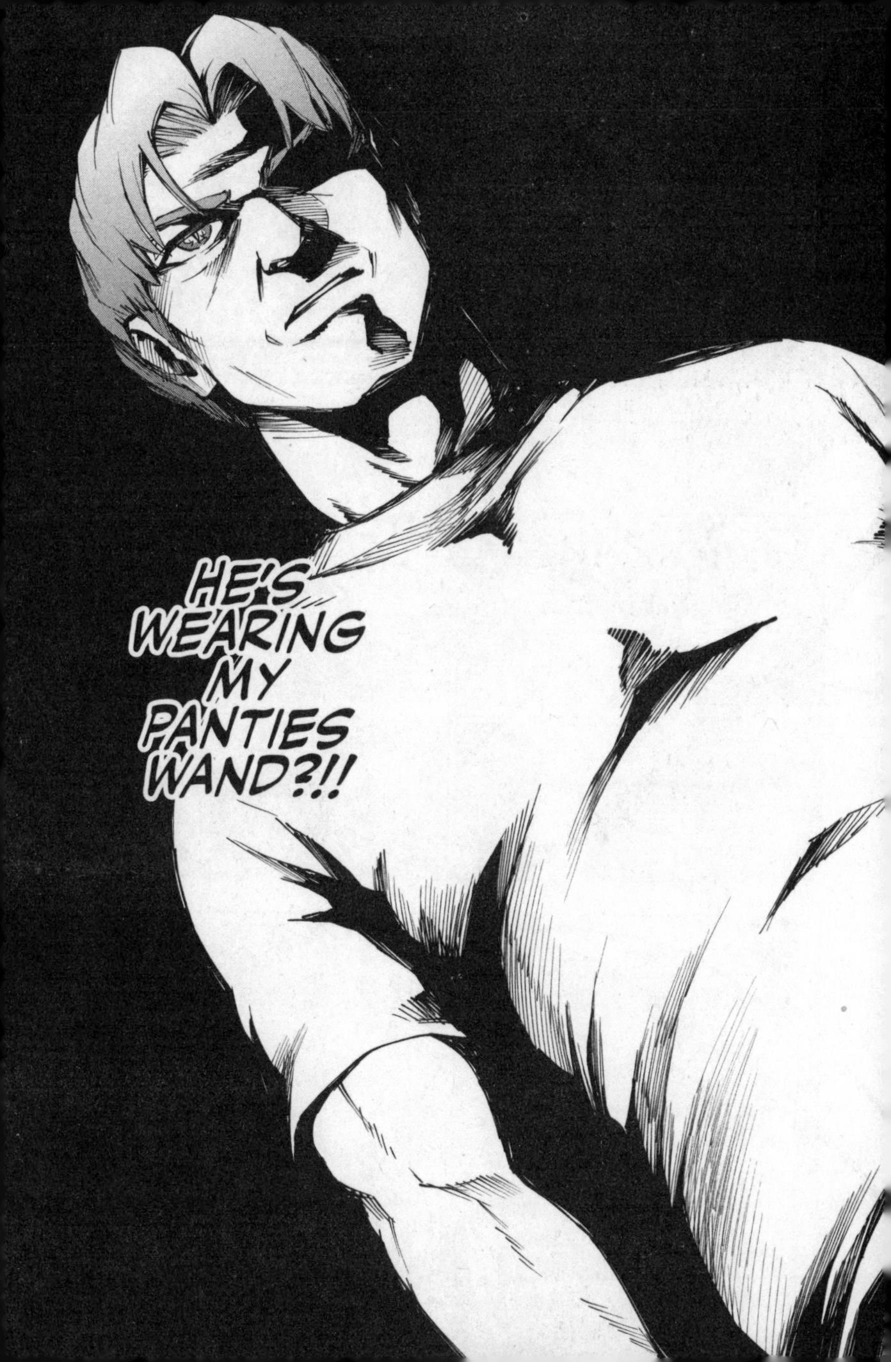
HE'S WEARING MY PANTIES WAND?!!

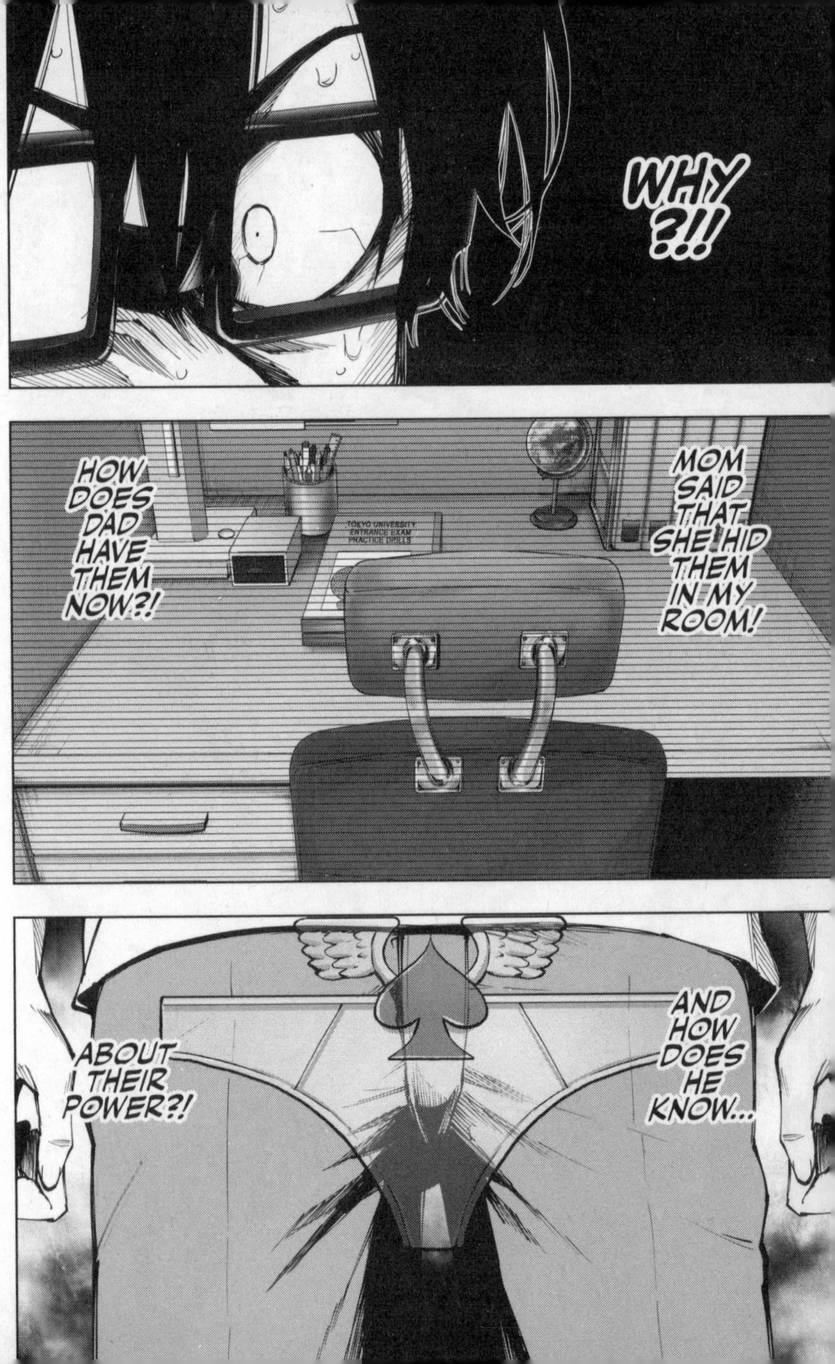
WHY ?!!
MOM SAID THAT SHE HID THEM IN MY ROOM!
HOW DOES DAD HAVE THEM NOW?!
TOKYO UNIVERSITY ENTRANCE EXAM PRACTICE DRILLS
AND HOW DOES HE KNOW...
ABOUT THEIR POWER?!

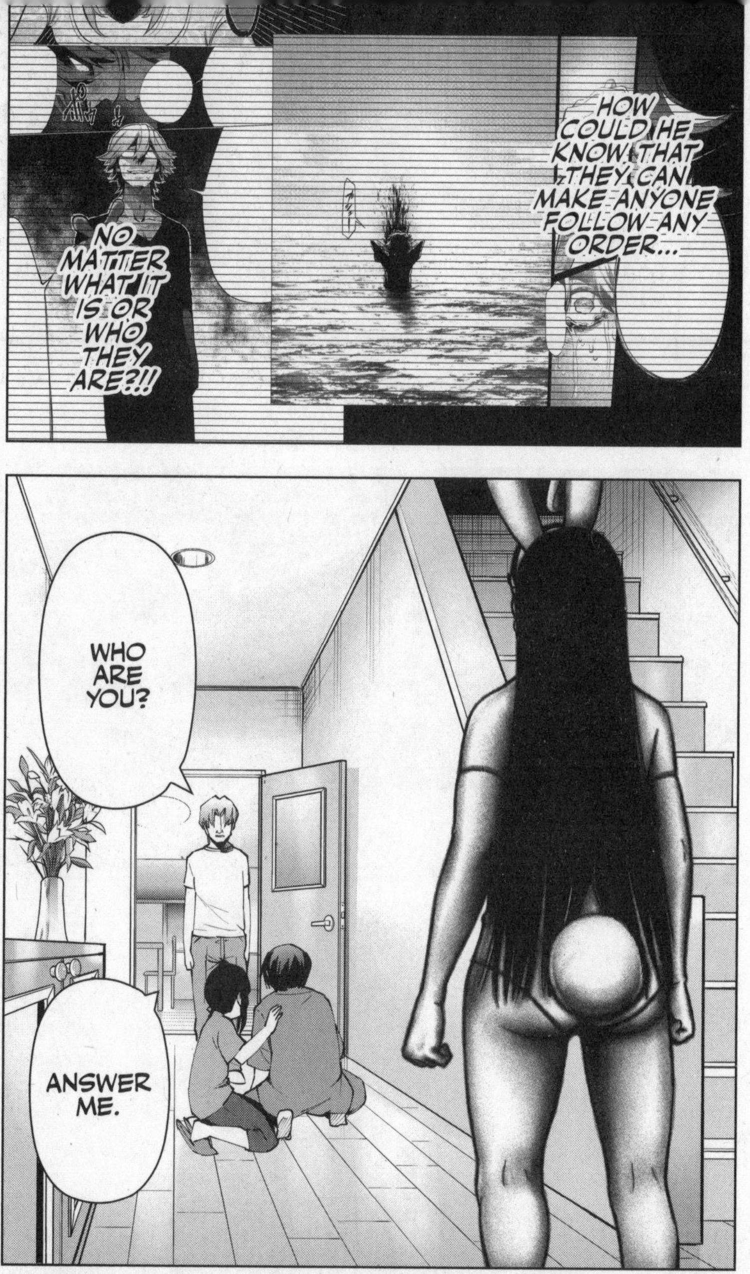
HOW COULD HE KNOW THAT THEY CAN MAKE ANYONE FOLLOW ANY ORDER...
NO MATTER WHAT IT IS OR WHO THEY ARE?!!
WHO ARE YOU?
ANSWER ME.

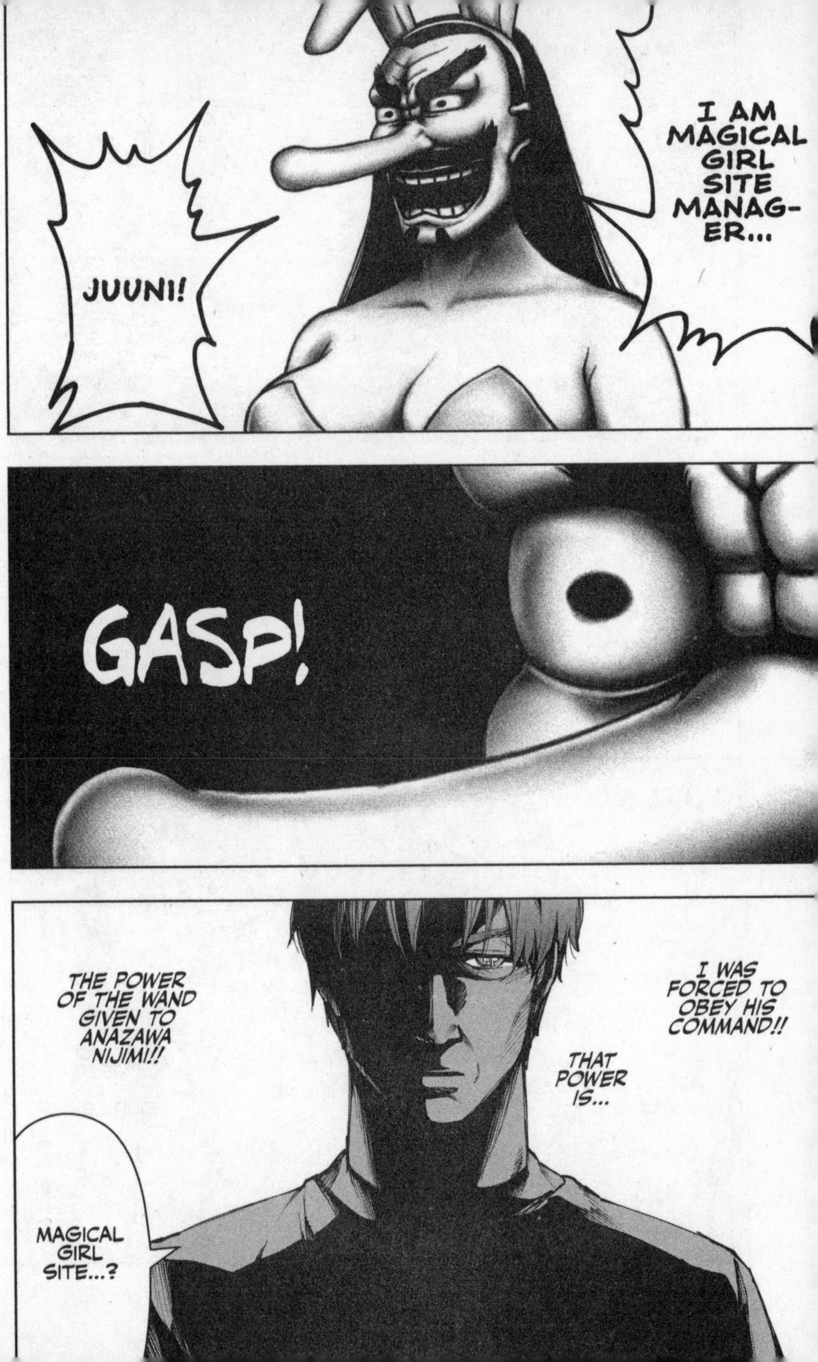
I AM MAGICAL GIRL SITE MANAGER...
JUUNI!
GASP!
I WAS FORCED TO OBEY HIS COMMAND!!
THAT POWER IS...
THE POWER OF THE WAND GIVEN TO ANAZAWA NIJIMI!!
MAGICAL GIRL SITE...?

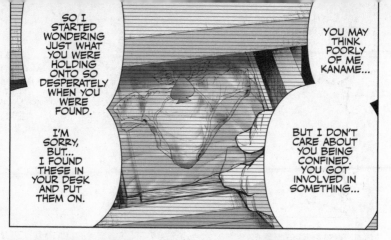

YOU MAY THINK POORLY OF ME, KANAME...
BUT I DON'T CARE ABOUT YOU BEING CONFINED. YOU GOT INVOLVED IN SOMETHING...
SO I STARTED WONDERING JUST WHAT YOU WERE HOLDING ONTO SO DESPERATELY WHEN YOU WERE FOUND.
I'M SORRY, BUT... I FOUND THESE IN YOUR DESK AND PUT THEM ON.
I... NEVER REALIZED...
I KNEW YOU MUST HAVE HAD A REASON... BUT FOR SOMETHING LIKE THESE TO EVEN EXIST...
ANYWAY, THESE WILL NO LONGER BE A PROBLEM.
THEY WILL NO LONGER DISTRACT YOU FROM YOUR STUDIES.

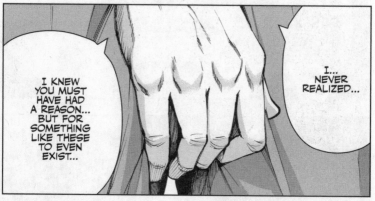

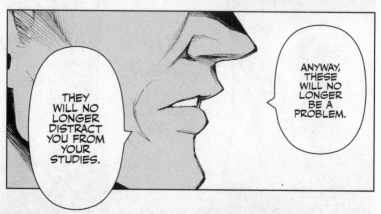

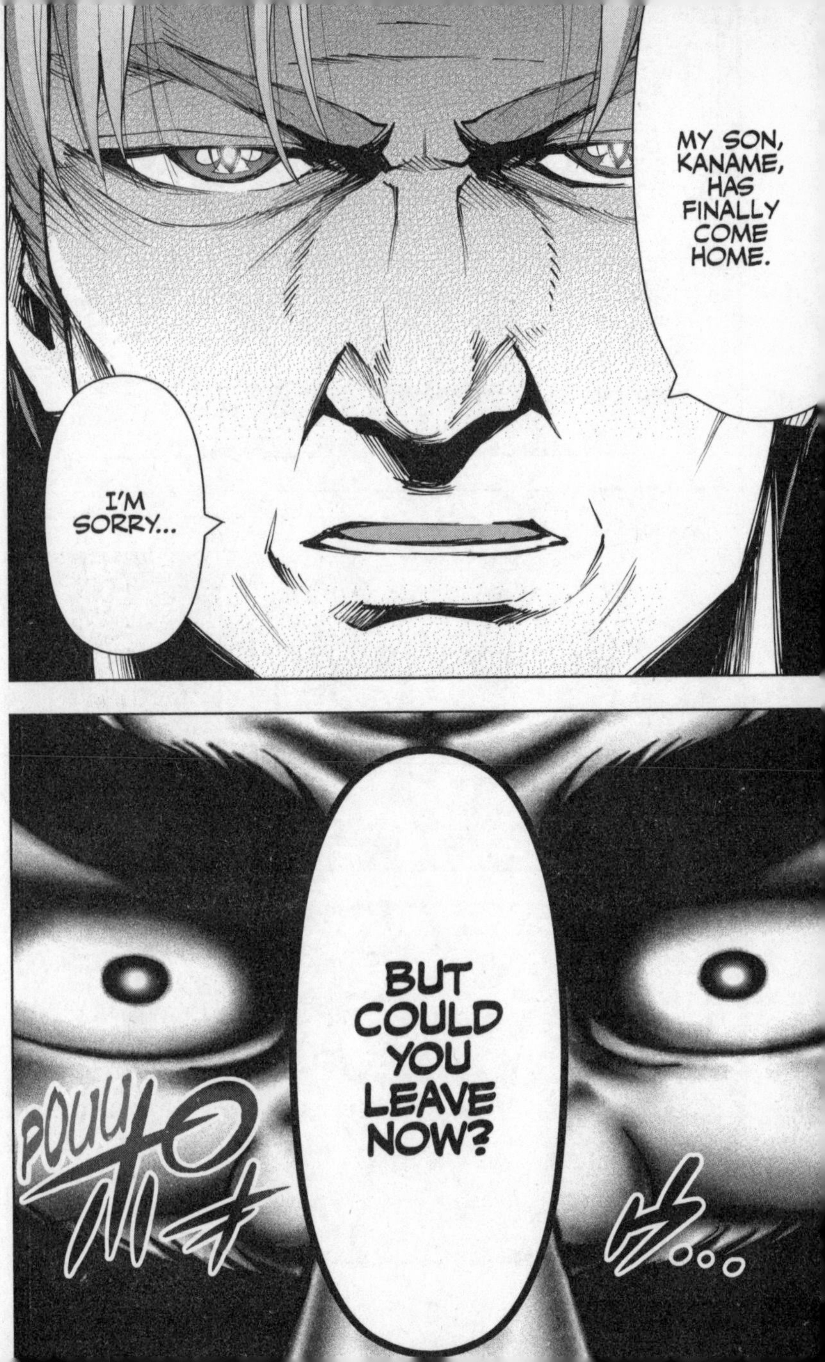
MY SON, KANAME, HAS FINALLY COME HOME.
I'M SORRY...
BUT COULD YOU LEAVE NOW?

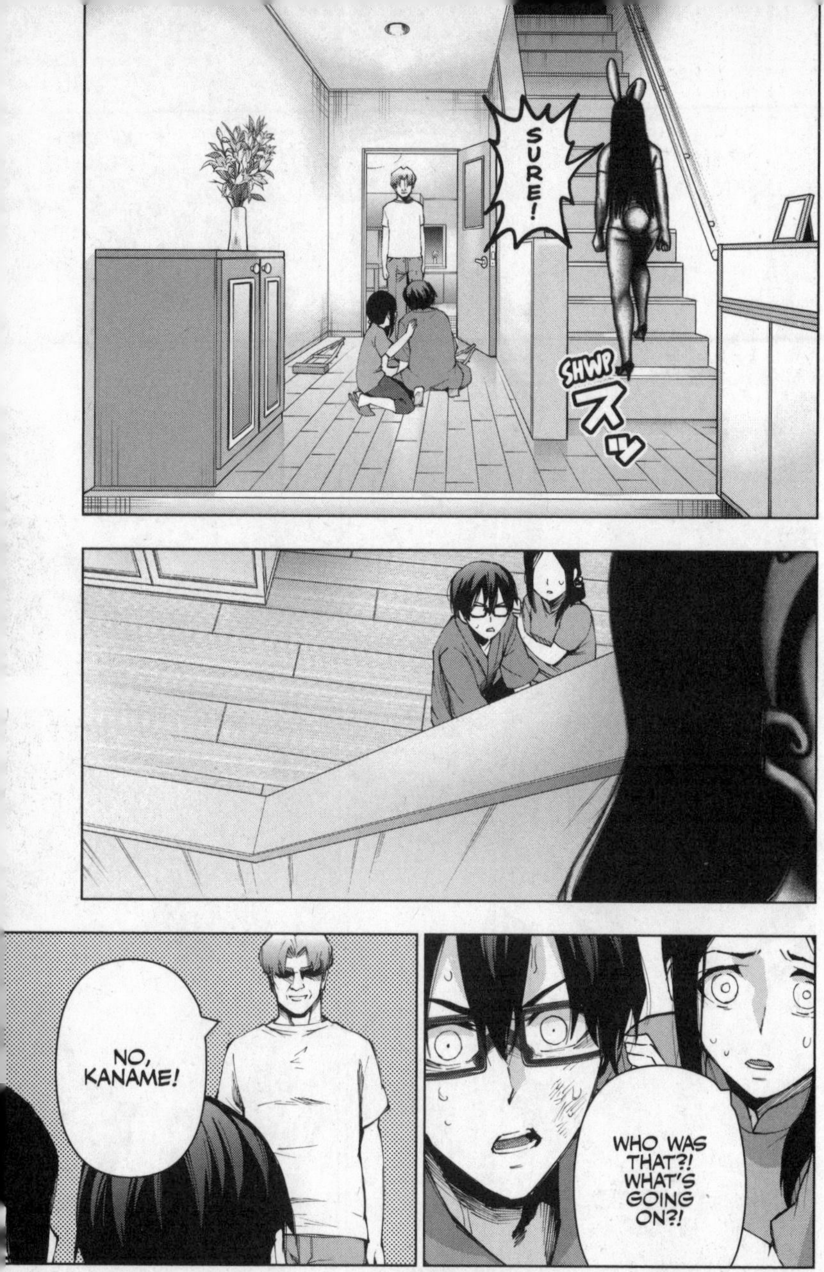
SURE!
SHWP
スッ
WHO WAS THAT?! WHAT'S GOING ON?!
NO, KANAME!

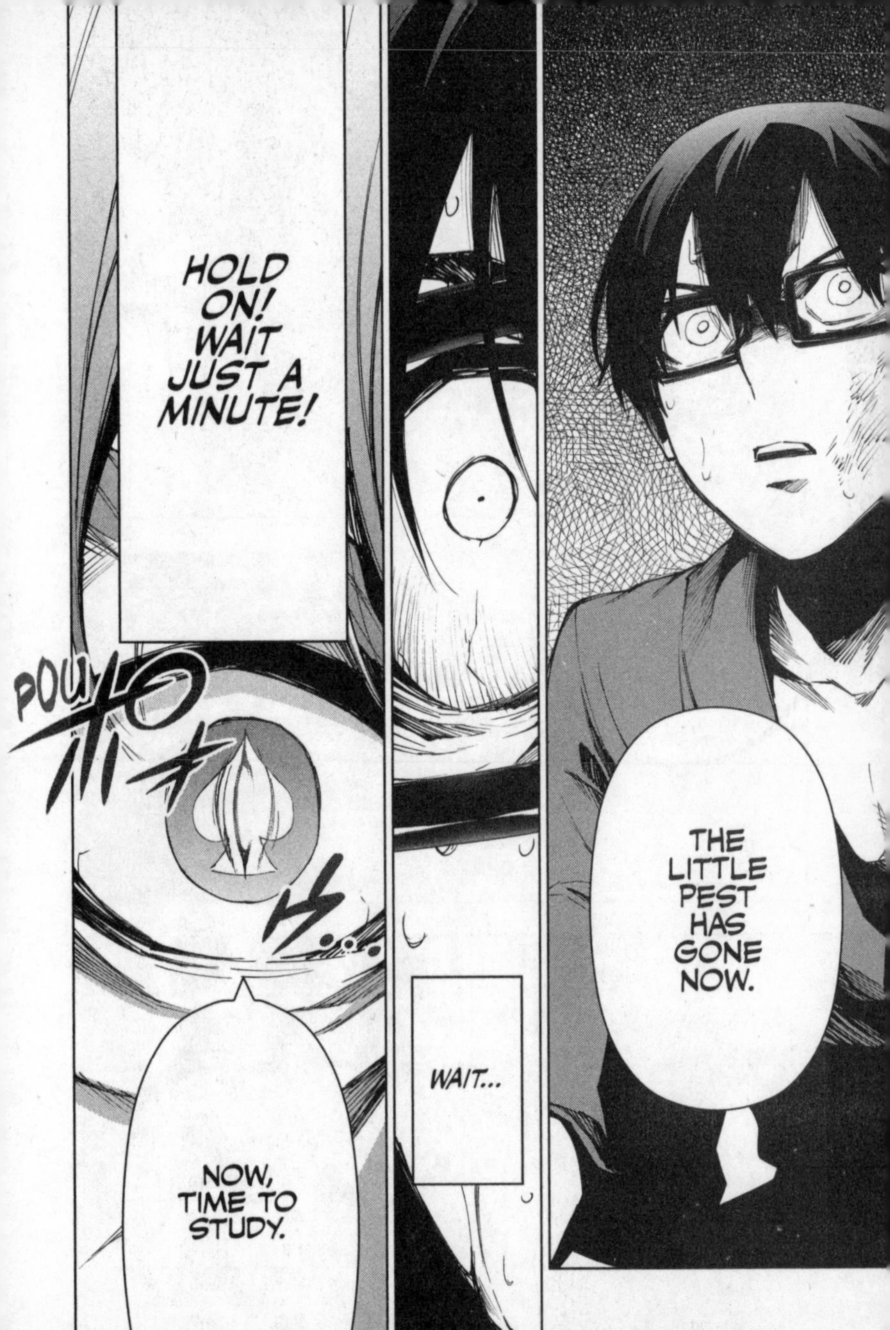
THE LITTLE PEST HAS GONE NOW.
WAIT...
HOLD ON! WAIT JUST A MINUTE!
POW
NOW, TIME TO STUDY.

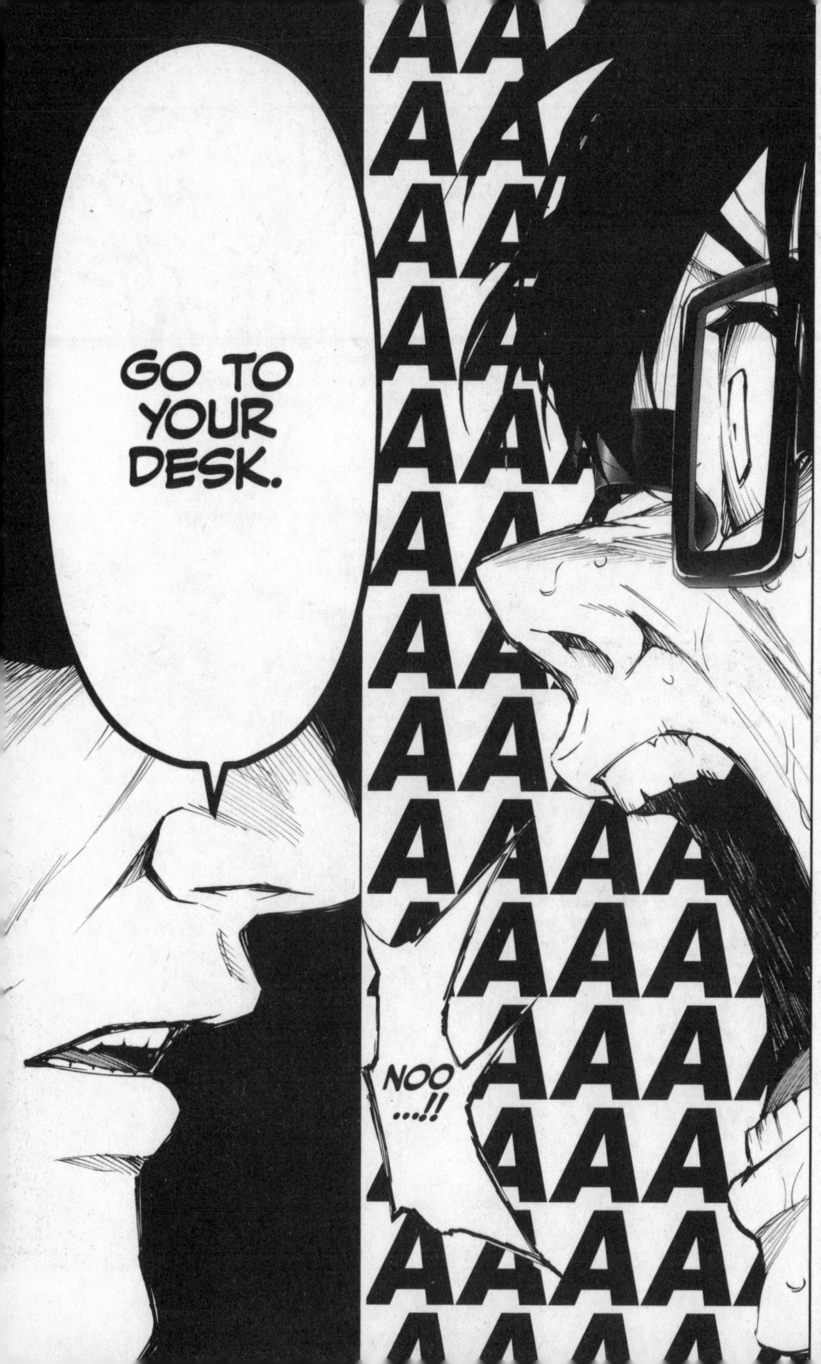
GO TO YOUR DESK.
NOO ...!!

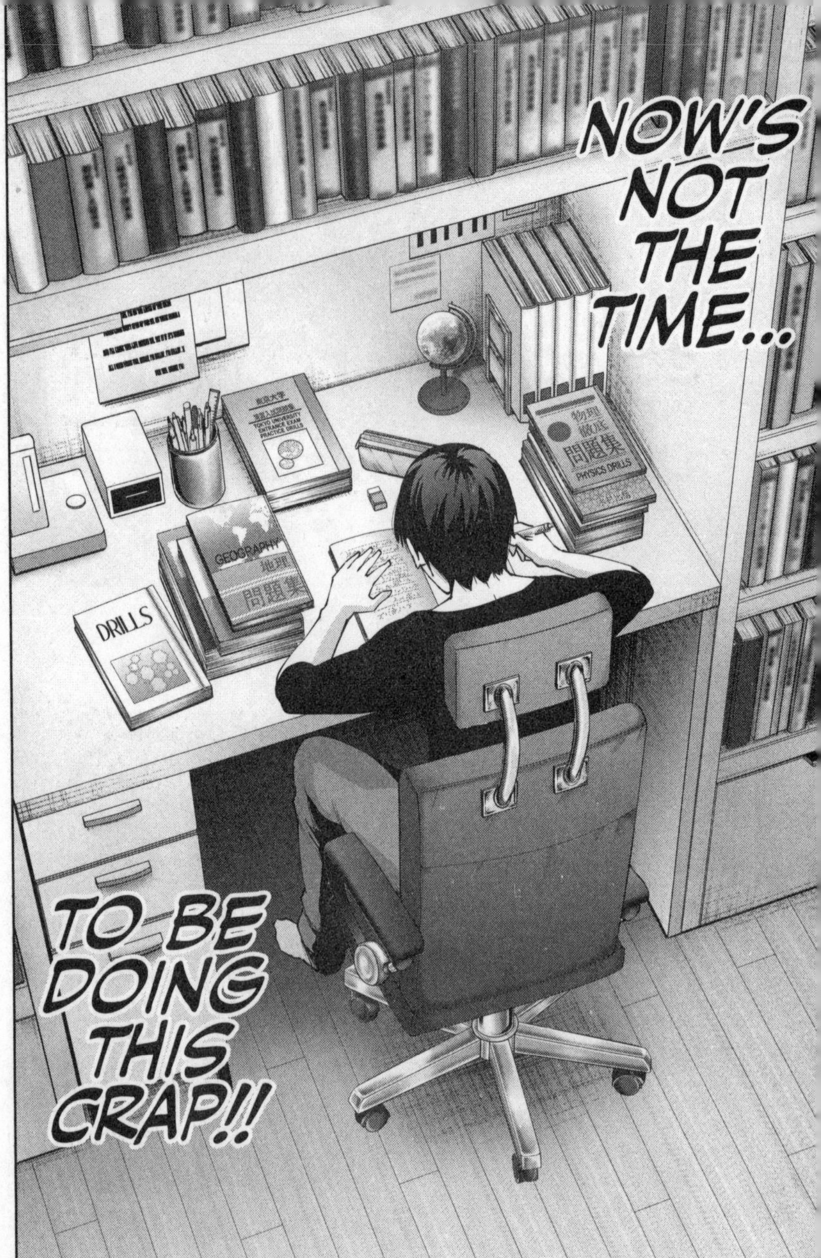
NOW'S NOT THE TIME...
TOKYO UNIVERSITY ENTRANCE EXAM PRACTICE DRILLS
物理 徹底 問題集
PHYSICS DRILLS
GEOGRAPHY
地理
問題集
DRILLS
TO BE DOING THIS CRAP!!

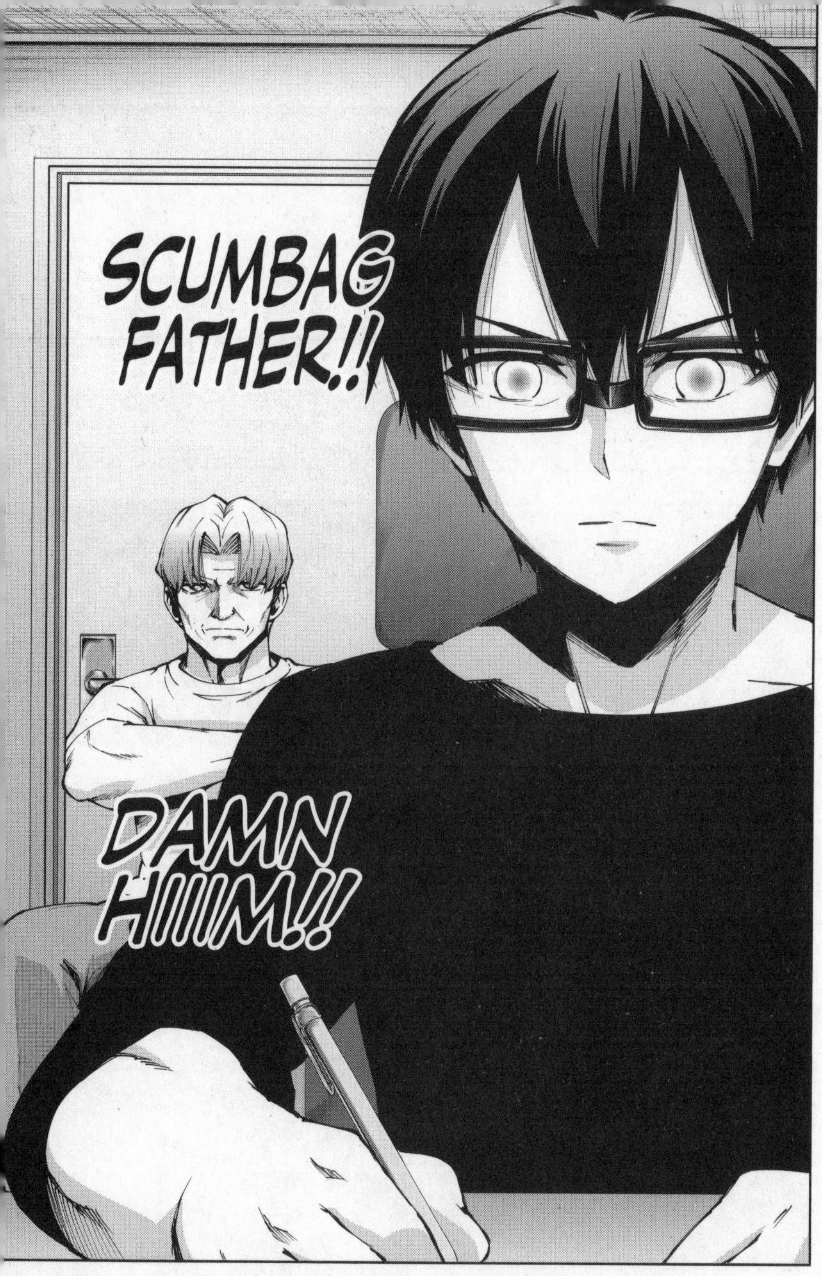
SCUMBAG FATHER!!
DAMN HIIIM!!

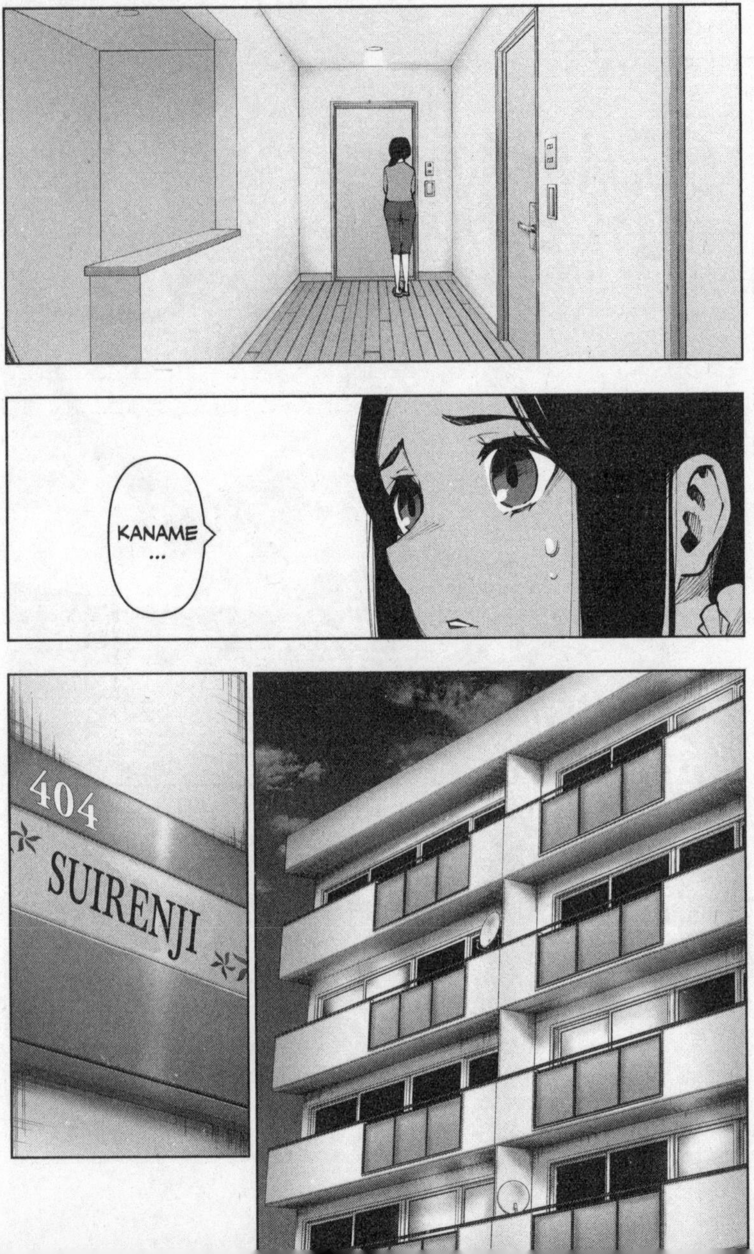
KANAME
...
404
SUIRENJI

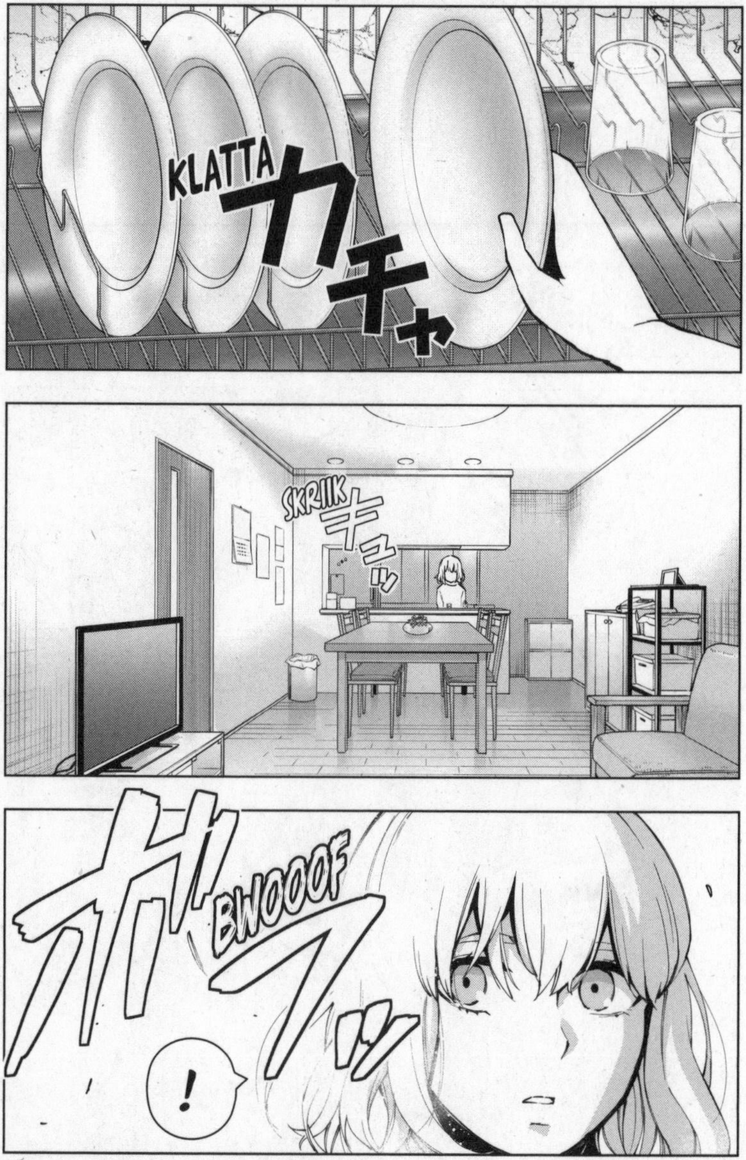
KLATTA
カチャ
SKRIIK
キュッ
ガバッ
BWOOOF
!

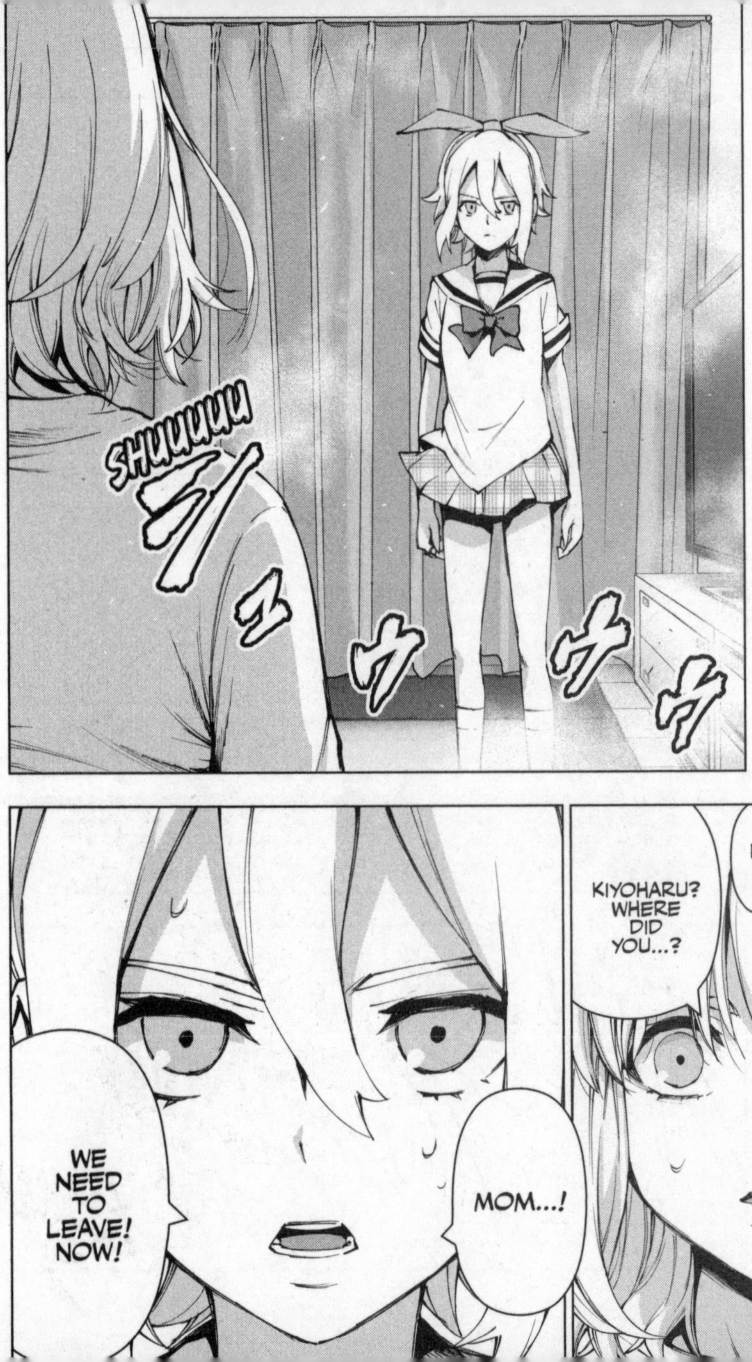
SHUUUUU
HUH ...?
KIYOHARU? WHERE DID YOU...?
MOM...!
WE NEED TO LEAVE! NOW!

zuず
zuず
zuず
zuず

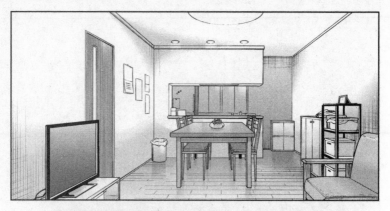

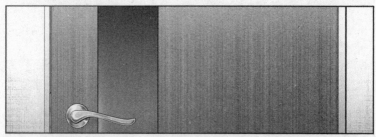

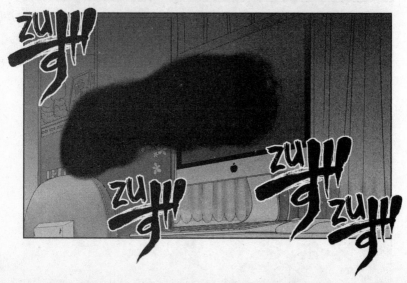

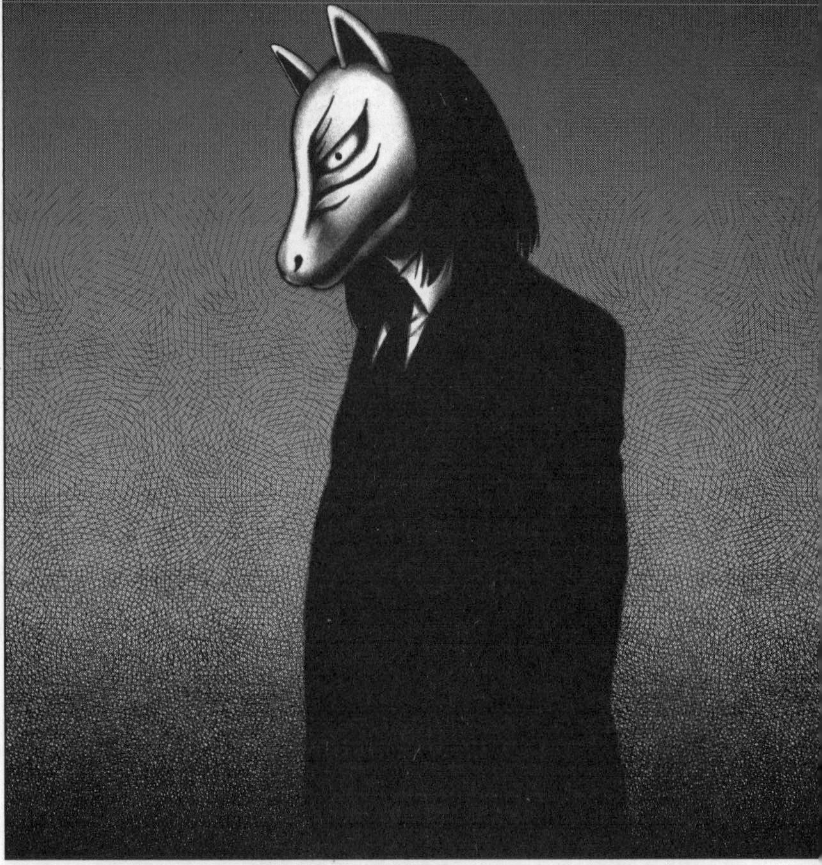

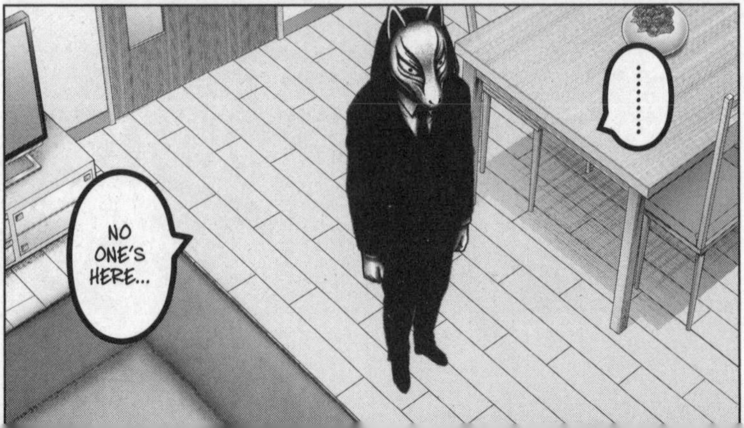
……
NO ONE'S HERE...

ENTER.95 PROFLIGATE VS. HERETIC

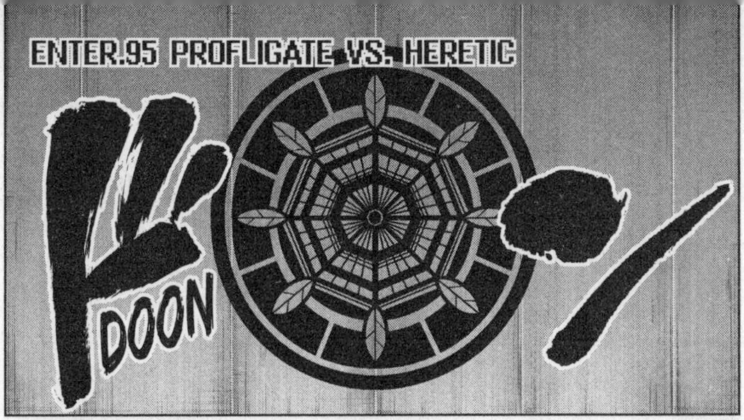
DOON

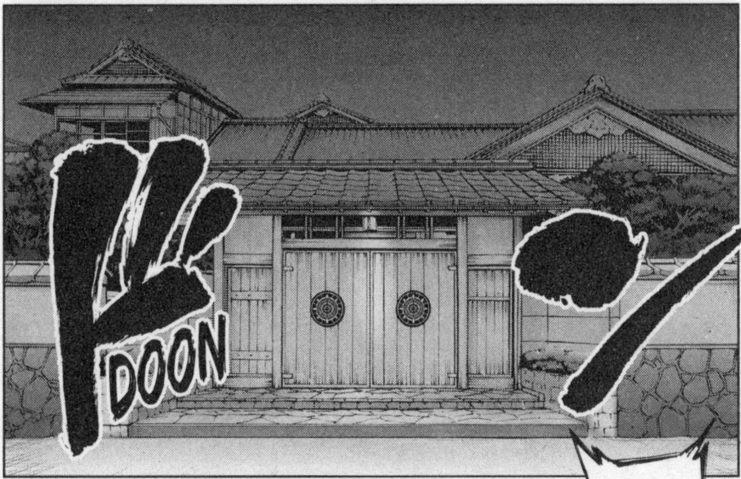
DOON

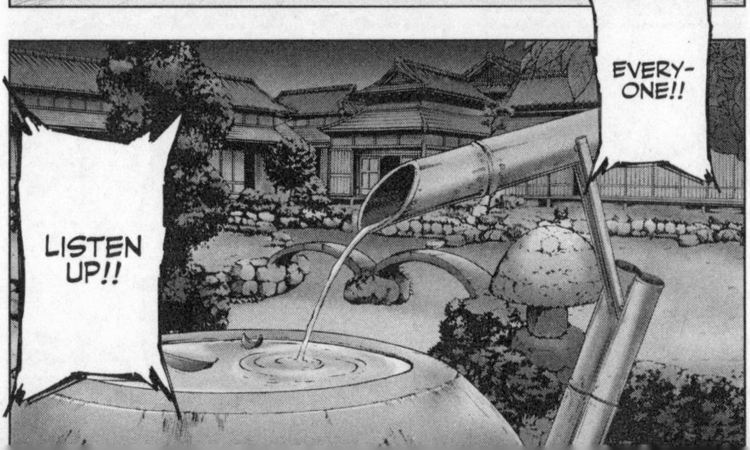
EVERY-ONE!!
LISTEN UP!!

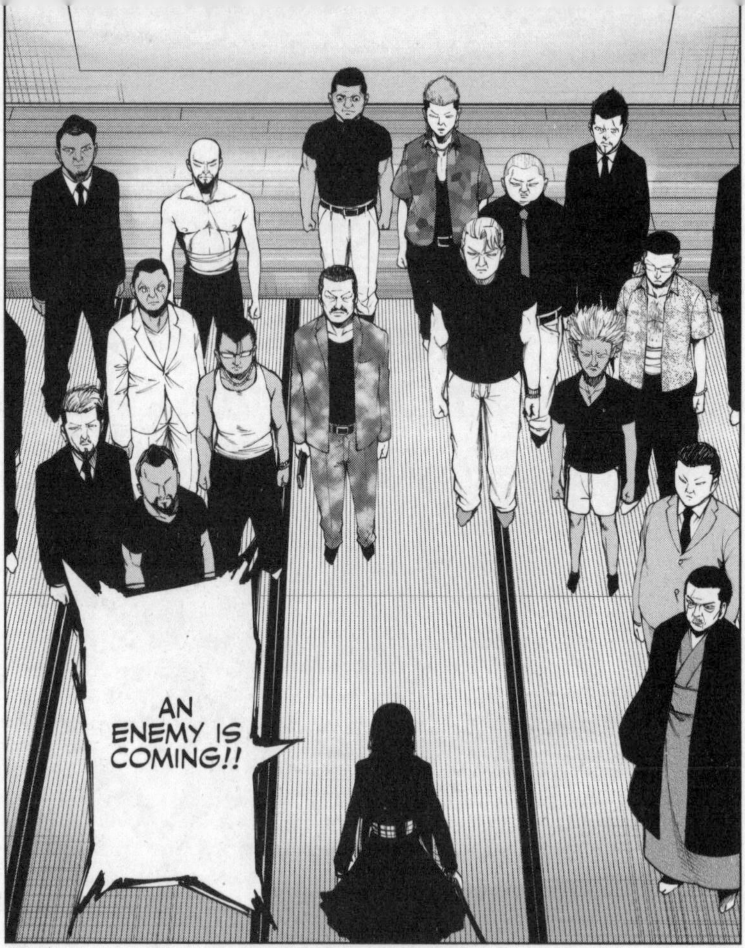
AN ENEMY IS COMING!!
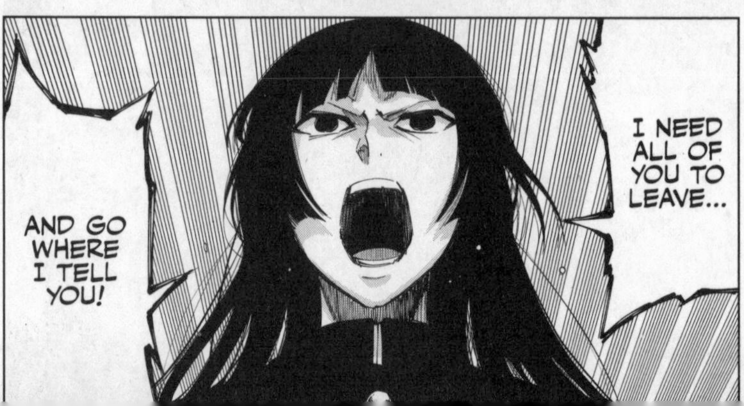
I NEED ALL OF YOU TO LEAVE...
AND GO WHERE I TELL YOU!

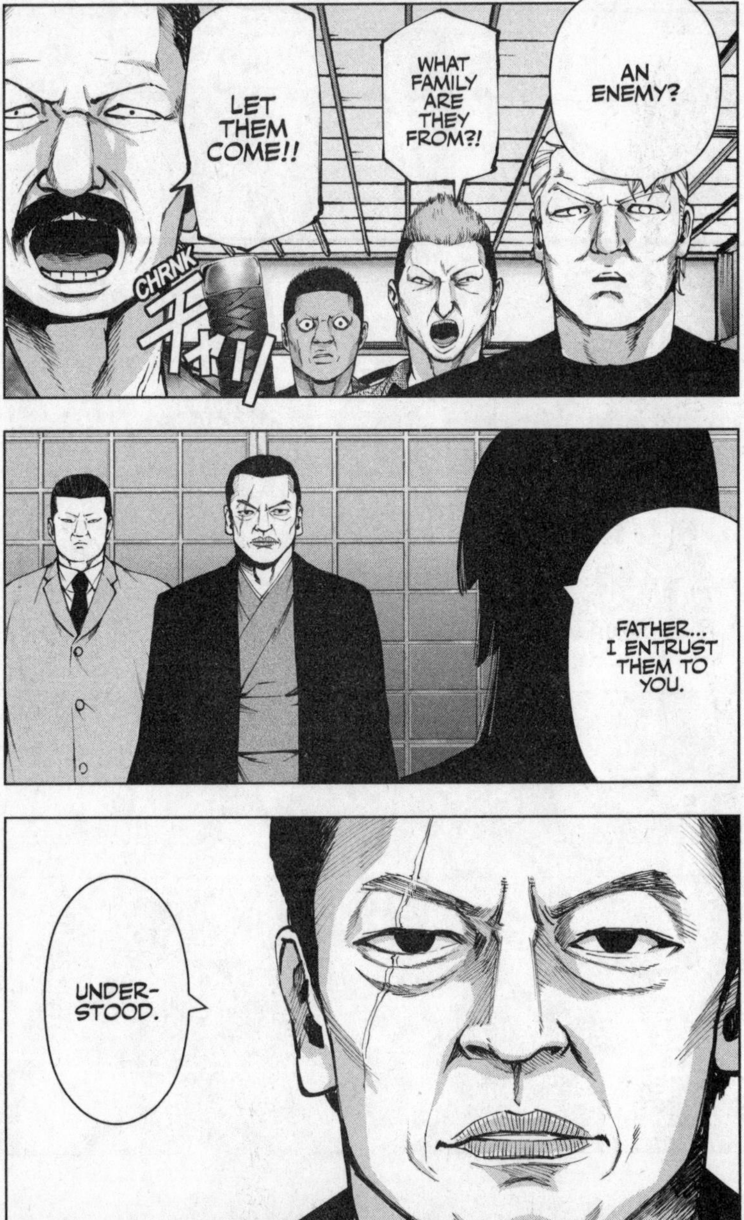
AN ENEMY?
WHAT FAMILY ARE THEY FROM?!
LET THEM COME!!
CHRNK
チャ
FATHER... I ENTRUST THEM TO YOU.
UNDER-STOOD.

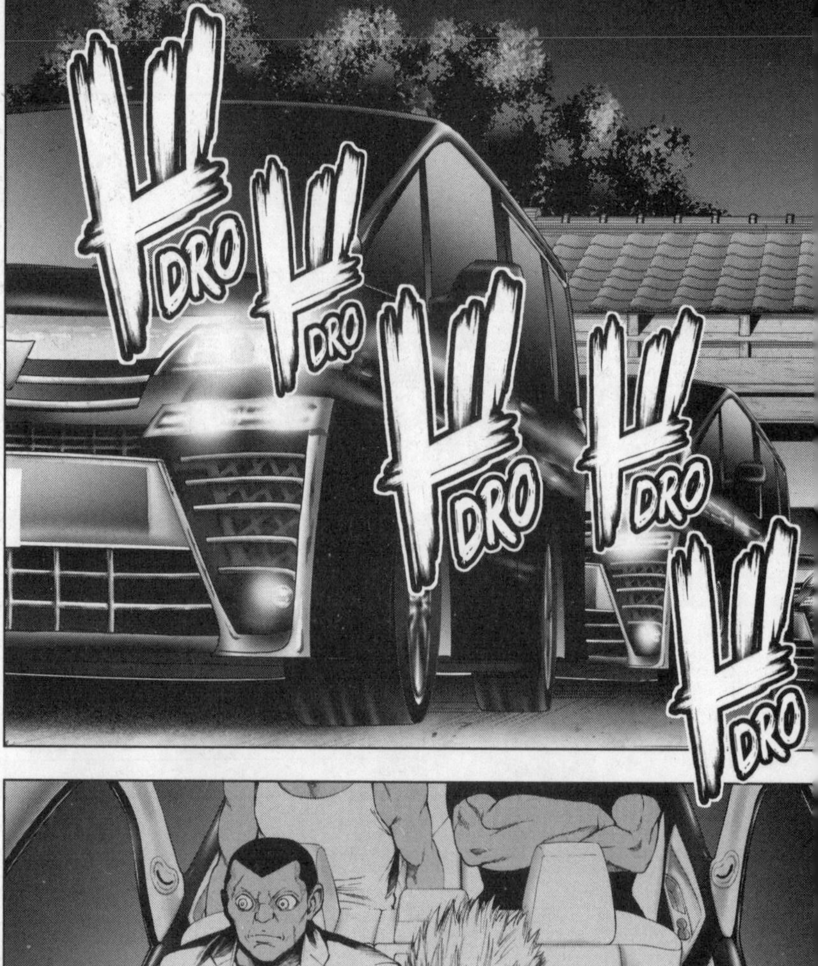
DRO
DRO
DRO
DRO
DRO
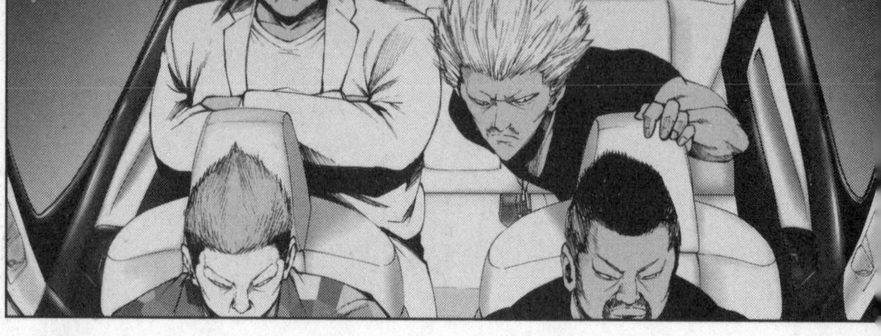

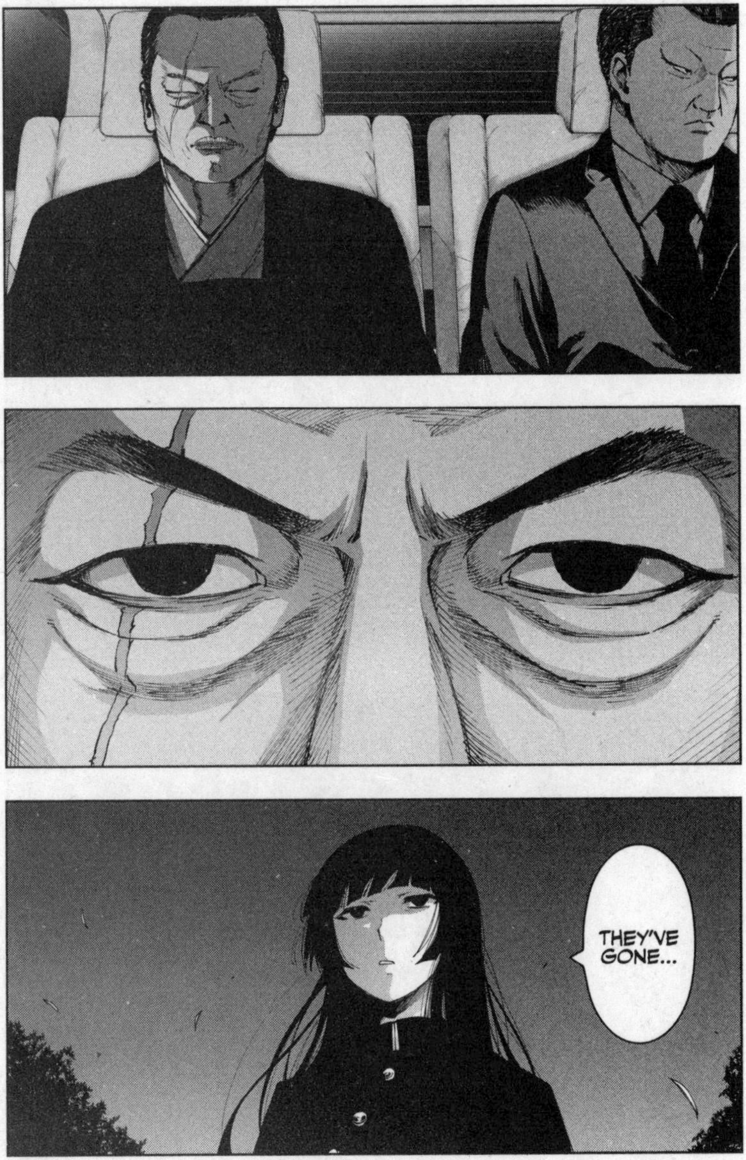
THEY'VE GONE...

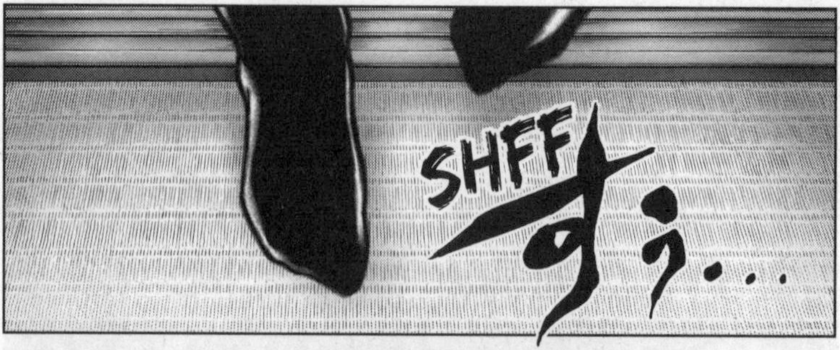
SHFF
すぅ...
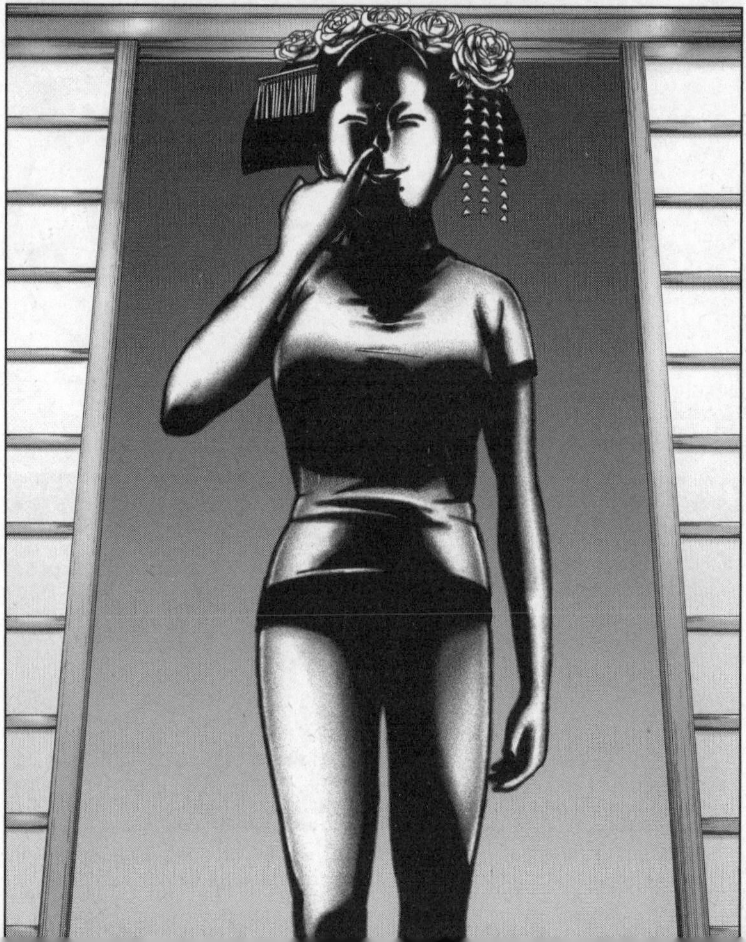

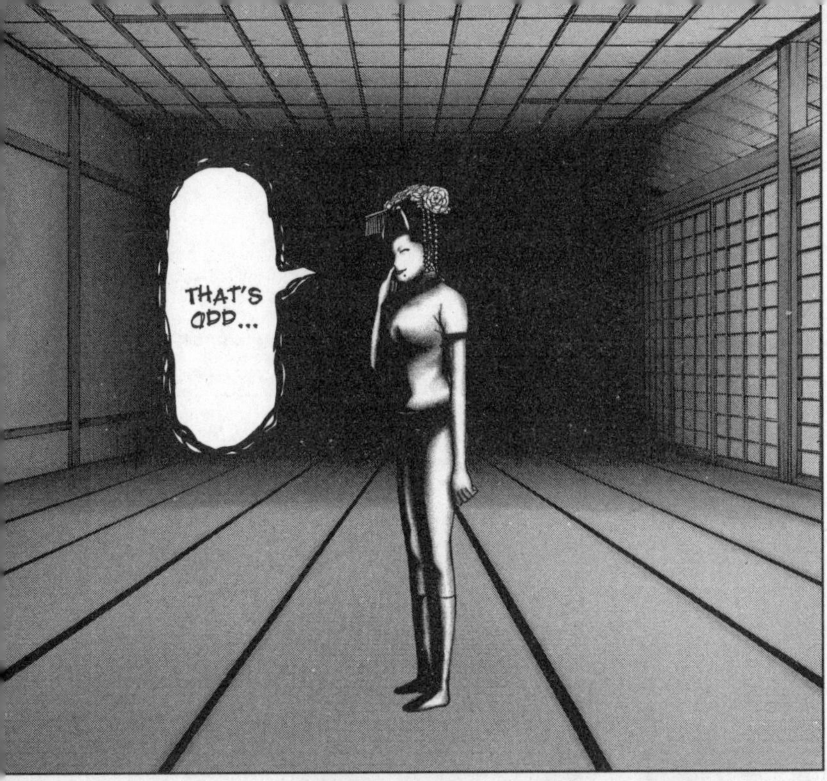
THAT'S ODD...

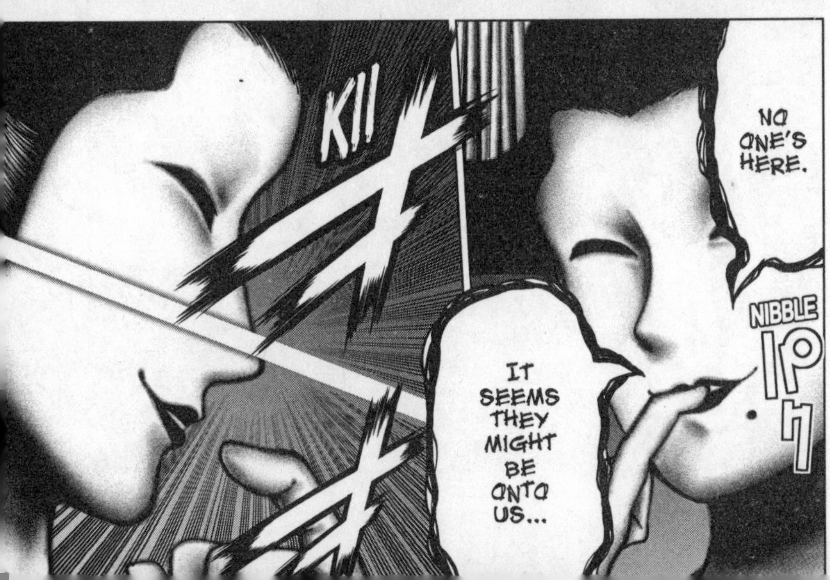
NO ONE'S HERE.
NIBBLE
IT SEEMS THEY MIGHT BE ONTO US...
KII

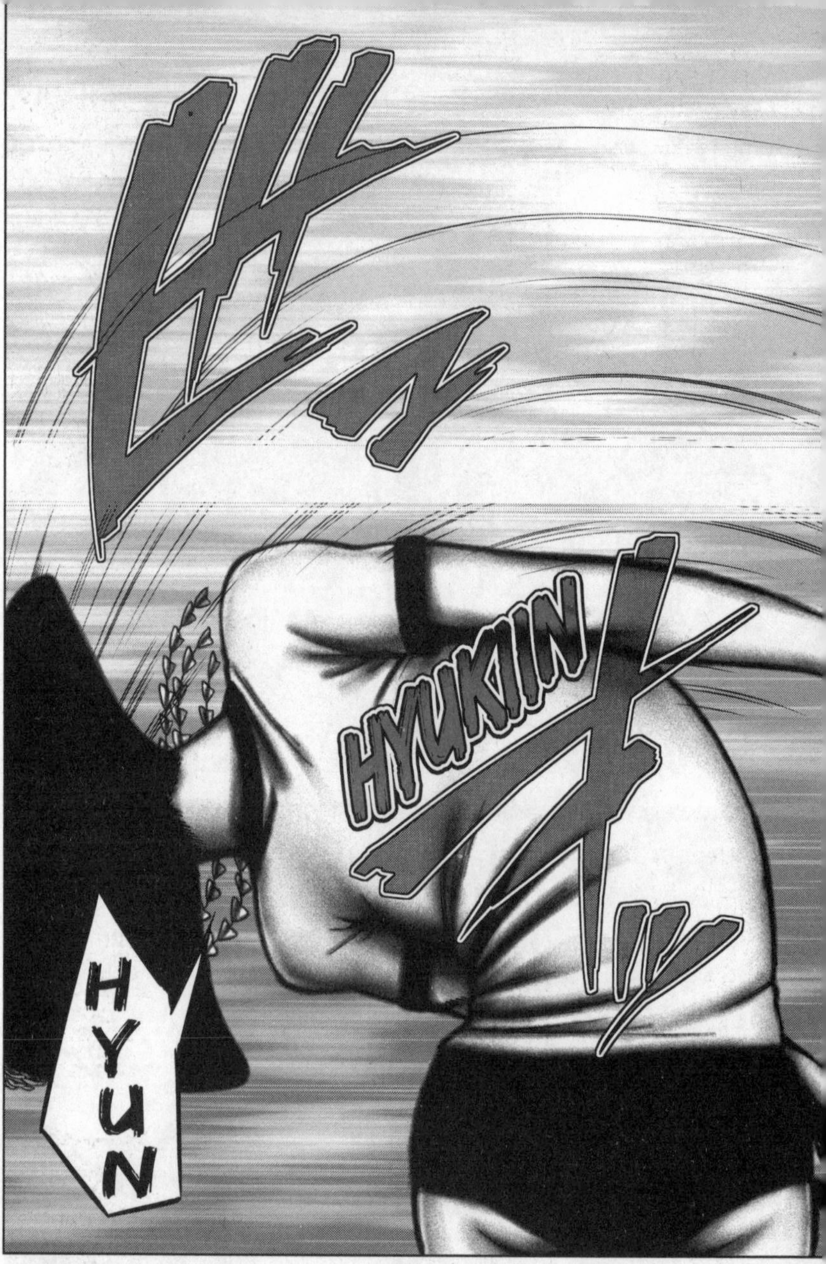
HYUKIIN
HYUN

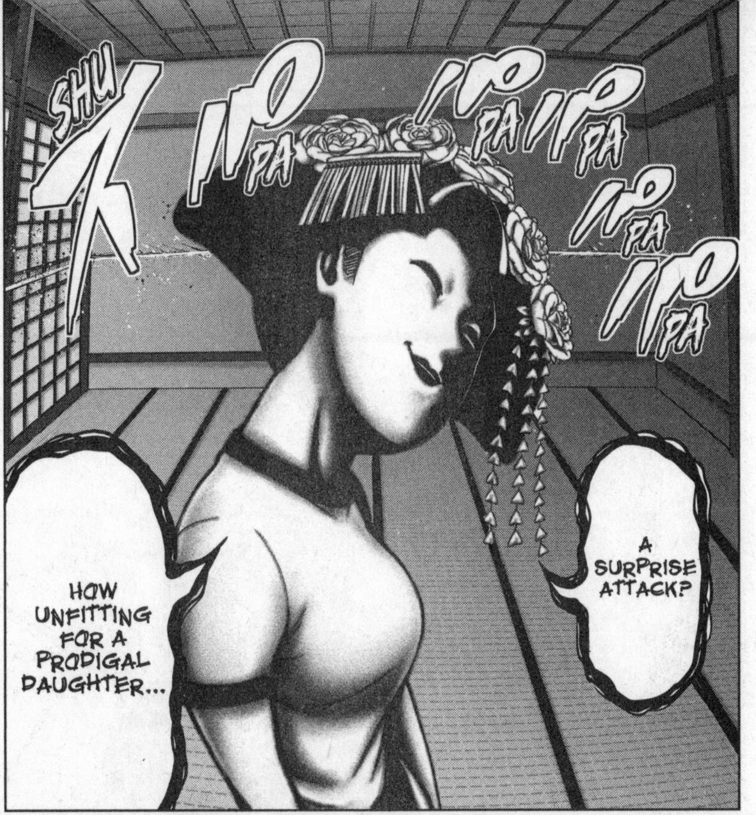
PA PA PA PA PA
SHU
A SURPRISE ATTACK?
HOW UNFITTING FOR A PRODIGAL DAUGHTER...
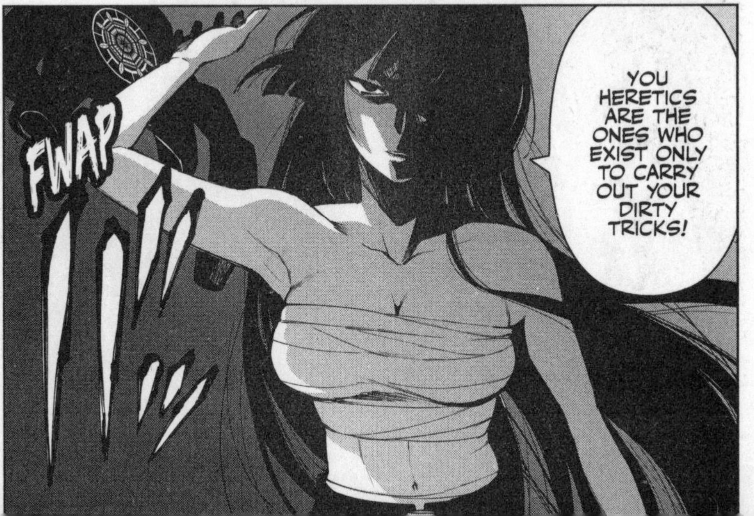
YOU HERETICS ARE THE ONES WHO EXIST ONLY TO CARRY OUT YOUR DIRTY TRICKS!
FWAP

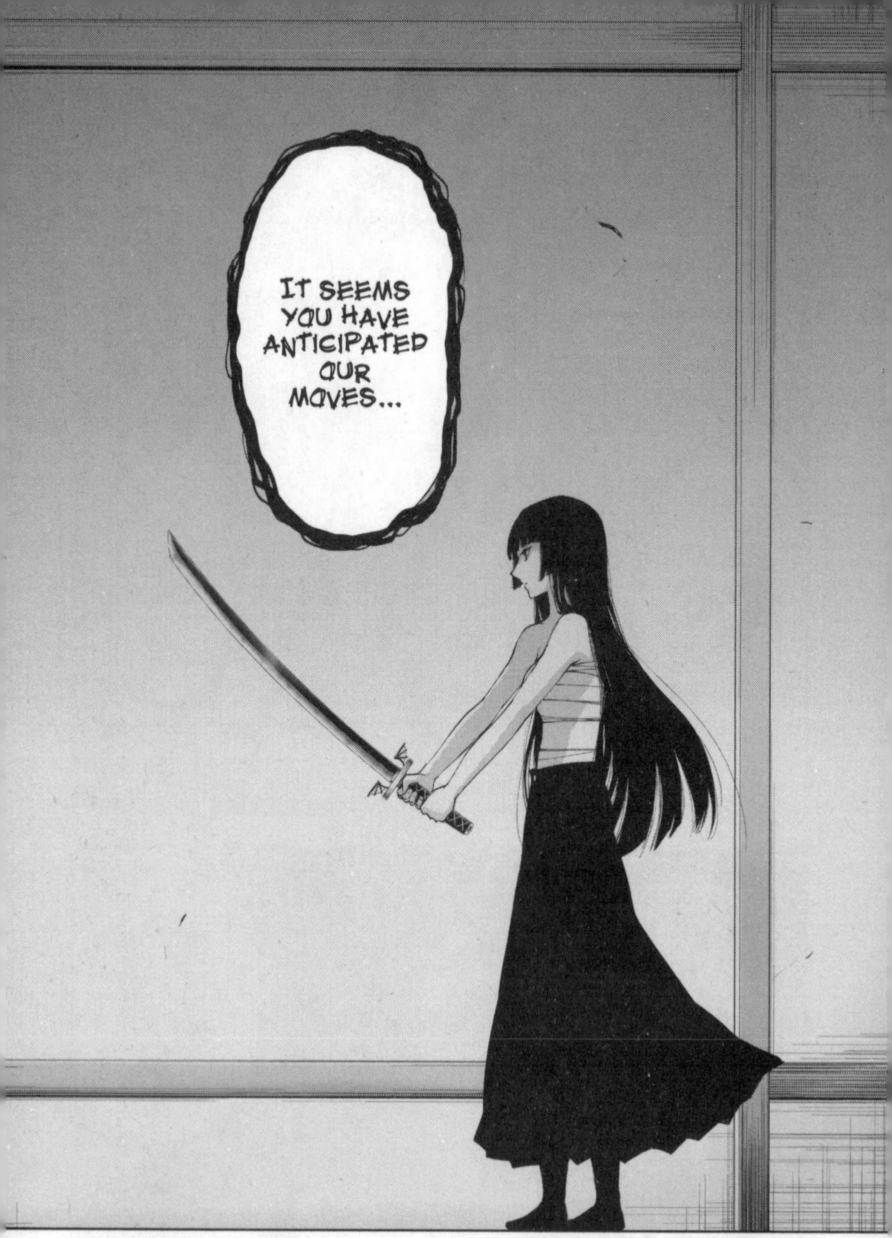
IT SEEMS YOU HAVE ANTICIPATED OUR MOVES...

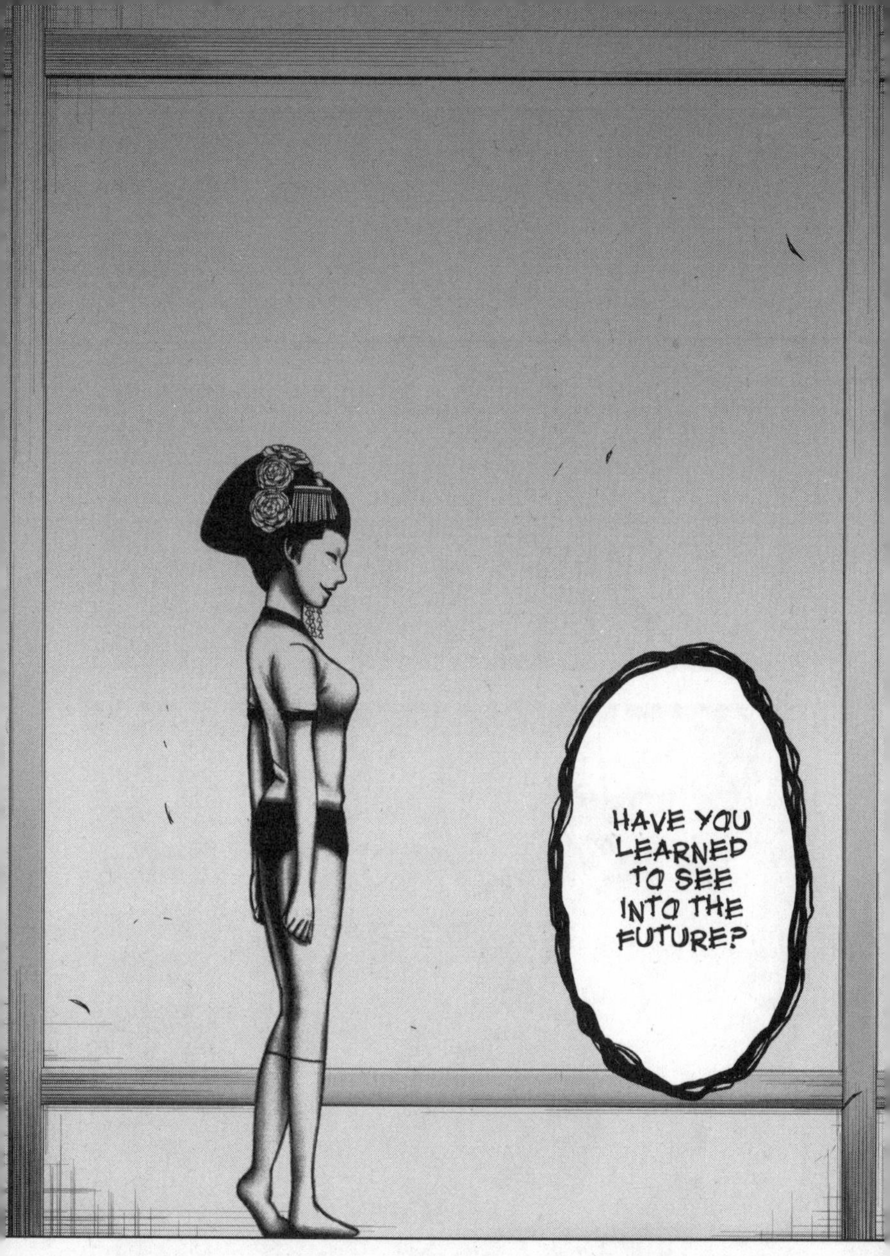
HAVE YOU LEARNED TO SEE INTO THE FUTURE?

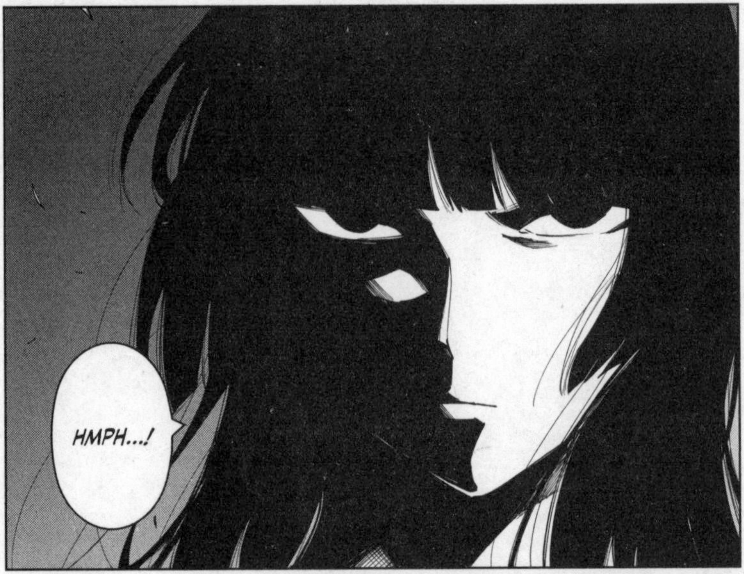
HMPH...!
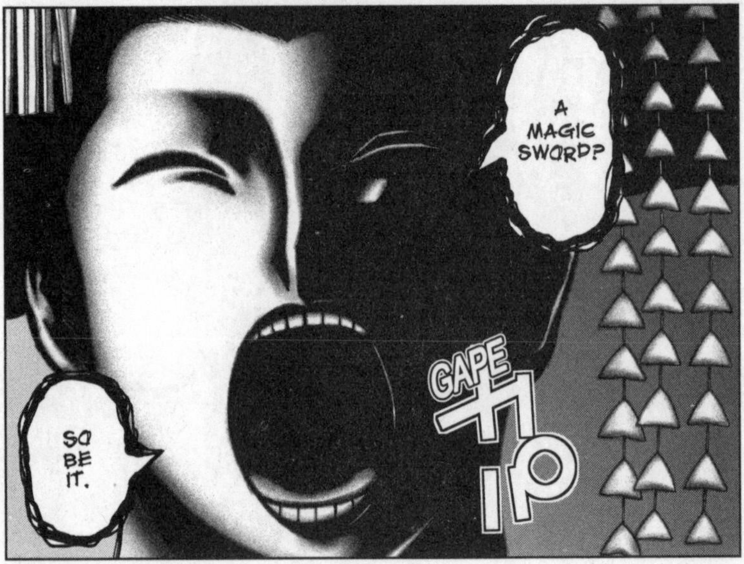
A MAGIC SWORD?
GAPE
SO BE IT.

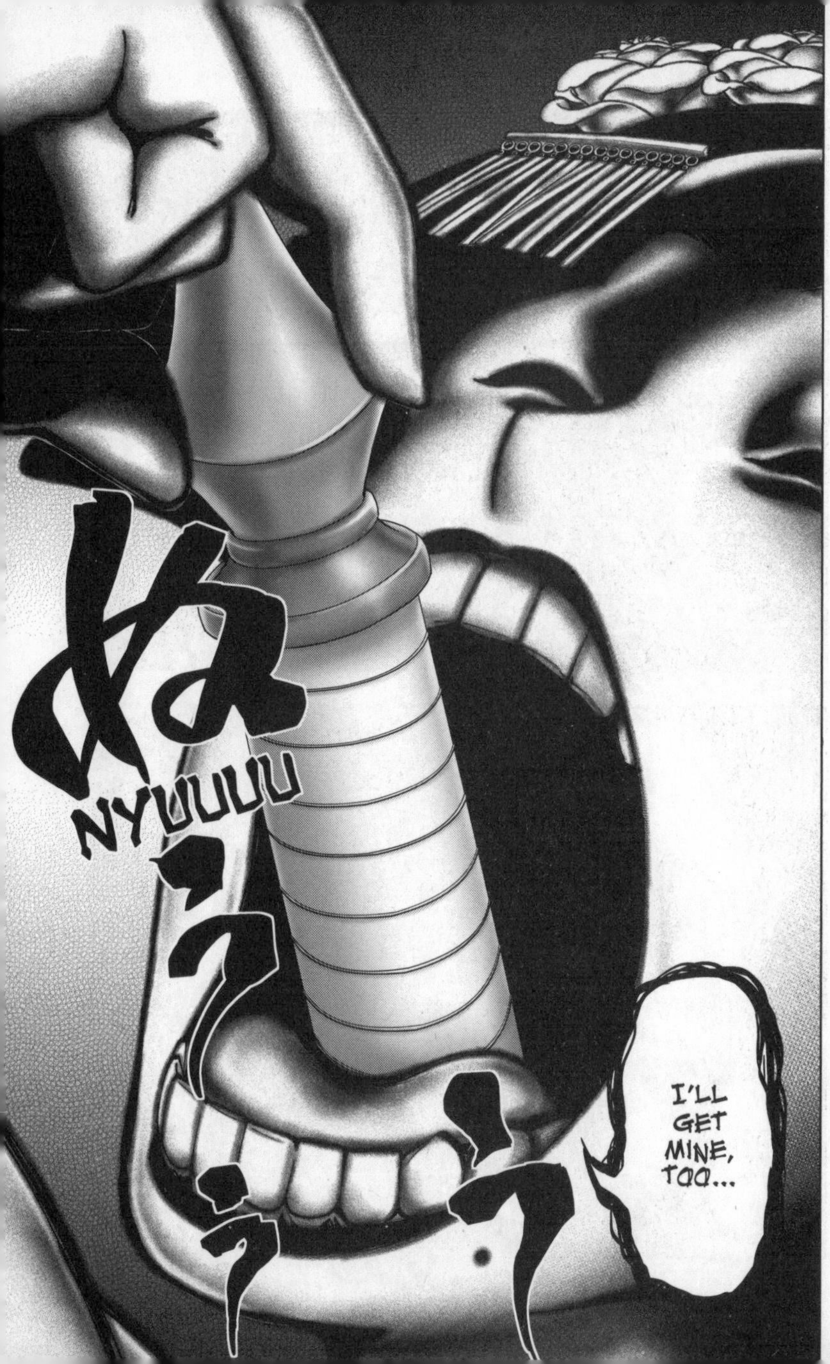
NYUUUU
I'LL GET MINE, TOO...

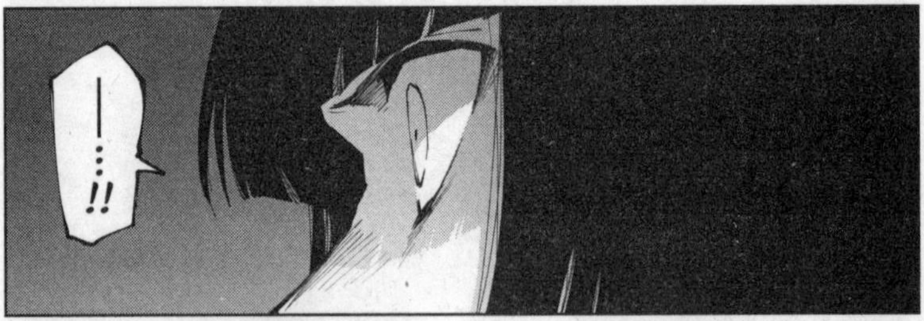
—…!!

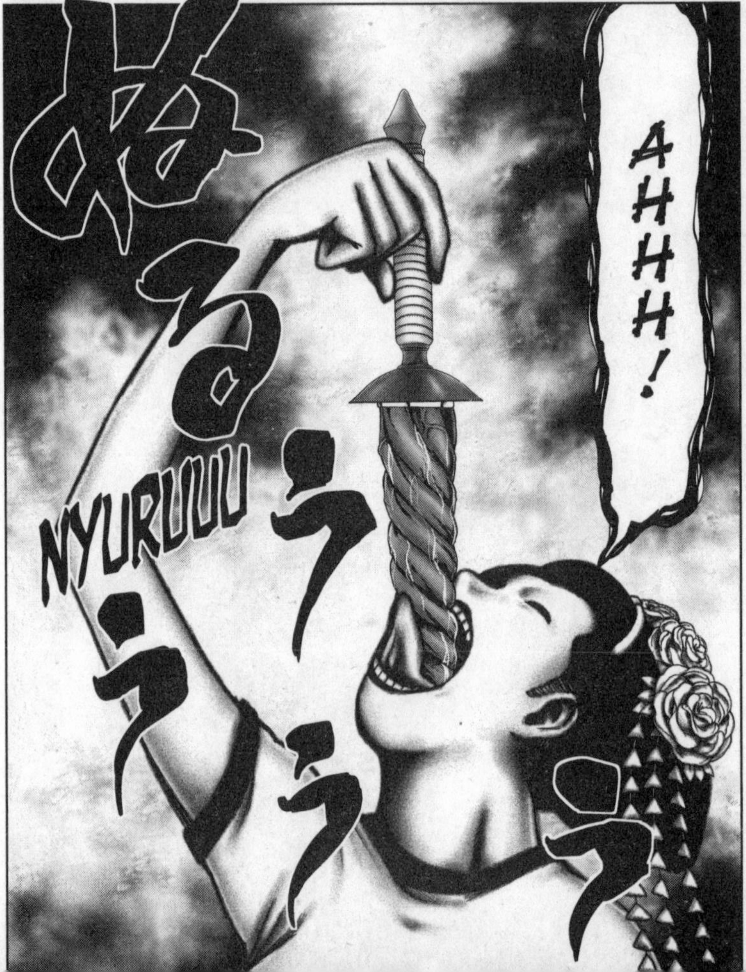
AHHHH!
ぬるうううう
NYURUUU

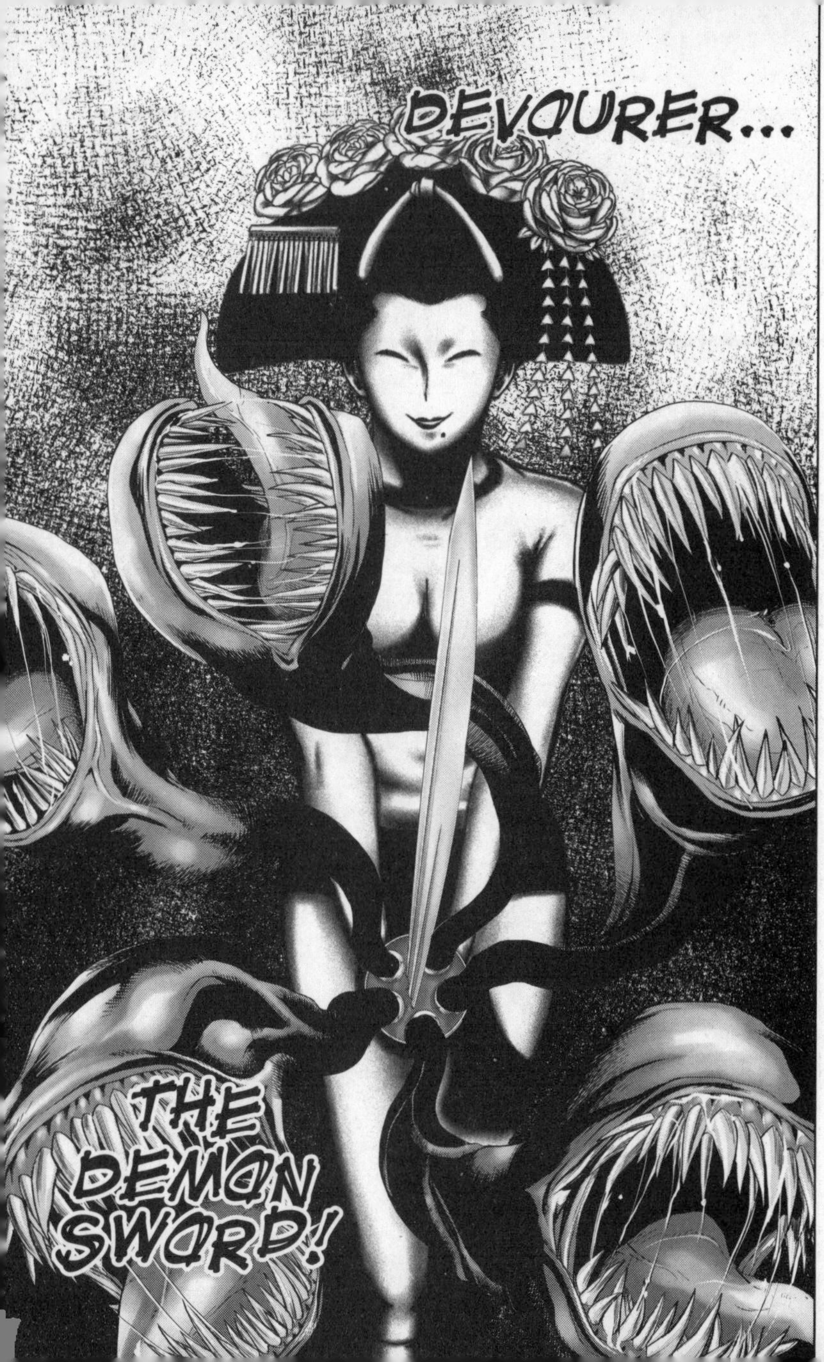
DEVOURER...
THE DEMON SWORD!

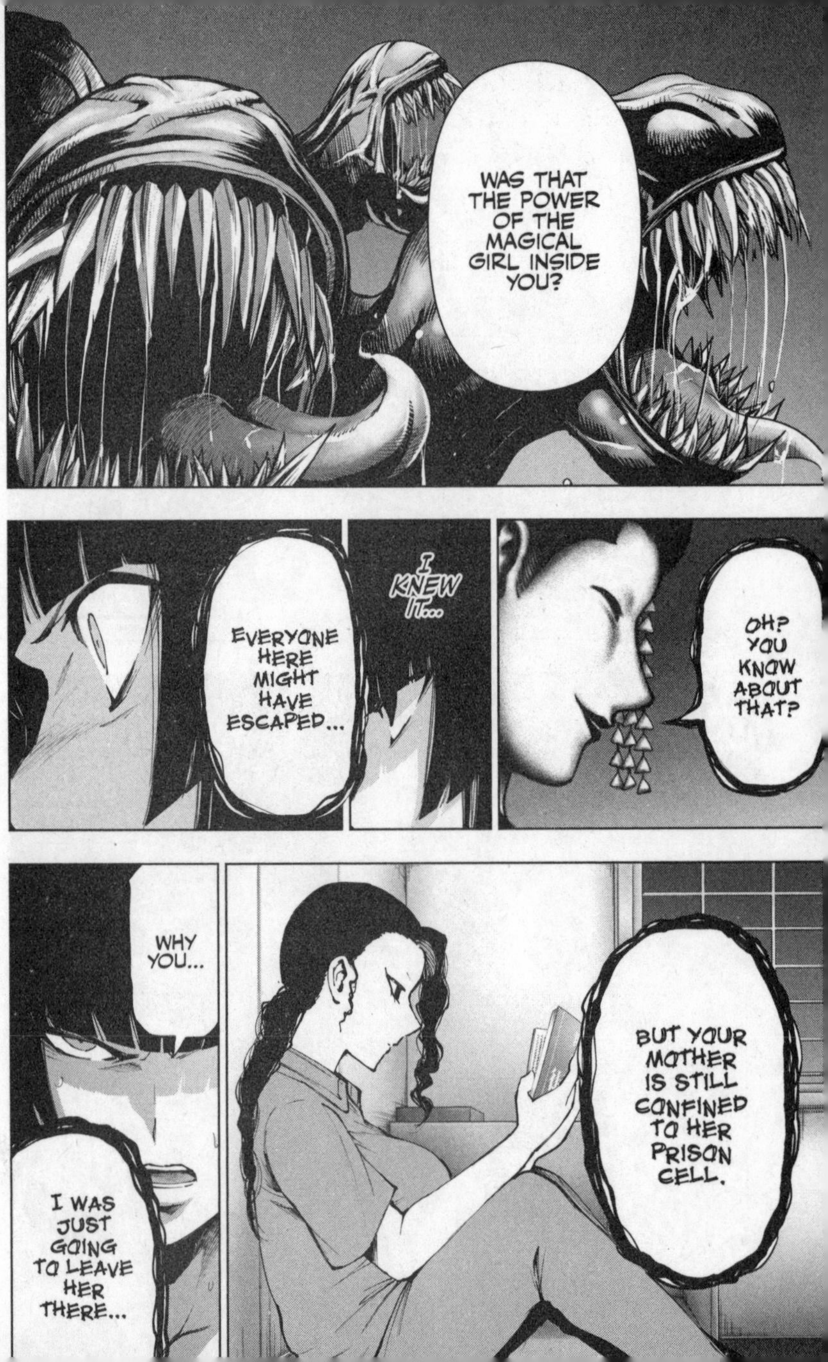
WAS THAT THE POWER OF THE MAGICAL GIRL INSIDE YOU?
OH? YOU KNOW ABOUT THAT?
I KNEW IT...
EVERYONE HERE MIGHT HAVE ESCAPED...
BUT YOUR MOTHER IS STILL CONFINED TO HER PRISON CELL.
WHY YOU...
I WAS JUST GOING TO LEAVE HER THERE...

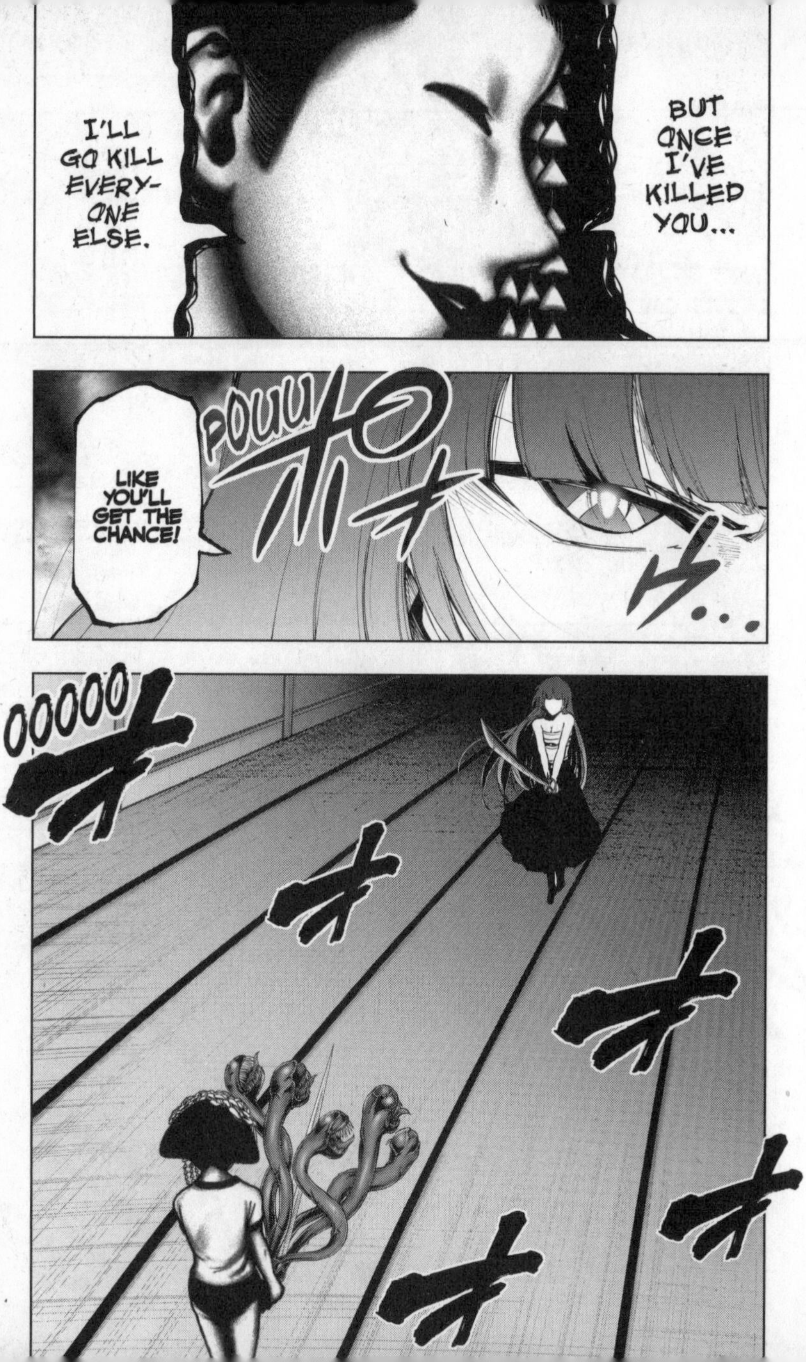
BUT ONCE I'VE KILLED YOU...
I'LL GO KILL EVERY-ONE ELSE.
POUU
LIKE YOU'LL GET THE CHANCE!
OOOOO

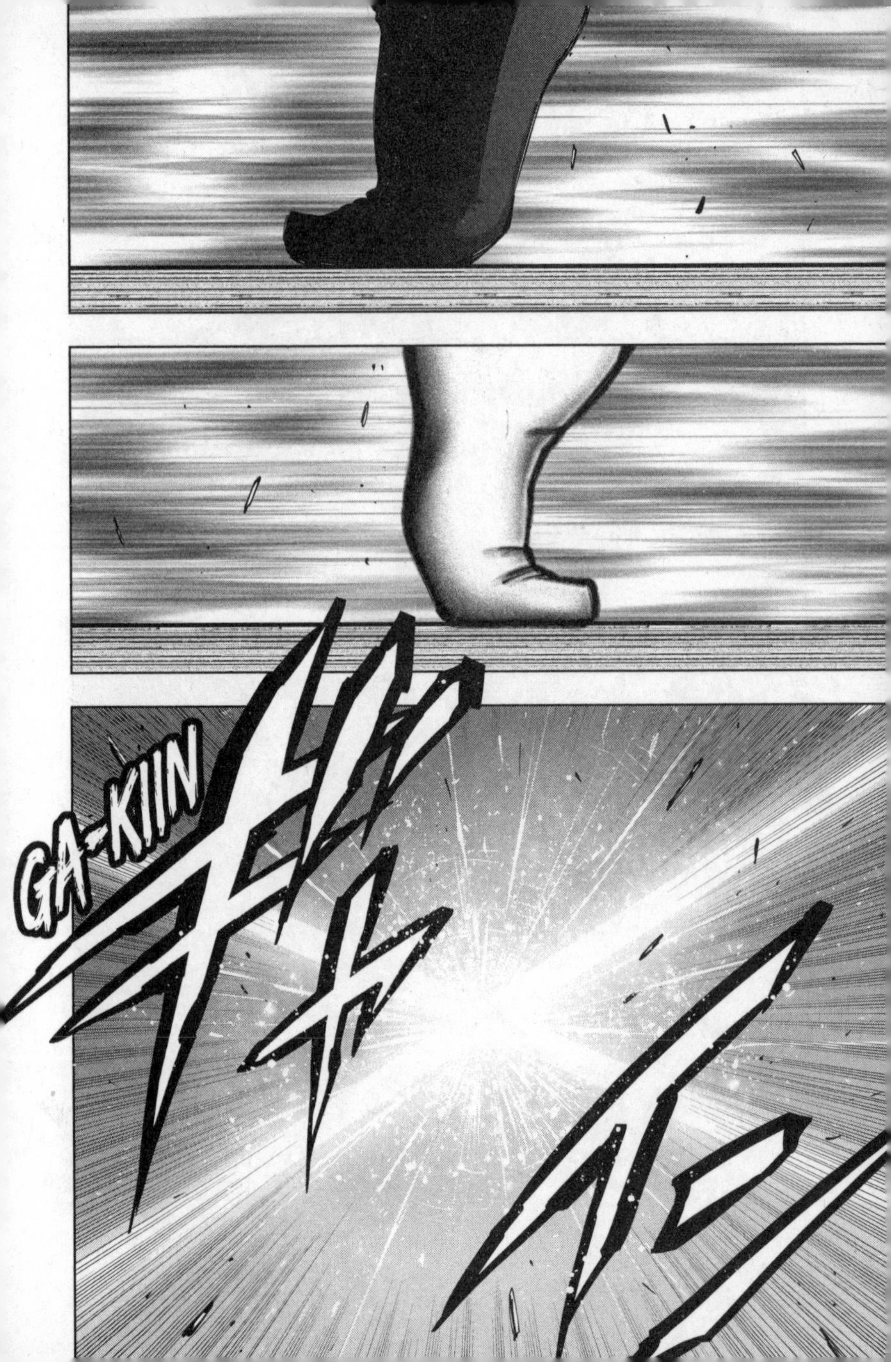
GA-KIIN

ENTER.96 SHARING WITH EACH OTHER

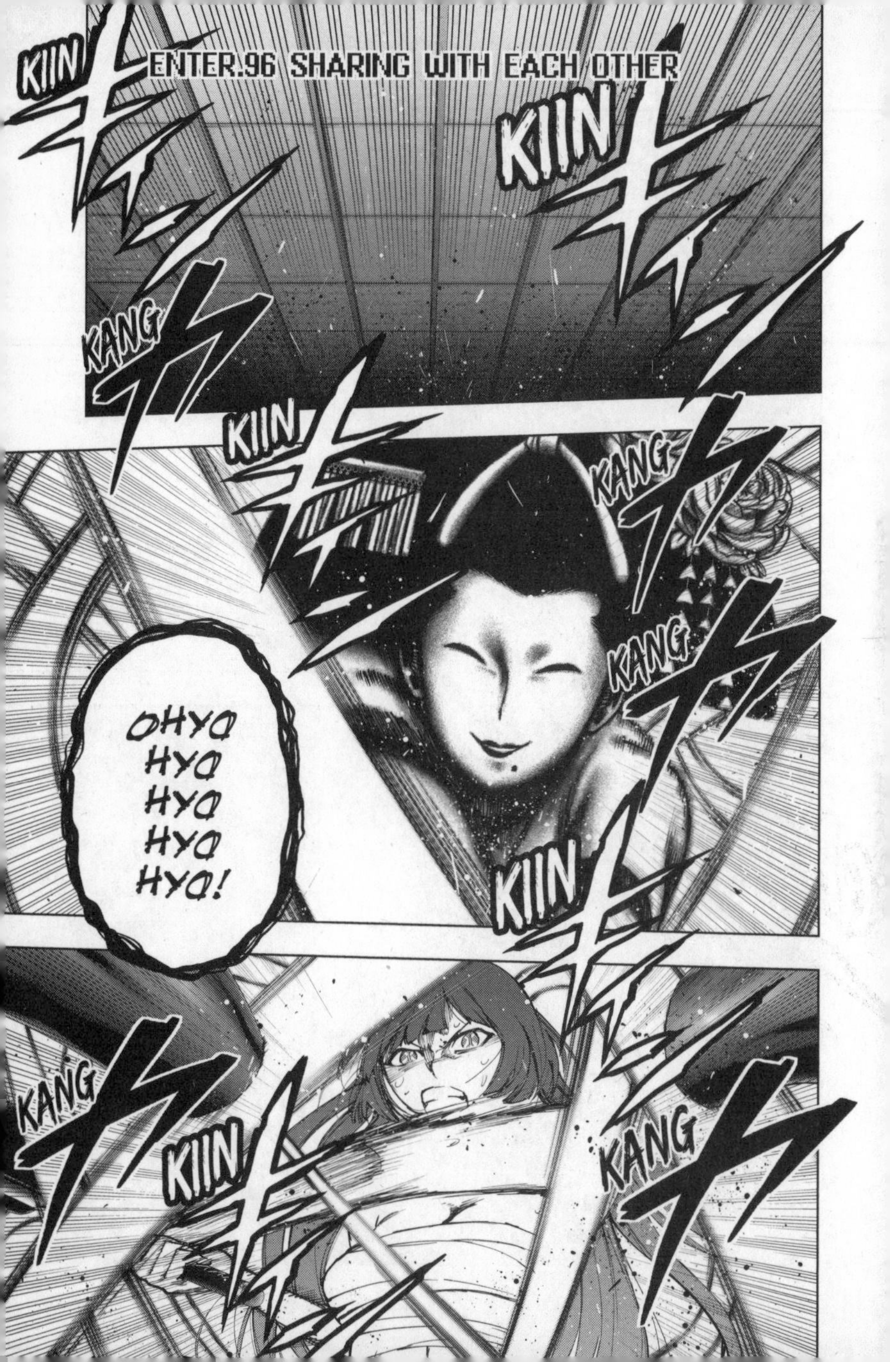
KIIN
KIIN
KANG
KIIN
KANG
KANG
OHYO HYO HYO HYO HYO!
KIIN
KANG
KIIN
KANG

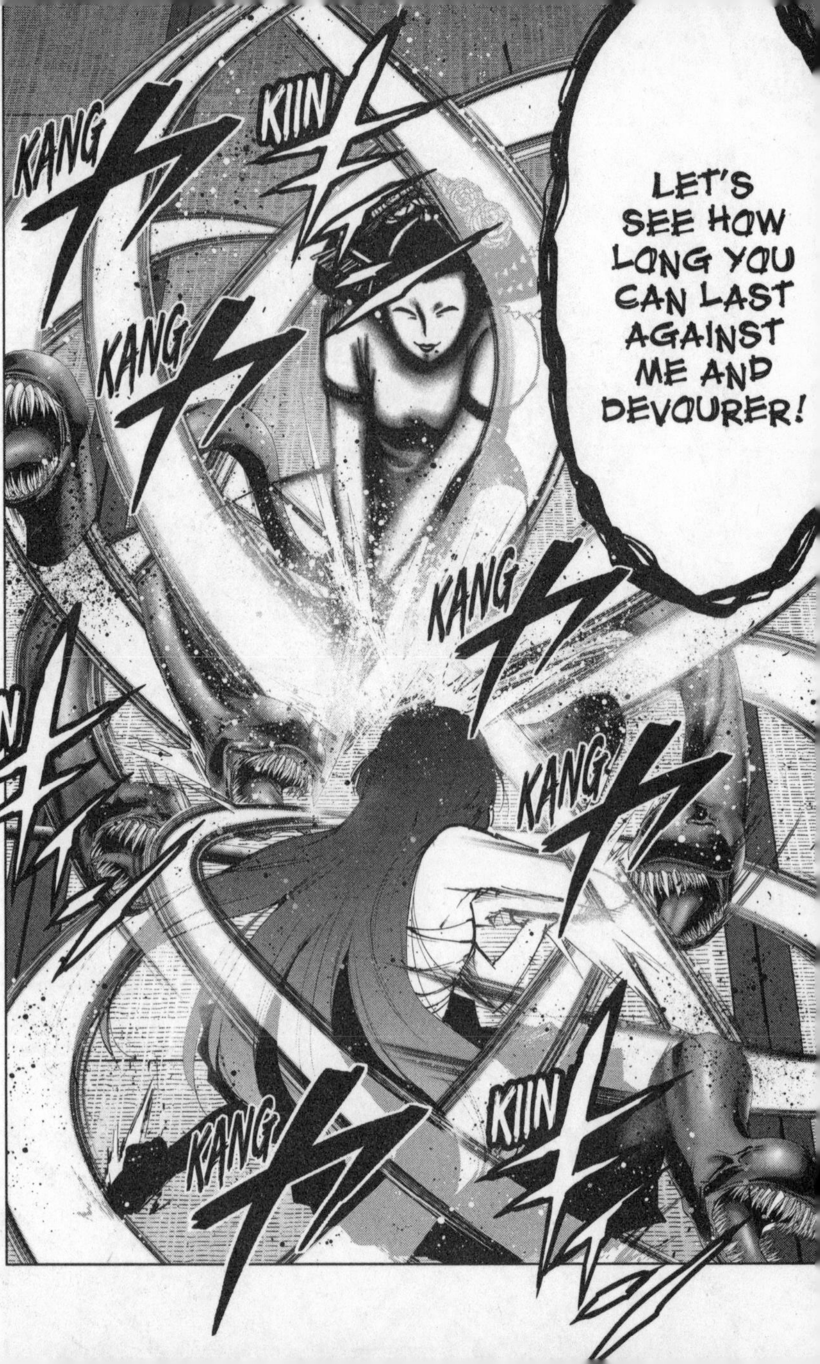
LET'S SEE HOW LONG YOU CAN LAST AGAINST ME AND DEVOURER!
KIIN
KANG
KANG
KANG
KANG
KIIN
KIIN
KANG

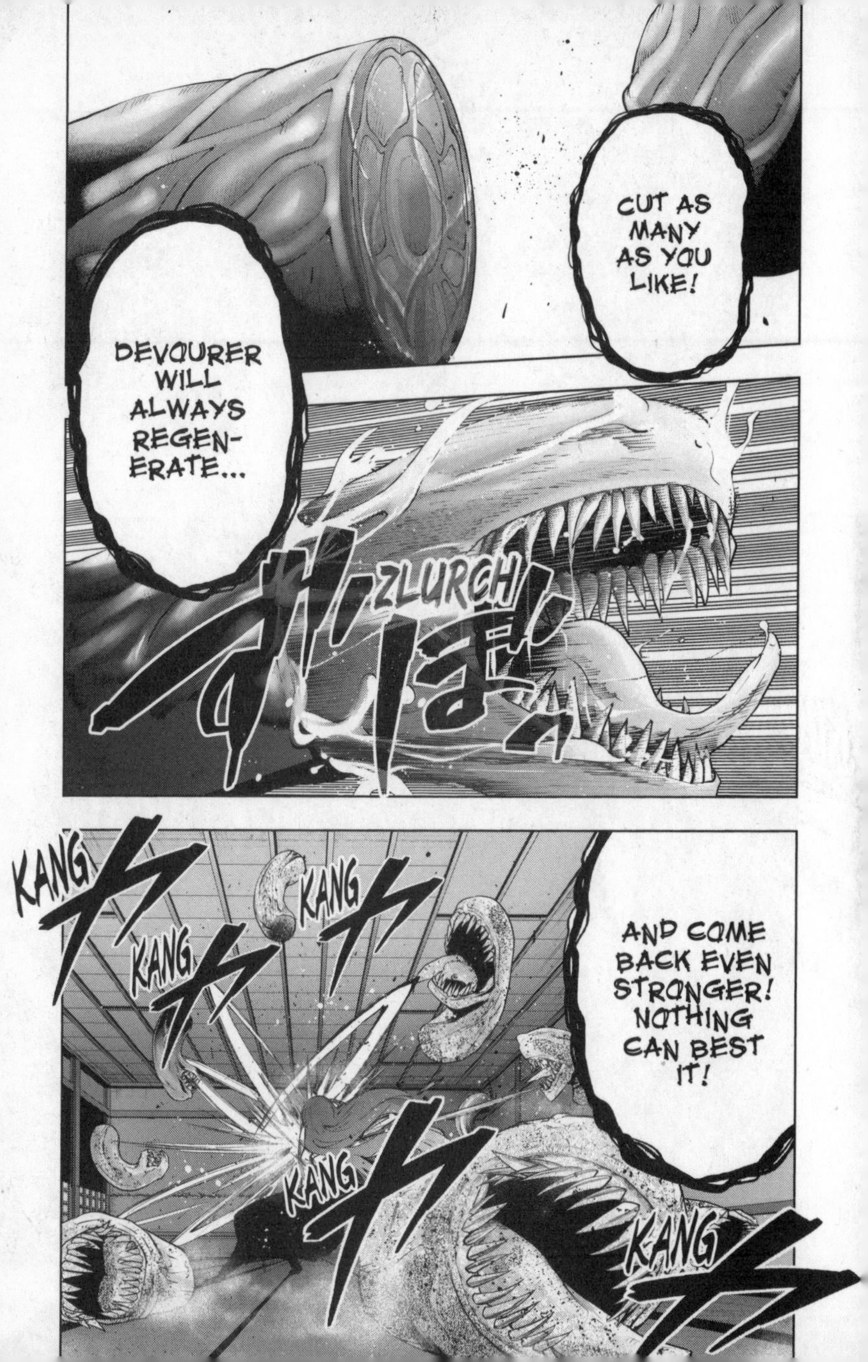
CUT AS MANY AS YOU LIKE!
DEVOURER WILL ALWAYS REGEN-ERATE...
ZLURCH
AND COME BACK EVEN STRONGER! NOTHING CAN BEST IT!
KANG
KANG
KANG
KANG
KANG

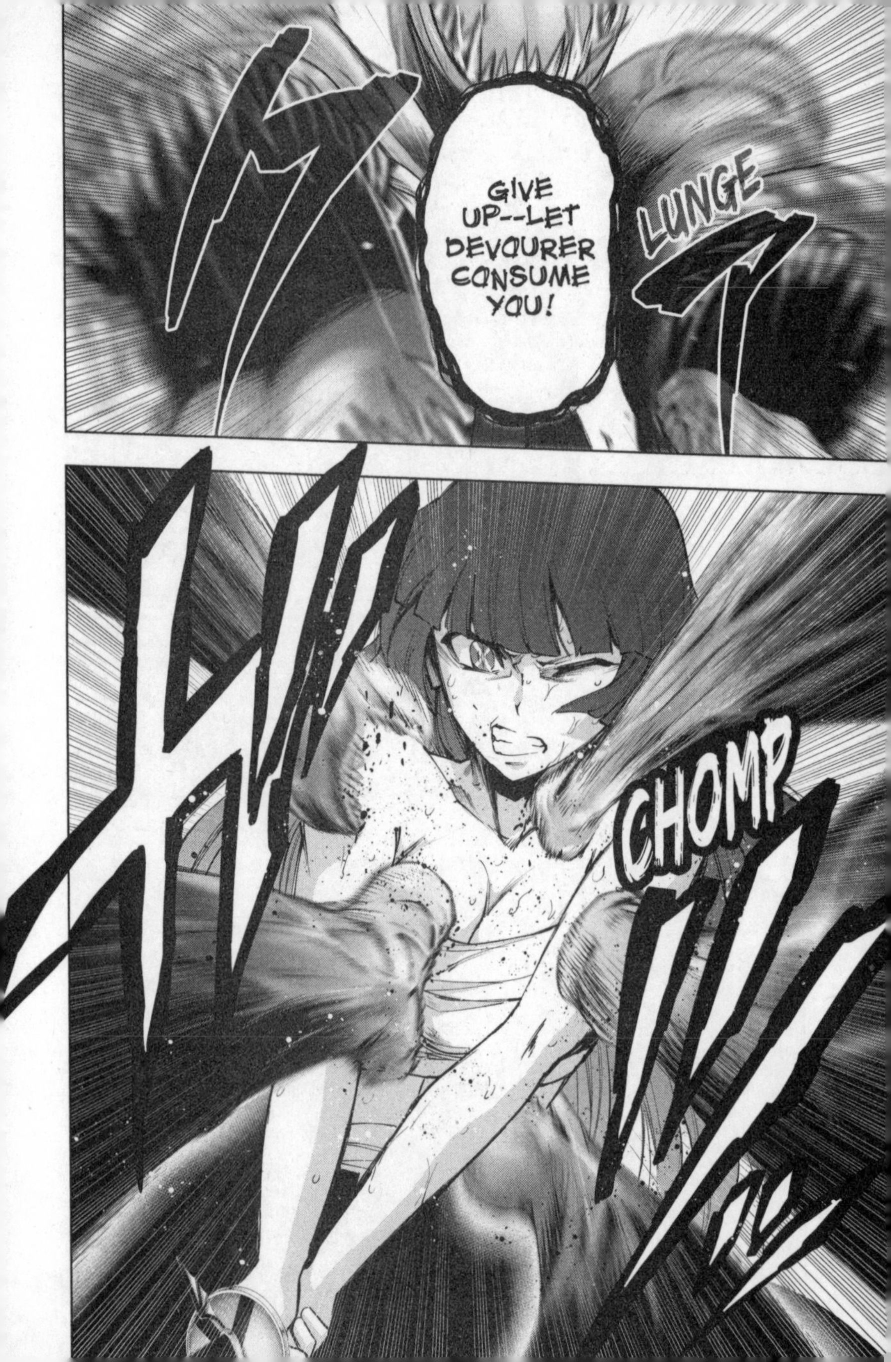
LUNGE
GIVE UP--LET DEVOURER CONSUME YOU!
CHOMP

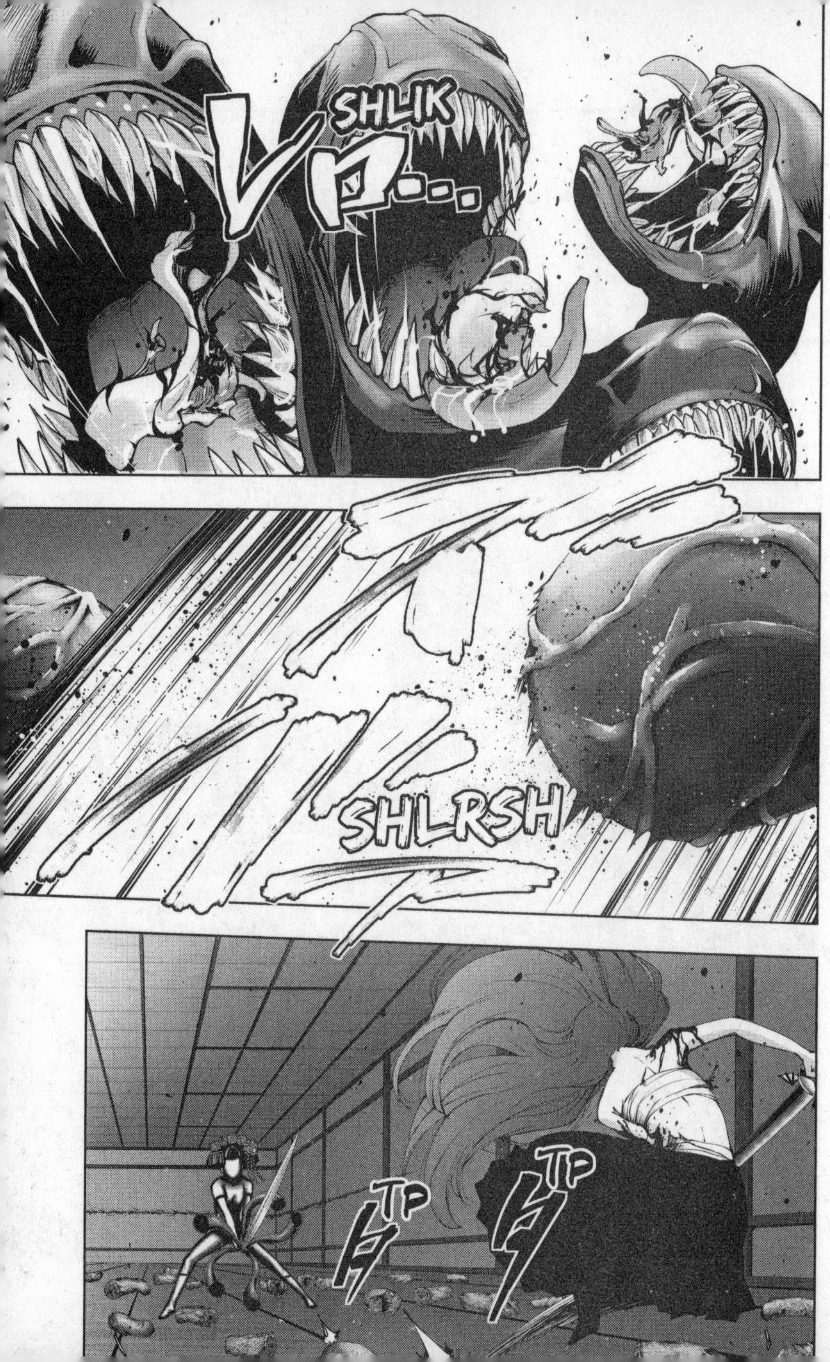
SHLIK
SHLRSH
TP
TP

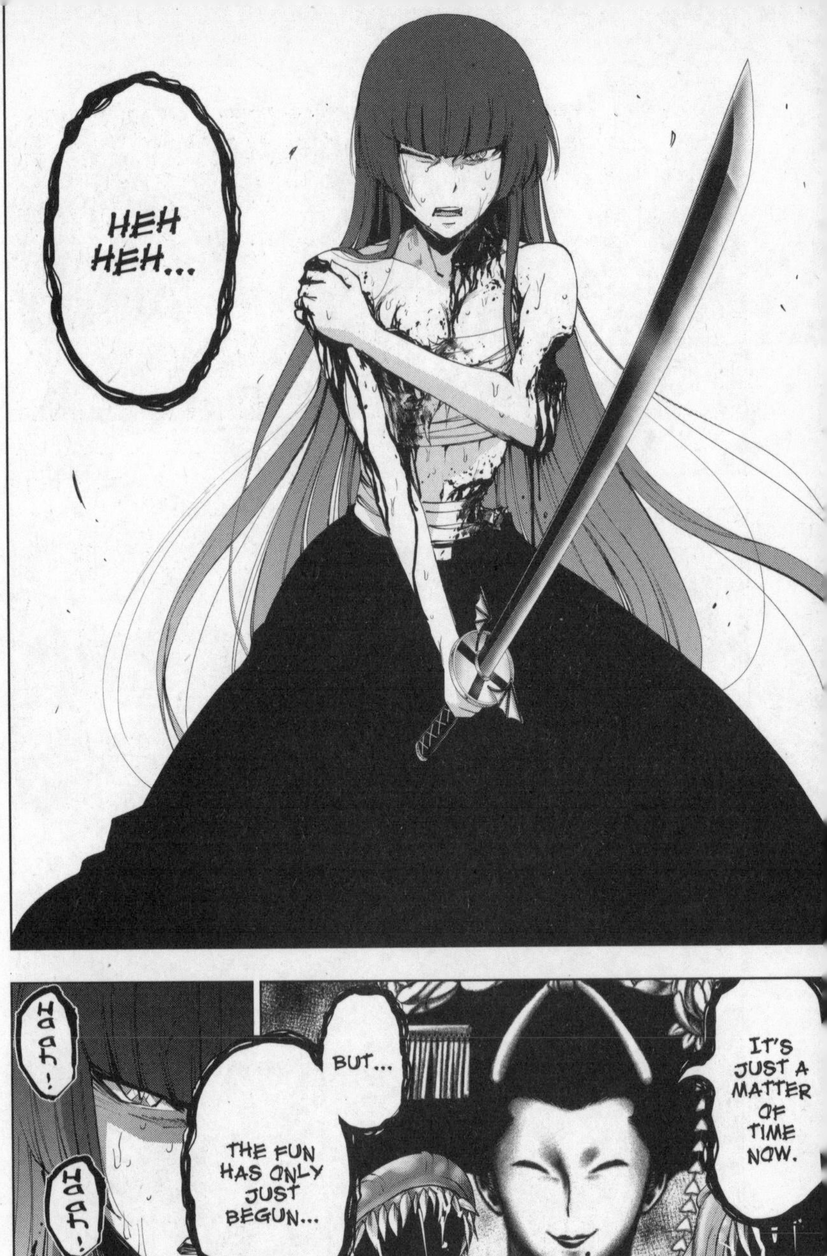
HEH HEH...
IT'S JUST A MATTER OF TIME NOW.
BUT...
THE FUN HAS ONLY JUST BEGUN...
Haah!
Haah!

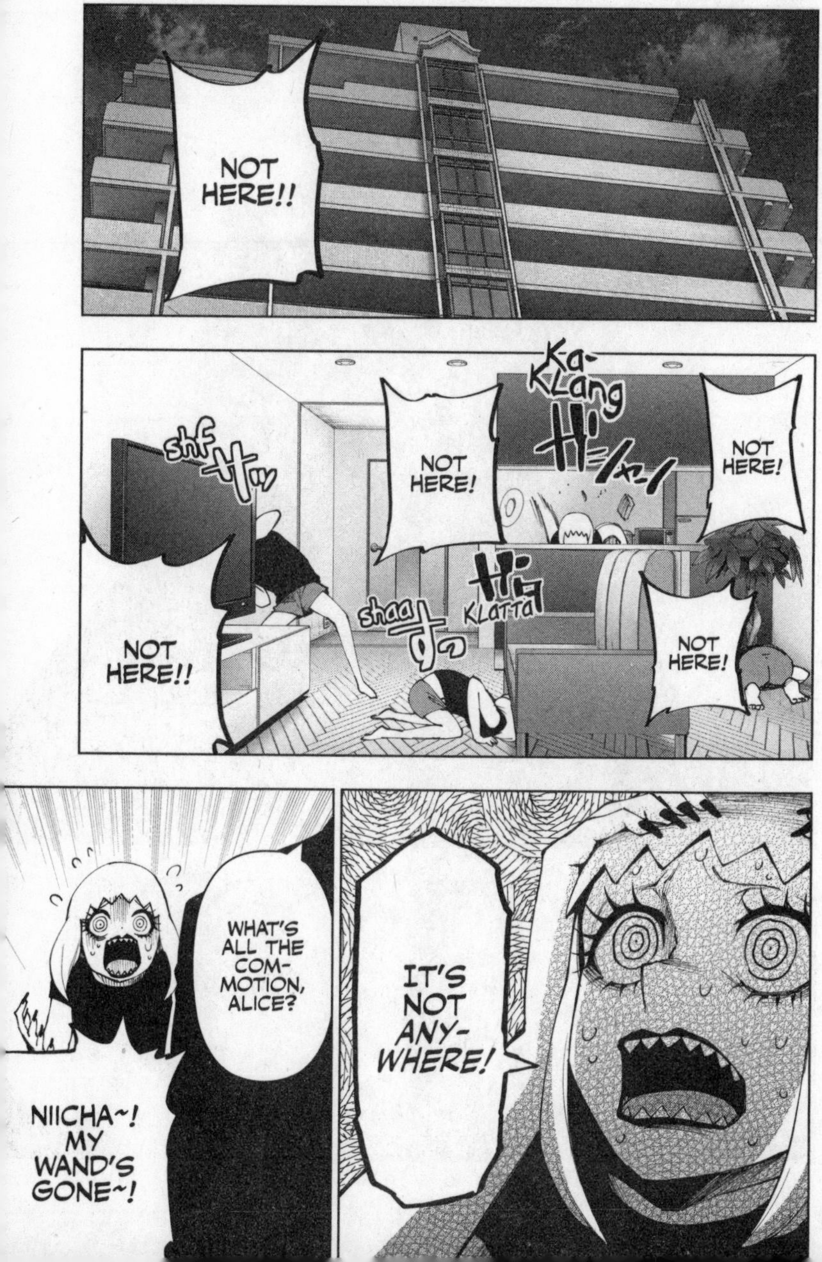
NOT HERE!!
NOT HERE!!
shf
NOT HERE!
shaa
KLATTA
Ka-Klang
NOT HERE!
NOT HERE!
NIICHA~! MY WAND'S GONE~!
WHAT'S ALL THE COM-MOTION, ALICE?
IT'S NOT ANY-WHERE!

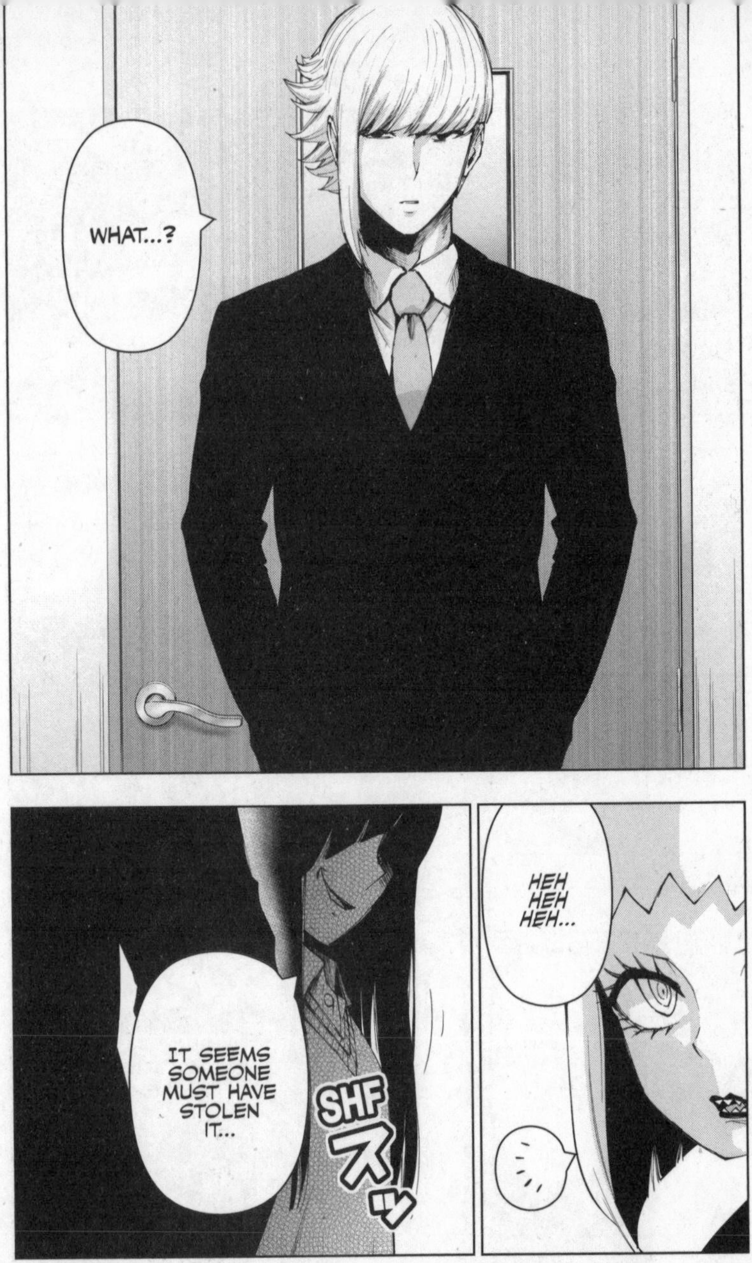
WHAT...?
HEH HEH HEH...
IT SEEMS SOMEONE MUST HAVE STOLEN IT...
SHF
スッ

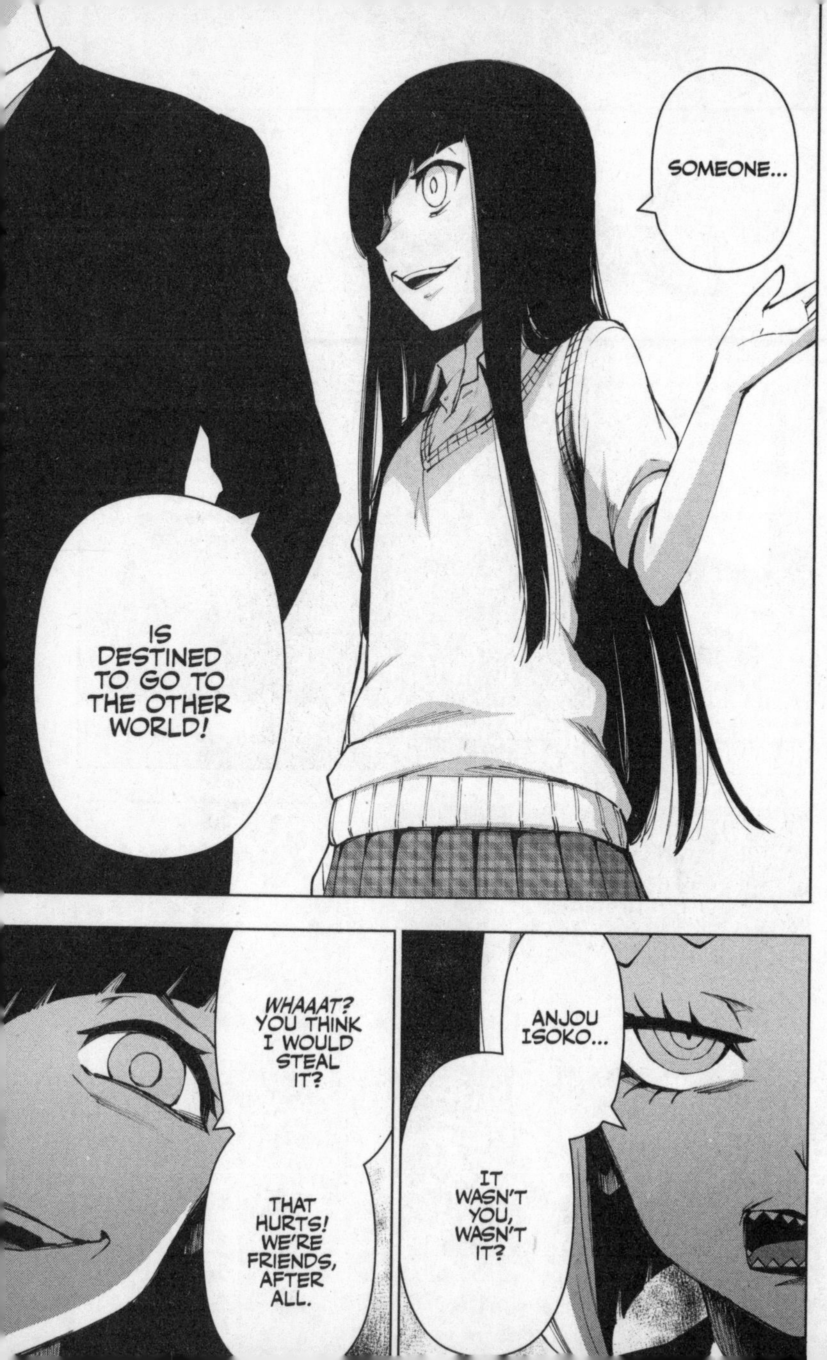
SOMEONE...
IS DESTINED TO GO TO THE OTHER WORLD!
ANJOU ISOKO...
IT WASN'T YOU, WASN'T IT?
WHAAAT? YOU THINK I WOULD STEAL IT?
THAT HURTS! WE'RE FRIENDS, AFTER ALL.

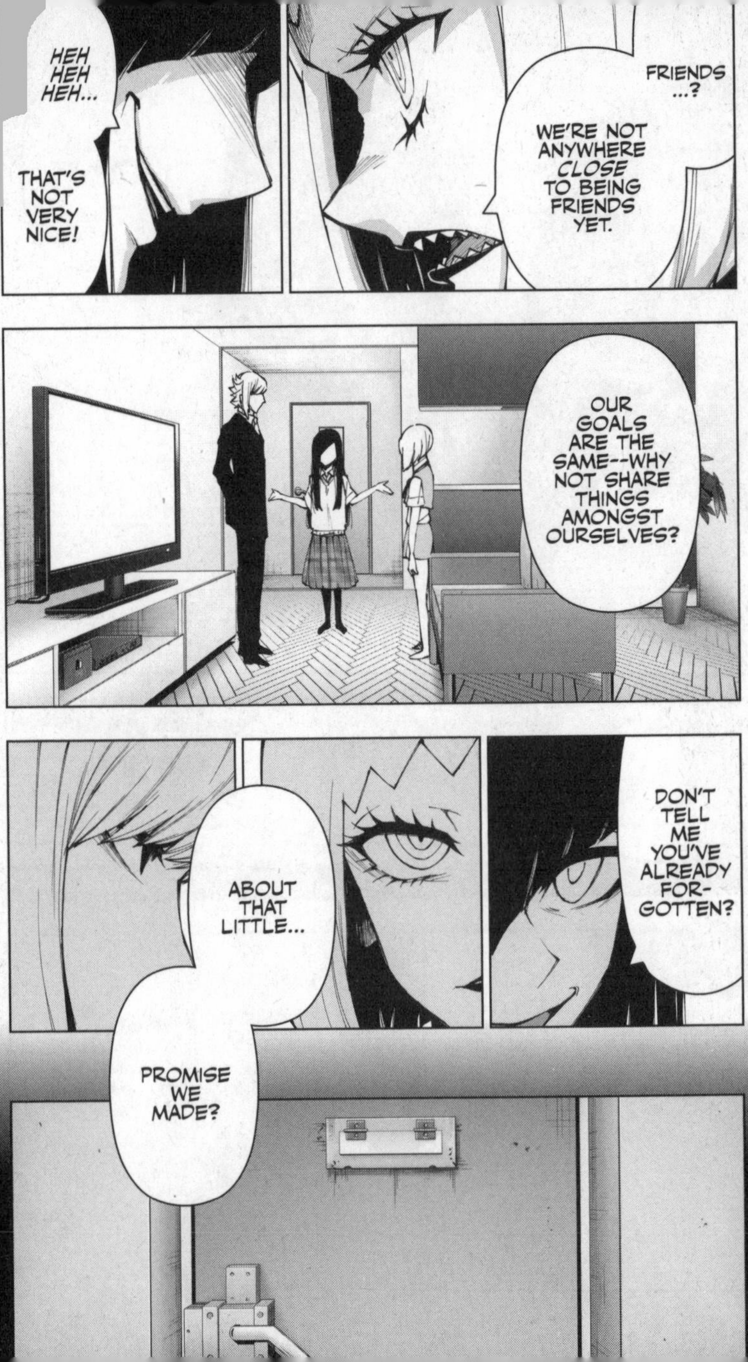
FRIENDS ...?
WE'RE NOT ANYWHERE *CLOSE* TO BEING FRIENDS YET.
HEH HEH HEH...
THAT'S NOT VERY NICE!
OUR GOALS ARE THE SAME--WHY NOT SHARE THINGS AMONGST OURSELVES?
DON'T TELL ME YOU'VE ALREADY FOR-GOTTEN?
ABOUT THAT LITTLE...
PROMISE WE MADE?

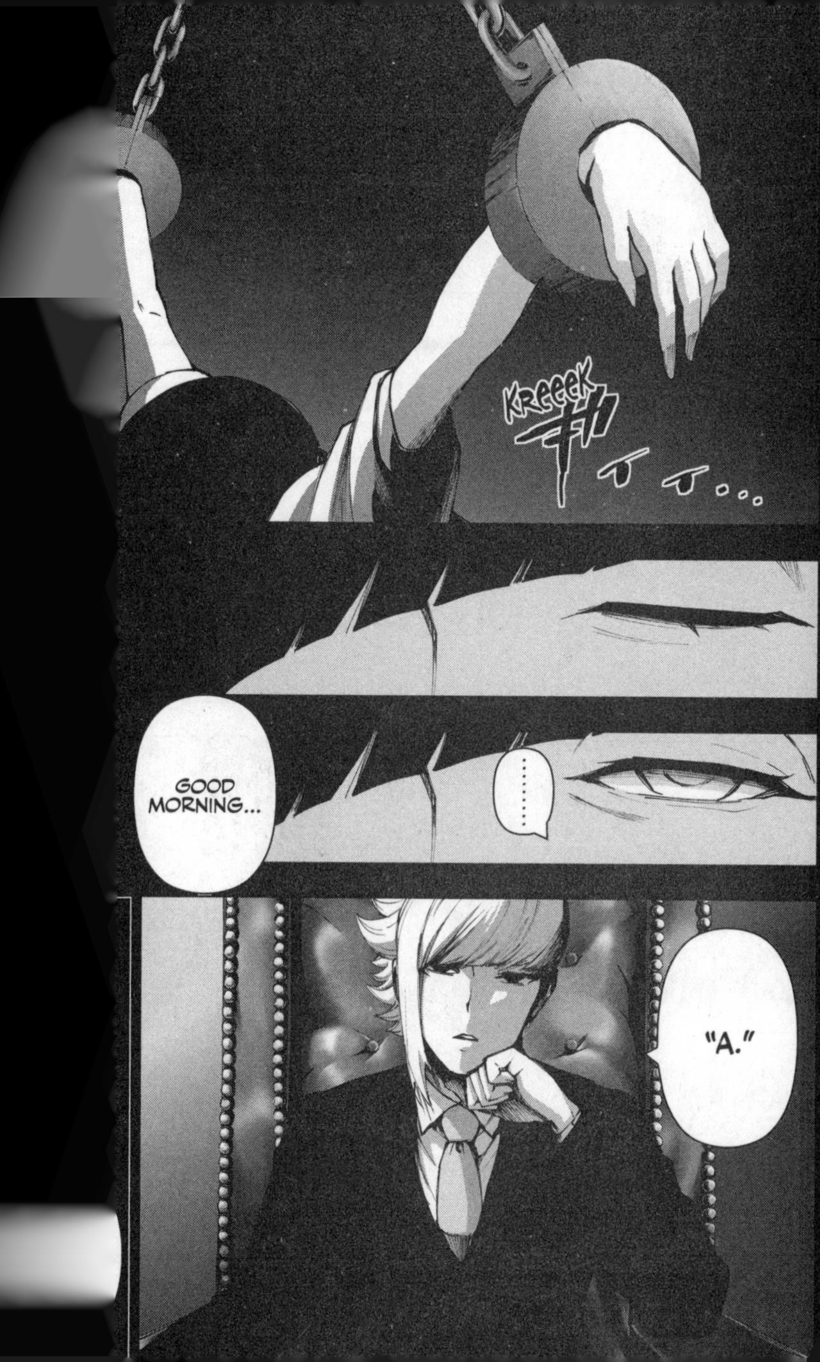
KREEEK
GOOD MORNING...
......
"A."

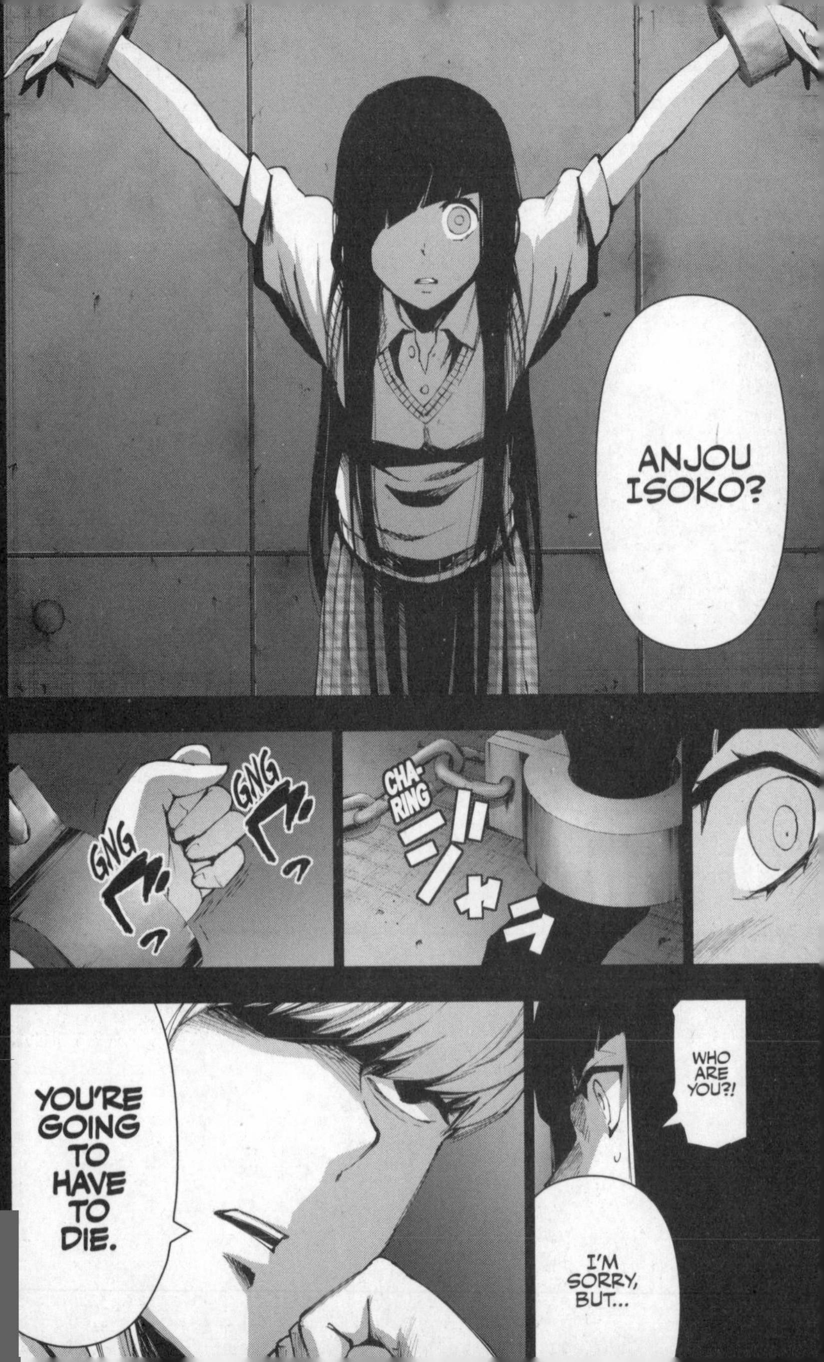
ANJOU ISOKO?
CHA-RING
GNG
GNG
WHO ARE YOU?!
I'M SORRY, BUT...
YOU'RE GOING TO HAVE TO DIE.

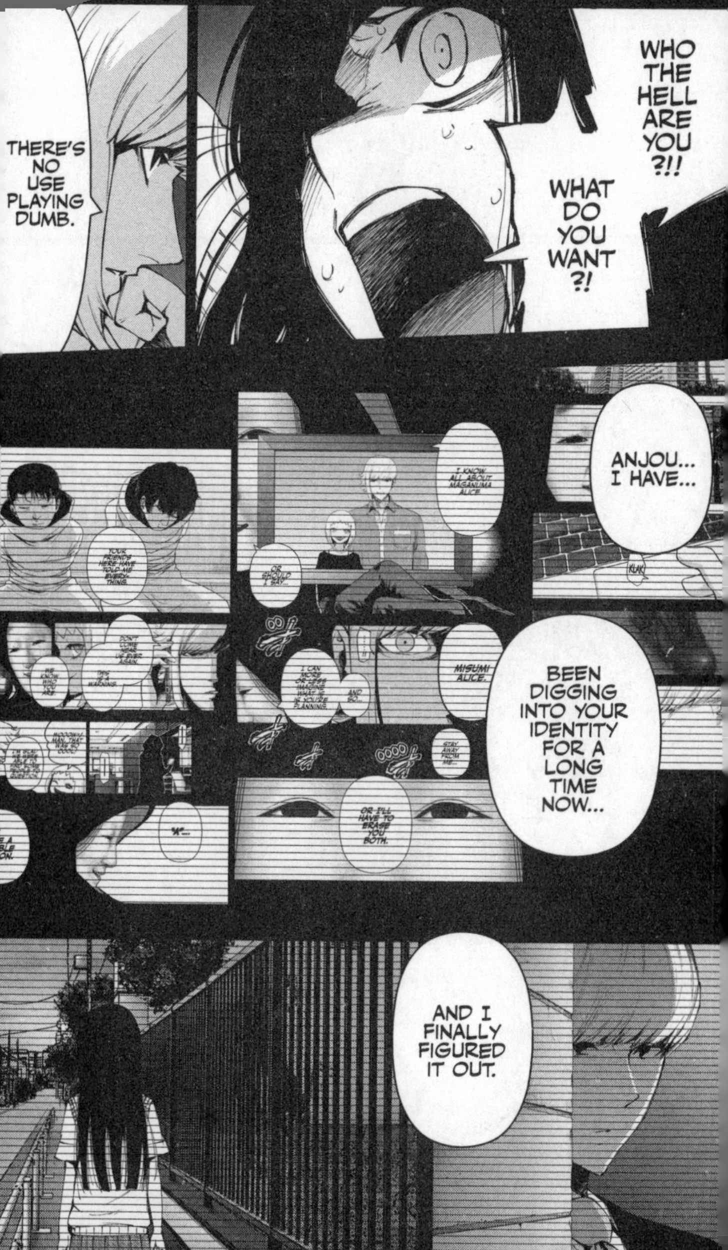
WHO THE HELL ARE YOU ?!!
WHAT DO YOU WANT ?!
THERE'S NO USE PLAYING DUMB.
ANJOU... I HAVE...
KLAK
I KNOW ALL ABOUT MAGANUMA ALICE.
OR SHOULD I SAY...
YOUR FRIENDS HERE HAVE TOLD ME EVERY-THING.
BEEN DIGGING INTO YOUR IDENTITY FOR A LONG TIME NOW...
MISUMI ALICE.
AND SO...
STAY AWAY FROM ME...
OR I'LL HAVE TO ERASE YOU BOTH.
AND I FINALLY FIGURED IT OUT.

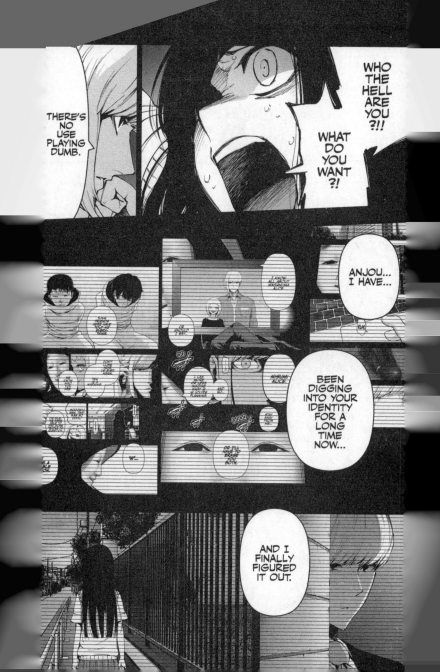

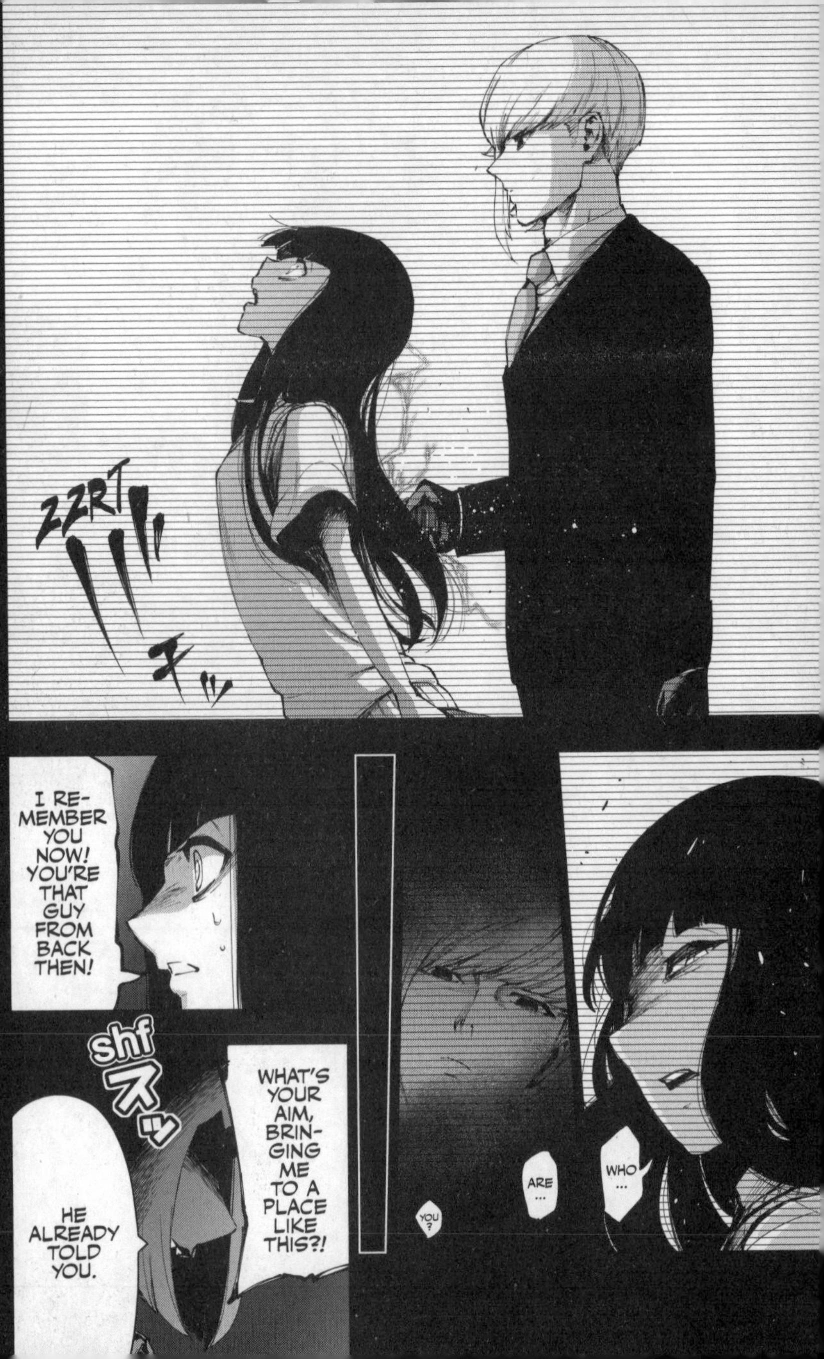
ZZRT
WHO... ARE... YOU?
I RE-MEMBER YOU NOW! YOU'RE THAT GUY FROM BACK THEN!
WHAT'S YOUR AIM, BRIN-GING ME TO A PLACE LIKE THIS?!
shf
HE ALREADY TOLD YOU.

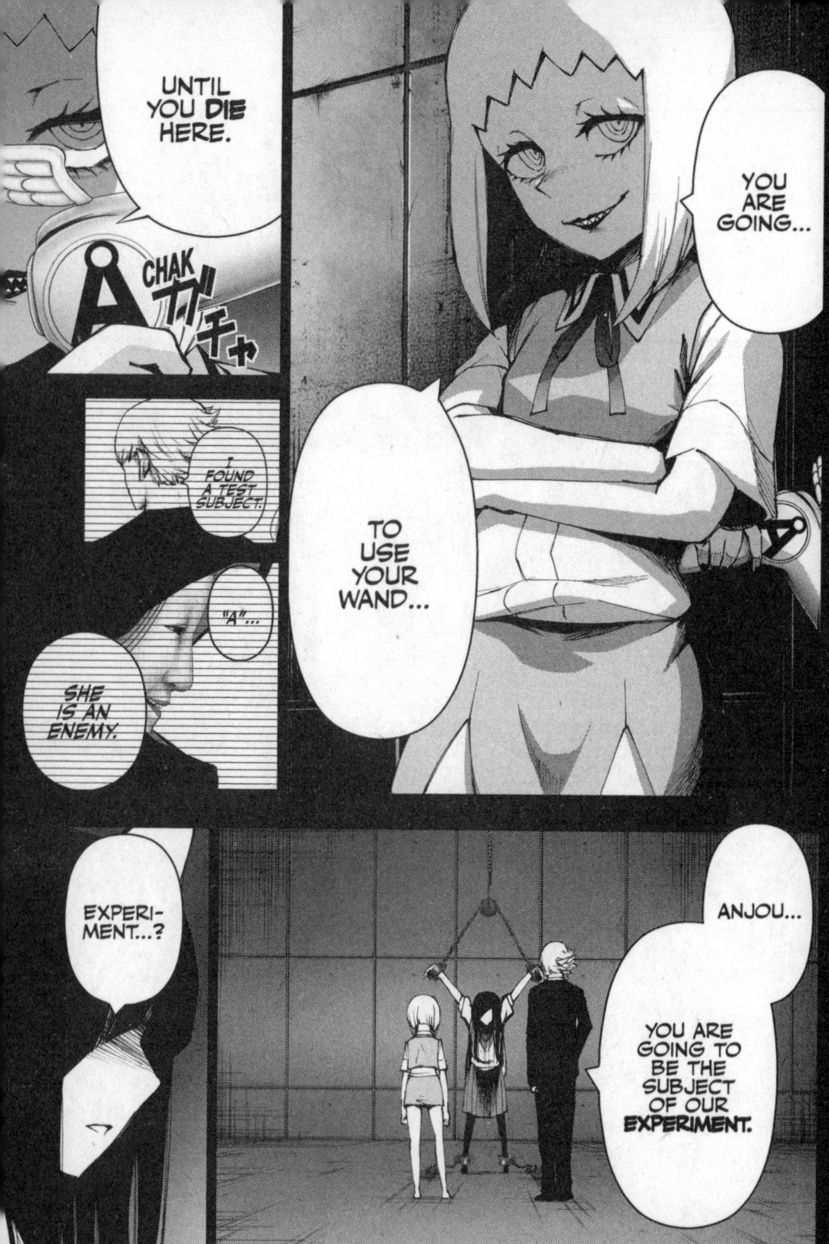
YOU ARE GOING...
TO USE YOUR WAND...
UNTIL YOU DIE HERE.
CHAK
ガチャ
I FOUND A TEST SUBJECT.
"A"...
SHE IS AN ENEMY.
ANJOU...
YOU ARE GOING TO BE THE SUBJECT OF OUR EXPERIMENT.
EXPERIMENT...?

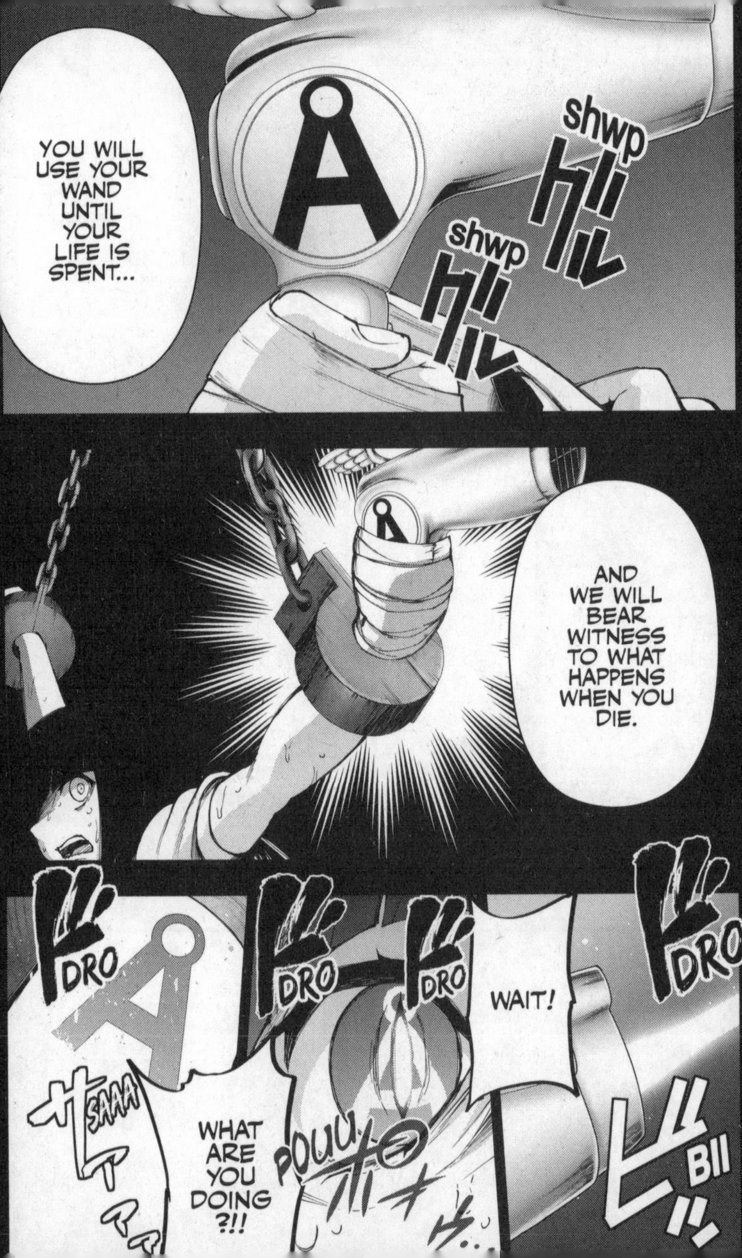
shwp
shwp
YOU WILL USE YOUR WAND UNTIL YOUR LIFE IS SPENT...
AND WE WILL BEAR WITNESS TO WHAT HAPPENS WHEN YOU DIE.
DRO
WAIT!
DRO
DRO
DRO
BII
POUU
WHAT ARE YOU DOING?!!
SAAA

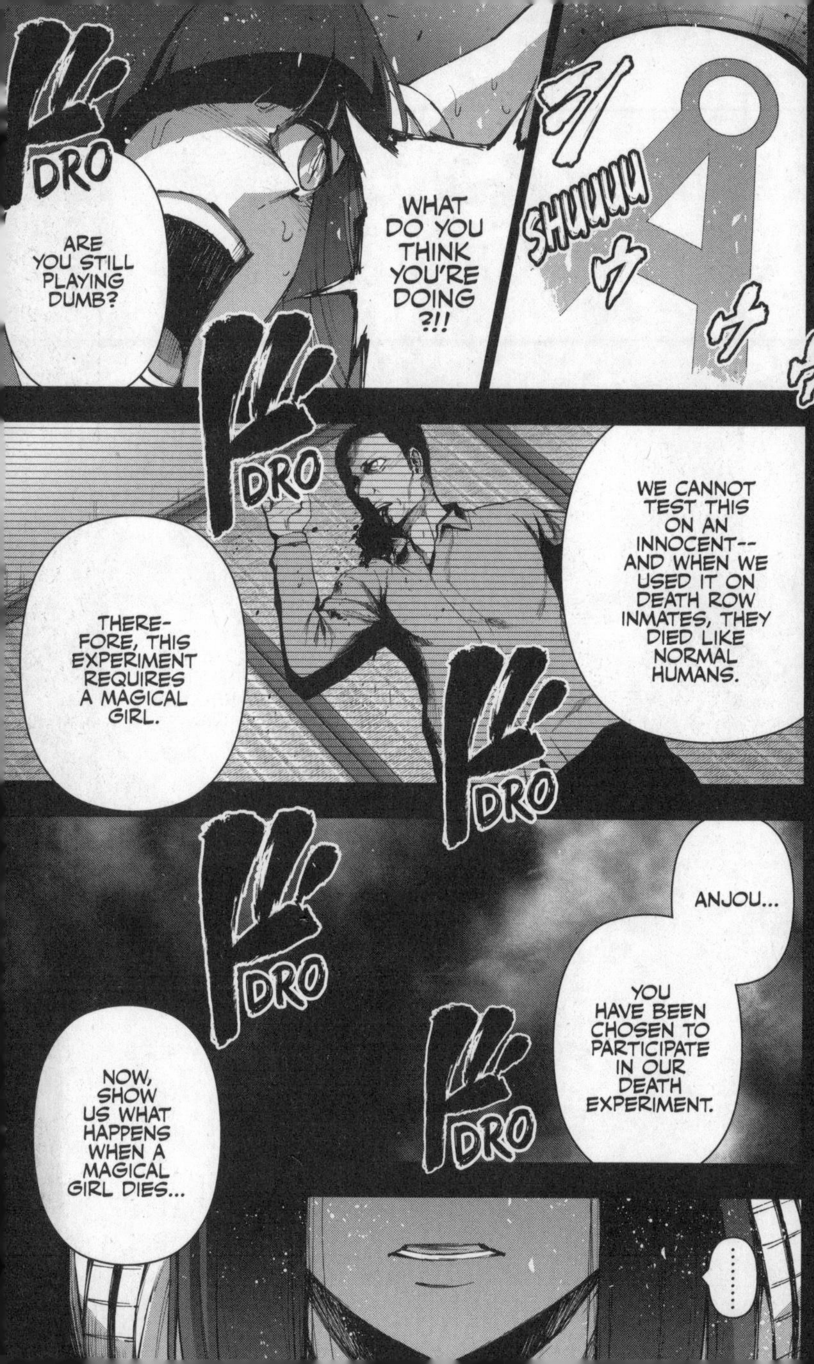
SHUUUU
WHAT DO YOU THINK YOU'RE DOING ?!!
DRO
ARE YOU STILL PLAYING DUMB?
DRO
WE CANNOT TEST THIS ON AN INNOCENT-- AND WHEN WE USED IT ON DEATH ROW INMATES, THEY DIED LIKE NORMAL HUMANS.
THERE-FORE, THIS EXPERIMENT REQUIRES A MAGICAL GIRL.
DRO
ANJOU...
YOU HAVE BEEN CHOSEN TO PARTICIPATE IN OUR DEATH EXPERIMENT.
DRO
DRO
NOW, SHOW US WHAT HAPPENS WHEN A MAGICAL GIRL DIES...
......

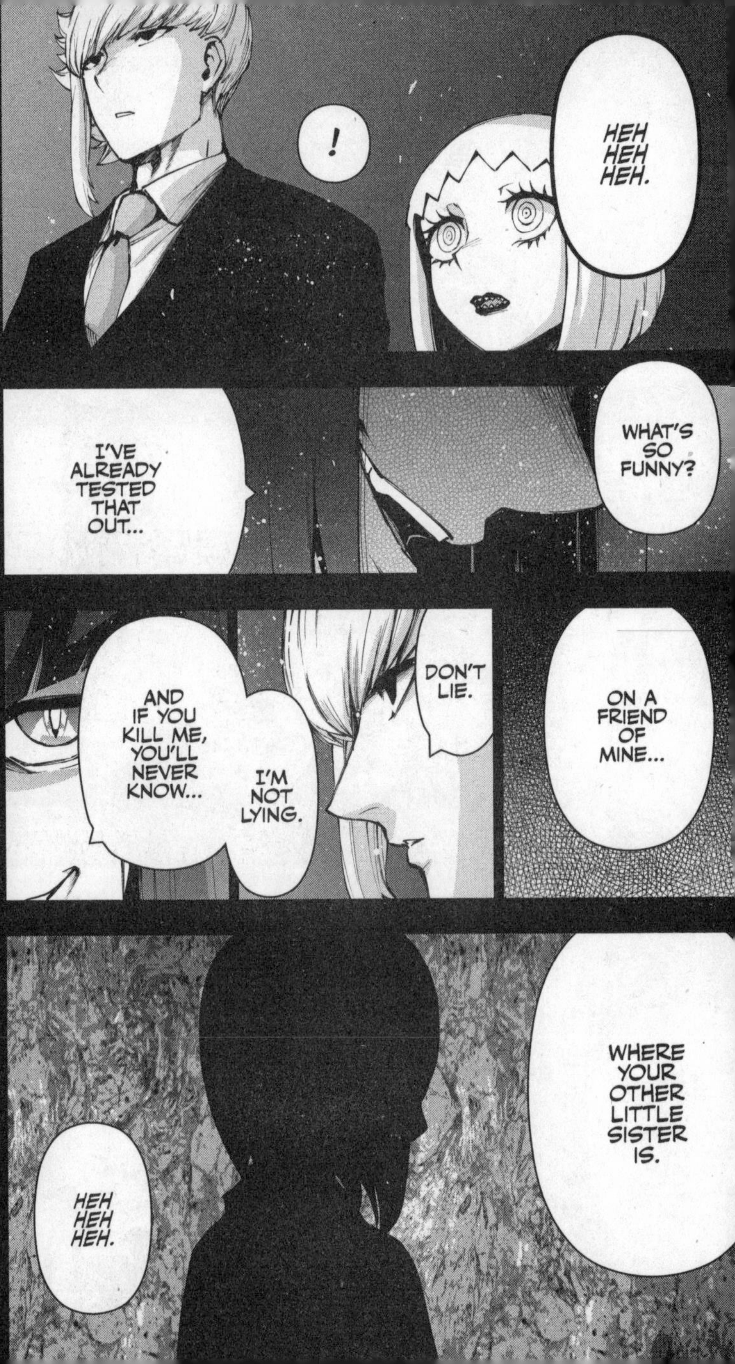
HEH HEH HEH.
!
WHAT'S SO FUNNY?
I'VE ALREADY TESTED THAT OUT...
ON A FRIEND OF MINE...
DON'T LIE.
I'M NOT LYING.
AND IF YOU KILL ME, YOU'LL NEVER KNOW...
WHERE YOUR OTHER LITTLE SISTER IS.
HEH HEH HEH.

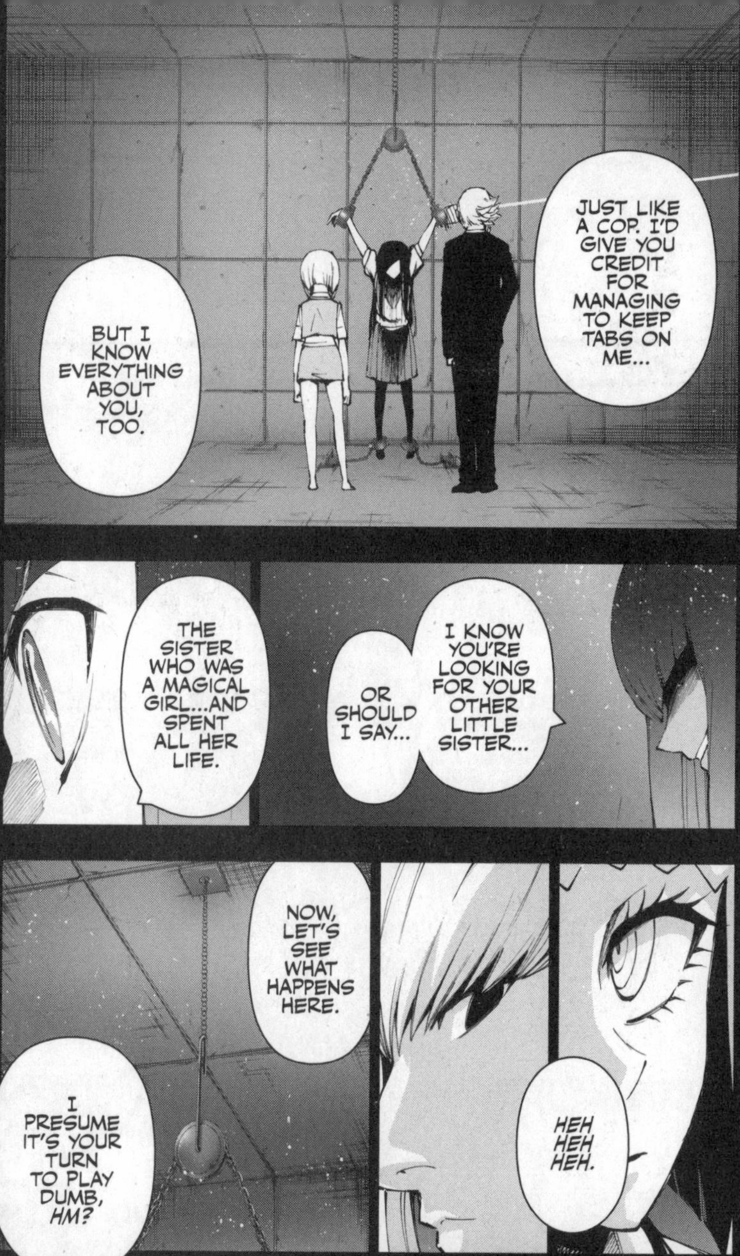
JUST LIKE A COP. I'D GIVE YOU CREDIT FOR MANAGING TO KEEP TABS ON ME...
BUT I KNOW EVERYTHING ABOUT YOU, TOO.
I KNOW YOU'RE LOOKING FOR YOUR OTHER LITTLE SISTER...
OR SHOULD I SAY...
THE SISTER WHO WAS A MAGICAL GIRL...AND SPENT ALL HER LIFE.
HEH HEH HEH.
NOW, LET'S SEE WHAT HAPPENS HERE.
I PRESUME IT'S YOUR TURN TO PLAY DUMB, *HM?*

ENTER.97 ANOTHER LITTLE SISTER

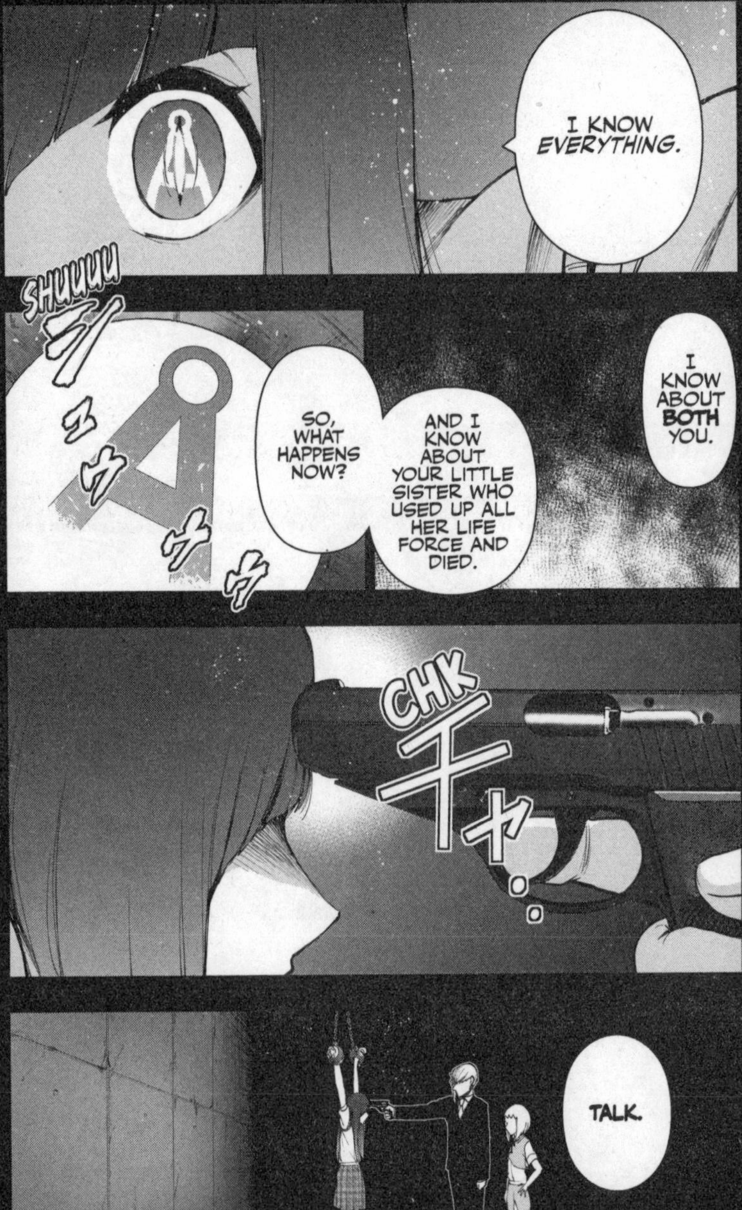
I KNOW EVERYTHING.
I KNOW ABOUT BOTH YOU.
AND I KNOW ABOUT YOUR LITTLE SISTER WHO USED UP ALL HER LIFE FORCE AND DIED.
SO, WHAT HAPPENS NOW?
SHUUUU
CHK
TALK.

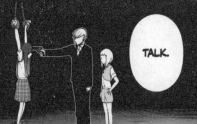

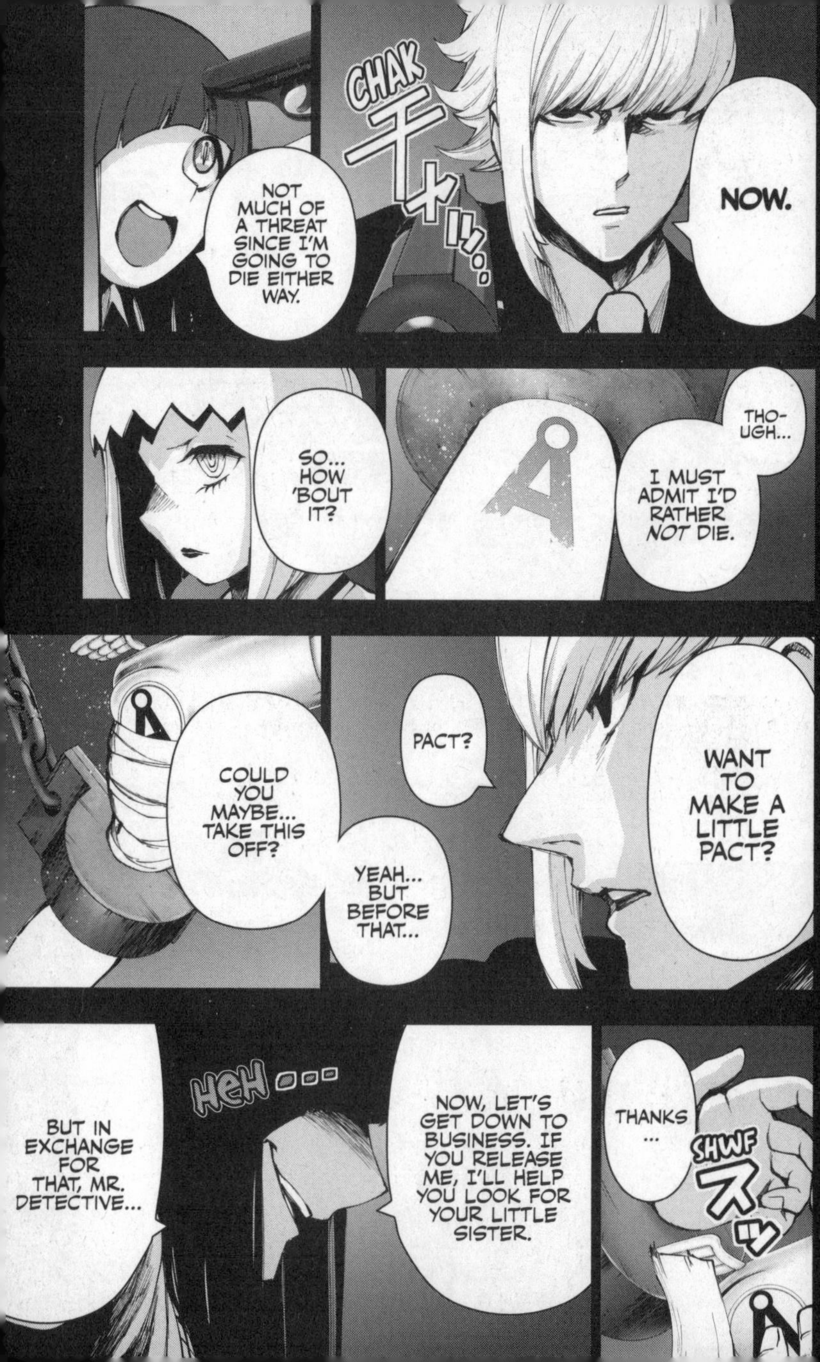
NOW.
CHAK
NOT MUCH OF A THREAT SINCE I'M GOING TO DIE EITHER WAY.
THOUGH...
I MUST ADMIT I'D RATHER *NOT* DIE.
SO... HOW 'BOUT IT?
WANT TO MAKE A LITTLE PACT?
PACT?
YEAH... BUT BEFORE THAT...
COULD YOU MAYBE... TAKE THIS OFF?
THANKS ...
SHWF
HEH...
NOW, LET'S GET DOWN TO BUSINESS. IF YOU RELEASE ME, I'LL HELP YOU LOOK FOR YOUR LITTLE SISTER.
BUT IN EXCHANGE FOR THAT, MR. DETECTIVE...

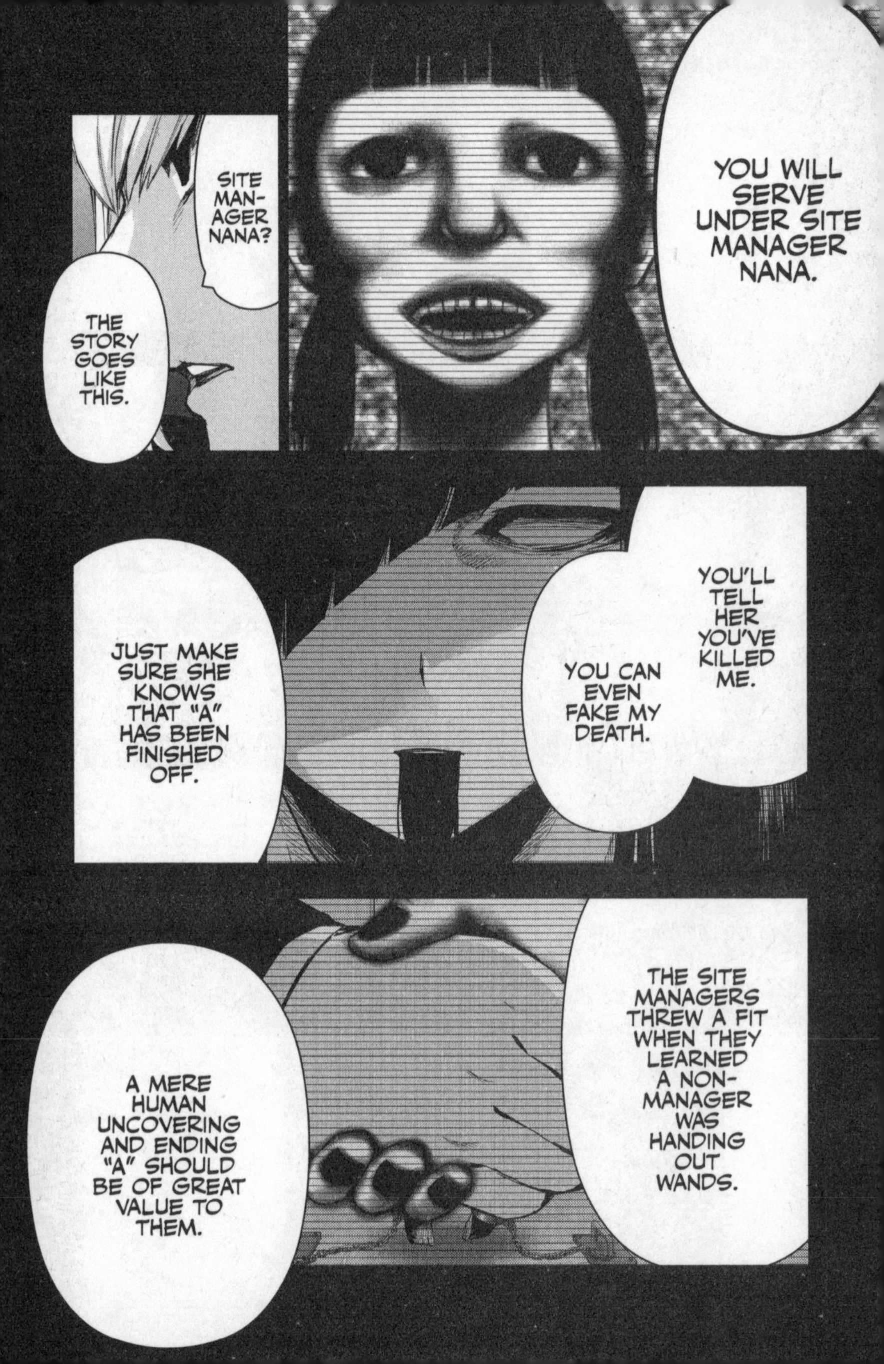
YOU WILL SERVE UNDER SITE MANAGER NANA.
SITE MAN-AGER NANA?
THE STORY GOES LIKE THIS.
YOU'LL TELL HER YOU'VE KILLED ME.
YOU CAN EVEN FAKE MY DEATH.
JUST MAKE SURE SHE KNOWS THAT "A" HAS BEEN FINISHED OFF.
THE SITE MANAGERS THREW A FIT WHEN THEY LEARNED A NON-MANAGER WAS HANDING OUT WANDS.
A MERE HUMAN UNCOVERING AND ENDING "A" SHOULD BE OF GREAT VALUE TO THEM.

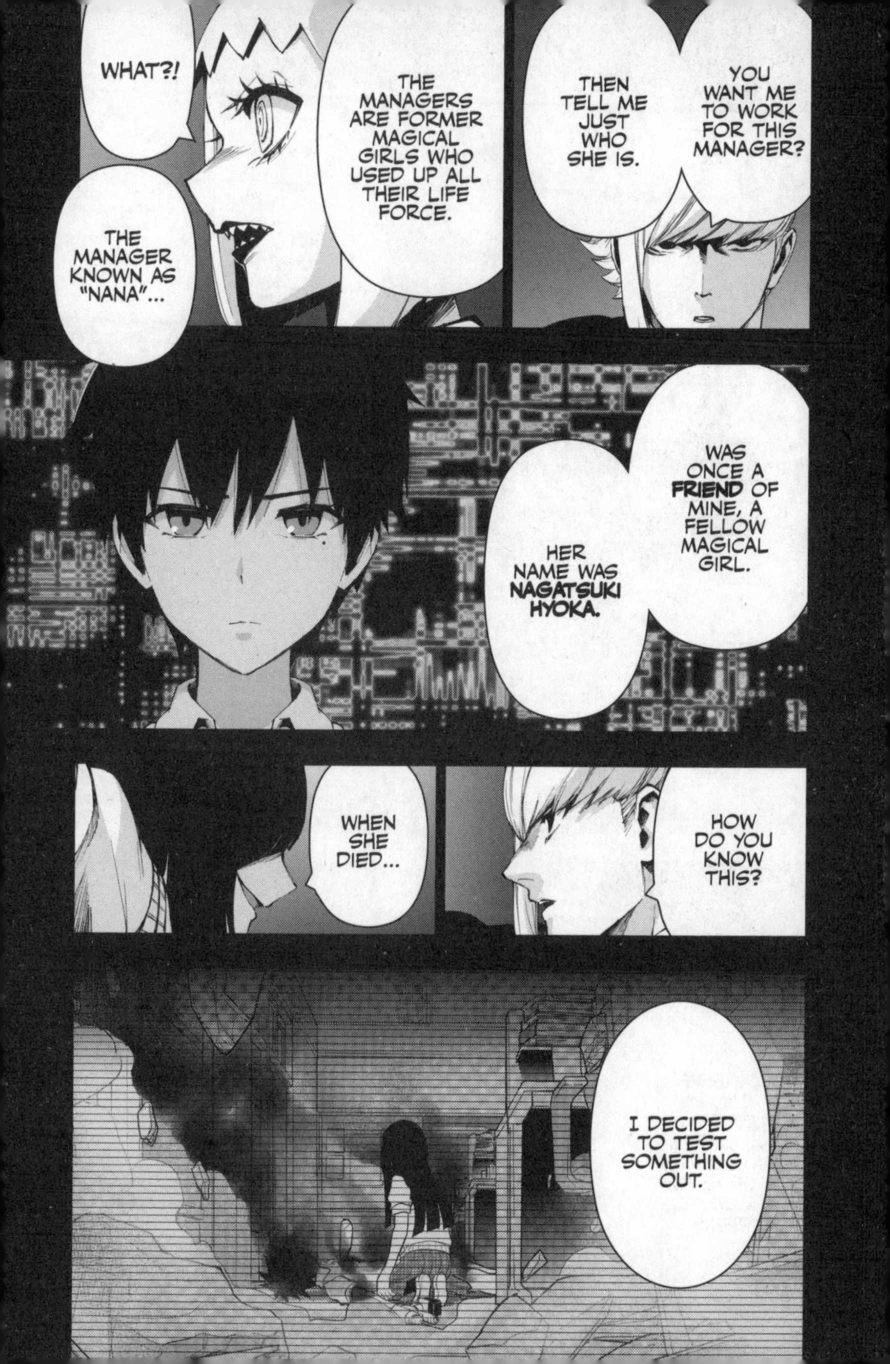
YOU WANT ME TO WORK FOR THIS MANAGER?
THEN TELL ME JUST WHO SHE IS.
THE MANAGERS ARE FORMER MAGICAL GIRLS WHO USED UP ALL THEIR LIFE FORCE.
WHAT?!
THE MANAGER KNOWN AS "NANA"...
WAS ONCE A FRIEND OF MINE, A FELLOW MAGICAL GIRL.
HER NAME WAS NAGATSUKI HYOKA.
HOW DO YOU KNOW THIS?
WHEN SHE DIED...
I DECIDED TO TEST SOMETHING OUT.

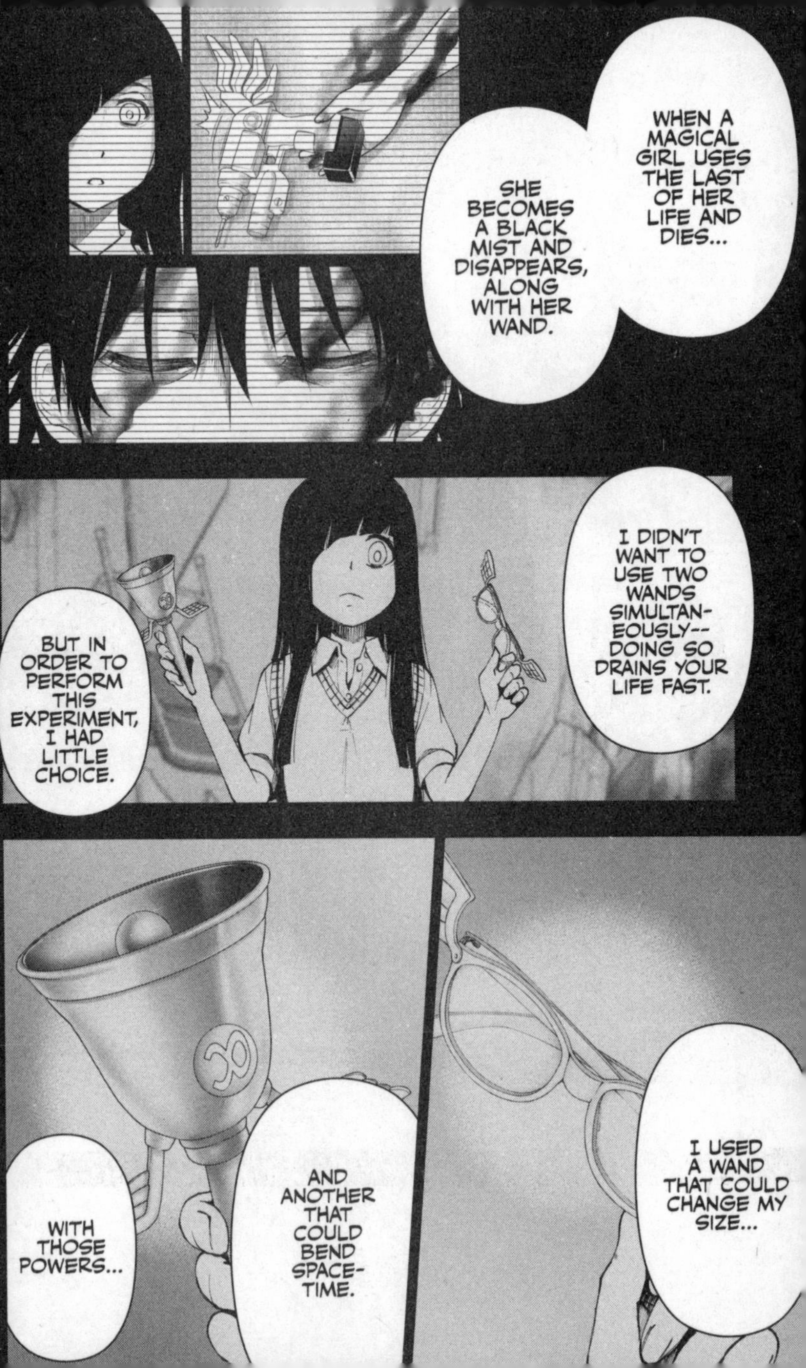
WHEN A MAGICAL GIRL USES THE LAST OF HER LIFE AND DIES...
SHE BECOMES A BLACK MIST AND DISAPPEARS, ALONG WITH HER WAND.
I DIDN'T WANT TO USE TWO WANDS SIMULTANEOUSLY-- DOING SO DRAINS YOUR LIFE FAST.
BUT IN ORDER TO PERFORM THIS EXPERIMENT, I HAD LITTLE CHOICE.
I USED A WAND THAT COULD CHANGE MY SIZE...
AND ANOTHER THAT COULD BEND SPACE-TIME.
WITH THOSE POWERS...

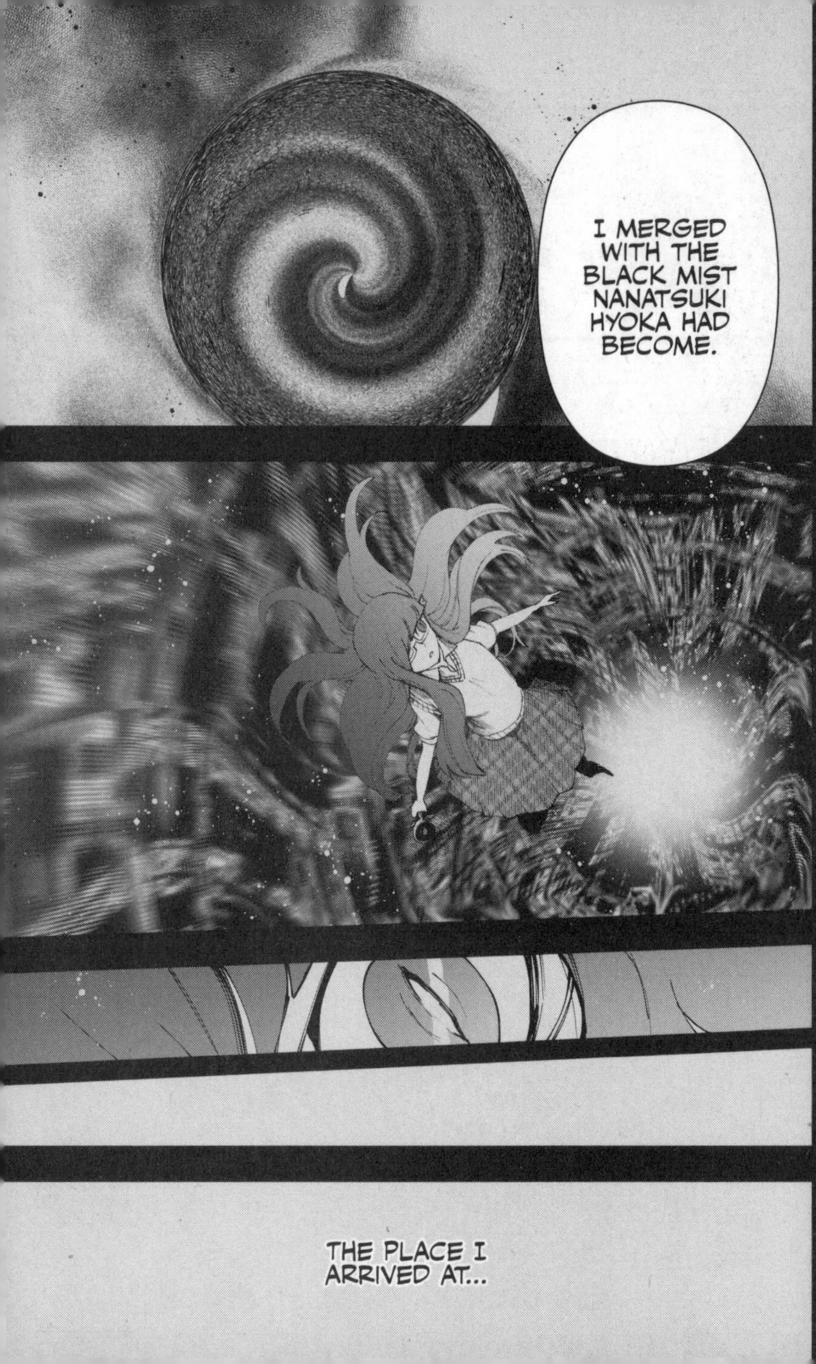
I MERGED WITH THE BLACK MIST NANATSUKI HYOKA HAD BECOME.
THE PLACE I ARRIVED AT...

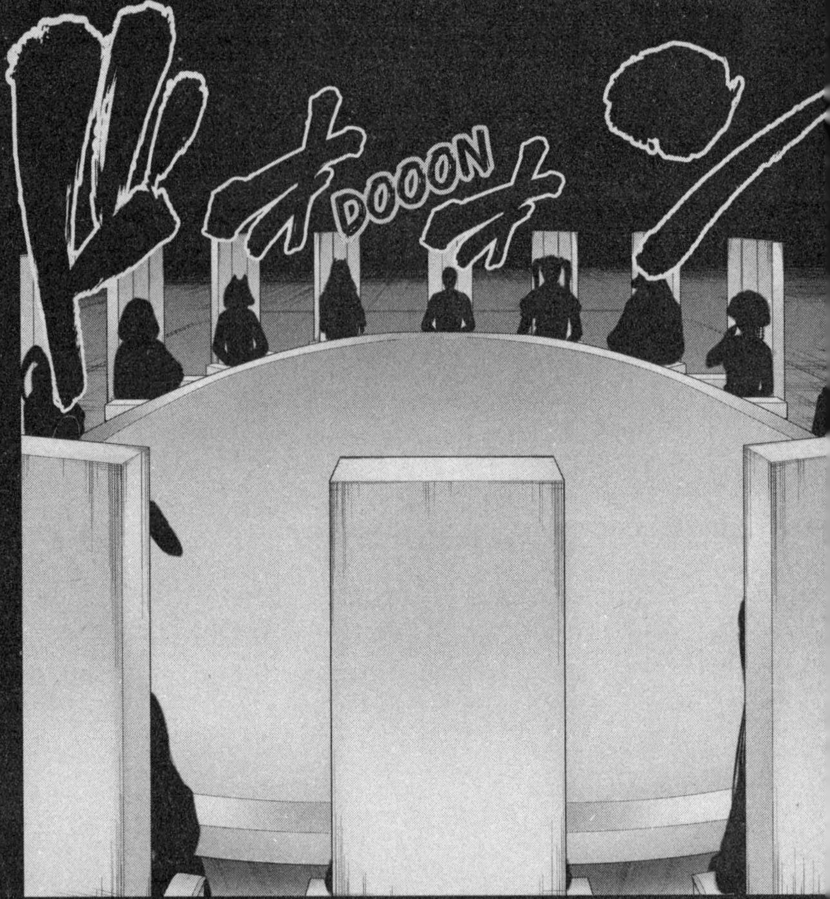
DOOON
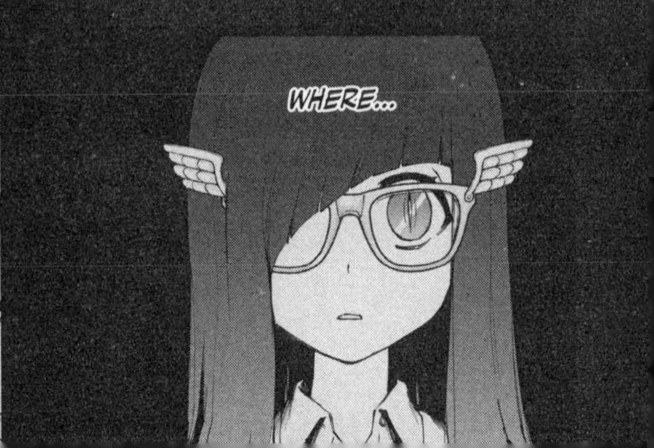
WHERE...
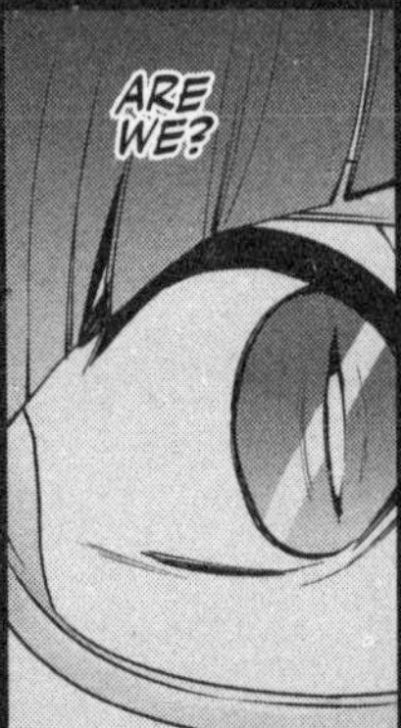
ARE WE?

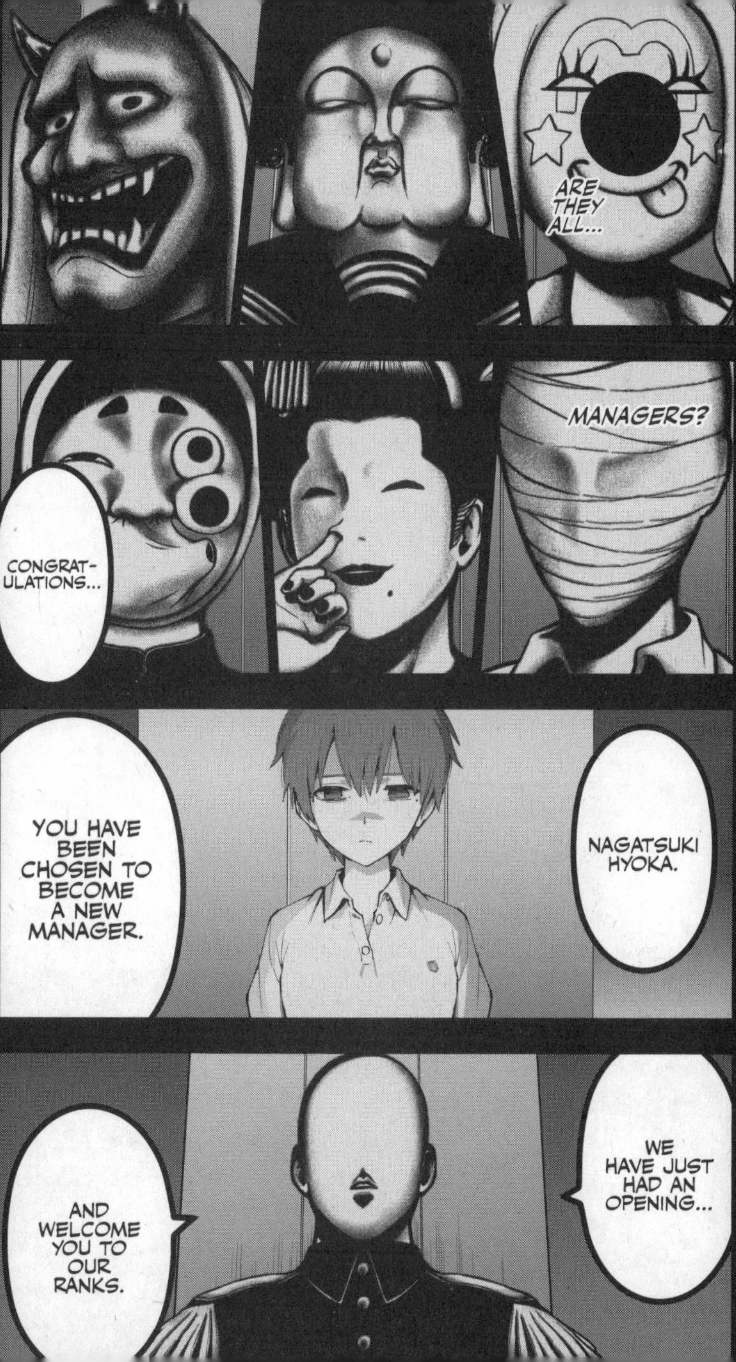
ARE THEY ALL...
MANAGERS?
CONGRAT-ULATIONS...
NAGATSUKI HYOKA.
YOU HAVE BEEN CHOSEN TO BECOME A NEW MANAGER.
WE HAVE JUST HAD AN OPENING...
AND WELCOME YOU TO OUR RANKS.

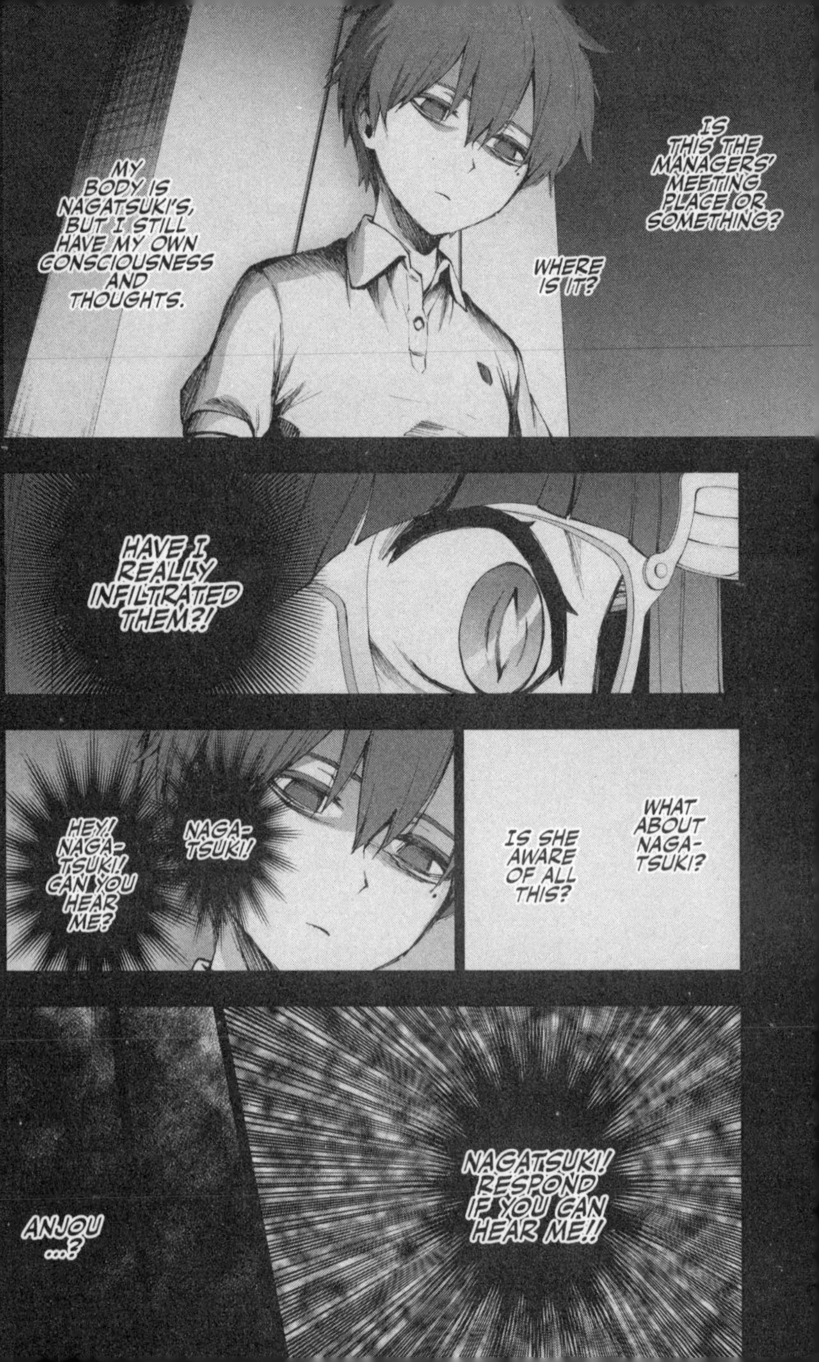
IS THIS THE MANAGERS' MEETING PLACE OR SOMETHING?
WHERE IS IT?
MY BODY IS NAGATSUKI'S, BUT I STILL HAVE MY OWN CONSCIOUSNESS AND THOUGHTS.
HAVE I REALLY INFILTRATED THEM?!
WHAT ABOUT NAGA-TSUKI?
IS SHE AWARE OF ALL THIS?
NAGA-TSUKI!
HEY! NAGA-TSUKI! CAN YOU HEAR ME?
NAGATSUKI! RESPOND IF YOU CAN HEAR ME!!
ANJOU ...?

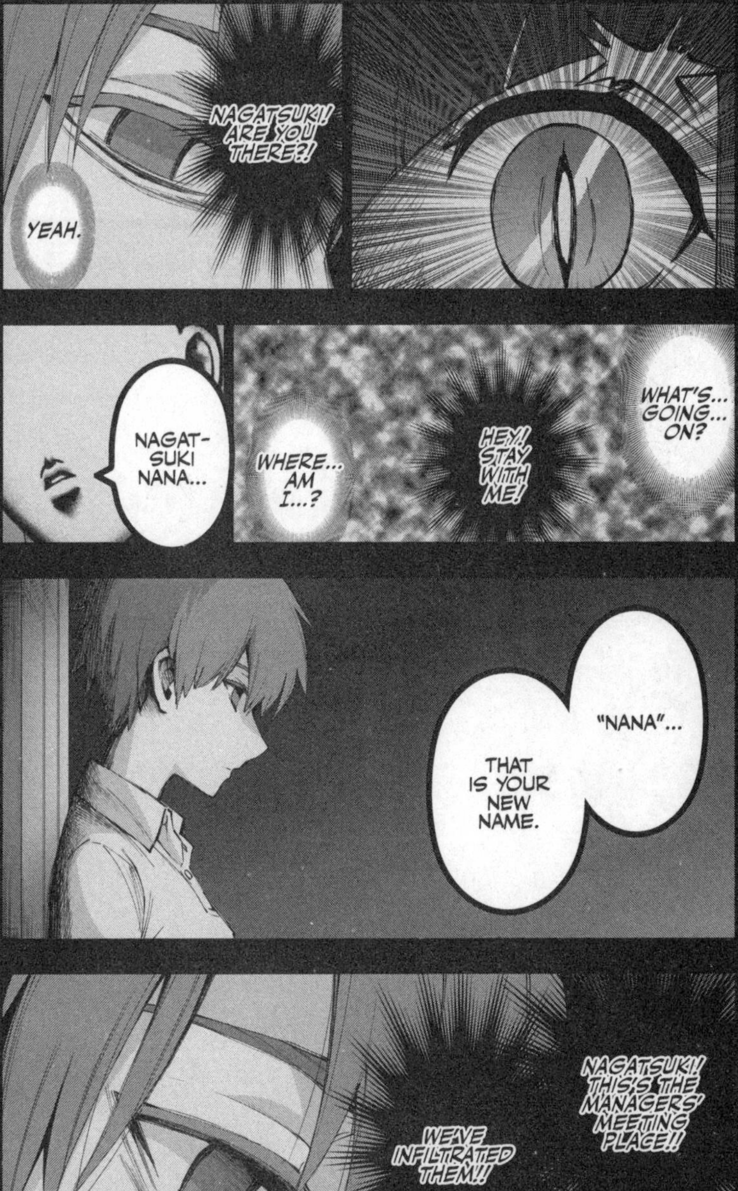
NAGATSUKI! ARE YOU THERE?!
YEAH.
WHAT'S... GOING... ON?
HEY! STAY WITH ME!
WHERE... AM I...?
NAGAT-SUKI NANA...
"NANA"... THAT IS YOUR NEW NAME.
NAGATSUKI! THIS'S THE MANAGERS' MEETING PLACE!!
WE'VE INFILTRATED THEM!!

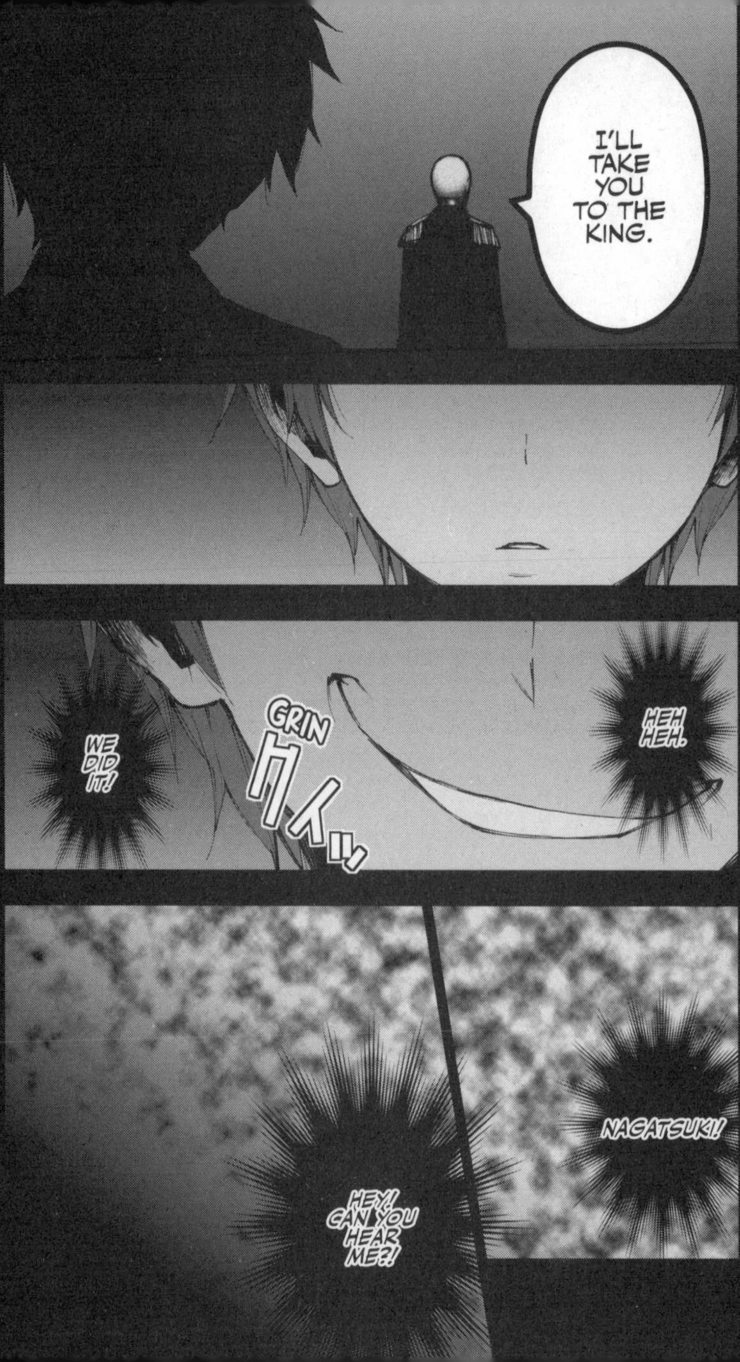
I'LL TAKE YOU TO THE KING.
HEH HEH.
GRIN
WE DID IT!
NAGATSUKI!
HEY! CAN YOU HEAR ME?!

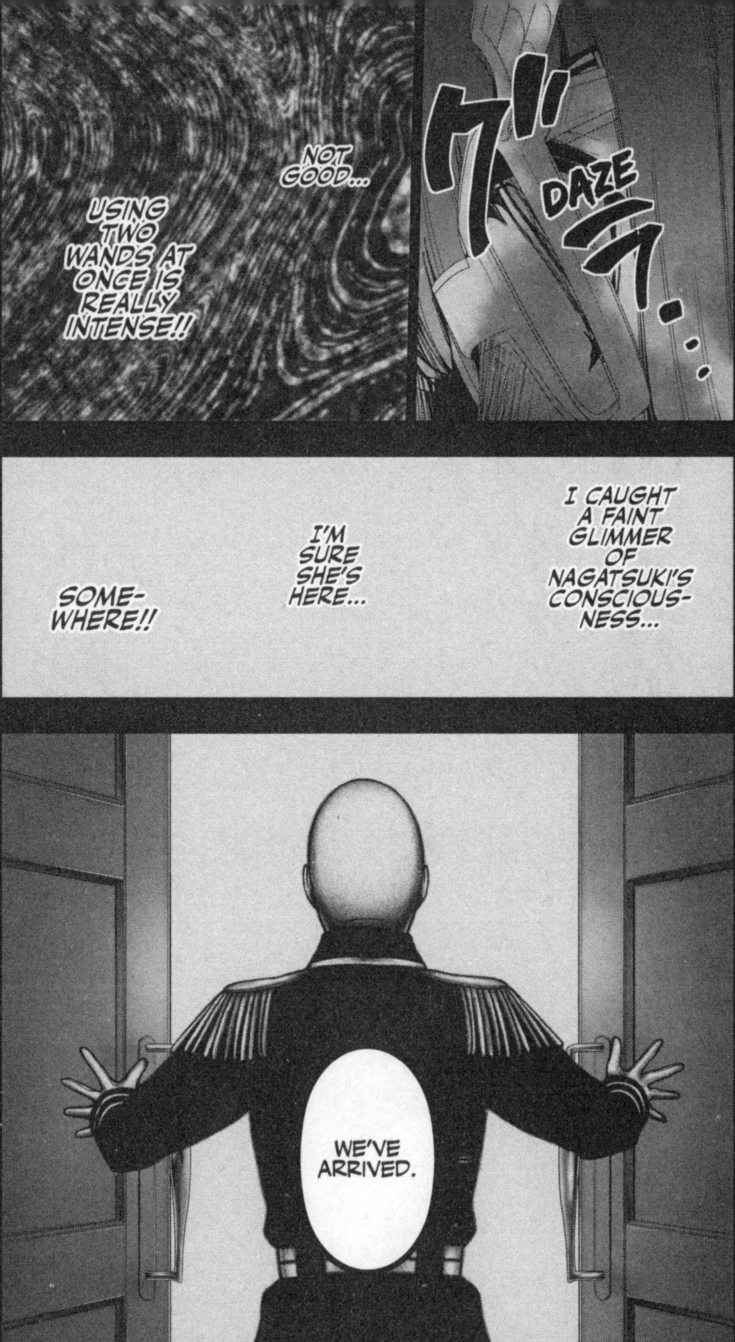
DAZE
NOT GOOD...
USING TWO WANDS AT ONCE IS REALLY INTENSE!!
I CAUGHT A FAINT GLIMMER OF NAGATSUKI'S CONSCIOUS-NESS...
I'M SURE SHE'S HERE...
SOME-WHERE!!
WE'VE ARRIVED.

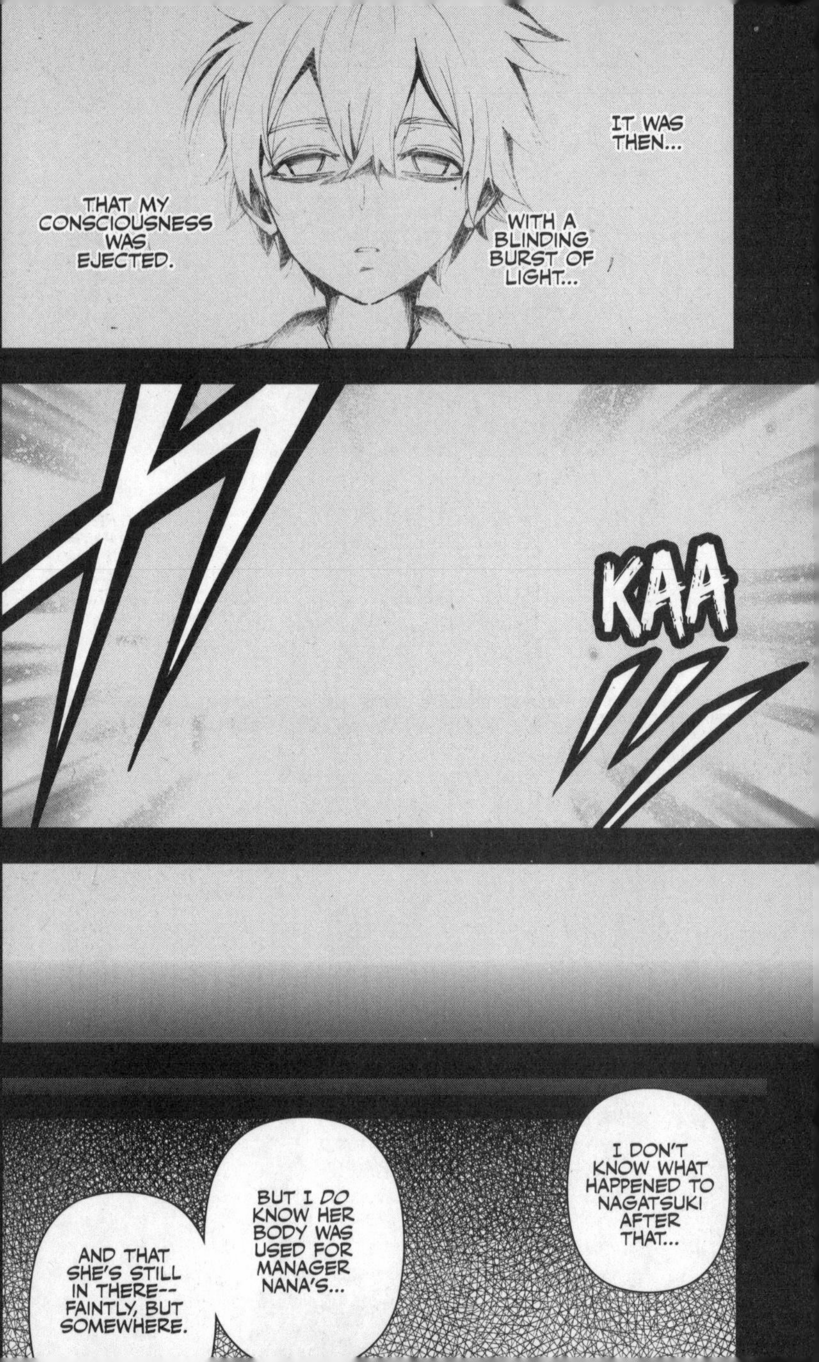
IT WAS THEN...
WITH A BLINDING BURST OF LIGHT...
THAT MY CONSCIOUSNESS WAS EJECTED.
KAA
I DON'T KNOW WHAT HAPPENED TO NAGATSUKI AFTER THAT...
BUT I *DO* KNOW HER BODY WAS USED FOR MANAGER NANA'S...
AND THAT SHE'S STILL IN THERE-- FAINTLY, BUT SOMEWHERE.

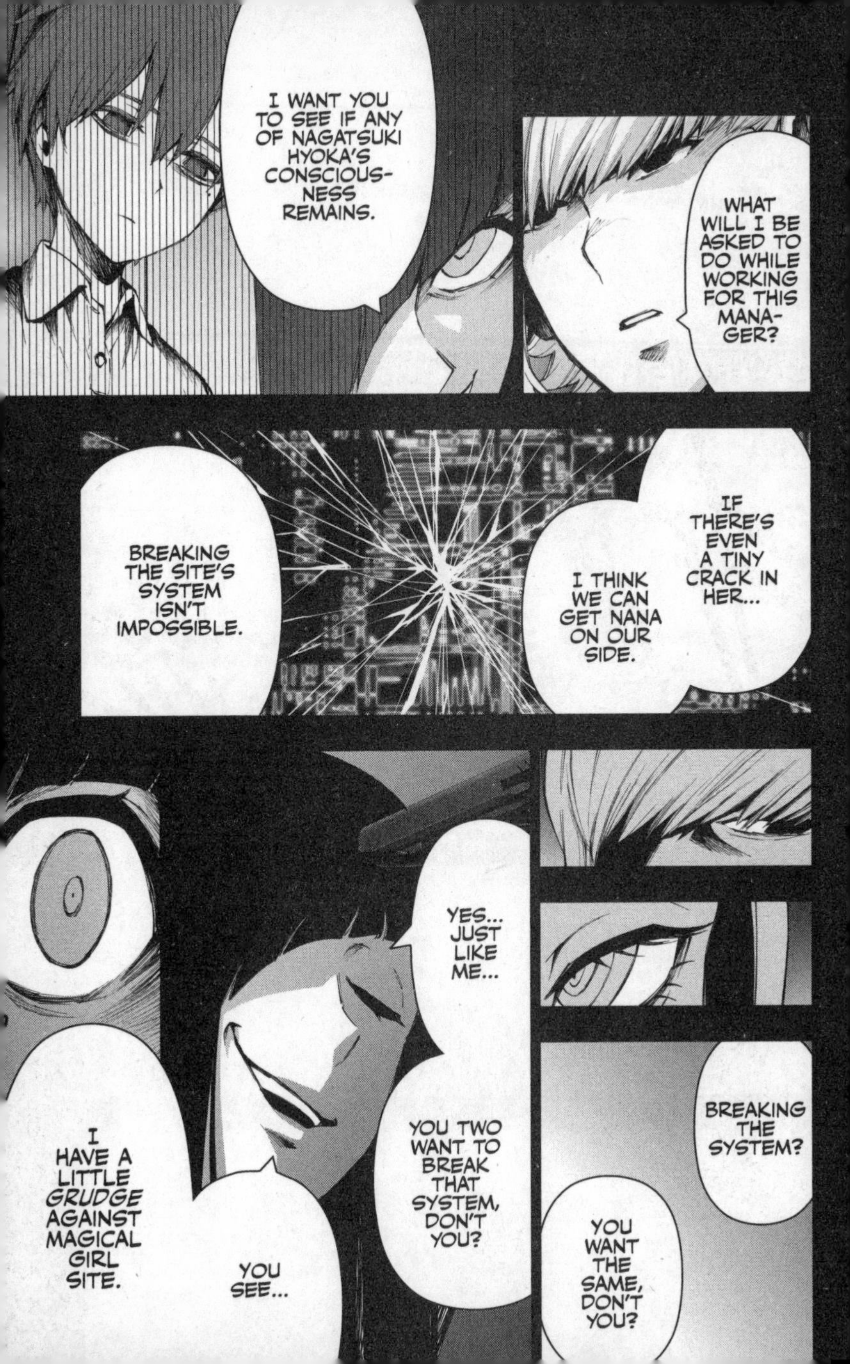
WHAT WILL I BE ASKED TO DO WHILE WORKING FOR THIS MANAGER?
I WANT YOU TO SEE IF ANY OF NAGATSUKI HYOKA'S CONSCIOUS-NESS REMAINS.
IF THERE'S EVEN A TINY CRACK IN HER...
I THINK WE CAN GET NANA ON OUR SIDE.
BREAKING THE SITE'S SYSTEM ISN'T IMPOSSIBLE.
BREAKING THE SYSTEM?
YOU WANT THE SAME, DON'T YOU?
YES... JUST LIKE ME...
YOU TWO WANT TO BREAK THAT SYSTEM, DON'T YOU?
YOU SEE...
I HAVE A LITTLE *GRUDGE* AGAINST MAGICAL GIRL SITE.

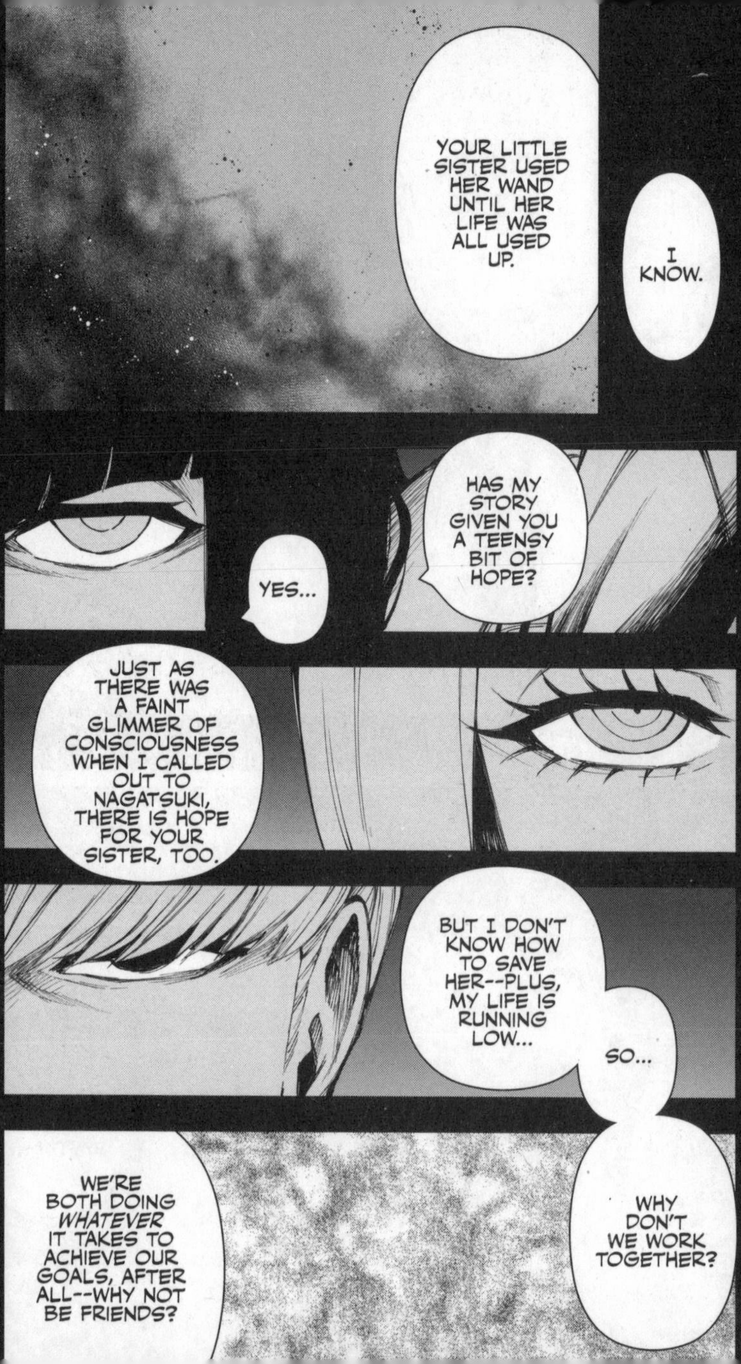
YOUR LITTLE SISTER USED HER WAND UNTIL HER LIFE WAS ALL USED UP.
I KNOW.
HAS MY STORY GIVEN YOU A TEENSY BIT OF HOPE?
YES...
JUST AS THERE WAS A FAINT GLIMMER OF CONSCIOUSNESS WHEN I CALLED OUT TO NAGATSUKI, THERE IS HOPE FOR YOUR SISTER, TOO.
BUT I DON'T KNOW HOW TO SAVE HER--PLUS, MY LIFE IS RUNNING LOW...
SO...
WHY DON'T WE WORK TOGETHER?
WE'RE BOTH DOING *WHATEVER* IT TAKES TO ACHIEVE OUR GOALS, AFTER ALL--WHY NOT BE FRIENDS?

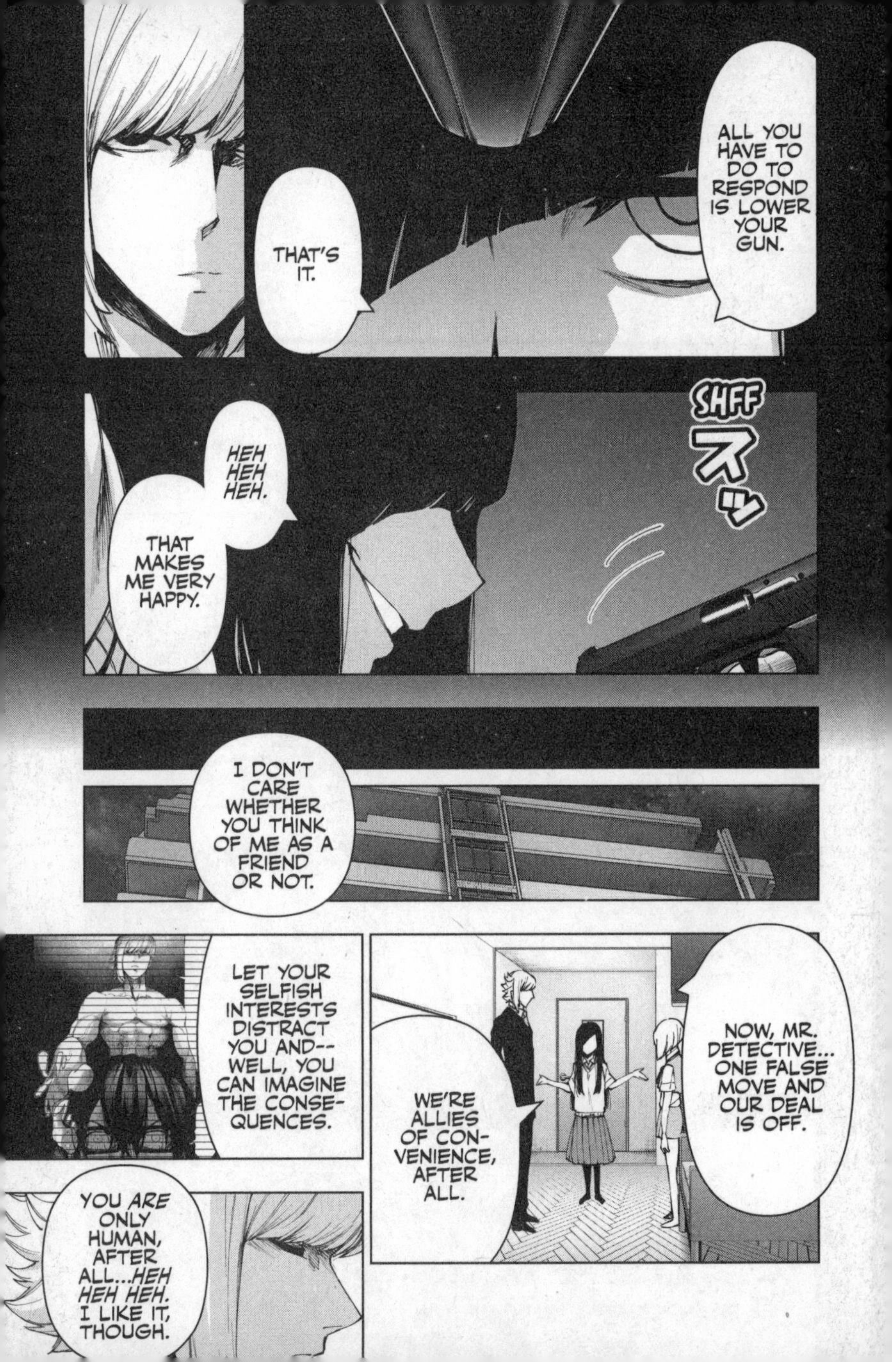
ALL YOU HAVE TO DO TO RESPOND IS LOWER YOUR GUN.
THAT'S IT.
SHFF
スッ
HEH HEH HEH.
THAT MAKES ME VERY HAPPY.
I DON'T CARE WHETHER YOU THINK OF ME AS A FRIEND OR NOT.
NOW, MR. DETECTIVE... ONE FALSE MOVE AND OUR DEAL IS OFF.
WE'RE ALLIES OF CON-VENIENCE, AFTER ALL.
LET YOUR SELFISH INTERESTS DISTRACT YOU AND-- WELL, YOU CAN IMAGINE THE CONSE-QUENCES.
YOU *ARE* ONLY HUMAN, AFTER ALL...*HEH HEH HEH.* I LIKE IT, THOUGH.

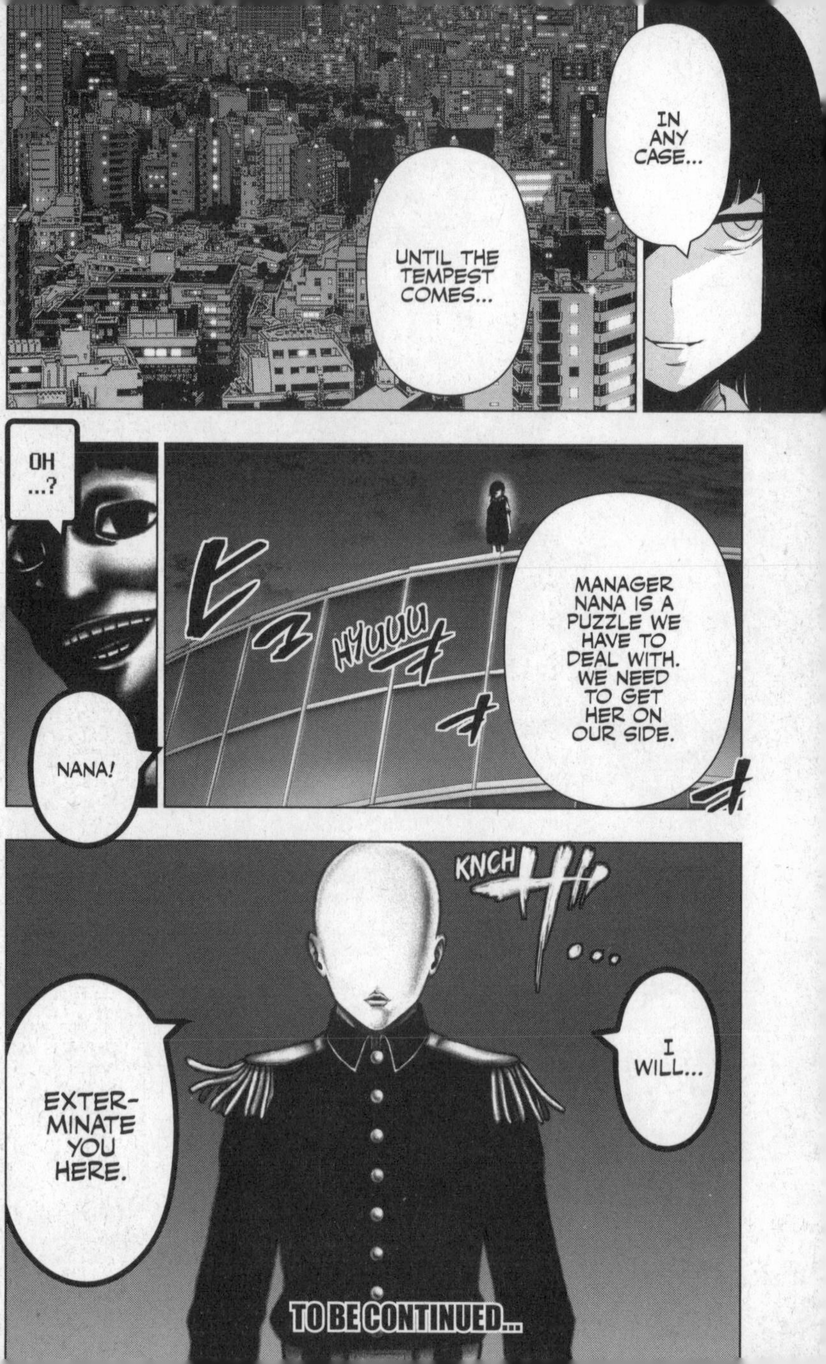
IN ANY CASE...
UNTIL THE TEMPEST COMES...
MANAGER NANA IS A PUZZLE WE HAVE TO DEAL WITH. WE NEED TO GET HER ON OUR SIDE.
HYUUU
OH ...?
NANA!
KNCH
...
I WILL...
EXTER-
MINATE
YOU
HERE.
TO BE CONTINUED...

Loading . . . Please Wait

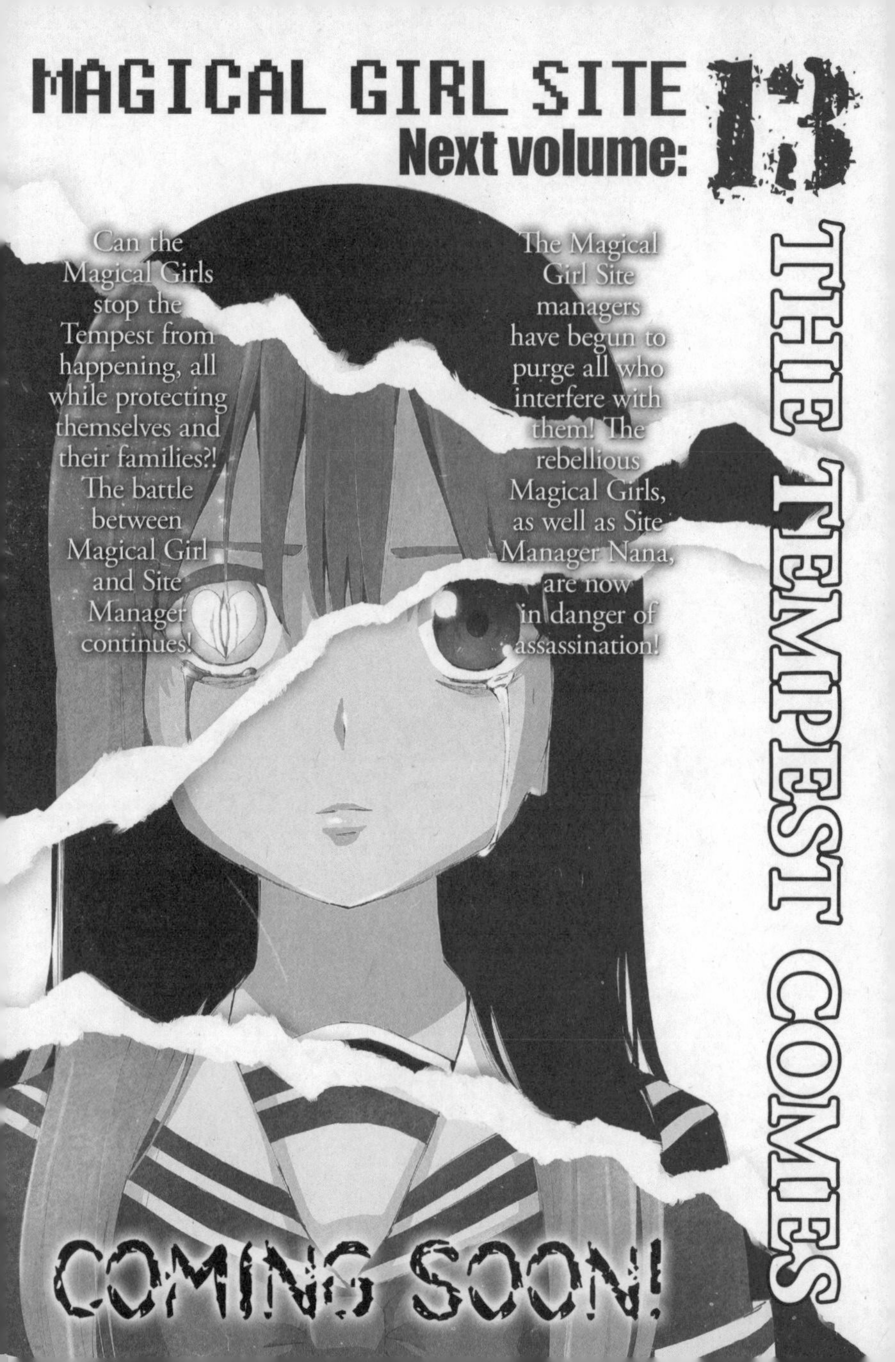
MAGICAL GIRL SITE
Next volume: 13
THE TEMPEST COMES
Can the Magical Girls stop the Tempest from happening, all while protecting themselves and their families?! The battle between Magical Girl and Site Manager continues!
The Magical Girl Site managers have begun to purge all who interfere with them! The rebellious Magical Girls, as well as Site Manager Nana, are now in danger of assassination!
COMING SOON!